life
APPLICATION®
Study Bible *Devotional*

life APPLICATION® Study Bible *Devotional*

Daily Wisdom from the Life of Jesus

TYNDALE HOUSE PUBLISHERS, INC.,
Carol Stream, Illinois

Visit Tyndale online at www.tyndale.com.

TYNDALE, Life Application, and Tyndale's quill logo are registered trademarks of Tyndale House Publishers, Inc.

Life Application Study Bible Devotional: Daily Wisdom from the Life of Jesus

Copyright © 2011 by Livingstone Corporation. All rights reserved.

Produced by the Livingstone Corporation: David Veerman and Neil Wilson, writers; Bruce Barton and Linda Taylor, editors.

Cover photograph of bread copyright © Isabelle Lafrance Photography/Gerry Images. All rights reserved.

Cover paper texture copyright © wrangler/Shutterstock. All rights reserved.

Cover border from Victorian Designs © Dover Publications. All rights reserved.

Designed by Jessie McGrath

Scripture quotations marked NLT are from the *Holy Bible,* New Living Translation, copyright © 1996, 2004, 2007 by Tyndale House Foundation. Used by permission of Tyndale House Publishers, Inc., Carol Stream, Illinois 60188. All rights reserved.

Scripture quotations marked NIV are from the Holy Bible, *New International Version,*® *NIV.*® Copyright © 1973, 1978, 1984, 2011 by Biblica, Inc.™ Used by permission of Zondervan. All rights reserved worldwide. www.zondervan.com.

Scripture quotations marked NKJV are from the New King James Version.® Copyright © 1982 by Thomas Nelson, Inc. Used by permission. All rights reserved. *NKJV* is a trademark of Thomas Nelson, Inc.

Scripture quotations marked KJV are from the *Holy Bible,* King James Version.

Library of Congress Cataloging-in-Publication Data

Life application study Bible devotional : daily wisdom from Jesus.
    p. cm.
  Includes index.
  ISBN 978-1-4143-4813-1 (sc)
1. Bible. N.T. Gospels—Chronology. 2. Bible. N.T. Gospels—Meditations. 3. Jesus Christ—Biography—Sources, Biblical. 4. Jesus Christ—Biography—Sources, Biblical—Meditations. I. Bible. N.T. Gospels. English. Selections. 2011.
  BS2559.L54 2011
  232.9007—dc22   2011016100

Printed in the United States of America

17   16   15   14   13   12   11
7   6   5   4   3   2   1

To one of the many behind the scenes, now with the Lord,
a relentless practitioner and enthusiastic spokesman
for Bible application

JAMES WINFIELD WILSON
1928–2009

PK, husband, father, grandfather, great-grandfather,
Bible translator, friend

TABLE *of* CONTENTS

Introduction

WEEK 1   Jesus' Coming Is Announced

WEEK 2   Jesus Is Born

WEEK 3   Jesus Grows Up

WEEK 4   Jesus Is Baptized

WEEK 5   Jesus Confronts Satan

WEEK 6   Jesus Meets Nicodemus

WEEK 7   Jesus Encounters a Samaritan Woman

WEEK 8   Jesus Heals

WEEK 9   Jesus Teaches about the Sabbath

WEEK 10   Jesus Preaches the Sermon on the Mount

WEEK 11   Jesus Teaches the Disciples about Prayer

WEEK 12   Jesus Is Wrongfully Accused

WEEK 13   Jesus Describes God's Kingdom

WEEK 14   Jesus Calms the Sea

WEEK 15   Jesus Commissions the Twelve

WEEK 16   Jesus Feeds the Five Thousand

WEEK 17   Jesus Challenges the Pharisees

WEEK 18   Jesus Reveals His Identity

WEEK 19   Jesus Tells What Following Him Will Mean

WEEK 20   Jesus Is Transfigured

WEEK 21   Jesus Presents the Realities of the Kingdom

WEEK 22   Jesus Describes Discipleship

WEEK 23   Jesus Tells the Parable of the Good Samaritan

WEEK 24   Jesus Talks about His Return

WEEK 25   Jesus Says He Is the Good Shepherd

WEEK 26   Jesus Attends a Banquet

WEEK 27   Jesus Talks about Being Lost and Found

WEEK 28   Jesus Raises Lazarus

WEEK 29   Jesus Speaks to the Rich Young Man

WEEK 30   Jesus Tells the Parable of the Vineyard Workers

WEEK 31   Jesus Heals a Blind Beggar

WEEK 32   Jesus Confronts Zacchaeus

WEEK 33   Jesus Is Anointed by Mary

WEEK 34   Jesus Enters Jerusalem

WEEK 35   Jesus Cleanses the Temple

WEEK 36   Jesus' Authority Is Challenged

WEEK 37   Jesus Teaches about the Future

WEEK 38   Jesus Is Betrayed

WEEK 39   Jesus Celebrates the Passover

WEEK 40   Jesus Washes the Disciples' Feet

WEEK 41   Jesus Promises the Holy Spirit

WEEK 42   Jesus Teaches about the True Vine

WEEK 43   Jesus Prays for His Followers

WEEK 44   Jesus Prays for Himself

WEEK 45   Jesus Is Arrested

WEEK 46   Jesus Is Denied by Peter

WEEK 47   Jesus Is Tried by Pilate

WEEK 48   Jesus Is Crucified

WEEK 49   Jesus Dies and Is Buried

WEEK 50   Jesus Is Resurrected

WEEK 51   Jesus Appears to the Disciples

WEEK 52   Jesus Gives Final Instructions

Topical Index
Scripture Index

They delight in the law of the LORD, meditating on it day and night. They are like trees planted along the riverbank, bearing fruit each season. Their leaves never wither, and they prosper in all they do. PSALM 1:2-3, NLT

The picturesque language of the first Psalm describes the potential impact of God's Word in people's lives. Meditating and delighting in God's Word produces trees of desirable and unusual character. These trees take their stand by a river that gives them life. You might call it a river of life, and you might also call what flows in that river "living water." These trees are described as "bearing fruit each season," which can mean, among other things, that whatever the season of life, the trees produce fruit appropriate for that season. These trees are also evergreen, since their leaves "never wither"—the seasons may come and go, and the fruit ripens and is harvested, but these trees persevere. They change and grow, yet remain the same. And these trees prosper.

The "trees" of Psalm 1 know what to do with God's Word. They live beside it, and it lives in them. They "delight" in what they discover from God's Word because they allow it to change the way they live. The results of their continual meditation are practical applications that lead to direction, change, truth, correction, and an increasing sense of God's involvement in their lives. We become those trees when we let Scripture speak into our lives that way—when we commit to becoming people who know what it means to both hear and do God's Word (James 1:19-25)—when we anticipate delight in God's Word.

The Birth of the LASB

The *Life Application Study Bible* (LASB) began during a coffee break. Someone asked a question, "If you could give students a Bible with built-in tools that would help them overcome unfamiliarity with Scripture and give them confidence to respond in obedience, what would you include in that Bible?"

Those of us sitting around the table that day were committed to communicating God's Word in ways that would give young people the best chance to experience its life-changing power. The coffee got cold as we brainstormed the kind of notes and other features that we were convinced might help people to come across the threshold of God's Word and into the life they could find in those pages. We were excited about the possibilities, but we had no idea what God would bring about as a result of that discussion. We also did not know what producing that Bible over the next several years would take. Our delighted naiveté was a tribute to the glory of God. We were about to join that throng of people through the ages who have been drawn into God's plans and purposes only to realize they had become part of something infinitely larger than themselves.

The point of the *Life Application Study Bible* wasn't to add to the Bible. Rather it was to provide people with tools that would help them experience the Bible. We didn't think the Bible needed help in being God's Word; we did think that people could use help in dealing with practical obstacles between themselves and God's Word. Judging from the responses to the LASB we've received over the years, God has used it in that way in countless lives.

The *Life Application Study Bible Devotional* was developed as one answer to the question: How can we encourage the readers of God's Word to *delight* in his Word? Application sounds like work—and often is. But it's the work we were designed to do. Rather than the frantic and hopeless work of trying to save ourselves, Bible application is the joyful work of gratitude for the priceless gift of salvation we have freely received through Christ (Ephesians 2:8-10)!

A metaphor similar to the psalm writer's picture of fruitful trees was used by Jesus to describe us. He spoke of vines and branches (John 15). Other places in the Bible point to the life God wants us to experience and uses the idea of roots (Ephesians 3:17-19; Colossians 2:6-7). The trees in Psalm 1 aren't running around the countryside getting good stuff done for God; rather they are healthy trees producing succulent fruit in season. What trees ultimately "do" is what God does in and through them. Good fruit is evidence of a tree or branch yielded to the purpose for which it was created. Attentive time spent in God's Word will bring about good fruit. The *Life Application Study Bible Devotional* is a tool to help you spend that time.

The Devotional Plan

This *Life Application Study Bible Devotional* allows you to spend time meditating day and night on the life of Jesus in order to thoroughly delight in that central part of God's Word. The pace is designed to take you through a year of concentrated reflection on the lessons found in Jesus' words and actions.

One of the features in the *Life Application Study Bible* is a "Harmony of the Gospels," located between the Gospel of John and the book of Acts. That extended chart offers a chronological list of 250 key events in the life of Jesus and where those events are found in each of the Gospels. (The Harmony is also built into the text of the Gospels; every paragraph mentions its possible Gospel parallels.)

Those 250 key events were organized into 52 larger sections to form the structure of this *Life Application Study Bible Devotional*. You will not only spend a year with Jesus; you will also spend each week in deliberate meditation on a specific event in his life.

We set out to avoid a typical devotional style, which can be light on Scripture and heavy on illustration. Many devotional books might be described as "hear and feel" approaches to God's Word, with an emphasis on feel. We wanted to aim at informed devotions—more of a read-hear-think-feel-and-do approach. The Bible has a captivating quality all its own, and we miss a lot when we move on to tangents too quickly. This *Life Application Study Bible Devotional* is for those who want to spend more time in God's Word than they have been spending, not less.

Each Week

Each week's six devotions concentrate on an event from Jesus' life, looking at the parallel passages in the Gospels related to that event. The accounts of Jesus' life vary in valuably revealing ways. Spending a week on each event will encourage deeper reflection and understanding. You will discover much more in any part of God's Word than can be exhausted by a few moments of reading.

Each Day

Each day's devotional reading includes four sections designed to establish a rhythm of reflection and ongoing meditation in your life. They will challenge you to personally respond to God's Word.

- Reading the Word—The day's focused selection from God's Word, chosen from that week's parallel passages from the Gospels.
- Setting the Scene—An extended reflection on the passage, highlighting details, background information, and other features that broaden the significance of the passage. Each Monday's devotional will be longer, introducing the major themes of the week.
- Getting Personal—Brief notes and questions to help you personalize the lessons of the daily Scripture reading.
- Talking to God—Suggestions for shaping an extended time of conversation with God each day.

The Scripture texts behind the *Life Application Study Bible Devotional* alternate among the New Living Translation, the New International Version, and the New King James Version. But the devotions can be used with any Bible.

We entrust this *Life Application Study Bible Devotional* to you with the same hope and prayer that has been wrapped around the *Life Application Study Bible*—that you would experience the root-deepening and fruit-ripening results of standing next to the waters of life in God's Word and delight as you meditate on them day and night.

Dave Veerman
Neil Wilson

SPRING 2011

JESUS' COMING IS ANNOUNCED
Week 1, Day 1

❋ *John 1:1-18; Luke 1:30-38; 1 John 1:1-3*

Because he is God, Jesus has always existed. This week, we will explore Jesus' true identity—before and after his earthly birth—and the announcement of his coming. We will discover the real Jesus and know how we should respond to him.

JESUS LIVES AND CREATES

Setting the Scene

Many believe that the apostle John, writer of the Gospel bearing his name, had first been a disciple of John the Baptist, who had pointed him to Jesus. Then John must have become an intermittent disciple of Jesus, for Scripture details another time when Jesus called John along the Sea of Galilee, where he had returned to his fishing trade with his brother, James, and their father, Zebedee. This time when Jesus called, John and James left everything, father and boat included, and followed him (Mark 1:19-20). At this point Jesus had already turned water into wine (John 2:1-11), cleared the Temple the first time (John 2:13-22), and been visited by Nicodemus at night (John 3:1-21). This calling of John and James also occurred after Herod had imprisoned John the Baptist (Luke 3:19-20), Jesus had spoken with the woman at the well (John 4:1-26), and Jesus had been rejected at Nazareth (Luke 4:16-30).

So John and his brother James became two of Jesus' original twelve disciples and, along with Peter, enjoyed a special relationship with Jesus. At times Jesus called just the three of them to see an important event, such as his Transfiguration.

John, therefore, was an eyewitness to Jesus' life and teachings. In his letter to the church, John wrote: "We saw him with our own eyes and touched him with our own hands" (1 John 1:1, NLT). As one who had seen Jesus up close, John wanted everyone to understand Jesus' true identity.

READING THE WORD

❋ *John 1:1-4, 14, NLT*

In the beginning the Word already existed. The Word was with God, and the Word was God. ²He existed in the beginning with God. ³God created everything through him, and nothing was created except through him. ⁴The Word gave life to everything that was created, and his life brought light to everyone.... ¹⁴So the Word became human and made his home among us. He was full of unfailing love and faithfulness. And we have seen his glory, the glory of the Father's one and only Son.

TALKING TO GOD

Thank God for sending his Son to earth. Ask him to deepen your understanding of Jesus as fully divine and yet fully human.

We learn in John 1:14 that "the Word" refers to Jesus. Theologians and philosophers, both Jews and Greeks, used the term "word" (in Greek, *logos*) in a variety of ways. In the Hebrew language of the Old Testament, "the Word" is described as an agent of creation (Psalm 33:6), the source of God's message to his people through the prophets (Hosea 1:1-2), and God's law, his standard of holiness (Psalm 119:11).

For Greeks, "the word" could mean a person's thoughts or reason, or might refer to a person's speech (the expression of thoughts). As a philosophical term, *logos* was the rational principle that governed the universe, even the creative energy that generated the universe.

In both the Jewish and Greek conceptions, *logos* conveyed the idea of beginnings, as in Genesis where the expression "God said" occurs repeatedly (Genesis 1:3ff). John may have had these ideas in mind, but his description shows he was speaking of Jesus as a human being he knew and loved, who was at the same time the Creator of the universe, the ultimate revelation of God, and the living picture of God's holiness, the one who "holds all creation together" (Colossians 1:17, NLT). Jesus as the *logos* reveals God's mind to us.

Clearly, John wanted everyone to know Jesus was not merely a man. Jesus was the eternal, all-powerful God who existed before time, created everything, and gave life.

Getting Personal

What qualities of Jesus convinced John that Jesus was divine, God in the flesh?

Why is Jesus' divinity crucial to the Christian faith?

If Jesus had been just a very good man, his life and death would have provided a great example of how a person should live. We could honor him and learn from his lifestyle. If Jesus had been only a great human teacher or orator, we could be motivated and inspired to work and achieve. But a great moral leader and powerful speaker can't save us from our sins, can't change us on the inside. Jesus can. As the divine Creator, he has the power to make us new.

JESUS BECOMES LIKE US

Setting the Scene

This week's passages reveal that Jesus was born as a baby. The divine Creator humbled himself and entered the human race as a flesh-and-blood human being. The apostle John knew Jesus man-to-man, having lived, eaten, conversed, and traveled with him. John had heard Jesus teach and heal, and had seen him suffer and die. According to John, "the Word became human and made his home among us" (John 1:14, NLT).

But no one was closer to Jesus than his mother, Mary. In this passage, an angel approached this startled teenager and explained that she would have a baby, but not just any baby, "the Son of God" (Luke 1:35, NLT). God would come to earth supernaturally but through natural means: conception, pregnancy, and birth. Jesus was (and is) both divine and human, the God-man. No one knows exactly how that works, but we see the evidence. Jesus was fully God and fully man—at the same time.

Imagine what Mary must have been thinking and feeling at this moment. Angel visits didn't happen every day! And Gabriel's message was even more startling—a virgin conceiving, by the Holy Spirit, and birthing God's Son. Yet Mary responded with faith and submission. No wonder she had "found favor with God."

Getting Personal

How does knowing that Jesus was human help you?

If you were in Mary's place, how would you have responded to the angel's announcement?

When do you find it difficult to submit to God's will?

Jesus was a living, breathing, and feeling human person. He wasn't a divine being dressed up like a human; he wasn't acting a part. Jesus fully took on flesh and experienced firsthand all that we experience. Thus, the Bible tells us, he can understand us and fully sympathize with us (Hebrews 4:15). Jesus, the Creator, became a baby, a child, an adolescent, an adult—with all of the human physical, psychological, and emotional qualities, but perfect, without sin. He knows us in every way. He knows you. And get this—he loves you and wants only the best for you. That's a truth almost as amazing as Gabriel's announcement.

READING THE WORD

❋ *Luke 1:30-38, NLT*

"Don't be afraid, Mary," the angel told her, "for you have found favor with God! 31You will conceive and give birth to a son, and you will name him Jesus. 32He will be very great and will be called the Son of the Most High. The Lord God will give him the throne of his ancestor David. 33And he will reign over Israel forever; his Kingdom will never end!" 34Mary asked the angel, "But how can this happen? I am a virgin." 35The angel replied, "The Holy Spirit will come upon you, and the power of the Most High will overshadow you. So the baby to be born will be holy, and he will be called the Son of God. 36What's more, your relative Elizabeth has become pregnant in her old age! People used to say she was barren, but she has conceived a son and is now in her sixth month. 37For nothing is impossible with God." 38Mary responded, "I am the Lord's servant. May everything you have said about me come true." And then the angel left her.

TALKING TO GOD

Meditate on Luke 1:37: "Nothing is impossible with God" (NLT). Pray for faith like Mary's to believe God in every situation.

READING THE WORD

✢ *John 1:10-13, NLT*
He came into the very world he created, but the world didn't recognize him. 11He came to his own people, and even they rejected him. 12But to all who believed him and accepted him, he gave the right to become children of God. 13They are reborn—not with a physical birth resulting from human passion or plan, but a birth that comes from God.

✢ *1 John 1:1-3, NLT*
We proclaim to you the one who existed from the beginning, whom we have heard and seen. We saw him with our own eyes and touched him with our own hands. He is the Word of life. 2This one who is life itself was revealed to us, and we have seen him. And now we testify and proclaim to you that he is the one who is eternal life. He was with the Father, and then he was revealed to us. 3We proclaim to you what we ourselves have actually seen and heard so that you may have fellowship with us.

TALKING TO GOD

Thank God for the gift of salvation through Jesus. Ask God to open your eyes and your ears to his work in the world, so that you can proclaim what you "have actually seen and heard."

JESUS SAVES

Setting the Scene

The divine Son of God, the true Light, came to the earth he had created but was rejected by most—but not everyone. All who put their faith in him, back then, today, and in the future, are reborn—spiritually, divinely transformed. John's letter affirms that Jesus is the "Word of life" and "eternal life." The salvation message is simple: Jesus, the God-man, entered human history, revealing sin and showing the way to eternal life. The first response is to recognize our sinfulness and to acknowledge that Jesus is the way. The second is to "believe" and "accept" the Savior.

When the first disciples believed and were regenerated by the Holy Spirit, they entered into a close relationship ("fellowship") with the Father and with his Son. The readers of 1 John had not seen and heard Jesus themselves, but they could trust that what John wrote was accurate. Believers today are like those second- and third-generation Christians. Though we have not personally seen, heard, or touched Jesus, we have the New Testament record of his eyewitnesses, and we can trust that these eyewitnesses spoke the truth about him.

Getting Personal

What convinced you to put your faith and trust in Christ?

How does being a child of God open up doors of fellowship with others?

When Jesus began his public ministry, many rejected him. Certain leaders felt his teaching threatened their status and authority. Some couldn't believe his claims—to be God in the flesh, their Messiah. Others couldn't get past Jesus' humble beginnings, which hardly befitted a king. Some struggled with Jesus' call to deny self. Today people reject Jesus for those same reasons. A man claiming to be God, the forgiver of sins, and the only way to heaven—that's tough to swallow. But now, just as then, many do believe and receive eternal life.

The word savior *means "one who saves, rescues, or delivers." Jesus the Savior has delivered you from your enemy, Satan, rescued you from sin's power, and saved you from sin's penalty. You're forgiven, free, and on your way to heaven.*

JESUS RELATES

Setting the Scene

Yesterday, we read John's declaration of his fellowship with the Father and the Son (1 John 1:1-3). Today's reading takes the relationship even closer: father and child. Those who believe in Jesus are "reborn" by God and become his children.

Family lineage and heritage were important to John and his fellow Jews. The Jews prided themselves on being God's chosen people through whom the whole world would be blessed. They knew, of course, that a person was Jewish by birthright. But they may have assumed that being born Jewish would also mean they automatically were God's children. Not so fast, John says. First, becoming a member of God's family is open to all who believe in Christ. Second, being of a specific race, nationality, family, or religion does not guarantee a spot at God's table. Only those who "believe" and "accept" are "reborn" into this family.

These days, many assume they have a relationship with God because they are relatively good people, attend church, or have a Christian family history. But God's family membership comes by faith alone. Each person is responsible for his or her own relationship with Christ.

The family analogy goes much further. As members of God's family, we have Jesus as our brother (Romans 8:29) and all other believers as our brothers and sisters. We're accepted; we're affirmed; we belong.

Getting Personal

How does knowing you are God's child affect your day-to-day choices?

According to this passage, how did you acquire "the right" to become God's child?

As God's children, we have a heavenly Father who cares about us and watches over us. We have an older Brother who is with us and who is interceding for us. We have the Holy Spirit inside us who comforts, guides, and leads us. We have brothers and sisters who encourage, teach, and assist us and hold us accountable. We're not alone.

We should relate well to other believers. This may seem like a tall order, but we don't pursue these relationships in our own power. With God's help we can be his kind of people.

READING THE WORD

❈ *John 1:12-13, NLT*
But to all who believed him and accepted him, he gave the right to become children of God. 13They are reborn—not with a physical birth resulting from human passion or plan, but a birth that comes from God.

TALKING TO GOD

Talk with God the Father about your relationship with your earthly father. Ask him for a greater understanding of what it means to be his child.

READING THE WORD

❋ *John 1:14-17, NLT*
So the Word became human and made his home among us. He was full of unfailing love and faithfulness. And we have seen his glory, the glory of the Father's one and only Son. 15John testified about him when he shouted to the crowds, "This is the one I was talking about when I said, 'Someone is coming after me who is far greater than I am, for he existed long before me.'" 16From his abundance we have all received one gracious blessing after another. 17For the law was given through Moses, but God's unfailing love and faithfulness came through Jesus Christ.

TALKING TO GOD

Thank God for the "gracious blessings" of his unfailing love and his faithfulness. Ask him to expand your vision of his glory and keep your focus on Jesus.

JESUS EXEMPLIFIES

Setting the Scene

John the Baptist (the "John" referred to in verse 15) acknowledges that Jesus existed long before him. From Luke 1:26, we learn that Elizabeth, John's mother, was six months pregnant when Gabriel made the grand announcement to Mary. So John was born at least six months before Jesus. But John knew that Jesus was much more than his blood relative through Mary; Jesus was the eternal Son of God, the Messiah. Truly Jesus is far greater than John and Moses and any other Old Testament prophet or king. John submitted himself to Jesus and sent his followers to him.

Because Jesus is God, he is perfect in every way. He is the perfect example, so we should look to him for an example of how to live. He is the perfect teacher, so we should listen to him and learn about God, morality, relationships, the meaning of life, and the future. He is the perfect sacrifice, fulfilling the requirements of the law, becoming sin, and dying in our place, so we should rest in him alone for salvation.

The apostle John affirms this by saying that Jesus was "full of unfailing love and faithfulness" and that he had given his people "one gracious blessing after another." That is, John had never found Jesus lacking in any way. John's description invites us to trust Jesus' ability to meet our needs. All believers receive Christ's blessings, but nothing can deplete Christ. No matter how much we receive of him, he keeps on giving. We don't need to seek any other source of spiritual power but Christ.

Getting Personal

What gracious blessings have you experienced because you know Jesus?

What other spiritual sources have you been tempted to consider recently (in the media, in books, in conversations)?

The author of Hebrews gives the secret to running the race of life. He says, "We do this by keeping our eyes on Jesus, the champion who initiates and perfects our faith" (Hebrews 12:2, NLT). Jesus is the initiator and the perfecter of our faith. He is all we need.

What helps you keep your eyes focused on Christ?

JESUS REPRESENTS

Setting the Scene

Gazing at the skies on a clear night, away from the city lights, we can feel overwhelmed by the vastness of space—and very small in comparison. God can seem distant. We can also feel far removed from the Father when we struggle with conflicts or grief. At those times we must remember to look to Jesus, who perfectly represents the Father. Only the Son communicates God's glory to us. The phrase "is near to the Father's heart" pictures Jesus as a child, enjoying a close and warm relationship with his Father. It also suggests the image of two companions enjoying a meal together. According to an ancient custom, the one who reclined next to the master at a meal was the one dearest to him. This is the Son who "has revealed God to us." The Son lived among people to explain God with his words and by his person. No one can know God apart from Christ. Later John writes about the time Philip said, "Lord, show us the Father, and we will be satisfied" (John 14:8, NLT). Jesus answered, "Anyone who has seen me has seen the Father!" (John 14:9, NLT).

Jesus is the visible, tangible image of the invisible God. He is the complete revelation of what God is like. This was startling news for Jews, who knew that no human could see God and live. Yet Jesus could say, "If you want to know what God is like, look at me!"

What is God's love like? Look at Jesus. How does God feel about hypocrisy? Look at Jesus. What about God's goodness, grace, and mercy? Look at Jesus.

Getting Personal

What can you do to focus more on Jesus?

God has revealed himself generally in nature and specifically in Scripture and perfectly in Christ. When you feel distant from the Father, remember that his Son is near you and his Spirit is in you.

As you share the faith with others, keep the focus on Jesus. People may believe in God as an idea, a concept, or even a Supreme Being—distant and unknowable. But they need to deal with Christ. What they do with him makes all the difference.

READING THE WORD

✹ *John 1:18, NLT*
No one has ever seen God. But the unique One, who is himself God, is near to the Father's heart. He has revealed God to us.

TALKING TO GOD

Pray that Jesus would make his character and presence real to you today.

JESUS IS BORN
Week 2, Day 1

❁ *Matthew 1:18-25; Luke 2:1-17*

It seemed as if all of earth and heaven got involved in the birth of Jesus. An angel visited in a dream to help Joseph make a tough decision. Caesar made a pronouncement that sent Mary and Joseph to their ancestral home in time to give birth to Jesus in Bethlehem, just as the prophet Micah had predicted. Angels sang from the heavens to shepherds in the fields, instructing them to go, see, and tell. The Savior, Jesus, was born as a baby and laid in a manger!

READING THE WORD

❁ *Matthew 1:18, NLT*
This is how Jesus the Messiah was born. His mother, Mary, was engaged to be married to Joseph. But before the marriage took place, while she was still a virgin, she became pregnant through the power of the Holy Spirit.

COMMITMENT AND CRISIS

Setting the Scene

After announcing the lineage of Jesus, Matthew introduces the two people who will be entrusted with God in the womb. Matthew wrote these words years after Jesus' death and resurrection, so the amazing climax of Jesus' life was already etched in the minds of his first readers. Matthew takes them (and us) back to the beginning to see how all the events unfolded that led to the overturning of the world.

Matthew doesn't mention a location, but we learn about Nazareth from Luke, though Matthew later (2:19-23) explains how Jesus came to be brought up in that northern town and why he was called a Nazarene. Matthew 1:18–2:23 includes aspects of Jesus' human origin that are not told anywhere else. Matthew gives us Joseph's perspective. As the story opens, an engagement (betrothal) has taken place, the first of several formal steps that will lead to the marriage of Joseph and Mary.

The reality of those times and that culture requires us to understand the "arranged" aspects of their relationship. Joseph would have met with Mary's father, not just to "ask for her hand in marriage" but to negotiate a bride-price (the financial commitment a groom made to his bride's family, demonstrating the seriousness of his intentions). Again the nearby record of genealogy reminds us that all the parties in these dealings would have been aware of the royal aspects of their mutual heritage. Such things were still important in a nation that continued to track an individual's connection with the original twelve tribes of

Israel. Both the prospective groom and bride traced their lineage to common points from Judah up through King David.

Mary might or might not have been allowed veto power in the arrangement, though the tone of the story leads us to believe she was in full agreement with her upcoming marriage to the local carpenter.

To the delightful news of the engagement of Mary and Joseph, Matthew adds three intriguing phrases: "before the marriage," "still a virgin," and "became pregnant through the power of the Holy Spirit." Luke has told us about the angel's visit with Mary. We can hardly imagine the conversation that must have followed if she tried to explain to her betrothed that she was with child and how the pregnancy had come about. The new circumstance could have created a strain on their relationship.

The cause may have been unique, but the results of change were the same we all experience—crisis. God's plan will involve crises in your life just as certainly as his arrival on earth created a series of crises for Mary and Joseph. Every crisis comes with the potential for God to do something great. How does that fact affect the way you respond to the crises in your life?

Getting Personal

What are some aspects of your life that seem to be going "according to plan" right now?

When did you last have to adapt to a significant unexpected change of plans?

God does exercise his sovereignty in our lives by overruling our plans. Proverbs reminds us repeatedly that we are free to make any plans we like, but to remember that God directs our steps. He is not limited to our plans. The challenge for us, then, is to develop God-oriented plans. Our responses to God-directed detours and obstacles tell us a lot about our progress in spiritual maturity.

THE STUNNED GROOM

READING THE WORD

❋ *Matthew 1:19-21, 24-25, NLT*
Joseph, her fiancé, was a good man and did not want to disgrace her publicly, so he decided to break the engagement quietly. 20As he considered this, an angel of the Lord appeared to him in a dream. "Joseph, son of David," the angel said, "do not be afraid to take Mary as your wife. For the child within her was conceived by the Holy Spirit. 21And she will have a son, and you are to name him Jesus, for he will save his people from their sins." . . . 24When Joseph woke up, he did as the angel of the Lord commanded and took Mary as his wife. 25But he did not have sexual relations with her until her son was born. And Joseph named him Jesus.

TALKING TO GOD

Ask God to help you follow him, even when his will leads you far from what others are doing or what others think should be done. Ask him to help you obey immediately, with determination, like Joseph.

Setting the Scene

The moment must have been intensely personal and painful for Joseph. Mary's unplanned pregnancy was a shock. We don't know how he reacted, but we are told how he planned to respond. Hurt and disappointed as he must have been, he still refused to take things out on Mary. The apparent death of their dreams and plans didn't need to result in Mary's actual death, which is probably what would have happened if Joseph had gone public with Mary's pregnancy and disavowed his own involvement. But Matthew tells us that Joseph could not set aside his personal character as a "good" (or righteous) man. But he did have to set aside pride and disappointment in order to practice compassion.

Joseph's intentions were correct according to the law, but God intervened with a better plan: "Do not be afraid to take Mary as your wife." If Joseph was not persuaded by Mary's explanation, then God provided the second witness that confirmed the story. Until Joseph faced the angel, the only possible explanations had been negatively human. Suddenly, with God in the picture, the shattering changes became filled with hope and promise.

Like Joseph, once we discover God's direction, our actions ought to be determined and immediate. Joseph married Mary and honored her special role by not physically consummating the marriage until after Jesus was born. Sooner or later, paying attention to God will lead us to take actions no one else seems to be taking. Following God's guidance may involve not following what others are doing or what others think should be done.

Getting Personal

Joseph's thoughtful approach rather than knee-jerk reaction gave God time to intervene. How could you practice this approach in challenging situations in your life?

When was the last time you changed course abruptly because of new information?

Waiting on God doesn't necessarily mean doing nothing. We want him to direct our lives and that may well mean taking the steps we know we can take. There are always obedient actions we can undertake while we are waiting for direction in some area. Like Joseph, move forward, trusting God's guidance.

ISAIAH'S GLIMPSE

Setting the Scene

Matthew wanted to make sure his Jewish readers (who were his primary original audience) saw the connection between the events in Jesus' life and the prophecies about the Messiah in their Scriptures, our Old Testament. The passage Matthew referred to came from the prophet Isaiah. While it likely had a short-term fulfillment, early Jewish scholars saw in passages like Isaiah 7:14 and 9:6 whispers from God about the promised Messiah. Until the discovery of the Dead Sea Scrolls in the middle of the twentieth century, the accuracy of messianic prophecies were often chalked up to Christians editing the ancient texts and "writing in" references to Jesus. But a complete scroll of Isaiah dating to before the time of Christ was part of the Qumran treasure trove, giving us documented evidence that prophecies about Jesus were on record long before he was born.

In Isaiah's immediate context, a young woman's life could have provided the timeline for the prophet's words to King Ahaz that his chief enemies would be defeated and an even more daunting enemy would rise. The woman would marry, bear a child, and wean the child while the events unfolded. She would name him Immanuel. The ultimate fulfillment of Isaiah's prophecy would occur when a virgin would actually conceive and bear a son who would be "God with us"—Immanuel.

Interestingly, the final verse in Matthew's Gospel records Jesus saying, "I am with you always"—he was not only born Immanuel, but he remains forever God with us among all peoples, to the end of the age.

Getting Personal

How do you live out in a daily way the fact that God is with you?

What does fulfilled prophecy tell you about the God you worship?

Because God foreknows, he can foretell. Because God is ultimately in control, what he foretells will come to be. These prophecies invite and test our trust in God. The accuracy of fulfillment that can be traced in Jesus' life leaves us without excuse when it comes to trusting God's plan for the world and his plan for our own lives. In what ways are you trusting God today?

READING THE WORD

❋ *Matthew 1:22-23, NLT*
All of this occurred to fulfill the Lord's message through his prophet: 23"Look! The virgin will conceive a child! She will give birth to a son, and they will call him Immanuel, which means 'God is with us.'"

TALKING TO GOD

Ask God to help you trust his plan for your life. Thank him for being "Immanuel," God with you personally.

CHANGE OF SCENES

Setting the Scene

Like a true historian, Luke paints in broad strokes the political landscape around the intimate scene in Bethlehem when Jesus was born. The Roman emperor Augustus set into motion a new program of taxation for the nations under his rule and caused a couple from Nazareth to travel to their ancestral home. Mary and Joseph didn't head for Bethlehem simply to fulfill the widely known prophecy that the Savior would be born in Bethlehem in Judea (Micah 5:2); they went to their family "hometown" because of the emperor's decree. God demonstrated his power and creativity in using the massive apparatus of the Roman government to move people into the places he wanted them to be for his own arrival on earth. Jerusalem was the great King David's capital, but his home was Bethlehem, and his descendant Joseph was required to report there.

Some might note all these converging developments and be amazed at the unusual number of coincidences, but those who keep God at the center of things know that the Creator of this world is also its Sustainer and Guide. The universe ship has a Captain, and the journey has a destination. The birth of Jesus was the most planned and prepared-for arrival in history. God's unfolding promise—first given to the fallen Adam and Eve that God would provide an answer for sin—was about to be fulfilled. As Joseph and Mary wearily approached Bethlehem, the final pieces of a complex plan fell quietly into place.

READING THE WORD

✽ *Luke 2:1-4, NLT*

At that time the Roman emperor, Augustus, decreed that a census should be taken throughout the Roman Empire. 2(This was the first census taken when Quirinius was governor of Syria.) 3All returned to their own ancestral towns to register for this census. 4And because Joseph was a descendant of King David, he had to go to Bethlehem in Judea, David's ancient home. He traveled there from the village of Nazareth in Galilee.

TALKING TO GOD

Ask God to help you trust in his sovereignty, even over the mundane and inconvenient events in life. Ask God to guide your steps today to glorify him and participate in his plans for the world.

Getting Personal

Where do you see God working on the world stage in our time in history?

What choices will you make today, depending on God to do his part?

It isn't all that easy to look at world events and understand how God is fitting them into his plan. But hindsight and continual observation of the flow of our own lives remind us that God is active and in control. The kind of trust we see in Joseph and Mary reveals the importance of obedience even when we can't see the immediate outcome of our next steps.

LABOR AND DELIVERY

Setting the Scene

Those who have lived with or been a woman in the final stages of pregnancy shake their heads in wonder over Mary and Joseph's journey from Nazareth to Bethlehem. Neither walking nor riding a donkey for several days could be described as anything but uncomfortable. Apparently the Romans had no provision in the taxation laws for filing a late return—Joseph and Mary were required to report, extenuating circumstances notwithstanding.

Countless tellings of the story have compressed the time between the couple's journey and Jesus' arrival. We usually picture the weary soon-to-be-parents wandering into Bethlehem in the evening, with Mary already feeling contractions, and the "No Vacancy" signs posted in the inn. Jesus was born in a little town, perhaps only large enough to have one inn. Necessity forced the couple to take shelter in some kind of alternative housing that had a manger. Since the "manger" indicates a place where animals were housed, it is likely that Jesus was born in a cave. This ironically means that Jesus spent both his arrival night and his departure night (following his death on the cross) in a cave.

Regardless of exact location, Jesus' birth went largely unnoticed by the world. The scant details point to the simplicity and commonness of his birth. God, taking on flesh, entered life in the same messy, painful, and wonder-filled way that every human does. The King of kings didn't get royal treatment at birth. Right from the start, only a few really understood and welcomed the Savior.

Getting Personal

Describe the time when you welcomed Jesus into your life. How has that decision changed you?

What aspects of the Christmas story affect you most profoundly? Why?

Familiarity with the story sometimes causes us to relive the events of Jesus' birth with mild indifference. But what would be our fate if the Savior had never been born? The wonder doesn't come from trying to imagine all the ways God might have arranged to rescue us; the wonder comes in realizing that this was, in fact, the way God fulfilled his promises.

READING THE WORD

✤ *Luke 2:5-7, NLT*
He took with him Mary, his fiancée, who was now obviously pregnant. 6And while they were there, the time came for her baby to be born. 7She gave birth to her first child, a son. She wrapped him snugly in strips of cloth and laid him in a manger, because there was no lodging available for them.

TALKING TO GOD

Ask God to make the story of his incarnation fresh for you as you study his Word. Ask him to help you appreciate the amazing juxtaposition of his glory and human labor and delivery and infancy.

PRESS RELEASE

✤ *Luke 2:8-17, NLT*

That night there were shepherds staying in the fields nearby, guarding their flocks of sheep. 9Suddenly, an angel of the Lord appeared among them, and the radiance of the Lord's glory surrounded them. They were terrified, 10but the angel reassured them. "Don't be afraid!" he said. "I bring you good news that will bring great joy to all people. 11The Savior—yes, the Messiah, the Lord—has been born today in Bethlehem, the city of David! 12And you will recognize him by this sign: You will find a baby wrapped snugly in strips of cloth, lying in a manger." 13Suddenly, the angel was joined by a vast host of others—the armies of heaven—praising God and saying, 14"Glory to God in highest heaven, and peace on earth to those with whom God is pleased." 15When the angels had returned to heaven, the shepherds said to each other, "Let's go to Bethlehem! Let's see this thing that has happened, which the Lord has told us about." 16They hurried to the village and found Mary and Joseph. And there was the baby, lying in the manger. 17After seeing him, the shepherds told everyone what had happened and what the angel had said to them about this child.

TALKING TO GOD

Ask God to make the wonder of his great good news fresh for you and to help you simply and joyfully let others know what you found when you acted on that good news.

Setting the Scene

Generally, the importance of an announcement is judged by the audience to which it is made. Today, significant proclamations call for a televised press conference with a written press release. God broke every rule of effective media management at the birth of his Son: He chose poor timing (the middle of the night), an insignificant audience (shepherds), an odd location (hillside pasture), and an over-the-top spokes-angel. Those inexplicable contrasts give Jesus' birth announcement a distinct ring of truth.

Happily, the angel's announcement included a note of "fear not" that applies far beyond the immediate circumstance and flows from the fact that the Savior's birth will bring "great joy" to "all people"—including us! As if unable to restrain themselves over the good news, the angelic choir breaks out with a song of confirmation and the hopeful word that the impact of the news will be "glory to God" and "peace" to people as a result of God's favor. The shepherds, untroubled by their low social status, set their feet in motion. And having received the truth they had been told by acting on it themselves, they then told others and they joyfully thanked God.

Shepherds were at the bottom of their societal structure. They knew their unworthiness as recipients of the news and its meaning. They simply accepted the fact that they now had a Savior, the Lord. We place ourselves in their sandals when we realize we are equally unworthy, and yet God has offered to us the same good news of a Savior.

Getting Personal

How do you identify with the shepherds who heard the news?

What do the inexplicable contrasts and unexpected qualities of the night of Christ's birth indicate about credibility of the account?

Luke tells us that those who heard the news secondhand from the shepherds "were amazed" (2:18, NIV). This response may or may not have been belief. The crucial lesson for us is not in the effect but in the effort. How often do you simply and joyfully let others know what you found when you acted on the news about Christ?

JESUS GROWS UP

✤ *Matthew 2:1-23; Luke 2:21-52*

After Jesus' birth in Bethlehem, he grew as an infant, toddler, child, and young man under the care of God-honoring parents. This week, we will examine those growing-up years, focusing especially on the people closest to him and those who interacted with him and his parents.

DOING GOD'S WILL

Setting the Scene

According to Leviticus 12:3, every Jewish boy was to be circumcised on the eighth day after his birth, and by custom he was given his name at that ceremony. Circumcision set Jews apart from Gentiles and was a sign of their unique, covenantal relationship with God (Genesis 17:9-14). Careful to obey Moses' law, Mary and Joseph took their son to the local priest to be circumcised, and there they named him Jesus, just as the angel had instructed Mary (Luke 1:31).

For forty days after the birth of a son and eighty days after the birth of a daughter, the mother was "unclean" according to the law and could not enter the Temple. After that time, the mother would make a purification offering. So Mary and Joseph traveled to Jerusalem for this ceremony. They were to bring a lamb for a burnt offering and a dove or pigeon for a sin offering. The priest would sacrifice these animals and declare the woman to be clean. If a lamb was too expensive, the law said that the parents could sacrifice "either a pair of turtledoves or two young pigeons."

In addition, a firstborn son was to be presented to God one month after birth (Exodus 13:2, 11-16; Numbers 18:15-16). The ceremony included buying back—"redeeming"—the child from God through an offering. Through this, the parents would publicly acknowledge that the child belonged to God, who alone has the power to give life.

Although Jesus was the Son of God, his earthly parents

READING THE WORD

✤ *Luke 2:21-24, 39-40, NLT*
Eight days later, when the baby was circumcised, he was named Jesus, the name given him by the angel even before he was conceived. 22Then it was time for their purification offering, as required by the law of Moses after the birth of a child; so his parents took him to Jerusalem to present him to the Lord. 23The law of the Lord says, "If a woman's first child is a boy, he must be dedicated to the LORD." 24So they offered the sacrifice required in the law of the Lord—"either a pair of turtledoves or two young pigeons." . . . 39When Jesus' parents had fulfilled all the requirements of the law of the Lord, they returned home to Nazareth in Galilee. 40There the child grew up healthy and strong. He was filled with wisdom, and God's favor was on him.

TALKING TO GOD

Give the Lord your anxieties about the uncertain future months, years, and decades. Ask him to lead you, step by step, into strong day-to-day decisions and holy living.

fulfilled everything God's law required regarding the birth of firstborn sons.

Eventually Mary and Joseph returned home to Nazareth, from where they had come to register for the census. A gap of several years separates verses 38 and 39 during which the family found a place to live in Bethlehem, fled to Egypt, and returned to Nazareth after Herod's death.

Getting Personal

What does this passage tell you about Mary and Joseph's values in bringing up Jesus?

When you face life's unknowns, what helps you choose to live God's way?

What an unusual introduction to parenting, beginning with angels' announcements, a divine conception, birth in a stable, and shepherds praising God. The Lord had revealed some of what would happen in the years to come, but like all parents, Mary and Joseph had a limited perspective. They couldn't see the future, and they must have wondered how they could possibly raise and parent the Son of God, their Messiah. Luke reports that they "fulfilled all the requirements of the law of the Lord" (2:39, NLT). Instead of worrying, wondering, and wavering, they took life one day and one decision at a time and obeyed God with each step.

BELIEVING GOD'S PROMISE

Setting the Scene

As Mary and Joseph entered the Temple, an old man, a stranger, took Jesus in his arms and began to praise God. Luke doesn't tell us much about Simeon except that he was "righteous and devout" and that he was "eagerly waiting for" the arrival of God's promised Messiah, the one foretold by the prophets. The Messiah would deliver God's people and establish God's Kingdom. All Jews hoped for the coming of their Deliverer, but God had told Simeon that he would see the Messiah in his lifetime. Simeon held on to this promise, so he had his eyes wide open, anticipating his Messiah's arrival. Simeon may not have known what age the Messiah would be at their meeting. So he may have been surprised and thrilled upon learning that this infant was God's Son. Just imagine how many babies Simeon had seen during this time, but he kept looking and trusting. And when Simeon saw Jesus, he knew this was the one.

After meeting Simeon, Mary and Joseph encountered Anna. This elderly Jewish woman spent most of her days worshiping and praying in the Temple. Seeing Jesus, Anna burst into praise, confirming what Simeon had said about the baby.

As we can certainly understand, "Jesus' parents were amazed at what was being said about him" by both Simeon and Anna.

Getting Personal

What might have caused Simeon and Anna to waver in their faith? How did the Holy Spirit help them?

In what ways do God's promises give you hope in times of waiting?

We probably won't find Simeon or Anna in any list of major Bible characters. Yet more than two millennia after this incident in the Temple, we know about them and their faith in God's promises. God's Word contains many promises, including God's continual presence, his sovereignty over world events, his Holy Spirit, his daily care, and his bringing us safely to heaven. During times of conflict, meager resources, loneliness, and suffering, God can seem distant. That's when we need to cling to the truth that God loves us so much that he sent Jesus.

READING THE WORD

✶ *Luke 2:25, 28-36, 38, NLT*
At that time there was a man in Jerusalem named Simeon. He was righteous and devout and was eagerly waiting for the Messiah to come and rescue Israel. . . . 28He took the child in his arms and praised God, saying, 29"Sovereign Lord, now let your servant die in peace, as you have promised. 30I have seen your salvation, 31which you have prepared for all people. 32He is a light to reveal God to the nations, and he is the glory of your people Israel!" 33Jesus' parents were amazed at what was being said about him. 34Then Simeon blessed them, and he said to Mary, the baby's mother, "This child is destined to cause many in Israel to fall, but he will be a joy to many others. He has been sent as a sign from God, but many will oppose him. 35As a result, the deepest thoughts of many hearts will be revealed. And a sword will pierce your very soul." 36Anna, a prophet, was also there in the Temple. . . . 38She came along just as Simeon was talking with Mary and Joseph, and she began praising God. She talked about the child to everyone who had been waiting expectantly for God to rescue Jerusalem.

TALKING TO GOD

Thank God for the example of Simeon's and Anna's faith in his promises. Ask God to give you a steadfast spirit in times of conflict, meager resources, loneliness, and suffering.

SEEKING GOD'S KING

READING THE WORD

✤ *Matthew 2:1-6, 9-11, NLT*

Jesus was born in Bethlehem in Judea, during the reign of King Herod. About that time some wise men from eastern lands arrived in Jerusalem, asking, 2"Where is the newborn king of the Jews? We saw his star as it rose, and we have come to worship him." 3King Herod was deeply disturbed when he heard this, as was everyone in Jerusalem. 4He called a meeting of the leading priests and teachers of religious law and asked, "Where is the Messiah supposed to be born?" 5"In Bethlehem in Judea," they said, "for this is what the prophet wrote: 6'And you, O Bethlehem in the land of Judah, are not least among the ruling cities of Judah, for a ruler will come from you who will be the shepherd for my people Israel.'" . . . 9The wise men went their way. And the star they had seen in the east guided them to Bethlehem. It went ahead of them and stopped over the place where the child was. 10When they saw the star, they were filled with joy! 11They entered the house and saw the child with his mother, Mary, and they bowed down and worshiped him. Then they opened their treasure chests and gave him gifts of gold, frankincense, and myrrh.

TALKING TO GOD

Thank God for the ways he draws you to himself. Ask him to show you how to use your gifts for his glory and service.

Setting the Scene

Several years passed between the events of Luke 2:38 and 39. During that time, Mary and Joseph found a place to live in Bethlehem, fled to Egypt to escape King Herod (Matthew 2:1-18), and returned to Nazareth after Herod's death (Matthew 2:19-23). Their flight to Egypt was precipitated by the arrival of wise men seeking "the newborn king of the Jews," which led to Herod's jealous rage.

The wise men seem to have specialized in astronomy, but they may have interpreted dreams and had other special knowledge and abilities. They referred to Jesus' "star." Numbers 24:17 mentions a "star" coming out of Jacob, but how would the wise men have known that the star represented the Messiah? Perhaps they were descendants of Jews who had remained in Babylon after the Exile and thus grew up knowing the Old Testament prophecies. Or they may have studied ancient manuscripts. Or perhaps God had given them a special message. In any case, they traveled to Jerusalem, the capital city, expecting to find a young king there. Herod had no idea what they were talking about but felt threatened by this talk of a "king." So he assembled the Jewish religious leaders and asked them.

Interestingly, the Jewish leaders told Herod and the wise men that the Messiah would be born in Bethlehem (see Micah 5:2), but they didn't go themselves. These visitors from faraway lands recognized Jesus as the Messiah when most of God's chosen people in Israel did not.

The wise men traveled thousands of miles searching for the one who had been born King of the Jews. And when they found him, they joyfully worshiped him and presented gifts fit for a king.

Getting Personal

What was your "star"—that is, what did God use to lead you to Jesus?

In what ways do you bow before your Savior? What gifts do you bring him?

God leads us to him through the Holy Spirit working in us and through choice relationships and circumstances. Wise people follow God's lead and find the Savior with great joy.

FOLLOWING GOD'S LEAD

Setting the Scene

Jesus' earthly father, Joseph, played a major role in the Incarnation story, but he is barely mentioned in Scripture. The Bible gives these facts: Joseph was a carpenter (Matthew 13:55), the son of Heli (Luke 3:23), and Mary's husband. We learn more about Joseph through his choices and actions. Matthew describes him as "a good man" (Matthew 1:19, NLT) and tells how he chose *not* to disgrace Mary publicly when he learned she was pregnant. Then, when God spoke to Joseph in a dream, he listened and obeyed, taking Mary to be his wife. In today's passage, we see other examples of this "good man" in action. God told Joseph, "get up," "flee to Egypt," and "stay." Joseph did exactly as he was told, leaving that very night and traveling with Jesus and Mary the seventy-five miles to Egypt, outside Herod's jurisdiction. Joseph followed God's instructions and remained in Egypt until the death of Herod, after which God told him to "get up" and return to the land of Israel.

Getting Personal

What is Joseph's unvarying response to God's directions to him through the angels' messages?

What may the Holy Spirit be telling you God wants you to do?

What steps can you take to follow his lead?

Joseph didn't doubt, question, or bargain with God. He obeyed—God led, and he followed. We probably won't receive a message from God through an angel or in a dream, but God has given us numerous instructions on what choices to make and actions to take. And we know from the Bible, from history, and from personal experience that his way is best.

READING THE WORD

❈ *Matthew 2:13-15, 19-23, NLT*
After the wise men were gone, an angel of the Lord appeared to Joseph in a dream. "Get up! Flee to Egypt with the child and his mother," the angel said. "Stay there until I tell you to return, because Herod is going to search for the child to kill him." 14That night Joseph left for Egypt with the child and Mary, his mother, 15and they stayed there until Herod's death. This fulfilled what the Lord had spoken through the prophet: "I called my Son out of Egypt." . . . 19When Herod died, an angel of the Lord appeared in a dream to Joseph in Egypt. 20"Get up!" the angel said. "Take the child and his mother back to the land of Israel, because those who were trying to kill the child are dead." 21So Joseph got up and returned to the land of Israel with Jesus and his mother. 22But when he learned that the new ruler of Judea was Herod's son Archelaus, he was afraid to go there. Then, after being warned in a dream, he left for the region of Galilee. 23So the family went and lived in a town called Nazareth. This fulfilled what the prophets had said: "He will be called a Nazarene."

TALKING TO GOD

Ask God to quicken your mind and spirit to see his instructions about your choices and actions as you read his Word and pray. Pray for the Lord to give you joy in following his lead.

READING THE WORD

❈ *Matthew 2:16-18, NLT*
Herod was furious when he realized that the wise men had outwitted him. He sent soldiers to kill all the boys in and around Bethlehem who were two years old and under, based on the wise men's report of the star's first appearance. 17Herod's brutal action fulfilled what God had spoken through the prophet Jeremiah: 18"A cry was heard in Ramah—weeping and great mourning. Rachel weeps for her children, refusing to be comforted, for they are dead."

TALKING TO GOD

Thank God that you have been rescued from the power of the evil one, and ask for his continued protection and guidance. Thank him for his ultimate power and authority—and that nothing can separate you from his love.

ASSESSING GOD'S ENEMIES

Setting the Scene

Evil is real. The Bible explains that ever since Adam and Eve disobeyed God and sin entered the world, people have been born sinners; thus, doing what is wrong comes naturally. We tend to look out for ourselves and our own interests first. Taken to the extreme, self-centeredness leads to every imaginable evil act. History documents the terrible acts of the evil king Herod, especially concerning potential rivals to the throne. In his later years, Herod had three of his sons killed as well as his wife and many actual or suspected conspirators. Herod didn't hesitate to spill blood to secure his power. Obsessed with himself, he felt threatened by a helpless baby who might one day become king.

Bethlehem was only a few miles from Jerusalem. Herod expected the wise men to return to him after finding the child they sought. When he learned they had gone home without reporting the location of the child, Herod took out his anger on innocent children.

We may question how God could permit such terrible atrocities, even as he allowed Jesus to escape. But Matthew, a Jew, knew all too well that the history of God's people was littered with evil acts against them. The Messiah's arrival caused Satan to unleash an arsenal of evil, in this instance using Herod.

The poetic quotation from the book of Jeremiah refers to Rachel, one of the wives of the Hebrew patriarch Jacob, also named "Israel." She symbolized the mother of the nation. The mothers of the murdered boys were inconsolable, so great was their grief.

Getting Personal

When you think of extreme evil, who or what comes to mind?

Jesus told his disciples to pray, "rescue us from the evil one" (Matthew 6:13, NLT). What historical examples of God's rescue can you list? How about for you personally?

Not only do human beings have an evil streak, but Satan is working overtime to thwart God's plans. We should always be on our guard, relying on God's strength, armor, and weapons (Ephesians 6:10-17). This world is not all there is; one day, God will be victorious (Romans 8:31-39).

DISCOVERING GOD'S SON

Setting the Scene

According to God's law, every male was required to go to Jerusalem three times a year for the great festivals. In the spring, the Passover was celebrated, followed immediately by the weeklong Festival of Unleavened Bread. Every year, Joseph, Mary, and Jesus celebrated Passover in Jerusalem.

At twelve years of age, Jesus would have been considered an adult, so Mary and Joseph weren't alarmed at first when he wasn't with them in the large caravan of people traveling home. When he didn't show up when they made camp in the evening, they returned to Jerusalem to look for him. After three long days of searching and worrying, they found him in the Temple, discussing theology with the religious teachers. During Passover, the greatest rabbis in Israel would assemble to teach and to discuss great truths. Certainly the coming Messiah would have been a discussion topic. Jesus would have been eager to listen and to ask probing questions. The depth of Jesus' wisdom at his young age amazed these teachers.

Mary and Joseph had looked for Jesus for three days, so her question is understandable: "Why have you done this to us?" Jesus simply replied, "Didn't you know that I must be in my Father's house?" Mary and Joseph didn't realize that Jesus was making a distinction between his earthly father and his heavenly Father. They knew Jesus was God's Son, but they didn't understand what his mission would involve. Joseph and Mary had to learn and observe the complex outworking of Jesus' special identity and calling, even as he lived in their family.

Getting Personal

When Jesus was a baby, what do you suppose Mary and Joseph imagined life would be like, having the Son of God in their home?

As you have grown, in what ways has your understanding of Jesus changed?

Mary did not completely understand her son, but she remembered these events and sought to find their meaning (Luke 2:51). Eventually Mary's son would become her Savior and she would understand.

READING THE WORD

❀ *Luke 2:41-49, NLT*

Every year Jesus' parents went to Jerusalem for the Passover festival. 42When Jesus was twelve years old, they attended the festival as usual. 43After the celebration was over, they started home to Nazareth, but Jesus stayed behind in Jerusalem. His parents didn't miss him at first, 44because they assumed he was among the other travelers. But when he didn't show up that evening, they started looking for him among their relatives and friends. 45When they couldn't find him, they went back to Jerusalem to search for him there. 46Three days later they finally discovered him in the Temple, sitting among the religious teachers, listening to them and asking questions. 47All who heard him were amazed at his understanding and his answers. 48His parents didn't know what to think. "Son," his mother said to him, "why have you done this to us? Your father and I have been frantic, searching for you everywhere." 49"But why did you need to search?" he asked. "Didn't you know that I must be in my Father's house?"

TALKING TO GOD

Express your joy in understanding who Jesus really is. Ask him to give you a mind that seeks after his truth with eagerness and pleasure.

JESUS IS BAPTIZED
Week 4, Day 1

❊ *Matthew 3:13-17; Mark 1:9-11; Luke 3:21-22*

From the moment Jesus stepped onto the dusty roads of Roman-occupied Palestine, he lived with purpose and in obedience to the will of his Father. He came to accomplish a task, and nothing would stop him from completing it. We can learn from Jesus' example of step-by-step daily obedience to the will of God. When we live in that kind of relationship, we bring him great joy.

READING THE WORD

❊ *Matthew 3:13, NLT*
Then Jesus went from Galilee to the Jordan River to be baptized by John.

INTENTIONAL LIVING

Setting the Scene

All three of the accounts from the Gospels that we will look at this week present Jesus as a grown adult. Mark's Gospel doesn't give any attention to the childhood events in Jesus' life, but moves quickly into the action that begins Jesus' public ministry—his baptism. In Luke, between the end of chapter 2 and the opening verses of chapter 3 a time gap of almost twenty years has passed—from the time Jesus visited the Temple as a youngster up to the beginning of his public ministry. For Matthew, the jump between the account of Jesus' earliest years and his arrival on the scene of John the Baptist's ministry covers almost thirty years.

Jesus was raised as an ordinary human child. Although there are certainly nonbiblical traditions about events in Jesus' childhood, the writers of the Gospels were not prompted to report anything unusual about those years. Even the incident at the Temple in Jerusalem when Jesus was twelve reads like a fairly typical exchange between an adolescent and his parents, except that Jesus demonstrated an awareness of his unique relationship with his Father (Luke 2:41-52). The summary statement in Luke 2:52 pictures Jesus as we meet him on the eve of his public ministry: "Jesus grew in wisdom and in stature and in favor with God and all the people" (NLT). What parents wouldn't want to describe their child as growing mentally, physically, spiritually, and socially?

By providing us few details about Jesus' adolescence, God has prevented us from thinking, *He didn't experience* what I experienced—how can he identify with me? But in speaking to this very point the book of Hebrews says about Jesus, "This High Priest of ours understands our weaknesses, for he faced all of the same testings we do, yet he did not sin" (Hebrews 4:15, NLT). We need not know the specifics of Jesus' development; God has given us enough to show us that Jesus was profoundly like us yet without sin. And like us, he was challenged to grow in all areas of life in order to become the man we can emulate and recognize as Master of our lives.

Based on Luke 2:52, we meet Jesus in Matthew 3:13 as a well-rounded adult making an intentional journey from Galilee south along the Jordan to the place where John the Baptist was performing baptisms of those who responded to his preaching. We know this was a familiar trip for Jesus. He had made it in the womb twice, and Luke 2:41 indicates that it was a family tradition to take a yearly trek from Nazareth to Jerusalem for Passover. This time, it appears that he made the trip alone. That forty-mile trip not only served to set Jesus' ministry in motion, it also foreshadowed the lifestyle Jesus would assume over the next three years.

Getting Personal

What does it mean to you that Jesus was human?

What encouragement does his normal development give you as you continue to grow spiritually, mentally, and emotionally?

At his every age and stage of development, we see Jesus active in doing his Father's will. Before we excuse ourselves by saying that he knew more than we know, we must account for the way God has provided in Scripture an abundance of examples and commands regarding his will. Whatever our circumstances, we are always able to do something that God has told us he wants us to do.

TALKING TO GOD

Take the Lord Jesus as your example of one who deliberately seeks to do the Father's will. Ask God to make you increasingly like him, ready and willing to obey.

THE SEDUCTION OF STARDOM

READING THE WORD

✶ *John 1:19-23, NLT*

This was John's testimony when the Jewish leaders sent priests and Temple assistants from Jerusalem to ask John, "Who are you?" 20He came right out and said, "I am not the Messiah." 21"Well then, who are you?" they asked. "Are you Elijah?" "No," he replied. "Are you the Prophet we are expecting?" "No." 22"Then who are you? We need an answer for those who sent us. What do you have to say about yourself?" 23John replied in the words of the prophet Isaiah: "I am a voice shouting in the wilderness, 'Clear the way for the LORD's coming!'"

TALKING TO GOD

Submit all of today's words and actions to the Lord. Ask him to provide real balance, with himself as the central focus of your life.

Setting the Scene

All four Gospels highlight the unique role of John the Baptist in the life of Jesus. Luke indicates that John and Jesus are distant cousins (see Luke 1:36, KJV).

Matthew interprets John's presence by quoting Isaiah 40:3, "He is a voice shouting in the wilderness, 'Prepare the way for the LORD's coming! Clear the road for him!'"(Matthew 3:3, NLT). Both Matthew and Mark describe John's appearance in a way that reminds us of Old Testament prophets whose ministry involved unorthodox outfits and unusual diets: "John's clothes were woven from coarse camel hair, and he wore a leather belt around his waist. For food he ate locusts and wild honey" (Matthew 3:4, NLT). Small wonder that the religious establishment sent a delegation to John to inquire about his identity. Would he claim to be a prophet? John made it clear he wasn't a prophet; he was the fulfillment of a prophecy!

John the Baptist knew his role and lived it. He was a charismatic figure whose life and message drew crowds, and he could have cashed in on his notoriety. Instead John used a striking word picture from Isaiah: "I am a voice shouting in the wilderness." To make sure they didn't miss the point, he added, "I'm not even worthy to be his slave and untie the straps of his sandal" (John 1:27, NLT). John was not seduced by his own stardom. He knew who the "star" really was and gladly pointed everyone toward the Savior.

Getting Personal

In what ways are you "preparing the way" for those around you to find the Savior?

How can you make Christ the central focus of your life?

"It's all about me" is the attitude of many in our world today. The bottom line for the Christian, however, is that it isn't all about me; it's all about Jesus. Every act, every word, every motive, every plan, every desire should revolve around the center, Jesus himself. Only then is life in balance. Only then can we point people to the Savior.

SIMPLE OBEDIENCE

Setting the Scene

Matthew 3:2 and 4:17 make it clear that John the Baptist and Jesus had a common message: "Repent of your sins and turn to God, for the Kingdom of Heaven is near" (NLT). For months before Jesus began his ministry, John had been confronting the crowds with their need to turn to God for forgiveness. When the Messiah arrived, John soon stepped aside, for his role was complete.

We don't know how many encounters John and Jesus had, but Christ's baptism stands out in the gospel story. John devoted his life to preparing the way for Jesus, but he clearly didn't expect Jesus to ask to be baptized along with the crowds. He knew Jesus had no reason to repent. So he suggested that Jesus baptize him.

Jesus' answer gives us a glimpse into his acceptance of God's will over the course of his life. The phrase "we must carry out all that God requires" is similar to Jesus' later words in the garden of Gethsemane, "I want your will to be done, not mine" (Luke 22:42, NLT). By insisting on baptism, Jesus was making public his identification with sinners. He went to the Cross as the ultimate act of substitution, but he began his ministry with this act of obedience that beautifully pictured his eventual purpose. Long before the nails were driven into his flesh, Jesus was taking steps that would make his sacrifice perfect and complete.

Getting Personal

If you had been there by the river that day, from what sins would you have needed to repent?

What makes submission to God difficult for you?

Both the King (Jesus) and his herald (John the Baptist) had the same message: repent. The herald invited people to demonstrate their inner response with an outward action in baptism. The King submitted to the outward action as a way to confirm that repentance makes a difference in God's eyes. This has always been the first step in responding to God—we must accept our hopeless condition apart from God's mercy and respond in simple obedience. The King welcomes the humble and needy who come to him.

READING THE WORD

❈ *Matthew 3:13-15, NLT*
Then Jesus went from Galilee to the Jordan River to be baptized by John. 14But John tried to talk him out of it. "I am the one who needs to be baptized by you," he said, "so why are you coming to me?" 15But Jesus said, "It should be done, for we must carry out all that God requires." So John agreed to baptize him.

TALKING TO GOD

As you come to the Lord today, recall your original understanding of your sin and your need for the saving mercy and grace of God. Tell God you need his healing mercy and grace just as much today!

READING THE WORD

✤ *Mark 1:10-11, NLT*
As Jesus came up out of the water, he saw the heavens splitting apart and the Holy Spirit descending on him like a dove. ¹¹And a voice from heaven said, "You are my dearly loved Son, and you bring me great joy."

TALKING TO GOD

Meditate on the mystery of the Trinity—God as Father, Son, and Spirit all at once. Thank the Lord for his all-encompassing forgiveness and his continual renewal in your life.

FROM THE INSIDE OUT

Setting the Scene

How do you picture this event? Some imagine Jesus standing waist-deep in the Jordan as John pours or sprinkles water over his head. Others imagine Jesus erupting from full immersion in the river. Either picture includes a similar point of identification—we know what it would be like to be suddenly wet on a hot day. We can sense the delightful refreshment of cold water and the satisfaction of publicly declaring our submission to God. For those who have struggled to surrender to God, the release that comes through baptism is often accompanied by laughter, tears, shouts, and even a holy sense of awe as the reality of the wetness connects with the reality of forgiveness.

John baptized hundreds, perhaps thousands, of people while he was preparing the way for Jesus; but no one experienced what Jesus did when he "came up out of the water." The Holy Spirit gave his dove-like approval, and God the Father voiced his pleasure in the moment. At Jesus' baptism, God unmistakably certified Jesus as his Son. The Trinity made an appearance. For those who wonder how God can be "three in one," Jesus' baptism captures the Trinity in action, expressing one mind and purpose yet in three distinct ways.

Getting Personal

What difference does it make that God the Father and God the Holy Spirit were present with Jesus at his baptism?

What does your baptism mean to you today?

We can guess at other reactions to baptisms. Notorious sinners may have been greeted with jeers of incredulity, and humble penitents may have been welcomed with encouraging cheers by those who had gone ahead of them. Others, like the Pharisees, stood to one side, refusing to repent and offering criticisms and ridicule of the whole process. But they could not deny what was happening in the lives of those who repented and prepared their lives for the one who was coming. That's what Jesus does—he comes into your life, forgives, cleanses, and renews from the inside out.

DIVINE JOY

Setting the Scene

We can almost hear that powerful voice "from heaven" saying, "You are my dearly loved Son, and you bring me great joy." God's words convey a dual expression of divine love and joy. Jesus was God's "dearly loved Son." We only need to chew on this concept for a few seconds to begin to understand both the depth of love and the depth of sacrifice.

A hymn from the early church describes the momentous significance of Jesus coming from heaven to the dusty roads of Judea: "Though he was God, he did not think of equality with God as something to cling to. Instead, he gave up his divine privileges; he took the humble position of a slave and was born as a human being. When he appeared in human form, he humbled himself in obedience to God and died a criminal's death on a cross" (Philippians 2:6-8, NLT).

The sacrifice was immense, and it was undertaken with purpose and conviction. We don't know at what point in his life Jesus fully understood his mission to die for the sins of all humanity. However, we do know that it was clear to him during his three years of traveling and teaching, for three separate times he told his disciples he was going to die and rise again. The events that unfolded did not take Jesus by surprise. He came to do what God had planned from ages past.

Jesus brought his Father great joy because he willingly took upon himself human form in order to die for sinful humanity—for us. The Father looked upon his human Son, fresh from the waters of baptism, and spoke from heaven of his love and joy for all to hear.

Getting Personal

What does the immensity of Jesus' sacrifice mean to you?

How might you bring great joy to God?

God's beloved children can bring him great joy as well. Many verses in the Bible describe God's great joy in his children, how he even rejoices over us with singing, how he smiles upon us and takes great joy in our love and worship. And in the end, we will hear his "well done."

READING THE WORD

✤ *Luke 3:21-22, NLT*
One day when the crowds were being baptized, Jesus himself was baptized. As he was praying, the heavens opened, 22and the Holy Spirit, in bodily form, descended on him like a dove. And a voice from heaven said, "You are my dearly loved Son, and you bring me great joy."

TALKING TO GOD

Praise God for the extraordinary gift of his Son. Ask him to help you pursue the godly, worshipful life that makes him rejoice over you.

BEGINNINGS

READING THE WORD

❋ *Matthew 3:16-17, NLT*
After his baptism, as Jesus came up out of the water, the heavens were opened and he saw the Spirit of God descending like a dove and settling on him. 17And a voice from heaven said, "This is my dearly loved Son, who brings me great joy."

TALKING TO GOD

Submit your goals to God, asking him to give you clear intention and determination to "carry out all that God requires."

Setting the Scene

The starter's gun marks the beginning of a race, but for the runners, weeks and months of preparation have come before that single shot. Likewise, the exchange of wedding vows begins a marriage that is part of an ongoing relationship that has been building. In many ways, the baptism of Jesus indicated the beginning of his public ministry. It marked the end of his private life and declared the start of his public life. He had already been living entirely for God; but with his baptism, that intention and direction came out in the open for the world to see.

Just as Jesus' actions provoked his Father to declare his pleasure, so Jesus' earlier words to John the Baptist, "It should be done, for we must carry out all that God requires" (Matthew 3:15, NLT) was Jesus' statement of love and delight at the prospect of moving into the intense period of work in the world that would lead to his death, resurrection, and return to his Father. This requirement of baptism was not imposed from the outside but was an internal deliberate intention to move consistently in a single direction. We imagine a twinkle in Jesus' eye as he said, "We must carry out all that God requires" to John. It was the same tone present in the young boy who said to his mother, "Didn't you know that I must be in my Father's house?" (Luke 2:49, NLT).

Getting Personal

What events in your life have marked times when you stopped focusing on yourself and started focusing on the needs of others?

What commitments have you made that you need to renew before others or before God?

Beginnings can be accompanied by fanfare or silence, but they are best marked by commitment. Those who start with an end in mind are much more likely to arrive than those who simply start without direction or destination. Jesus wasn't uncertain about where his life was headed. As we trace his steps, we will see intentional decisions all along the way. His declaration "We must carry out all that God requires" is a purpose statement all believers could adopt and follow.

JESUS CONFRONTS SATAN

Week 5, Day 1

❋ *Matthew 4:1-11; Mark 1:12-13; Luke 4:1-13*

Immediately following his baptism by John the Baptist and the Father's public declaration of his identity, Jesus was tempted by Satan. This week we will examine Satan's tactics, the specific temptations, and Jesus' responses.

GOING ALONE

Setting the Scene

Jesus' baptism marked the beginning of his public ministry. John had been the talk of Israel, and hundreds were going out to see him, hear him preach, and be baptized as a sign of repentance from sin. John told the crowd, "Someone is coming soon who is greater than I am—so much greater that I'm not even worthy to stoop down like a slave and untie the straps of his sandals" (Mark 1:7, NLT). When Jesus arrived at the Jordan River where John was baptizing, John exclaimed, "Look! The Lamb of God who takes away the sin of the world!" (John 1:29, NLT). Jesus requested baptism as well. Although reticent at first, John baptized him, and when Jesus came up out of the water, the heavens opened, the Holy Spirit descended, and a voice from heaven declared, "You are my dearly loved Son, and you bring me great joy" (Mark 1:11, NLT).

From a purely human standpoint, that would have been an ego moment: dramatic entrance, great crowds, heavenly declaration. Often a high point like that is followed by a low, as the person at the peak begins to think too highly of him- or herself and tumbles.

But there was no ego trip for Jesus. Immediately following this dramatic event, empowered by the Holy Spirit, Jesus left the crowds behind and took the offensive against the enemy, Satan, by going into the lonely and desolate wilderness to fight temptation. The fact that Jesus was "compelled" to go there doesn't mean he was reluctant but rather that Jesus was determined to go, in agreement with the Spirit.

READING THE WORD

❋ *Mark 1:12-13*, NLT

The Spirit then compelled Jesus to go into the wilderness, 13where he was tempted by Satan for forty days. He was out among the wild animals, and angels took care of him.

TALKING TO GOD

Pray, as Jesus taught his disciples, that God would lead you away from temptation and deliver you from evil. Thank Jesus for being willing to suffer temptation in order to understand you and to show you the way to stand against it.

Notice that Satan is real and personal, not an idea or force. A fallen angel, Satan, the devil, is the powerful enemy of God and his people. He should be taken seriously.

The "wilderness" could be dangerous, inhabited by wild animals such as boars, jackals, wolves, foxes, leopards, and hyenas. The fact that the "angels took care of him" probably refers to meeting Jesus' spiritual needs. Just as Satan's temptations lasted continuously for the forty days, so did the support and comfort of the angels.

Getting Personal

Why do you think Jesus chose this time for his confrontation with Satan?

What would have made Jesus susceptible to temptation?

When are you most vulnerable to making sinful choices?

How does knowing that Jesus faced the same types of pressures and choices help you resist temptation?

Jesus would have been very vulnerable: suddenly alone—away from his followers and the crowd, in a hostile environment, and hungry.

The writer of Hebrews explains that Jesus "faced all of the same testings we do, yet he did not sin" (4:15, NLT). When Jesus became a living, breathing human being, he submitted himself fully to human limitations. He would have felt elation at his baptism, sensing the closeness of his Father and excitement about beginning his public ministry. Then he would have felt the chill of the wind as he sat on the hard ground and heard the night howls of prowling animals. He would have experienced gnawing hunger and thirst. The temptations were real.

From Jesus' experience we learn that God may lead us into dangerous and intense spiritual battles. We won't always feel good; in fact, we will have times of deprivation, loneliness, and hostility. It also teaches us that Jesus did, in fact, experience extreme temptations; he knows what we're facing, and he knows how we feel.

FEELING HUNGRY

Setting the Scene

During Jesus' forty days in the wilderness, he fasted. Fasting, the practice of going without food, and perhaps even water, was used as a way to focus on prayer and preparation. As a human being, Jesus experienced hunger and thirst; in fact, he must have been famished and physically weak after forty days. Satan's first temptation hit Jesus where he was most vulnerable.

This is Satan's typical method of operation, attacking where we are vulnerable and making the choice seem simple and logical: "Just turn some of these stones into bread and have yourself a small meal." What could possibly be so wrong about that? But more was going on here than a seemingly compassionate suggestion for a hungry person to have lunch.

Satan began by saying, "*If* you are the Son of God" (emphasis added). Satan was tempting Jesus with his own power. Satan did not doubt that Jesus was the Son of God or that he could indeed make bread from stones. He wanted Jesus to use his power in the wrong way at the wrong time—to meet his own needs rather than fulfill his God-given mission. But instead of getting into a discussion with Satan (as Eve had done; see Genesis 3:1-7), Jesus refused to entertain any doubt of God's loving provision. He answered by quoting Scripture (Deuteronomy 8:3).

Jesus came to earth to accomplish the Father's mission. Everything he said and did was directed toward that goal. For Jesus, obedience to the Father's mission was more important than food—no matter how he felt, no matter what Satan said.

Getting Personal

What are some common physical temptations?

How might meeting a physical need distract us from focusing well on God?

What physical temptation troubles you most? What can you do to resist?

This first temptation was physical, often called "the lust of the flesh" (1 John 2:16, KJV). Eating is not wrong; we have to eat to live. But one of Satan's strategies is to take something natural and good and tempt us to use it the wrong way or at the wrong time. Our natural desires are good, but they can drive us to sin if we're not careful.

READING THE WORD

❋ *Matthew 4:1-4, NLT*
Then Jesus was led by the Spirit into the wilderness to be tempted there by the devil. 2For forty days and forty nights he fasted and became very hungry. 3During that time the devil came and said to him, "If you are the Son of God, tell these stones to become loaves of bread." 4But Jesus told him, "No! The Scriptures say, 'People do not live by bread alone, but by every word that comes from the mouth of God.'"

TALKING TO GOD

Consider a short fast—perhaps skipping only one meal. Use your hunger as a reminder to focus on a specific area of need or temptation. Ask God to help you fulfill your natural physical desires only in the right ways, at the right time.

READING THE WORD

❂ *Luke 4:5-8, NLT*

Then the devil took him up and revealed to him all the kingdoms of the world in a moment of time. 6"I will give you the glory of these kingdoms and authority over them," the devil said, "because they are mine to give to anyone I please. 7I will give it all to you if you will worship me." 8Jesus replied, "The Scriptures say, 'You must worship the LORD your God and serve only him.'"

TALKING TO GOD

Focus on Christ and his Kingdom as you worship in prayer. Ask God to deepen your allegiance to him.

LOOKING DOWN

Setting the Scene

In this temptation, Satan showed Jesus all that the world had to offer, in terms of power and possessions. Satan was offering Jesus "authority" in exchange for worship. Jesus didn't argue with Satan about who owned the world. In fact, later he stated that Satan is, in fact, the "ruler of this world" (John 12:31, NLT). Satan was tempting Jesus to take the world as an earthly kingdom right then, without carrying out God's plan of salvation. For Jesus, that would mean obtaining his promised dominion over earth without experiencing the Cross. Satan offered Jesus a painless shortcut. In addition, in order to worship Satan, Jesus would have had to denounce his loyalty to the Father; Satan's goal always has been to replace God as the object of worship.

It's really a matter of perspective. Anyone who looks down from a mountain, airplane, or skyscraper can be overwhelmed by the sights below—and to have it all! To rule an earthly empire. So much for so little—or so it seems . . . looking down.

But Jesus looked up. That is, he didn't allow the earthly perspective to entice him to make a terrible decision. For Jesus to take a shortcut to ruling the world by worshiping Satan would be to break the first commandment (Exodus 20:3). Jesus resisted this temptation, rejecting Satan's offer.

Getting Personal

In what ways does this temptation to "have it all" reflect what many people desire these days?

What have people sacrificed to "gain the whole world" (Matthew 16:26, NLT)?

What makes this temptation so strong?

This temptation is the "lust of the eyes" (1 John 2:16, KJV), or "a craving for everything we see" (NLT). Satan was saying, "You can have it all, and you can have it now. It's easy—just switch your allegiance to me." Sound familiar? When tempted to compromise your values for money or power, remember who really controls the universe. Look up, focus on Christ and his Kingdom, and find true riches.

LIVING HIGH

Setting the Scene

In this final temptation, Satan took Jesus to the top of the Temple, the tallest building in the area. The "highest point of the Temple" probably would have been the corner wall that jutted out of the hillside, overlooking the valley below.

Satan changed his tactics as he tried to appeal to ego, to pride. He challenged Jesus to prove his identity, to show the world that he was God's Son. "Do something spectacular," Satan was saying. "Make a grand entrance to let everyone know who you are! You're more than a carpenter's son—you are the Son of God! You'll be famous. Display your power!" And what a great show it would have been: Jesus hurtling toward the ground but rescued dramatically, at the last moment, by angels!

This temptation epitomizes the third category of what "the world offers"—pride in who we are and what we have done (1 John 2:16). This was another blatant attempt to sidetrack Jesus from fulfilling his purpose, which was to humble "himself in obedience to God" and die "a criminal's death on a cross" (Philippians 2:8, NLT).

Jesus rebuffed this temptation by affirming his deity as he quoted Deuteronomy 6:16: "You must not test the LORD your God" (NLT).

Getting Personal

Why might this suggestion by Satan have been tempting at this stage in Jesus' life?

What temptations do you face that involve pride?

When might you have to humble yourself for God's sake?

The appeal to pride is a huge temptation in our society. Everyone seems to be seeking the spotlight, trying to gain that moment of fame, to be the next big thing, to be a star. Many people, even believers, will compromise their morals, values, faith, and goals to fulfill this lust for popularity, significance, and fame.

Jesus' way is humility, and he promises that "those who are last now will be first then, and those who are first will be last" (Matthew 20:16, NLT). Many of the most "insignificant" people in this world will be great in Christ's Kingdom. What matters is how we measure up to God's standards, not the world's.

READING THE WORD

✤ *Luke 4:9-12, NLT*
Then the devil took him to Jerusalem, to the highest point of the Temple, and said, "If you are the Son of God, jump off! [10]For the Scriptures say, 'He will order his angels to protect and guard you. [11]And they will hold you up with their hands so you won't even hurt your foot on a stone.'" [12]Jesus responded, "The Scriptures also say, 'You must not test the LORD your God.'"

TALKING TO GOD

Before the Lord, examine your own pursuits of popularity or relevance. Ask God to shift your personal longings to a strong desire for his glory and his purposes in the world.

READING THE WORD

❁ *Matthew 4:6-7, NLT*
[Satan] said, "If you are the Son of God, jump off! For the Scriptures say, 'He will order his angels to protect you. And they will hold you up with their hands so you won't even hurt your foot on a stone.'" 7Jesus responded, "The Scriptures also say, 'You must not test the LORD your God.'"

TALKING TO GOD

Pray for an increased hunger for the truths in God's Word. Thank God for Scripture's ultimate authority, power, and reliability.

GIVING THE WORD

Setting the Scene

In this final temptation, Satan quoted Psalm 91:11-12, trying to appeal to the authority of Scripture to make the temptation more reasonable. Psalm 91 describes God's protection of those who trust him. Satan was quoting the passage out of context, implying that God would protect his people even as they sin or make foolish choices, removing the natural consequences of those sinful acts and bad choices. Jumping off the Temple in a public display of God's supernatural protection would not have been part of the Father's will for his Son.

In context, Psalm 91 promises God's protection for those who, while living in his will and serving him, find themselves in danger. It does not promise protection for artificially created crises in which Christians call out to God in order to test his love and care. God has built natural laws into our universe that we need to respect. We should not test God, asking him to suspend his natural laws to keep us from our foolishness. And that's exactly the point made by Jesus in refuting Satan's statement. He quoted Deuteronomy 6:16: "You must not test the LORD your God" (NLT).

By quoting Scripture, Jesus was affirming the authority of God's Word. If God has said something, then that settles it. We should also see, however, that the Bible can be twisted and misused. Satan enjoys presenting half-truths or twisting God's words to make them say something entirely different than their intended meaning.

Getting Personal

What examples have you heard or read when Scripture has been twisted or taken out of context to teach something contrary to God's laws?

What can you do to guard against falling for Satan's Bible-twisting lies?

Anyone can pull out a string of words or a short passage to support almost any action. When a verse is quoted or a passage referenced, we must make sure it reflects the actual meaning. God has given us an amazing resource. We must read and study it to learn his timeless truths. Then we should change our lives to conform to what God is telling us.

DEFEATING THE ENEMY

Setting the Scene

During this entire wilderness episode, Jesus endured Satan's unrelenting temptation. He held strong, defeating Satan at every point. But when Jesus told the devil to leave, Satan "went away." Jesus is Satan's superior. Satan must do as Jesus commands.

But then the Gospel of Luke adds this ominous phrase, "[Satan] left him until the next opportunity came." This wilderness experience was just the first of many encounters Jesus would have with Satan and his power. Jesus' personal victory over the devil at the very beginning of his public ministry set the stage for his command over demons throughout his life on earth, but it did not keep Satan from continuing to try to sabotage Jesus' mission. In other words, Jesus' defeat of the devil at this time was decisive but not final. Throughout the next three years, Jesus would confront Satan in many other ways and circumstances. Satan is relentless and always looks for opportunities to exploit.

Without question, Satan is also powerful. Jesus called him "the ruler of this world" (John 12:31, NLT). So we should take Satan seriously and never fool around with occult practices. And we should make no mistake about his intentions: Satan is at war with God and his people and will do everything in his power to thwart God's purposes on earth.

Getting Personal

In what ways is the devil pictured in today's culture so that people fail to take him seriously?

What could cause a Christian to be vulnerable to temptation?

What can you do to be ready to resist Satan?

Just because we win a victory doesn't mean the battle is over. Satan is relentless. He always does whatever he can to mess with God's people. Jesus has given us armor and weapons to use in this spiritual battle (Ephesians 6:10-20), but they won't do us any good if we don't use them. Peter writes, "Stay alert! Watch out for your great enemy, the devil. He prowls around like a roaring lion, looking for someone to devour. Stand firm against him, and be strong in your faith" (1 Peter 5:8-9, NLT).

READING THE WORD

✤ *Matthew 4:10-11, NLT*
"Get out of here, Satan," Jesus told him. "For the Scriptures say, 'You must worship the LORD your God and serve only him.'" 11Then the devil went away, and angels came and took care of Jesus.

✤ *Luke 4:13, NLT*
When the devil had finished tempting Jesus, he left him until the next opportunity came.

TALKING TO GOD

Thank God that you are never alone in your spiritual battle against God's enemy, Satan. Ask God to help you continually remember his presence and increasingly depend on his power.

❀ *John 3:1-21*

Jesus met many people during his three years of public ministry, and most walked away from him with their lives utterly and completely changed. Nicodemus was part of the ruling class of religious leaders. He was well read and well educated, and he was curious about Jesus' message, so he came with his questions. Jesus answered his questions—and changed his life.

READING THE WORD

❀ *John 3:1, NLT*
There was a man named Nicodemus, a Jewish religious leader who was a Pharisee.

JESUS AND THE PHARISEES

Setting the Scene

Before we can learn from this conversation between Jesus and Nicodemus, we must appreciate what it took for this Pharisee to approach Jesus that evening. John's inclusion of the man's name and his party affiliation is significant. There is much to learn and apply from this twilight talk as we also consider the rapidly deteriorating relationship between Jesus and this major group within Judaism in the first century.

The Pharisees were the cultural and religious traditionalists of Jesus' day. Like Jesus, they took God's Word seriously. In their zealous efforts to live by God's Word, they had identified so many minute standards of obedience that they obliterated the spirit of God's instructions. Joyful obedience was replaced by legalistic and crushing rule-keeping. The Pharisees were control-driven people. They defined their relationship with God to the smallest detail, and they imposed their standards on others. In fact, one of the charges Jesus leveled against the Pharisees as a group was, "You are careful to tithe even the tiniest income from your herb gardens, but you ignore justice and the love of God. You should tithe, yes, but do not neglect the more important things" (Luke 11:42, NLT). Jesus confronted their focus on minutiae while ignoring major points of obedience to God. Jesus' point wasn't to ignore the discipline of tithing but to show the Pharisees that God was more concerned for justice and love.

In Jesus' day, the line between religious and political authority was certainly blurred. Frustrated by the rule of the Roman Empire, leaders among the Jewish people tended to come from religious groups. Alongside the Pharisees were the Sadducees, people who treated the law of Moses primarily as a governmental document rather than a spiritual one. They operated within a civil form of religion in which God was little more than a figurehead. The Pharisees and Sadducees competed for power in the Sanhedrin, the highest Jewish governmental body under Roman control. Nicodemus was a member of that body.

The Pharisees could also be described as the group most officially in favor of the coming Messiah. The fulfillment of this promise would not only expel the Romans from the Promised Land, but it would also place the Pharisees firmly in power as the religious leaders of God's people. Publicly, the Pharisees could not accept Jesus' claim to be the Messiah. Not only did he fail to fit their notions of who and what the Savior would be, he also offended them by treating lightly the very traditions they felt made them unique—primarily their highly ritualized observance of the Sabbath. Privately, individual Pharisees demonstrated a hunger for righteousness that drew them to Jesus. Some sensed hypocrisy in themselves that Jesus confronted. And so the Pharisee named Nicodemus arranged to meet Jesus one evening.

Jesus unsettles people. He unsettled Nicodemus, and he continues to unsettle us. Just when we think we have Jesus figured out, he surprises us. He tells us the things we need to hear, even when we don't want to hear them. Nicodemus didn't know what to expect when he approached Jesus that night.

Getting Personal

When has defending a tradition kept you from seeing the real Jesus?

How has Jesus overcome stereotypes you've had of him?

How has Jesus transcended your expectations of him?

The living Lord smashes stereotypes and glib descriptions. Jesus comes personally and speaks personally—right to your needs, your hang-ups, your heart. What is Jesus saying to you these days?

TALKING TO GOD

Come to God today with confidence because you are his child, but without an arrogance that assumes you know everything there is to know about him and his ways. Express your willingness to be surprised by Jesus—to be unsettled and changed by him.

SEARCHING IN THE DARK

READING THE WORD

❋ *John 3:2, NLT*
After dark one evening, [Nicodemus] came to speak with Jesus. "Rabbi," he said, "we all know that God has sent you to teach us. Your miraculous signs are evidence that God is with you."

TALKING TO GOD

Day or night, the Lord is always with you. Recall the time, if you can, when you were—like Nicodemus—on the brink of Christ's Kingdom. Thank God for his saving grace that drew you in and made you his own.

Setting the Scene

Instead of asking a question, Nicodemus offered a compliment to Jesus. We don't know if he wanted to make a good impression or whether he simply wanted to get to the heart of the matter. But as we will see, Jesus responded with an answer to the question that Nicodemus was *really* asking but hadn't put into words.

John mentions that Nicodemus came to Jesus by night. The setting tells us Nicodemus wasn't eager to be seen. He didn't approach Jesus at high noon because he was a man trying to make up his mind about Jesus. He knew what many of his fellow Pharisees were saying about Jesus, but he wasn't sure who Jesus was. (The "we all know" hints that he was not the only Pharisee who felt this way). Nicodemus was close to the Kingdom, but he hadn't stepped over the border yet.

Nicodemus used two phrases to describe how he understood Jesus: "God has sent you" and "God is with you." This was about as far as an Old Testament Jew could allow himself to go in acknowledging divine approval over someone's life and work. For devout Jews the question was, "If I believe in you, Jesus, how does that change my view of God?" Nicodemus was willing to recognize that Jesus' words and works originated with God, but he wasn't sure what to do with Jesus himself.

Jesus responded to Nicodemus's compliment by giving him an unexpected message from God.

Getting Personal

If you suddenly found yourself alone with Jesus, what would be the first thing you would say to him?

What people in your life have no idea that you really believe in Jesus? How can you let them know?

Contrary to most of us, Nicodemus was risking his reputation and perhaps his life by being with Jesus. Our standards of privacy protect our freedom to believe, but they also make it very easy to hold beliefs that fail to change us or to change our lifestyles. Nicodemus knew that what he did about Jesus would change everything else. He just didn't know how—yet.

BLINDED BY LIGHT

Setting the Scene

Jesus got to the heart of the matter at once. Nicodemus spoke as "we" and "us," but Jesus looked him in the eyes and said, "Unless *you* are born again." Caught off guard, Nicodemus could only imagine one kind of birth, and the ludicrous picture of an adult receiving a second birth from his mother prompted Nicodemus's question.

Jesus clarified by rephrasing and expanding his first statement. "Born again" was a new way to describe spiritual regeneration and conversion. Instead of "You cannot *see* the Kingdom of God," Jesus said, "No one can *enter* the Kingdom of God" (emphasis added). And "born again" becomes "born of water and the Spirit." Many see here a reference to baptism (in water) and baptism by the Spirit. But the immediate context supports the interpretation of physical birth and spiritual birth. The "again birth" follows the first birth that humans can produce. The change is so radical that it is equal in importance to our original birth. So, Jesus said, we shouldn't be surprised by the standard: "You must be born again."

Jesus equated "born again" with "born of the Spirit." He was no longer speaking of the ultimate results of spiritual rebirth (citizenship in the Kingdom of God), but about how the Spirit works in someone's life. The effects of God's transforming power are like the evidence for the wind: You can hear it and see its effects, but you can't see the wind itself.

We often explain our own conversion experience by focusing on what we did—prayed the prayer, raised the hand, knelt at the altar, wept in repentance—but those actions were a response to what God was doing.

Getting Personal

For you personally, how was becoming a Christian like being "born again"?

How has the Holy Spirit produced spiritual life in you?

If you have experienced being born again, you have a story to tell. Whether that experience produced a radical shift in your life or reflected more subtle and quiet changes, life became different. This is what conversion does—converts you to God's way of thinking and living. Nicodemus had to question long-held beliefs and reexamine his priorities. What has the Spirit been saying to you?

READING THE WORD

✸ *John 3:2-8, NLT*

After dark one evening, he came to speak with Jesus. "Rabbi," he said, "we all know that God has sent you to teach us. Your miraculous signs are evidence that God is with you." 3Jesus replied, "I tell you the truth, unless you are born again, you cannot see the Kingdom of God." 4"What do you mean?" exclaimed Nicodemus. "How can an old man go back into his mother's womb and be born again?" 5Jesus replied, "I assure you, no one can enter the Kingdom of God without being born of water and the Spirit. 6Humans can reproduce only human life, but the Holy Spirit gives birth to spiritual life. 7So don't be surprised when I say, 'You must be born again.' 8The wind blows wherever it wants. Just as you can hear the wind but can't tell where it comes from or where it is going, so you can't explain how people are born of the Spirit."

TALKING TO GOD

Reexamine your own long-held beliefs and priorities. Ask God to make clear what his Spirit is asking of you today. Thank him again for the second birth he's given you.

READING THE WORD

❊ *John 3:9-15, NLT*

"How are these things possible?" Nicodemus asked. 10Jesus replied, "You are a respected Jewish teacher, and yet you don't understand these things? 11I assure you, we tell you what we know and have seen, and yet you won't believe our testimony. 12But if you don't believe me when I tell you about earthly things, how can you possibly believe if I tell you about heavenly things? 13No one has ever gone to heaven and returned. But the Son of Man has come down from heaven. 14And as Moses lifted up the bronze snake on a pole in the wilderness, so the Son of Man must be lifted up, 15so that everyone who believes in him will have eternal life."

TALKING TO GOD

Come to the Lord today in a fresh spirit of openness and willingness, asking for his lordship and direction over your life.

Setting the Scene

Nicodemus asked the obvious question: "How are these things possible?" Nicodemus, a scholar in religious matters, was suddenly a student in basic spiritual realities. Now it was Jesus' turn to compliment Nicodemus as a "respected Jewish teacher." This wasn't derision, but gentle and persistent revelation of the truth: Pedigrees carry little weight when we stand as individuals before God. Nicodemus's position among his people didn't give him standing before God. He may have been a capable instructor on the contents of the Old Testament, but his teaching ultimately failed if he didn't understand the main point.

Jesus answered the question first by pointing to the failure of so many people to accept the evidence of the Spirit's work. He was saying to Nicodemus, "Look, if I tell you about things here on earth (like people being radically reborn by the Spirit) that you can verify for yourself and yet you don't believe me, then how can I expect you to accept what I tell you about heavenly things?" Jesus didn't wait for an answer but pointed out that his own knowledge of spiritual reality was based on the fact that he had "come down from heaven" and knew firsthand whereof he spoke. Jesus was deepening the significance of Nicodemus's earlier descriptions, "God has sent you" and "God is with you," which would put Jesus in the category of prophet. But claiming to originate in heaven put Jesus in a category of his own.

Then, in a stunning segue that revealed Jesus' central purpose, he showed Nicodemus that a classic moment in Old Testament history was actually a foreshadowing of God's ultimate plan to rescue humanity by means of the Cross.

Getting Personal

How often do you approach Jesus as a person willing to learn from him?

What was the last life-changing lesson you learned from Jesus?

Jesus doesn't have to live up to our expectations or even answer our questions. We're accountable to him, not the other way around. If we don't have this servant-Master, creature-Creator relationship clear, we will never recognize our need to receive all Christ has for us.

HIS ONE AND ONLY SON

Setting the Scene

Here we read God's motive for giving that gift of eternal life, of being born again: He "loved the world so much." The quantitative statement raises the question: How much did God love the world? God's action answers the question: "He gave his one and only Son." This is giving, not as in "sharing for a time" but as in allowing the Son of Man to be "lifted up" like Moses' serpent on a pole. This is the kind of ultimate giving Paul described in Romans 5:8, "But God showed his great love for us by sending Christ to die for us while we were still sinners" (NLT).

After declaring God's motive and action, John 3:16 then defines the breadth of the opportunity (everyone) and the mode of response (who believes in him). The classic English "whosoever" here conveys the thought that anyone and everyone who believes in Jesus becomes a candidate to receive certain benefits and avoid certain consequences. This conveys the same certainty as the "must" Jesus used when he told Nicodemus "you must be born again" in order to "enter the Kingdom of God." So "believes in him" becomes a crucial phrase to understand. Believing in Jesus doesn't mean attraction to his personality or recognition of his existence; believing in Jesus means believing in the significance of his work at the Cross, where he died for our sin.

"Will not perish" refers to the fact that without Jesus' intervention, we have no hope. Perishing is the human condition. The gospel is good news because it tells us there's one way to avoid perishing—believing in Jesus.

Getting Personal

How did you first realize God's love for you?

Why is it difficult for people to believe in Jesus today?

At some point in your life you may have memorized this verse. It represents one of the clearest summaries of the gospel in the New Testament. Accepting its meaning and committing to it lead to second birth. By personalizing these words, we allow God to do his birthing work in us.

READING THE WORD

✤ *John 3:16, NLT*
For God loved the world so much that he gave his one and only Son, so that everyone who believes in him will not perish but have eternal life.

TALKING TO GOD

Thank God for providing a way of salvation and for making it available to all who believe. Acknowledge the greatness of a love that would go so far to save you and make you his own.

COME TO THE LIGHT

READING THE WORD

❈ *John 3:17-21, NLT*
God sent his Son into the world not to judge the world, but to save the world through him. 18There is no judgment against anyone who believes in him. But anyone who does not believe in him has already been judged for not believing in God's one and only Son. 19And the judgment is based on this fact: God's light came into the world, but people loved the darkness more than the light, for their actions were evil. 20All who do evil hate the light and refuse to go near it for fear their sins will be exposed. 21But those who do what is right come to the light so others can see that they are doing what God wants.

TALKING TO GOD

Bring your own feelings of cowardice or courage to the Lord as you ask him to help you grow into a champion of the gospel message.

Setting the Scene

In the verses after John 3:16, Jesus corrects several misunderstandings that might rise from the gospel summary he has just given. The world's judgment is a done deal, dating back to the fall of humanity in Genesis. Jesus came to provide salvation from the judgment already in place.

John does not record how the conversation with Nicodemus ended. Nicodemus may have told Jesus he had just heard a lot he needed to think about. Perhaps he rushed back to locate a scroll and read again Numbers 21:4-9, the vivid account of the agony caused by the snakes and God's instructions to Moses to cast a bronze snake and hang it on a pole. Nicodemus surely had to reflect on Jesus' multiple claims of his unique relationship as the Son of God the Father. Jesus' description of three discernible parties (God as Father, Son, and Spirit) in the spiritual rebirth process would not have been easy to consider. In Nicodemus's circles, Jesus' claims seemed not only different but blasphemous.

Yet we know the Spirit flowed into Nicodemus's life and changed him. He became one of the reborn ones. John 7:50-51 describes his participation in an intense discussion about Jesus in the Sanhedrin. When someone made the argument that not a single Pharisee believed in Jesus, Nicodemus spoke up, at great danger to himself. Other circumstances forced Nicodemus gradually to take a public stand with Jesus. After the Crucifixion, while Jesus' disciples hid in fear, Nicodemus joined Joseph of Arimathea to ask for Jesus' body to bury it (John 19:38-42). Nicodemus's actions revealed him to be not only a believer, but also a champion of the gospel message.

Getting Personal

How do you experience the tension between the desire for light and the love of darkness in your own life?

What has been your developmental journey of faith since the point when you were born again?

Nicodemus is an easy target to hit with accusations of cowardice or shyness in proclaiming his faith. But given the almost limitless freedoms we have to express and declare our faith, how bold are we being in our times and culture?

JESUS ENCOUNTERS A SAMARITAN WOMAN

❋ *John 4:1-42*

After being baptized by John and being tempted by Satan, Jesus began his public ministry in Galilee, where he visited Nazareth, Cana, and Capernaum before returning to Jerusalem for the Passover. There he threw the money changers out of the Temple and spoke with Nicodemus. Then he and the disciples planned to return to Galilee. This week we'll focus on a dramatic meeting between Jesus and a woman he met on the way.

GOING GOD'S WAY

Setting the Scene

The Pharisees were wrong about Jesus baptizing people, but they were right in realizing that he was drawing larger crowds than John the Baptist. That shouldn't have been surprising since John was pointing people to Jesus. The vigilant Pharisees would have turned their attention to Jesus, so Jesus decided to leave Judea and return to Galilee.

Although the most direct route from Judea to Galilee is through Samaria, many strict Jews would travel east of the Jordan River through Perea, miles out of the way, to prevent contact with any despised Samaritans. Jews hated Samaritans because they weren't pure-blooded Jews, having intermarried with Assyrians and other foreigners through the years after the nation's exile. When the remnant of Jews returned from captivity in Babylon, for example, they refused to allow the Samaritans living in the land to help rebuild the Temple or the city of Jerusalem, even though they claimed to worship the same God. The Samaritans had adopted the Pentateuch (first five books of the Old Testament) as their Scriptures and had set up a place for worship on Mount Gerizim. They knew about a coming Messiah but were far from having an accurate knowledge of the truth.

Jacob's well was highly valued by the Samaritans, who claimed Jacob as their father just as the Jews did. Jesus was thirsty because of the long walk and because noon would have been the hottest part of the day. His weariness and thirst show his true humanity.

READING THE WORD

❋ *John 4:1-9, NLT*

Jesus knew the Pharisees had heard that he was baptizing and making more disciples than John 2(though Jesus himself didn't baptize them—his disciples did). 3So he left Judea and returned to Galilee. 4He had to go through Samaria on the way. 5Eventually he came to the Samaritan village of Sychar, near the field that Jacob gave to his son Joseph. 6Jacob's well was there; and Jesus, tired from the long walk, sat wearily beside the well about noontime. 7Soon a Samaritan woman came to draw water, and Jesus said to her, "Please give me a drink." 8He was alone at the time because his disciples had gone into the village to buy some food. 9The woman was surprised, for Jews refuse to have anything to do with Samaritans. She said to Jesus, "You are a Jew, and I am a Samaritan woman. Why are you asking me for a drink?"

TALKING TO GOD

God sees people in terms of his love for them and their need of him. Lay your personal biases before the Lord and ask him to help you see those around you as he does.

Two facts are unusual about the Samaritan woman drawing water. First, she could have gone to a well closer to her town. Second, women generally would draw water later in the day, when the temperature was cooler. Because of her reputation, this woman may have chosen this well and time of day to avoid other women.

Since Jesus did not have a container, he asked the woman for a drink. This request drew her into conversation. The woman was surprised that Jesus, a Jewish male, would speak to her and, even more shocking, that he would drink from her cup. The explanatory phrase "to have anything to do with Samaritans" literally means "to share the use of anything with Samaritans." John may have been saying that Jews and Samaritans would not share the same utensils or facilities. In strictly religious terms, many Jews of Jesus' time considered the Samaritans permanently unclean.

Jesus crossed those barriers to strike up a conversation with this woman. He wanted more than water; he was reaching out to a person in need. Everything Jesus did and said had a purpose. He didn't just wander into Samaria; Jesus chose to make contact with Samaritans, to bring the Samaritans what he had given Nicodemus— the offer of eternal life. Jesus didn't hold the Jewish prejudices. Throughout his ministry, Jesus continually reached out to all kinds of people—Jews, Samaritans, Gentiles, men, women, rich, poor, religious, and totally irreligious.

Getting Personal

What religions or types of people are subjected to prejudice these days?

When have you been looked down on for what you believe? How did you feel? How did you react?

Jesus sees each individual as someone who needs him. Nothing keeps Jesus from loving people and bringing them his good news. Nothing could keep Jesus from coming and dying for us.

Jesus has come to your well, and he sees you—not as a race, nationality, gender, political party member, or any other social category. He sees you as someone who needs him, and he wants to come close to you.

GETTING SERIOUS

Setting the Scene

Rather than answer the woman's question directly, Jesus piqued her interest with an intriguing comment, taking their common interest in water and thirst and transitioning to a more serious topic. His goal was to tell her about eternal life, and thirst provided that opportunity.

Jesus' remark produced several practical questions in the mind of the Samaritan woman. Just as Nicodemus didn't understand Jesus' reference to being born again, she did not immediately sense the depth of Jesus' words about "living water." Was this water at the bottom of this spring-fed well? If so, how could Jesus offer it with no container for drawing it? She began to wonder if Jesus had access to some source of water other than Jacob's well. *Who is this stranger?* she thought.

Jesus explained that his "water" flowed from a never-ending spring and quenched spiritual thirst. That definitely got the woman's attention. And though she didn't understand what Jesus meant, she wanted his "water."

Getting Personal

What do you remember about being spiritually thirsty? How did you feel? What did you do to try to quench that thirst?

Who first shared the Good News about Jesus with you? What did the person say, and how did you respond?

What might be a good way for you to begin a conversation with an unbelieving friend that might lead to telling that person about Christ?

Although Jesus' goal in his various conversations was always the same—to share the truth about himself and the way to obtain eternal life—his approaches varied greatly, with each one tailored to the individual. He told Nicodemus, a spiritual leader, that he needed a spiritual rebirth; he told this Samaritan woman about "living water." With others, Jesus used salt, seeds, doors, riches, sheep, and other word pictures. Just as every individual is unique, so, too, was the gospel presentation. With the woman at Jacob's well, Jesus began with their common thirst for H$_2$O, then directed her to deeper realities. Jesus didn't blast the woman with the truth or talk down to her. He shared a natural conversation, person-to-person, treating her with respect.

READING THE WORD

✤ *John 4:10-15, NLT*

Jesus replied, "If you only knew the gift God has for you and who you are speaking to, you would ask me, and I would give you living water." [11]"But sir, you don't have a rope or a bucket," she said, "and this well is very deep. Where would you get this living water? [12]And besides, do you think you're greater than our ancestor Jacob, who gave us this well? How can you offer better water than he and his sons and his animals enjoyed?" [13]Jesus replied, "Anyone who drinks this water will soon become thirsty again. [14]But those who drink the water I give will never be thirsty again. It becomes a fresh, bubbling spring within them, giving them eternal life." [15]"Please, sir," the woman said, "give me this water! Then I'll never be thirsty again, and I won't have to come here to get water."

TALKING TO GOD

Remember how astonishing it is that the Creator initiated a relationship with you. Praise him for his love and persistence in your life.

READING THE WORD

✤ *John 4:16-18, NLT*
"Go and get your husband,"
Jesus told her. 17"I don't have
a husband," the woman replied.
Jesus said, "You're right! You
don't have a husband— 18for you
have had five husbands, and
you aren't even married to the
man you're living with now. You
certainly spoke the truth!"

TALKING TO GOD

*Put aside any fears you may feel
today as you come in prayer to
the one who loves you without
conditions. Thank God that he
sees you through the cleansing
power of Christ's blood, fully
forgiven.*

GOING DEEPER

Setting the Scene

The woman was receptive to whatever Jesus had to offer,
especially if it meant not having to walk to the well
whenever she needed water. She didn't understand Jesus,
but she was open to having her life changed.

Then Jesus abruptly shifted the subject from water to
lifestyle. The woman knew she needed living water at one
level, but Jesus knew she had a far deeper need. So he
turned the conversation to her personal life. When the
woman replied, "I don't have a husband," she was speaking the truth without any explanation. Jesus' response
must have startled her even more than his claim to have
an endless source of water, revealing his knowledge of her
checkered past and her sin of adultery. Jesus wanted this
woman to recognize her sin and her need for forgiveness.
Then she would be ready to receive soul-quenching living
water—salvation, total forgiveness, and eternal life.

Getting Personal

*What might the Samaritan woman have been
thinking when Jesus mentioned her previous
marriages and current living situation?*

*Imagine Jesus looking at you right now—what does
he see? How do you think Jesus feels about you?*

*What, if anything, keeps you from being totally open
with God? What could help you be more honest with
him?*

*Every person, regardless of how he or she looks and
talks, harbors past hurts and sins and present fears,
dreams, desperate choices, and conflicts. Even those
who seem to have life figured out and their act
together have secrets. We may be able to hide our
true selves from others, but Jesus knows what we've
done and what we're planning—what we're really
like. And he cares. Nothing we have done shocks
Jesus or drives him away. We can be totally honest
with this one who loves us unconditionally.*

POINTING TO CHRIST

Setting the Scene

By saying that Jesus "must be a prophet," the woman was admitting he had been correct in his statements about her personal life. Instead of continuing along this line of conversation, however, she shifted the discussion away from herself to religion in general. Jesus let it go, keeping the woman's interest by letting her direct the discussion.

To both Jews and Samaritans the correct way to worship God depended on geography, a physical place. But Jesus pointed to a new worship approach—not at Mount Gerizim or in Jerusalem, but in the Spirit of God. Jesus explained that the Samaritans' system of worship was incomplete and flawed because it had no clear object. The Jews, however, did know whom they worshiped because they had the full revelation in the Old Testament Scriptures. Jesus presented the gospel not as a criticism of the desire and need to worship but to reveal the nature of true worship. For both Samaritans and Jews, the message was: "It's great to desire to worship, but your worship is misdirected. The perfect Object to be worshiped has come."

Talk of a new kind of worship must have reminded the Samaritan woman about the coming of the Messiah. Having already expressed that Jesus must be a prophet, she expressed her wish for the coming Prophet who would explain everything. Then Jesus clearly stated, "I AM the Messiah!" Although Jesus avoided telling the Jews directly that he was the Christ, he revealed his identity to this Samaritan woman.

Getting Personal

Why does talking about God seem easier than submitting to him?

When do forms of worship sometimes get in the way of the central focus of your worship, Jesus himself?

Jesus cares for us, and he offers us living water—himself. But he expects us to be open with him—and that can be threatening. We can more easily discuss churches, doctrines, and worship styles. Too often we miss Jesus in our hairsplitting theological discussions and religious analyses. We do need answers to questions about church and worship, but more than anything we need Jesus.

READING THE WORD

✤ *John 4:19-26, NLT*

"Sir," the woman said, "you must be a prophet. 20So tell me, why is it that you Jews insist that Jerusalem is the only place of worship, while we Samaritans claim it is here at Mount Gerizim, where our ancestors worshiped?" 21Jesus replied, "Believe me, dear woman, the time is coming when it will no longer matter whether you worship the Father on this mountain or in Jerusalem. 22You Samaritans know very little about the one you worship, while we Jews know all about him, for salvation comes through the Jews. 23But the time is coming—indeed it's here now—when true worshipers will worship the Father in spirit and in truth. The Father is looking for those who will worship him that way. 24For God is Spirit, so those who worship him must worship in spirit and in truth." 25The woman said, "I know the Messiah is coming—the one who is called Christ. When he comes, he will explain everything to us." 26Then Jesus told her, "I AM the Messiah!"

TALKING TO GOD

Don't hold back from full disclosure with God, who knows you better than you know yourself. Thank him for the living water—himself!—that will ultimately satisfy.

READING THE WORD

✤ *John 4:27-30, NLT*
Just then his disciples came
back. They were shocked to find
him talking to a woman, but none
of them had the nerve to ask,
"What do you want with her?"
or "Why are you talking to her?"
28The woman left her water jar
beside the well and ran back
to the village, telling everyone,
29"Come and see a man who told
me everything I ever did! Could
he possibly be the Messiah?"
30So the people came streaming
from the village to see him.

TALKING TO GOD

*Remember the many ways God
has changed and blessed your
life, and take time to thank him for
each remembered circumstance.
Ask God to restore your enthusiasm for the message of his
living water.*

SPREADING THE NEWS

Setting the Scene

The disciples had been following Jesus just a short time.
Every day they were learning more about their leader
and his mission. Seeing Jesus break two cultural taboos
(speaking with a Samaritan and speaking with a female
stranger) must have confused them. If they had been at
the well a bit earlier to hear the discussion, they would
have been even more shocked to learn that this was a
woman of questionable reputation. They must have
thought Jesus knew what he was doing, however, because
no one questioned his actions or motives. The disciples
did witness what happened next, though.

The woman abruptly left her water jug at the well,
ran into town, and told everyone about the man she had
just met. This man was different. He knew her, and instead of judging and rejecting her, he offered her real life.

People followed the woman back to meet this intriguing stranger. Knowing the woman's moral history, they
may have come to see someone who "told [her] everything [she] ever did." Some may have come simply because of the woman's enthusiasm.

The woman had dropped everything to spread the
news about Jesus. She had come to an out-of-the-way
well in the middle of the day to avoid embarrassing contact with those who knew her history. But after meeting Jesus, she didn't care who met her. She sought out
people and told everyone about what had happened.
Her message was personal: "Come meet the one who has
changed my life!"

Getting Personal

*What part of your personal history would you like
to keep hidden?*

In what ways are you different because you met Jesus?

Who needs to know your story about meeting Jesus?

*We have the advantage of knowing what transpired
soon after this meeting at the well. We know about
the Cross and Resurrection. We know Jesus truly is
the Christ, the Way, the Truth, and the Life (John
14:6). And we have the advantage of knowing that
for two thousand years, millions of lives (partakers
of the "living water") have been changed by God's
Spirit. With the energy and urgency of this unnamed
Samaritan woman, we could change the world.*

SEEING THE HARVEST

Setting the Scene

Jesus told his disciples that the fields were "ripe for the harvest" and they were the harvesters. He was speaking of the work of evangelism, of bringing people into the Kingdom. In telling the disciples to "wake up" and look at the fields, Jesus may have been directing them to look at the approaching Samaritans. The word "ripe" has also been translated "white." Harvests in Palestine do not look white, but Samaritans often dressed in white. They were ready to be "harvested."

Jesus was teaching them about his identity and mission and their calling. Here he explained about the important roles of sowing spiritual seed and harvesting. Both roles are crucial for spreading the gospel. Jesus, as both sower and harvester, sowed the seed through a single Samaritan woman and reaped a harvest from many in a Samaritan city. This sowing and harvesting transpired so quickly that the sower and harvester could rejoice together. Usually, the sower's joy is hopeful, for it is based on a future harvest. But in the context of eternity, the sower and harvester will be together and can rejoice over the harvest they both accomplished.

Many of the Samaritans who believed in Jesus were first drawn by the testimony of the woman he met at the well. The last statement—"Now we know that he is indeed the Savior of the world"—proclaims that Jesus had come to be not just the Jews' Messiah, but the world's Savior as well.

Getting Personal

What concerns and issues can keep us from seeing the spiritual harvest all around us?

In what ways do you "sow" in the work of spreading the Good News about Jesus?

If you could see an obvious "harvesting" opportunity, how would you respond?

What a contrast in vision. The disciples saw a Samaritan woman; Jesus saw a hurting person needing forgiveness. The disciples thought about physical needs; Jesus focused on spiritual nourishment. Jesus was telling these companions, "Change your perspective. Open your eyes. Look at the wonderful ministry opportunity right here, right now. This is why I called you. Let's get busy . . . and rejoice!"

READING THE WORD

✢ *John 4:35-42, NLT*

"You know the saying, 'Four months between planting and harvest.' But I say, wake up and look around. The fields are already ripe for harvest. 36The harvesters are paid good wages, and the fruit they harvest is people brought to eternal life. What joy awaits both the planter and the harvester alike! 37You know the saying, 'One plants and another harvests.' And it's true. 38I sent you to harvest where you didn't plant; others had already done the work, and now you will get to gather the harvest." 39Many Samaritans from the village believed in Jesus because the woman had said, "He told me everything I ever did!" 40When they came out to see him, they begged him to stay in their village. So he stayed for two days, 41long enough for many more to hear his message and believe. 42Then they said to the woman, "Now we believe, not just because of what you told us, but because we have heard him ourselves. Now we know that he is indeed the Savior of the world."

TALKING TO GOD

Ask God to give you his view of the people you see regularly, and pray for the Spirit's prompting to show you opportunities for sowing or harvesting in the fields "ripe for harvest."

JESUS HEALS
Week 8, Day 1

✤ *Mark 1:32-34; 2:1-12; Luke 4:31-39, 42-44; 5:12-16*

Jesus came to bring the Good News of the Kingdom of God, and as part of that message he brought spiritual healing for people's hearts. To help people understand that he could indeed forgive sins, he did miraculous signs and wonders. This week we'll look at some of the healings Jesus performed.

READING THE WORD

✤ *Mark 1:32-34, NLT*
That evening after sunset, many sick and demon-possessed people were brought to Jesus. 33The whole town gathered at the door to watch. 34So Jesus healed many people who were sick with various diseases, and he cast out many demons. But because the demons knew who he was, he did not allow them to speak.

SURROUNDED BY NEEDS

Setting the Scene

Once Jesus embarked on his public ministry with the miracle at the Cana wedding, he was rarely far from people in need. Mark provides a revealing glimpse of Jesus at the end of his day. This particular day was a Sabbath, and Jesus, along with his disciples, began the day in the local synagogue in Capernaum. People from all around the city were in attendance since this was the local gathering place for studying the law of Moses. Jesus was teaching that morning when a demon made a sudden appearance, protesting Jesus' interference (see Mark 1:21-25). The way Jesus expelled the demon made quite an impression on those at the synagogue. Mark mentions that "news about Jesus spread quickly throughout the entire region of Galilee" (Mark 1:28, NLT).

Apparently the crowd at the synagogue set off a local news grapevine. By nightfall, when the strict restrictions on travel during the Sabbath ended, people descended on Capernaum, hoping for help from Jesus. That single phrase, "The whole town gathered at the door to watch," captures the intense interest that drew people to Jesus. In the glare of the evening fires, the joyful faces of people freed from captivity to sickness and to demonic influence glowed even brighter. The night echoed both with the cries of demons and with shouts of praise to God. Those who came or were brought to Jesus were healed. He did not let the demons identify him because he was not ready to reveal his true identity as the Son of God.

If we assume that Jesus performed miracles in order

to prove who he was, we will be somewhat confused when we read that he refused to do a miracle on command (Matthew 16:1-4), that he forbade demons from speaking (Mark 1:34), and that he asked those he had healed not to tell anyone (Mark 1:44). Why would he not take advantage of every marketing opportunity? Because his identity didn't depend on people believing he could do miracles! Jesus didn't work miracles to *prove* he was the Son of God; he did miracles because he *was* the Son of God. He didn't go around "flashing credentials"; he responded to genuine needs and didn't exploit those he was helping. He wouldn't be pressured or bullied into performing miracles. He didn't heal everyone.

Jesus made it very clear that he could perceive a person's real need, even when that person asked only for physical healing. So he greeted the man lowered through the roof on a stretcher with a word of forgiveness. He knew the man needed forgiveness even more than he needed to be able to walk (Mark 2:3-5). There was a specific purpose behind every miracle Jesus performed, but it was never simply to prove who he was.

Earlier that day in the Capernaum synagogue, Jesus was teaching and those who listened were amazed at the authority of his words. Not long after this, when it became clear Jesus wouldn't settle for being a miracle worker, Simon Peter described why real disciples follow Jesus. He said, "Lord, to whom [else] would we go? You have the words that give eternal life" (John 6:68, NLT).

Getting Personal

In what way is Jesus' true identity greater than that of a mere miracle worker?

How does Jesus' healing power increase your faith?

Belief in Jesus is not a razor-thin line we straddle depending on how compelling the reasons for faith appear to us today. We don't trust in Jesus because of this or that specific proof. That is conditional, fluctuating faith. We trust in Jesus beyond our capacity to disbelieve. We stand before Jesus and say, "Lord, I believe, help my unbelief."

TALKING TO GOD

Focus your personal worship today on who Jesus is, beyond what he has done for you. Celebrate his deity, his love, his sovereignty, and his truth.

TEACHING AND HEALING

READING THE WORD

✤ *Luke 4:31-37, NLT*

Then Jesus went to Capernaum, a town in Galilee, and taught there in the synagogue every Sabbath day. 32There, too, the people were amazed at his teaching, for he spoke with authority. 33Once when he was in the synagogue, a man possessed by a demon—an evil spirit—began shouting at Jesus, 34"Go away! Why are you interfering with us, Jesus of Nazareth? Have you come to destroy us? I know who you are—the Holy One of God!" 35Jesus cut him short. "Be quiet! Come out of the man," he ordered. At that, the demon threw the man to the floor as the crowd watched; then it came out of him without hurting him further. 36Amazed, the people exclaimed, "What authority and power this man's words possess! Even evil spirits obey him, and they flee at his command!" 37The news about Jesus spread through every village in the entire region.

TALKING TO GOD

As you pray today, commit yourself confidently to the Lord, whose power and authority triumph over every enemy.

Setting the Scene

Jesus actually moved to Capernaum, making that village in Galilee his base of operations during much of his ministry years. He became a regular teacher in the local synagogue "every Sabbath day" when he was in town. The brevity of the Gospel accounts often leads us to picture Jesus continually on the move, at times almost driven from place to place by the crowds that followed him. But Jesus lived at the normal speed of life, walking from place to place. One of the easy-to-miss lessons from Jesus' life is that when we follow him, we must slow down.

Jesus taught with authority, unlike other spiritual teachers of his day. While they quoted various authorities, he spoke as one intimately aware of the meaning of God's Word, with confidence and clarity, connecting the content of Scripture with the lives of his hearers.

The rude interruption by the demon-possessed man shows us spiritual realities that seem foreign to us. We wonder, *Could this happen today?* C. S. Lewis pointed out that Satan knows enough to go undercover when it suits him. In our current society, too many simply dismiss the possibility of the satanic or see it merely as fodder for movies and TV shows with no real base in reality. Here, Jesus' presence forced the demon out of hiding. We discover with certainty that demons do exist and that their purpose is to destroy. Against Jesus, however, they have no power or authority.

Getting Personal

What amazes you about Jesus' teaching?

What evidence do you see of Satan at work in the world?

Ignoring demonic activity and the other ways Satan is active in the world means we would have to ignore a great deal of Scripture. Treating God's Word seriously means we have to conclude that Satan and his demons are real, dangerous, and powerful. They are not to be trifled with or taken lightly. We take them seriously because, as Christians, we put on the armor of God specifically for this battle (Ephesians 6:10-16).

A HOSPITABLE MIRACLE

Setting the Scene

Several of Jesus' disciples were businessmen in Capernaum. Four were fishermen; one was a local tax collector. At least Matthew (Matthew 9:10) and Simon Peter owned homes. Mark 1:29 tells us that the brothers Simon and Andrew owned the home together. The reference to Simon's mother-in-law indicates that he was a married man, and others of Jesus' disciples probably were too. Paul mentions in 1 Corinthians 9:5 that Peter and "other apostles" traveled with wives.

Going to Simon and Andrew's home involved certain strict rules of hospitality. Visitors were to be welcomed, protected, fed, and treated with respect. Having a sick mother-in-law in the home made the situation awkward and difficult; Simon was going to have difficulty providing hospitality. Having just seen Jesus heal a man in the synagogue, those with Jesus asked him to heal the ill woman.

Matthew, Mark, and Luke all record what follows, but each supplies a unique detail. Matthew noticed that Jesus touched the woman's hand (8:15); Mark adds that Jesus helped her stand (1:31); and Luke used the same Greek word "rebuked" to describe how Jesus dealt with the demon in the synagogue and the woman's fever at Simon's house. While some might conclude that Jesus was dealing with demonic forces in both cases, we need to remember that Jesus also "rebuked" the wind while he stood in a storm-tossed boat on Galilee (Luke 8:24). The one who spoke the world into existence has authority to correct the natural world. But he also treated Simon's mother-in-law with a compassionate touch.

The woman was healed immediately. Her raging fever left her, and she was refreshed enough to help entertain Simon's guests. Jesus had delivered a housewarming gift none of them would ever forget.

Getting Personal

What rules of hospitality do you practice in your home?

How have you experienced Jesus' healing touch?

In Jesus' day, the rules of hospitality required people to relate to each other in ways we forego by our tendency toward privacy and separate lives. It isn't easy to make others feel at home, but the practice of hospitality often opens doors for God to work in special ways.

READING THE WORD

❀ *Luke 4:38-39, NLT*
After leaving the synagogue that day, Jesus went to Simon's home, where he found Simon's mother-in-law very sick with a high fever. "Please heal her," everyone begged. 39Standing at her bedside, he rebuked the fever, and it left her. And she got up at once and prepared a meal for them.

TALKING TO GOD

Commit your home, its uses, and your family who live there to the Lord today. Put all you have at God's disposal for his purposes and his glory.

HABITS OF THE HEART

READING THE WORD

✸ *Luke 4:42-44, NLT*
Early the next morning Jesus went out to an isolated place. The crowds searched everywhere for him, and when they finally found him, they begged him not to leave them. 43But he replied, "I must preach the Good News of the Kingdom of God in other towns, too, because that is why I was sent." 44So he continued to travel around, preaching in synagogues throughout Judea.

TALKING TO GOD

As you pray today, try to balance speaking with listening. Practice being alone with God, and ask him to speak to you.

Setting the Scene

We move from a late evening when Jesus deals with crowds of curious and needy people to the quiet dawn hours after Jesus leaves Simon's home. He finds "an isolated place." This gives us another glimpse into the way Jesus lived intentionally. In his Gospel, Mark adds the note that Jesus' purpose was "to pray" at the beginning of the day (1:35). Jesus didn't seek solitude to be alone with himself; he found a quiet place to be alone with his Father. Time apart allows us to focus our prayer by minimizing distractions. It offers God time to speak to us. The impression we get from Jesus' life is that these times away were essential to his spiritual well-being.

The parallel accounts in the different Gospels give a more complete picture of this event. Mark tells us the disciples were the first to notice Jesus missing and searched for him. "When they found him, they said, 'Everyone is looking for you.' But Jesus replied, 'We must go on to other towns as well, and I will preach to them, too. That is why I came'" (Mark 1:37-38, NLT). Luke provides the atmosphere of the moment, telling us that the people "begged him not to leave them." Jesus informed those seeking him that his priority was delivering the "Good News of the Kingdom of God" as widely as possible. He refused to be distracted. The apparent urgency of people's needs would not keep him from his primary task.

Getting Personal

What would improve the regularity and quality of your time alone with God?

What most distracts you from keeping your spiritual priorities?

Habits like prayer and carrying out God's priorities in life will be limited if we consistently yield to distractions. Growing in our relationship with God doesn't happen by accident. We must imitate the intentional way Jesus carried out daily living. Most positive habits begin as deliberate actions. We don't accidentally fall into the habit of prayer. We grow into the habit of prayer by repeated practice. Prayer becomes habitual when we discover it is crucial to our spiritual health.

WILLINGNESS

Setting the Scene

Jesus healed many people, but some of those cases stood out to the disciples. This particular one caught the attention of Dr. Luke. An "advanced case of leprosy" usually results in grotesque injury and disfigurement. A leper suffers from loss of feeling. Nerve endings that lie just below the surface of the skin all over the body gradually become dead. A leper cannot feel a pebble in his shoe or sense that she has grasped a hot object that is burning her hand. The pain that triggers an instant jerk from us is absent in leprosy.

A leper's life was marked by other pain. In Jesus' day, lepers were required to maintain a personal quarantine, keeping their distance from others and loudly announcing that they were "Unclean!" to anyone who might come near. This man had advanced leprosy, meaning people gave him a wide berth. It's quite possible this man had gone years without personal contact with another human being. His humble request to Jesus might sound tentative to us, but it combines a balance of respect ("if you are willing") with a profound recognition of Jesus' abilities.

Jesus responded without a word. He moved toward the man and touched him. He treated him as clean before he actually healed him. His words "I am willing" must have simply confirmed for this man what was already happening in his mind and body. Wholeness is much more than physical health. In fact, wholeness is more important than the condition of our bodies. Even under the best circumstances, our bodies age and wear out; only God can provide wholeness of heart, mind, and soul. Fortunately, God is willing.

Getting Personal

What diseases today compare to leprosy in Jesus' time?

Which of your friends need the wholeness of heart, mind, and soul that God provides?

We are not yet whole. Sometimes we require adjustments; at other times only radical transformation will bring about God's purposes in us. Every glimpse of our incompleteness can be an invitation to join the leper at Jesus' feet to humbly ask for healing and cleansing.

READING THE WORD

✤ *Luke 5:12-16, NLT*

In one of the villages, Jesus met a man with an advanced case of leprosy. When the man saw Jesus, he bowed with his face to the ground, begging to be healed. "Lord," he said, "if you are willing, you can heal me and make me clean." 13Jesus reached out and touched him. "I am willing," he said. "Be healed!" And instantly the leprosy disappeared. 14Then Jesus instructed him not to tell anyone what had happened. He said, "Go to the priest and let him examine you. Take along the offering required in the law of Moses for those who have been healed of leprosy. This will be a public testimony that you have been cleansed." 15But despite Jesus' instructions, the report of his power spread even faster, and vast crowds came to hear him preach and to be healed of their diseases. 16But Jesus often withdrew to the wilderness for prayer.

TALKING TO GOD

Bring your personal brokenness to the Healer today, with confidence that he is willing to make you whole.

DEEP HEALING

Setting the Scene

Meditating on this story allows us to marvel over the ingenuity, friendship, and trust displayed by the four men who brought their paralyzed friend to Jesus.

It helps to know a little about house architecture in the Middle East. This was likely a mud-brick home with a flat roof made out of grass-reinforced mud laid over a lathwork of tree trunks and branches. Roofs in this part of the world often did double duty as elevated decks removed from the dust and heat of the street level. Faced with a wall-to-wall crowd in the house and limited access to the doorways, the friends devised a desperate plan. They would go up on the roof, figure out where Jesus was standing below, punch a hole through the rafters, and lower their friend in front of the Lord.

Imagine the scene indoors. Those listening to Jesus began to notice sounds overhead, and then pieces of the ceiling started to rain down. Moments later, an opening appeared and a stretcher was lowered. The crowd, driven back by the debris, had cleared a landing area.

Looking down at the man clearly in need of one kind of healing, Jesus chose instead to offer him first a deeper healing—the forgiveness of sins! Some religious experts accused him of blasphemy, since if he claimed to be able to forgive sins he claimed to be God. Of course, that is exactly who Jesus is.

Jesus added significance to his statement of forgiveness. He knew talk was cheap unless he could back it up with action—which he did by freeing the man to skip home joyfully!

Getting Personal

How have you personally experienced Jesus' healing power?

At what point in your life did you understand that "your sins are forgiven"?

Jesus honored the faith of those friends. The paralysis of sin is the most debilitating human disease, and people all around us are walking by with the symptoms every day. How much trouble are we willing to undertake to get our friends to Jesus?

READING THE WORD

❋ *Mark 2:2-12, NLT*

Soon the house where he was staying was so packed with visitors that there was no more room, even outside the door. While he was preaching God's word to them, 3four men arrived carrying a paralyzed man on a mat. 4They couldn't bring him to Jesus because of the crowd, so they dug a hole through the roof above his head. Then they lowered the man on his mat, right down in front of Jesus. 5Seeing their faith, Jesus said to the paralyzed man, "My child, your sins are forgiven." 6But some of the teachers of religious law who were sitting there thought to themselves, 7"What is he saying? This is blasphemy! Only God can forgive sins!" 8Jesus knew immediately what they were thinking, so he asked them, "Why do you question this in your hearts? 9Is it easier to say to the paralyzed man 'Your sins are forgiven,' or 'Stand up, pick up your mat, and walk'? 10So I will prove to you that the Son of Man has the authority on earth to forgive sins." Then Jesus turned to the paralyzed man and said, 11"Stand up, pick up your mat, and go home!" 12And the man jumped up, grabbed his mat, and walked out through the stunned onlookers.

TALKING TO GOD

Express your gratitude to God for the healing you have personally received from him, sometimes at great cost to himself. Ask him to help you extend the grace you've received to those around you who also need his healing.

JESUS TEACHES ABOUT THE SABBATH

❋ *Matthew 12:1-14; Mark 2:23-28; 3:1-6; Luke 6:1-11*

Jesus had been teaching and healing throughout Galilee, so more and more people were hearing about him. Alerted to Jesus' growing popularity, the Pharisees decided to check him out. This week, we'll look in on some of Jesus' first confrontations with the Pharisees, the Jewish religious leaders.

ENCOUNTERING CRITICS

Setting the Scene

Well-known rabbis used to walk and teach with their students following. Although Jesus had not yet chosen the Twelve, at this time two former disciples of John the Baptist and others were following him. The Gospels report the occasions that Jesus met and called Andrew, Simon Peter, Philip, and Nathanael (John 1:35-51); James and John (Matthew 4:18-22); and Matthew, also known as Levi (Mark 2:13-17). So those men would have been among the disciples with Jesus in the fields. But the group would have been larger than just those few. Certainly some in the crowd were following Jesus out of curiosity, to learn more about this charismatic figure. Others would have been following because they knew they had found the Messiah.

Jesus and his disciples, still in Galilee (most likely outside of Capernaum), were "walking through some grainfields." Because the disciples were hungry, they began to pluck heads of grain and eat them. They weren't stealing (Deuteronomy 23:25): God had told farmers not to harvest the edges of their fields, so travelers and the poor could partake (Leviticus 23:22). On any other day, no one would have questioned Jesus about what the disciples were doing. Because this was the Sabbath, however, the Pharisees accused them of breaking God's law about not working on the day they were supposed to keep holy.

The Pharisees had separated themselves from anything non-Jewish and carefully followed both the Old Testament laws and the oral traditions handed down

READING THE WORD

❋ *Matthew 12:1-2, NLT*
At about that time Jesus was walking through some grainfields on the Sabbath. His disciples were hungry, so they began breaking off some heads of grain and eating them. ²But some Pharisees saw them do it and protested, "Look, your disciples are breaking the law by harvesting grain on the Sabbath."

❋ *Exodus 20:8-11, NLT*
"Remember to observe the Sabbath day by keeping it holy. ⁹You have six days each week for your ordinary work, ¹⁰but the seventh day is a Sabbath day of rest dedicated to the LORD your God. On that day no one in your household may do any work. This includes you, your sons and daughters, your male and female servants, your livestock, and any foreigners living among you. ¹¹For in six days the LORD made the heavens, the earth, the sea, and everything in them; but on the seventh day he rested. That is why the LORD blessed the Sabbath day and set it apart as holy."

TALKING TO GOD

Before the Lord today, examine your own spirit of criticism or judgment of others. Ask God to fill you with his love for others and help you extend his grace to them.

through the centuries. They were exacting and scrupulous in their attempts to follow God's law as well as hundreds of those traditional laws. And they expected all Jews to do the same.

According to Exodus 34:21, harvesting grain was forbidden on the Sabbath, and picking the grain and rubbing it could have been interpreted as "harvesting." But, as was often the case, the Pharisees were missing the spirit of the law and focusing on the letter. The disciples were picking the grain because they were hungry, not to harvest the grain for profit. The disciples were not breaking God's law as recorded by Moses, just violating one of the Pharisees' many rules. Obviously the Pharisees must have been following Jesus to find an offense worthy of accusation. They expected to put Jesus on the defensive. Instead, he refuted their specific accusation and their interpretation of the Sabbath.

Getting Personal

The Pharisees saw themselves as guardians of God's law, so they were quick to judge and condemn anyone who might break even a minor interpretation and tradition. Emphasizing laws and rules is called "legalism," and it's easy to slip into, especially if we're trying to justify our own behavior. In the process, we can miss what's really important. The Pharisees tried to create a religious crisis over a few heads of grain. Soon we'll see them argue about whether or not to heal someone on the Sabbath.

When do you tend to be legalistic—at home, in traffic, at church, in the neighborhood?

When have you been on the other end, accused of breaking someone's rule or going against an accepted practice?

Nobody's perfect, so we can always find something to criticize if we look hard enough. Jesus was perfect, yet the Pharisees thought they had caught him breaking one of the Ten Commandments. Jesus said that he didn't come to abolish the law but to fulfill it (Matthew 5:17). Instead of condemning us for our lawbreaking, he treats us with mercy and grace, giving us what we could never earn by our own efforts. Based on our merits, we wouldn't have a chance for redemption and eternal life. The Pharisees focused on the law and missed the Savior.

RESPECTING THE LAW

Setting the Scene

In answering these critics, Jesus pointed them to the Scriptures they professed to know so well. By comparing himself and his disciples to David and his men, Jesus was saying, in effect, "If you condemn me, you must also condemn David." Jesus was not discarding the law and advocating disobedience. Instead, he pointed to a higher law and emphasized discernment and compassion, something the self-righteous Pharisees did not comprehend. People's needs are more important than technicalities.

In calling himself Lord over the Sabbath, Jesus claimed the authority to overrule the Pharisees' traditions and regulations because he had created the Sabbath. Jesus, therefore, could interpret the meaning of the Sabbath and all the laws pertaining to it. Through their confusing system of Sabbath laws, the religious leaders had made themselves lords of the Sabbath and thus lords over the people. In claiming to be Lord over the Sabbath, Jesus was stating his divinity and confronting the position of the religious leaders.

Jesus believed in the Sabbath and lived it. But he knew Sabbath observance must point to the Sabbath Maker and not focus on technical, hairsplitting definitions of "work" and "rest." By remaking the Sabbath into a day of refreshment, worship, and healing, he was prying open the tightfisted control the Pharisees held on the people.

Getting Personal

Why is Sabbath rest important to us?

What needs to change in your routine or lifestyle to honor God on the Sabbath?

Some people may think that because believers are no longer "under law," we can live any way we please (referencing Jesus' comments in this passage as proof). But this story doesn't make that point. God's moral laws—the Ten Commandments (including the one about the Sabbath)—still apply. Jesus was highlighting the fact that even well-intentioned, religious people can add rules and restrictions to God's laws and totally miss their meaning. Those added-on, human-made regulations are not inspired and inviolable. God wants us to study and apply his Word, but we must not project our personal applications onto others.

Jesus must be Lord over everything in our lives, including the Sabbath.

READING THE WORD

❁ *Luke 6:1-5, NLT*

One Sabbath day as Jesus was walking through some grainfields, his disciples broke off heads of grain, rubbed off the husks in their hands, and ate the grain. 2But some Pharisees said, "Why are you breaking the law by harvesting grain on the Sabbath?" 3Jesus replied, "Haven't you read in the Scriptures what David did when he and his companions were hungry? 4He went into the house of God and broke the law by eating the sacred loaves of bread that only the priests can eat. He also gave some to his companions." 5And Jesus added, "The Son of Man is Lord, even over the Sabbath."

TALKING TO GOD

Put your own day-of-rest practices before the Lord today. Ask him to help you shape and improve that day for worship and rest, and listen for the Spirit's prompting for changes that may need to take place.

REMEMBERING THE PURPOSE

READING THE WORD

❊ *Luke 6:6-9, NLT*

On another Sabbath day, a man with a deformed right hand was in the synagogue while Jesus was teaching. 7The teachers of religious law and the Pharisees watched Jesus closely. If he healed the man's hand, they planned to accuse him of working on the Sabbath. 8But Jesus knew their thoughts. He said to the man with the deformed hand, "Come and stand in front of everyone." So the man came forward. 9Then Jesus said to his critics, "I have a question for you. Does the law permit good deeds on the Sabbath, or is it a day for doing evil? Is this a day to save life or to destroy it?"

TALKING TO GOD

Praise God today that he is relational and personal. Beyond any set of religious rules and traditions, you have a relationship with God himself—how wonderful!

Setting the Scene

The religious leaders were continuing to scrutinize Jesus' ministry. Here they were in the synagogue, not to worship, but to watch Jesus closely. And they wondered how he would deal with the man with the "deformed right hand." Their interpretation of keeping the Sabbath prohibited healing except in life-threatening situations; thus, if Jesus were to heal the man, instead of rejoicing in the relief of human suffering, they could accuse Jesus of breaking the Sabbath.

Jesus could have avoided conflict by healing the man on another day. If he had waited, however, he would have been submitting to the Pharisees and showing that their made-up rules were equal to God's law. But the commandment about the Sabbath was never meant to oppress people.

Jesus met needs, regardless of the day or time. Healing the man revealed Jesus' authority over the Sabbath and showed that in the new Kingdom, every day is holy; salvation and healing can come to anyone on any day. The Sabbath, while given to God's people as a day of rest and worship, was also a day for people to be merciful and kind to those in need. And that is exactly what Jesus intended to show the Pharisees when he asked the man to step forward.

Getting Personal

How can we glorify God by obeying the Ten Commandments?

What can you do to restore, reconcile, and rebuild relationships, even on Sunday?

Jesus clearly framed the issue with his questions to the Pharisees: "Does the law permit good deeds on the Sabbath, or is it a day for doing evil? Is this a day to save life or to destroy it?" Honoring God's laws should be positive and life-giving, not negative and oppressive. Yet many Christians seem to be joyless rule-keepers, afraid of God's judgment and punishment. When we focus on the commandments instead of the Commandment Giver and on the letter of the law instead of its spirit, we lose sight of the law's ultimate purpose—to glorify God. The emphasis should be off us and on him.

SEEING THE VALUE

Setting the Scene

Mark points out that Jesus "noticed" the man with the deformity. The synagogue must have been filled, especially since this was the Sabbath and Jesus had been drawing crowds because of his healing and teaching. Add to that number the disciples and Pharisees. Yet Jesus saw this man. Perhaps the man was near Jesus and his entourage, or maybe he walked up to Jesus. Or he may have approached Jesus after Jesus looked at him. Whatever the case, Jesus noticed him.

The Pharisees did, too, but they did not see a man in need; they saw only an opportunity for possibly accusing Jesus of wrongdoing as a Sabbath-breaker. They were more concerned about protecting their laws than freeing a person from suffering.

Jesus knew the value of this man (Matthew 10:31; 12:12). He was not an object or discussion topic but one of God's special creations—and Jesus acted accordingly.

Getting Personal

In what ways can you identify with this man in the synagogue?

When have you felt lost in a crowd, alone, and carrying a heavy burden?

When have you felt especially valued by God?

Nothing escapes Jesus' notice. Regardless of the circumstances or surroundings, he sees us. Whether our needs are obvious, as in the case of the man and his deformed hand, or hidden, Jesus knows about them. And he sees us with compassion.

He sees you. Imagine him looking at you, smiling, and gesturing for you to come to him. How do you feel? What happens next?

You are important to Jesus.

READING THE WORD

❋ *Mark 3:1-4, NLT*
Jesus went into the synagogue again and noticed a man with a deformed hand. 2Since it was the Sabbath, Jesus' enemies watched him closely. If he healed the man's hand, they planned to accuse him of working on the Sabbath. 3Jesus said to the man with the deformed hand, "Come and stand in front of everyone." 4Then he turned to his critics and asked, "Does the law permit good deeds on the Sabbath, or is it a day for doing evil? Is this a day to save life or to destroy it?" But they wouldn't answer him.

TALKING TO GOD

Bring all your burdens and cares to God because he cares for you (1 Peter 5:7).

READING THE WORD

✤ *Matthew 12:9-13, NLT*
Then Jesus went over to their synagogue, 10where he noticed a man with a deformed hand. The Pharisees asked Jesus, "Does the law permit a person to work by healing on the Sabbath?" (They were hoping he would say yes, so they could bring charges against him.) 11And he answered, "If you had a sheep that fell into a well on the Sabbath, wouldn't you work to pull it out? Of course you would. 12And how much more valuable is a person than a sheep! Yes, the law permits a person to do good on the Sabbath." 13Then he said to the man, "Hold out your hand." So the man held out his hand, and it was restored, just like the other one!

TALKING TO GOD

Tell God you confidently trust his sovereignty and goodness over issues of suffering, whether your own or those of someone you love. Praise the Lord for his authority over all your days and circumstances.

MEETING A NEED

Setting the Scene

We don't know if the man in the synagogue was born with a deformed hand or had acquired it by an accident or disease. Whatever the cause, the hand was useless, and the man's condition would have greatly affected his ability to live a normal life. Although the man didn't ask Jesus for anything, he needed healing.

After Jesus announced that doing good on the Sabbath was lawful, he did exactly that. Jesus told the man to hold out his hand. In response and with everyone watching, the man stretched his hand in front of him. In faith, the man, submitting his will to Jesus, obeyed.

The moment he did so, the hand "was restored, just like the other one!"

Getting Personal

When have you asked God for healing for yourself or someone else? What happened?

When has someone's healing strengthened your faith in God?

Jesus sees, and he acts. Bringing the man to the front of the assembly, Jesus healed his hand. As with the leper (Matthew 8:3) and the paralyzed man (Matthew 9:6-7), Jesus gave this man his life back. The man would be able to work again and no longer have to face the embarrassment of his deformity.

Jesus mends broken lives—physically, emotionally, and spiritually. And he restores us. Jesus told the man to stretch out his arm. In faith, the man, submitting his will to Jesus, obeyed.

Jesus still heals. He still sees us as individuals and asks us to trust in him, to give him our deformities, our sorrows. Jesus forgives our sins and restores our relationship with him. And he can heal our hands, legs, minds, and hearts. Jesus didn't heal every lame person in Palestine, but he healed this man. Whether or not he makes whole our deformed hands right now, eventually he will—we will be made new.

CONFRONTING POWER

Setting the Scene

Putting these three Gospel accounts together, we see that the Pharisees were furious with Jesus. At first these religious leaders had been merely curious about Jesus, but their curiosity turned to hatred. They were "wild with rage" because Jesus had openly confronted their authority and placed himself above them. Jesus had looked them in the eyes, flouted their laws, and exposed the hatred in their hearts to the entire crowd in the synagogue.

These Jewish religious leaders were so jealous of Jesus' popularity, his miracles, and his authority that they missed who he was—the Messiah for whom they had been waiting. They refused to acknowledge Jesus because they were not willing to give up their treasured positions and power. When Jesus exposed their attitudes, he became their enemy, and they began looking for ways to destroy him. Ironically, they began planning *on the Sabbath* to kill him. Their hatred drove them to plot murder—an act clearly against the law.

The Pharisees "met with the supporters of Herod." This was an unlikely (and unholy) alliance. This group, also called the "Herodians," was made up of Jews who hoped to restore Herod the Great's line to the throne, so they usually stood in direct conflict with the Jewish religious leaders. But Jesus threatened the authority of both groups, so they began working together to rid themselves of this threat.

Getting Personal

When have you encountered opposition because of your desire to follow Jesus' example and teachings in your lifestyle?

How will you respond the next time you are "persecuted for doing right" and for following Jesus (Matthew 5:10-12)?

Either Jesus is who he said he is, or he is a fraud. The Pharisees chose the latter. We who follow Jesus can also be seen as threats. When we stand up for compassion and justice, we will be opposed by many who profit from oppression and discrimination. We may even encounter opposition from religious leaders who see their grip loosening. Jesus turns the world's values upside down, but his way is true and right. It is the only path to eternal life.

READING THE WORD

❊ *Matthew 12:14, NLT*
Then the Pharisees called a meeting to plot how to kill Jesus.

❊ *Mark 3:6, NLT*
At once the Pharisees went away and met with the supporters of Herod to plot how to kill Jesus.

❊ *Luke 6:11, NLT*
At this, the enemies of Jesus were wild with rage and began to discuss what to do with him.

TALKING TO GOD

Express to the Lord your whole-hearted commitment to Jesus and his teachings, no matter what consequences arise from your obedience and loyalty.

JESUS PREACHES THE SERMON ON THE MOUNT

Week 10, Day 1

❊ *Matthew 5:1-48; Mark 4:21-23; Luke 6:27-36; 11:33*

Many of us think we know all about Jesus' Sermon on the Mount because we've heard snippets of it preached in various sermons. The truths Jesus taught about the Kingdom of God were undeniably shocking to his listeners and freeing at the same time. This week we'll take a look at the most famous sermon ever preached and see what fresh truths God has for us today.

READING THE WORD

❊ *Matthew 5:1-10, NIV*

Now when Jesus saw the crowds, he went up on a mountainside and sat down. His disciples came to him, 2and he began to teach them. He said: 3"Blessed are the poor in spirit, for theirs is the kingdom of heaven. 4Blessed are those who mourn, for they will be comforted. 5Blessed are the meek, for they will inherit the earth. 6Blessed are those who hunger and thirst for righteousness, for they will be filled. 7Blessed are the merciful, for they will be shown mercy. 8Blessed are the pure in heart, for they will see God. 9Blessed are the peacemakers, for they will be called children of God. 10Blessed are those who are persecuted because of righteousness, for theirs is the kingdom of heaven."

TO BE OR NOT TO BE

Setting the Scene

This section in the Gospel of Matthew is traditionally known as the Sermon on the Mount. If these chapters represent notes taken during one specific occasion, then it probably involved several days of sessions in which Jesus interacted with the crowds that followed him. This concentrated section presents verse after verse of timeless truth. Here we get to experience firsthand what people had been reporting about Jesus' words—that he taught with authority. Some of the most familiar phrases connected with Jesus can be found in these chapters. It isn't surprising that this section of the New Testament is often considered among the finest pieces of literature in history.

The Sermon on the Mount begins with an overview by the Master. The Beatitudes can be summarized in several ways. Some readers focus on the obvious applications of the verses, seeing them as a code of behavior for believers in all times and places. Others point to the phrases as declarations of the ultimate values of the Kingdom of God, differing sharply from earthly values and ideals. Those who want to emphasize what Jesus' words meant to his immediate audience focus on how Jesus' views contrasted with those of the other religious teachers of his day. Still others see Jesus' statements connected to the ethical and spiritual ideals of the Old Testament, but now revealed as a seamless description of God's ultimate purposes for his people. All agree, however, that these verses are not random or optional pursuits for followers of Jesus—each one of them captures an important component of the life of faith.

We respond to the Beatitudes by reflecting on the sequence of Jesus' statements and using them as a road map to spiritual maturity. God blesses every step we take along our journey of faith. With poverty of spirit, we realize our spiritual bankruptcy and desperate need for God's intervention. Access to owning the Kingdom of Heaven is rooted in the shattering awareness that we can never earn it or buy it. Mourning relates to our repenting over our spiritual bankruptcy. Recognition of sin requires the follow-up of repentance. The next two steps combine humility (meekness) with a strong desire for right living (righteousness). They are introduced in their true role as by-products in the lives of recipients of God's blessings. Next come mercy and purity, requiring us to reduce our expectations of others and increase the expectations we place on ourselves. We practice mercy toward others, but strive for purity and transparency before God. The last two steps present a surprising contrast. We are active in making and keeping peace yet must also anticipate a harsh response, or persecution, from others who reject Christ's Kingdom.

We experience these steps repeatedly in life. Each time we make peace and experience rejection in the world, we gain a fresh awareness of our need for humility and trust in our own lives. The journey lasts a lifetime.

Getting Personal

Which Beatitude seems the most difficult for you?

Based on your growth and experiences to date, which Beatitude most represents your life?

Jesus ended the Sermon on the Mount by inviting his audience to identify themselves in one of two groups (Matthew 7:24-27). Are we people who listen to Christ's teaching and follow it, or are we people who hear his teaching and ignore it? Exposure to Jesus' teaching isn't enough; the truth must be acted upon.

TALKING TO GOD

Acknowledge the Lord's countercultural set of values as expressed in the Beatitudes. Pray through them, seeking God's work in your life at every step.

READING THE WORD

✤ *Matthew 5:11-12, NIV*
Blessed are you when people insult you, persecute you and falsely say all kinds of evil against you because of me. 12Rejoice and be glad, because great is your reward in heaven, for in the same way they persecuted the prophets who were before you.

TALKING TO GOD

Pray through these compelling guidelines for living, meditating on the short-term and long-range costs and rewards of each. Ask God for courage and strength to live according to his Word in this sermon.

HARD TIMES

Setting the Scene

To make sure we catch the ominous tone of the eighth Beatitude, Jesus rephrased the blessing with specifics. The description "persecuted because of righteousness" expanded to "persecute you and falsely say all kinds of evil against you," which adds up to a thorough rejection. This is news we don't want to hear. Do we really want to follow Jesus into a life of blessing that also promises difficulty and pain? Jesus instructed those considering becoming his disciples to count the cost (Luke 14:28), and he provided a clear idea of what that cost might be. There will always be some who decide the price tag for spiritual maturity and God's blessing is too high.

Jesus helped by giving us a more long-range view. Costs and rewards may be present or future. One choice may yield great short-term rewards followed by long-term regrets; another may be difficult at first but generate years of great reward. Jesus applied the principle to all of life. He warned that the immediate results of following him may be hard, but the reward of heaven will make the hardships worthwhile.

If we read through the first seven Beatitudes with costs in mind, we discover that each one requires an uncomfortable investment, beginning with coming clean about spiritual poverty. Repentance (mourning) may not be a cost we're eager to bear. Humbling ourselves will take a toll on pride, and longing for justice will be frustrating in a fallen world. Mercy will cost us our strong desire for revenge. And the desire for purity and peace will be costly to our tendency toward self-centeredness. But Jesus has promised that God blesses those who make the difficult investments in his way of living. God will bring lasting satisfaction into your life as a long-term result.

Getting Personal

Which Beatitude seems most costly to you?

Which blessing do you most eagerly desire?

Jesus was certainly speaking with the end of life in mind; much of the blessing from the Beatitudes will come to us in eternity. Yet there are clearly lifelong benefits that come to us on our present journey with Jesus.

TASTE AND SIGHT

Setting the Scene

After several verses on persecution, Jesus portrays the effects his followers ought to have on the world around them. Like salt and light, which are useful only when properly *applied*, our lives bring praise to God only as we acknowledge Jesus as Lord, submit ourselves to his active leadership, and then mix and mingle in the world. Just as salt and the lamp are objects to be used for a purpose—one enhancing flavor and the other providing visibility in a dark place—our lives are intended for a purpose, as well; namely, bringing glory to God.

Salt has limitations. It can lose its flavor or become impure. Yet the apostle Paul encouraged the Colossians to "let your conversation be gracious and attractive so that you will have the right response for everyone" (Colossians 4:6, NLT). The word "attractive" in this verse was translated from the same word used for "salt" in Matthew 5. Salt preserves as well as enhances food while maintaining its own distinctness. Christians are to season the world by their presence and yet maintain a distinction from the ways of the world.

Light has limitations too. It is useless if no one can see it. Jesus' picture of hidden light shows the folly of Christians living isolated from the world. We are to be the means by which others might see God.

Getting Personal

Which of these two pictures, salt or light, most represents your interaction with non-Christians?

In what ways do Christians hide their lamp under a bowl?

John Wesley was asked about the effectiveness of open-air preaching and the public proclamation of the gospel in eighteenth-century England. Wesley apparently smiled and said something to the effect that "when you light yourself on fire, people will show up to watch you burn." We will not be effective unless we are willing to be seen by others and consumed in his service. Neither salt nor light has to be perfect in order to be useful.

READING THE WORD

✵ *Matthew 5:13-16, NIV*
You are the salt of the earth. But if the salt loses its saltiness, how can it be made salty again? It is no longer good for anything, except to be thrown out and trampled underfoot. 14You are the light of the world. A town built on a hill cannot be hidden. 15Neither do people light a lamp and put it under a bowl. Instead they put it on its stand, and it gives light to everyone in the house. 16In the same way, let your light shine before others, that they may see your good deeds and glorify your Father in heaven.

TALKING TO GOD

Confess to God your reluctance to be persecuted or consumed in his service. Submit yourself, consciously, to his command, despite any shortcomings and fears. Ask him for courage to do his will.

THE LAW ABOVE THE LAW

READING THE WORD

✢ *Matthew 5:17-20, KJV*
Think not that I am come to destroy the law, or the prophets: I am not come to destroy, but to fulfil. 18For verily I say unto you, Till heaven and earth pass, one jot or one tittle shall in no wise pass from the law, till all be fulfilled. 19Whosoever therefore shall break one of these least commandments, and shall teach men so, he shall be called the least in the kingdom of heaven: but whosoever shall do and teach them, the same shall be called great in the kingdom of heaven. 20For I say unto you, That except your righteousness shall exceed the righteousness of the scribes and Pharisees, ye shall in no case enter into the kingdom of heaven.

TALKING TO GOD

Talk with the Lord about your own relation to his law—how these standards help you understand God's will but also frustrate you in your inability to live up to them on your own. Thank God for imputing his righteousness to you and for empowering you by his Spirit to live for him.

Setting the Scene

For the average person listening to Jesus, the law of Moses was the huge elephant in every room. The Law, the shorthand term for the first five books of the Hebrew Old Testament, was undeniably present in every situation people encountered. That law, with the multiplied traditions surrounding it, governed almost any action a person might need to take each day. Already Jesus' challenging of traditions was being seen as an attack on the underlying law of Moses. Here Jesus formally disarmed those who would accuse him of trying to destroy or replace what God had already given his people.

Jesus warned anyone speaking on his behalf to take care not to ignore the least commandment or influence others to do so, because they would not have standing in God's Kingdom. God's laws were still to be taught as the ultimate standard for behavior.

Then Jesus shifted the focus slightly to include the idea of righteousness. Jesus was not exactly complimenting the teachers of religious law and the Pharisees as paragons of righteousness; he was pointing out that genuine obedience to God would require greater and substantially different righteousness than these current leaders could muster. As guardians of the law, these leaders claimed to be obedient to it, yet Jesus pointed out on numerous occasions that these guardians invalidated the law by their contrived interpretations.

At the heart of this statement is Jesus' claim to fulfill the law and prophets. He was deliberately pointing to himself as the living standard. He also warned the scribes and Pharisees that their brand of righteousness would not gain them access to heaven.

Getting Personal

What does Jesus mean that our righteousness must be better than the righteousness of the scribes and Pharisees?

How did Jesus accomplish the purpose of the law?

The Pharisees were proud of their reputation. Yet the Old Testament prophet Isaiah declared that "all our righteousnesses are as filthy rags; and we all do fade as a leaf; and our iniquities, like the wind, have taken us away" (Isaiah 64:6, KJV). In other words, we can't save ourselves by our good works.

BOUNDARIES OF PASSION

Setting the Scene

Right after pointing to the righteousness of the Pharisees and teachers of the law, Jesus launches into some vivid examples that would have cut close to his audience: murder, legal actions, and adultery. It appears there were plenty of twenty-first-century problems back in the first century.

Instead of discussing when someone falls off a cliff, Jesus points out how long someone has walked along the edge before he fell off. When he brings up murder, he doesn't question the law but instead draws attention to the motives leading up to murder. Hatred, insults, and curses are shown to be various expressions of the same danger of destructive passion.

When it comes to reconciliation, Jesus asks for more than a willingness to forgive if approached. He calls on his followers to initiate the peacemaking process. Forgiveness is important. Humility and vulnerability are necessary to make the first move.

And to those who might think to reduce God's commands to the letter of overt action, Jesus points out the futility of such a course. While one might not commit adultery, one might still lust after someone.

In Matthew 5:29-30, Jesus uses the hyperbole of the ancient code of Hammurabi ("an eye for an eye") to point out the seriousness of sin. His death on the cross was not about sins in the causal sense but about sin that infects us to the core of our being. Without Jesus, even the loss of an eye would not ensure our forgiveness. Only his righteousness earns us God's forgiveness and cleanses us thoroughly.

Getting Personal

What is your definition of sin? Based on today's passage, what do you think Jesus would say about your definition of sin?

When have you avoided a sin overtly only to realize that you committed it in your heart?

Sometimes we might shrug away a "minor" sin, thinking we're in the clear as long as we don't break God's "major" laws. But no sin is "minor" or "major" in God's sight. As Romans 3:23 reminds us, all have sinned and fallen short of the glory of God. Every infraction points to the need of a Savior.

READING THE WORD

❋ *Matthew 5:21-28, NIV*
You have heard that it was said to the people long ago, "You shall not murder, and anyone who murders will be subject to judgment." 22But I tell you that anyone who is angry with a brother or sister will be subject to judgment. Again, anyone who says to a brother or sister, "Raca," is answerable to the court. And anyone who says, "You fool!" will be in danger of the fire of hell. 23Therefore, if you are offering your gift at the altar and there remember that your brother or sister has something against you, 24leave your gift there in front of the altar. First go and be reconciled to them; then come and offer your gift. 25Settle matters quickly with your adversary who is taking you to court. Do it while you are still together on the way, or your adversary may hand you over to the judge, and the judge may hand you over to the officer, and you may be thrown into prison. 26Truly I tell you, you will not get out until you have paid the last penny. 27You have heard that it was said, "You shall not commit adultery." 28But I tell you that anyone who looks at a woman lustfully has already committed adultery with her in his heart.

TALKING TO GOD

Admit your tendency to arrange your own sins on a sliding scale of bad to worst. Ask God to help you turn away from all attitudes and actions that displease him; ask him to give you his own view of sin.

READING THE WORD

✤ *Matthew 5:31-34, 37-39, 43-45, NLT*

You have heard the law that says, "A man can divorce his wife by merely giving her a written notice of divorce." 32But I say that a man who divorces his wife, unless she has been unfaithful, causes her to commit adultery. 33You have also heard that our ancestors were told, "You must not break your vows; you must carry out the vows you make to the LORD." 34But I say, do not make any vows! . . . 37Just say a simple, "Yes, I will," or "No, I won't." Anything beyond this is from the evil one. 38You have heard the law that says the punishment must match the injury: "An eye for an eye, and a tooth for a tooth." 39But I say, do not resist an evil person! If someone slaps you on the right cheek, offer the other cheek also. . . . 43You have heard the law that says, "Love your neighbor" and hate your enemy. 44But I say, love your enemies! Pray for those who persecute you! 45In that way, you will be acting as true children of your Father in heaven. For he gives his sunlight to both the evil and the good, and he sends rain on the just and the unjust alike.

TALKING TO GOD

Before the Lord, examine yourself to see if you have been applying the law to the lives of others while exempting yourself from God's call to deep personal integrity. Thank him for his continual mercy, and ask for his power to heal your own attitudes and actions.

WHAT HAVE YOU HEARD?

Setting the Scene

Three times in today's passage we read of Jesus stating, "You have heard the law that says." In each case, Jesus repeated the common understanding of one of God's laws and then showed how it had been distorted by widespread misinterpretation. The laws for divorce had gradually been reshaped into a freewheeling policy in which men could obtain divorce on a whim. In other settings (see Matthew 19:1-9), Jesus referred to the origin of marriage in the Garden and the designed lifelong nature of the relationship. Marriage, like everything else in creation, was marred by the fall of humanity. While stating what the law allowed due to the sins of people, Jesus still maintained the value of the commitment. Although unfaithfulness might be a reason for a divorce, the damage of adultery also could be repaired with genuine repentance, forgiveness, and reconciliation.

A person's plainspoken "yes" or "no" ought to be as dependable as any elaborate vow. If someone can't depend on our word, a vow does not increase our integrity.

Jesus also rejected the idea that offenses of any kind must be retaliated. He showed his followers a radical alternative: going the second mile, turning the other cheek, loving one's enemies. The idea of loving enemies goes against common sense. Jesus knew that common sense may cause us to respond contrary to God's heart in a matter.

Getting Personal

Which of today's guides to extraordinary living seems most difficult to you? Why?

If Jesus said these words to you personally, how might your priorities change?

Jesus must have had a twinkle in his eye when he pointed out that God "sends rain on the just and the unjust alike," thereby sparing a lot of us from a good deal of embarrassment. Few of us can escape the reality of today's passage. Jesus exposes the raw edge of many lives. His words uncover what we might try to keep hidden.

JESUS TEACHES THE DISCIPLES ABOUT PRAYER

Week 11, Day 1

❀ *Matthew 6:5-15*

Continuing his Sermon on the Mount, Jesus taught his close followers about prayer. This week we will explore Jesus' model for the manner, attitude, and content of our prayers.

HUMILITY

Setting the Scene

In using the word *hypocrites*, Jesus referred to many of the Pharisees and other religious leaders who wanted people to think they were holy. They even used public prayer to get attention. Jesus called them hypocrites because they were not actually praying to God; instead, they were putting on a show for an audience who would revere them for their apparent holiness. Their motive was pride.

By saying, "when you pray," Jesus was assuming that his followers would pray. He wasn't saying people shouldn't pray in the synagogues (or church) or even on "street corners" for that matter, but that prayers shouldn't be done for show. We find the reality and depth of prayer not in public but in private communication with God. Corporate, public prayer can be powerful, and such prayers were vital to the early church and have an important place in churches today. But people who pray more in public than in private should consider their motives. If they really want to communicate and fellowship with God, they should go alone into a room, "shut the door," and pray. Praying only where others will notice may indicate that their real intention is to please people, not God. The only "reward" or results from the prayers of hypocritical religious leaders would be esteem from their earthly audience.

The prayer life of Jesus' followers should differ radically. When we pray in public, pride can easily creep in. We can be overly concerned with using the right words and phrases, or about being politically and religiously

READING THE WORD

❀ *Matthew 6:5-6, NLT*
When you pray, don't be like the hypocrites who love to pray publicly on street corners and in the synagogues where everyone can see them. I tell you the truth, that is all the reward they will ever get. 6But when you pray, go away by yourself, shut the door behind you, and pray to your Father in private. Then your Father, who sees everything, will reward you.

TALKING TO GOD

Do your best to eliminate pride as a motive as you meet with God to pour out your emotions, express your thoughts, and listen in the quietness for God's answers.

correct. We may even be tempted to use prayer to spread gossip about others or to let everyone know of our spiritual accomplishments. But in private prayer, we eliminate pride from our motives; we humbly pour out our emotions to God, express our true thoughts and feelings, and listen in the quiet for God's answers.

Getting Personal

In what public settings do you pray or hear others pray? When have those prayers been helpful to you?

When have you had extended times of private prayer? How does your approach and content in those prayers differ from your public prayers?

Where will you choose as your place of private prayer? When will you begin to spend personal time with your Father?

Prayer should be a habit and a vital part of our lives. Paul wrote that Christians should "never stop praying" (1 Thessalonians 5:17, NLT), implying that we should pray at all times of the day and in all locations, including home, office, school, malls, and presumably, "street corners." Most believers today probably won't shout out prayers in a crowded mall or business district, but we may be tempted to make a show of our piety in religious settings (worship services, small groups, Sunday school classes, prayer meetings, etc.). At those times, we should guard our motives, remembering that God is our primary audience, not the people in the group.

Our biggest problem, however, is that we may limit our prayers to those locations. Instead, God wants to hear from us as we drive, before and during important meetings, while working in the kitchen or garden—in all of life's routines. We also need to spend extended time with the door closed behind us, listening to our Father and humbly presenting ourselves and our needs to him.

SINCERITY

Setting the Scene

After discussing hypocrisy, Jesus next pointed to the practices of "other religions" and highlighted another truth about prayer. To "babble on and on" is to repeat the same words over and over, like a magic incantation. Many pagan worshipers believed that saying certain words and phrases and repeating them often would help them get through to their gods.

Jesus wasn't belittling prayer or even the idea of being persistent in prayer, something that he would later encourage his disciples to do (Luke 18:1-8). And the prayer that Jesus taught his disciples has been repeated by church congregations and individual believers for twenty centuries. Instead, Jesus condemned the shallow repetition of words by those who don't have a personal relationship with God and who are not thinking about what they are saying. Prayer isn't magic, like waving a wand and saying "Abracadabra," and God doesn't offer secret formulas for us to use. Prayer is communication, one person talking to another. As this passage shows us, God is more interested in our hearts (our focus and motives) than our words. He wants us to approach him with openness, honesty, and sincerity, engaging our minds and emotions.

Getting Personal

How can your prayers be more open and honest?

How can you be more focused on God and aware of him as you pray?

"Your Father knows exactly what you need even before you ask him!" How should that truth affect the way your pray?

Believers should come to God as to their loving Father, sincerely bringing specific needs. This statement that "the Father knows exactly what you need even before you ask him" doesn't excuse believers from praying; it's just that we don't have to spend a long time reciting our needs. God doesn't need our prayers, but he wants our prayers and knows that we need them.

God knows you outside and in: thoughts, feelings, relationships, conflicts, dreams, anxieties, hopes, and needs. As your loving Father, he cares about you, his child. And as his child, you can approach your Father at any time and anywhere, coming boldly into his presence (Hebrews 4:16). Open your heart to him.

READING THE WORD

❋ *Matthew 6:7-8, NLT*
When you pray, don't babble on and on as people of other religions do. They think their prayers are answered merely by repeating their words again and again. [8]Don't be like them, for your Father knows exactly what you need even before you ask him!

TALKING TO GOD

Focusing on the person and character of Christ will help you communicate in prayer in a more natural, person-to-person way. Begin your prayer time today by directing your focus on God, praising him for aspects of his character that you have recognized or learned.

READING THE WORD

✱ *Matthew 6:9, NLT*
Pray like this: Our Father in heaven, may your name be kept holy.

TALKING TO GOD

God's ultimate holiness and supremacy makes our finitude and neediness seem even more desperate. Remember both his glory and your need as you enjoy the incredible blessing today of being welcomed into the presence of the Almighty with all the love and affection of a Father.

HONOR

Setting the Scene

In saying, "May your name be kept holy," Jesus opens his model prayer with an attitude of praise and honor to God. The first-person plural pronoun may indicate that believers could pray it corporately.

The very first phrase of this prayer contains a profound tension: We should approach God as "Father" while recognizing that he is "holy." To be "holy" means to be sacred, perfect, and totally set apart. But "Father" refers to a close relationship. God is majestic and holy, transcending everything on earth, but he is also personal and loving. Many religious people understand that God is totally other, and they approach him with caution, with fear, and sometimes with complex rituals. This would have been the attitude of Jews in Jesus' day. The book of Leviticus highlights God's holiness and provides detailed instructions for entering into his presence. Because of Jesus and his work on the Cross as the final sacrifice, we can now come to God directly and boldly. He is our Father, and we are his children. But the last half of this statement—"may your name be kept holy"—indicates that we shouldn't come to him flippantly or casually. God wants to hear and listen as a loving Father, but our being able to approach him is an awesome privilege. We must enter the King's throne room respectfully. When we pray for God's name to be "kept holy," we are praying that this world will honor his name. And we look forward to Christ's return when that will be a reality and all the world will recognize the power of his name.

Getting Personal

When have you felt almost overwhelmed with the sense of God's holiness? How did that affect your prayers?

When have you felt extremely close to God, almost as if you were being cradled in his arms? How did that affect your prayers?

The first line of this model prayer is a statement of commitment to honor God's holy name in how we live. As Christians, we bear the name of Christ; thus, our words and actions reflect on him.

SUBMISSION AND DEPENDENCE

Setting the Scene

The Jewish people knew the prophecies of a coming Messiah, whom they expected to throw off the nation's oppressors, defeat her enemies, and restore Israel to her former glory under David and Solomon. God had announced his Kingdom in the covenant with Abraham (Genesis 17:7-8; referenced in Matthew 8:11 and Luke 13:28), and pious Jews were still waiting for it. So most Jews found accepting Jesus as their Messiah to be very difficult because Jesus preached a spiritual kingdom, not an earthly, physical one.

When Jesus told his disciples to pray, "May your Kingdom come soon," he was referring to God's spiritual reign, not Israel's freedom from Rome. To pray, "May your Kingdom come soon," is to ask that more and more people will enter God's Kingdom and to ask God to rule in their lives. It also reaffirms belief in the coming of a future Kingdom, when all evil will be destroyed, God will establish the new heaven and earth, and his glory will be known to all the nations (Psalm 110:1; Revelation 21:1).

Saying "May your will be done" acknowledges total submission to God's rule, praying that God's perfect purpose will be accomplished in this world ("on earth") as it already is in heaven.

With submission to God and his rule comes total dependence. The next request regards personal needs and provisions. "Food" refers to food in general, though it could also refer to spiritual nourishment. Notice that we must trust God "today" to provide what he knows we need.

Getting Personal

When have you seen a dramatic instance of God providing for you?

How do you balance depending on God and relying on yourself?

Believers must trust God for provision and not worry. The fact that God provides daily food does not mean we should just sit back, relax, and wait for food (or money) to drop into our laps. We need to work to earn enough to pay for what we eat. Praying for daily food acknowledges that God is Sustainer and Provider. He gives us ability and opportunities to work. He provides.

READING THE WORD

❋ *Matthew 6:10-11, NLT*
May your Kingdom come soon. May your will be done on earth, as it is in heaven. 11Give us today the food we need.

TALKING TO GOD

Thank God specifically for the ways he has been providing for you and for those who depend on you. Don't hesitate to ask him to provide for you even today.

READING THE WORD

❋ *Matthew 6:12, 14-15, NLT*
Forgive us our sins, as we have
forgiven those who sin against
us.... ¹⁴If you forgive those who
sin against you, your heavenly
Father will forgive you. ¹⁵But if
you refuse to forgive others, your
Father will not forgive your sins.

TALKING TO GOD

*If there is someone you've been
having a hard time forgiving,
picture that person beside you
at the foot of Jesus' cross—both
of you needing forgiveness. Then
focus in prayer on your own need
for the Lord's forgiveness—which
is already yours because of the
Cross.*

FORGIVENESS

Setting the Scene

The next line of the Lord's Prayer makes an important request but adds a significant condition. Sin includes both active *and* passive resistance to God. Instead of submitting to him, we turn away, disobey, and live the way we want. Because we are sinners, cut off from God, we are helpless and hopeless—unless he forgives us. Even as believers, we sin each day, so we must come to him for forgiveness, cleansing, and strength to go on. In prayer we humbly ask God to forgive our sins. But then Jesus' prayer adds a condition, "Forgive us . . . as we have forgiven." Jesus meant our forgiveness of others should reveal our understanding of God's forgiveness of us. When believers understand the greatness of the forgiveness they have received, they willingly extend such forgiveness to others.

Jesus gave this startling warning: If we refuse to forgive others, God will also refuse to forgive us. This does not refer to salvation, because salvation is not dependent on anything people can do. But living in relationship with God requires constant repentance of the sins that plague us. Because believers must come to God constantly for confession and forgiveness, refusing to forgive others reveals a lack of appreciation for the mercy received from God. All people are on common ground as sinners in need of God's forgiveness. If we are unwilling to forgive others, we are denying and rejecting God's forgiveness of us (see Ephesians 4:32; Colossians 3:13). Later, Jesus would tell a parable depicting such a situation (Matthew 18:23-35).

Getting Personal

*When have you held a grudge against someone—
that is, you found forgiveness difficult to give?*

*How can remembering that God has forgiven you
help you to forgive others?*

*Be careful what you pray for! When we so easily repeat
the Lord's Prayer, we pray, "Forgive us our sins, as we
have forgiven those who sin against us." But do we
really want God to hold us that accountable? May we
be quick to forgive, extending grace to others in the
same way God has extended grace to us.*

DELIVERANCE

Setting the Scene

Traditionally the first half of this verse asks, "Lead us not into temptation" (KJV), but a more accurate translation is "Don't let us yield to temptation." God doesn't tempt us, as James clearly states: "When you are being tempted, do not say, 'God is tempting me.' God is never tempted to do wrong, and he never tempts anyone else. Temptation comes from our own desires, which entice us and drag us away" (James 1:13-14, NLT). At times God allows us to be tempted, as a test. But this testing always has a purpose. God continually works to refine his people, teach them to depend on him, and strengthen their character to be more like him. How he does this differs in every person's life.

The next line has been translated "Deliver us from evil" (KJV), but the more accurate translation is "Rescue us from the evil one." Satan is actively looking for ways to harm God's people, to throw them off course. Jesus wanted his followers to place their trust in God during trying times and to pray for deliverance from "the evil one" and his deceit. We can't resist temptation or defeat in our own strength; we must depend on God working in us and in our situation.

Believers who pray these last lines of the Lord's Prayer realize their sinful nature and their need to depend on God in the face of temptation.

Getting Personal

What types of temptations are most tempting to you?

When might you encounter temptations today, both the trivial and the serious? What can you do to resist?

All Christians struggle with temptation. A temptation can be so subtle that we don't even realize what is happening. Yet hear this promise: "God is faithful. He will not allow the temptation to be more than you can stand. When you are tempted, he will show you a way out so that you can endure" (1 Corinthians 10:13, NLT). When temptations hit, thank God for trusting you that much, ask him to show you what to do, and pray for his strength to deliver you from the evil one.

READING THE WORD

❃ *Matthew 6:13, NLT*
And don't let us yield to temptation, but rescue us from the evil one.

TALKING TO GOD

As you pray, use the phrase "Don't let me yield to" and list your own specific temptations. Ask God to show you ways to resist and endure, and thank him in advance for his promise of deliverance.

JESUS IS WRONGFULLY ACCUSED
Week 12, Day 1

❁ *Matthew 12:22-50; Mark 3:20-35; Luke 8:1-3, 19-21*

When we think about Jesus and those closest to him, we usually include the twelve disciples, and after that the list is short. The Gospels, however, do give us glimpses into some of the background relationships in Jesus' life. There were other disciples. Jesus' family members were on the scene. When we look closely, we see Jesus fully engaged in healthy relationships. His life modeled the boundaries between support from friends and family and the separation that makes ministry possible.

READING THE WORD

❁ *Luke 8:1-3, NLT*
Soon afterward Jesus began a tour of the nearby towns and villages, preaching and announcing the Good News about the Kingdom of God. He took his twelve disciples with him, 2along with some women who had been cured of evil spirits and diseases. Among them were Mary Magdalene, from whom he had cast out seven demons; 3Joanna, the wife of Chuza, Herod's business manager; Susanna; and many others who were contributing their own resources to support Jesus and his disciples.

ENTOURAGE

Setting the Scene

Women played a leading role in the Gospel of Luke. Beginning with the story of Jesus' birth, the Greek physician included women as active participants in Jesus' ministry. The Nativity is seen through Mary's eyes, with such intimate notes that Mary may have been one of Luke's many eyewitness sources for compiling his record of Jesus' life and ministry.

As the eighth chapter of Luke opens, Jesus leaves Capernaum, his home base, and leads a group of followers on a ministry "tour" of surrounding cities. This preaching trip included stops in cities around the northern end of the Sea of Galilee. By now the twelve disciples have been chosen. A number of women also join the group, including three who are named: Mary Magdalene, Joanna, and Susanna.

People have often wondered why Jesus never called any women in the way he called the twelve disciples. Knowing the character of the disciples as we do, Jesus' invitation to "follow me" wasn't given based on some kind of impressive résumé. In the culture of the day, established businesspeople and leaders would be prohibited from the traveling lifestyle the disciples had. Peter, James, John, and the rest needed a specific challenge; the women simply responded to Jesus' character and words—they followed. Women were at the cross, while many disciples hid. They were also at the tomb early while the eleven grieved, and so they were the first to discover the joyful truth of the Resurrection.

The three women Luke names came with history. Mary Magdalene had been afflicted with multiple demons, which Jesus expelled. Luke captures the basis for this Mary's connection with Jesus. She filled the void evil left behind with devotion to the one who set her free. Joanna was a woman with social influence and an important husband, which shows that Jesus drew followers from every strata of society. Susanna, who is not mentioned anywhere else in Scripture, may have been a person widely known to Luke's original audience, since Luke doesn't mention her town of origin or a male relative.

These three and other women would probably not have been allowed to carry out public duties like preaching, but Luke notes that they used their personal means to support the efforts of Jesus' traveling band. They partnered in ministry with their money. Yet these women also bore witness to Jesus' power in their lives. Their presence made practical the "preaching and announcing the Good News about the Kingdom of God." Citizenship in Jesus' Kingdom was open to women also. Jesus was not simply speaking about an ideal that might be achieved at some future date. He was modeling the diversity, unity, and love of people whose connection to one another through Jesus Christ overcame any other barrier. Luke was describing an early form of community that would later be called the church (*ekklesia*), the ones called out by God for his purposes.

Getting Personal

Who are some of the most diverse people you have come to know because of your mutual connection with Jesus Christ?

In what ways are your resources being used to support the ministry of Christ's Kingdom?

As he invested in the lives of others, Jesus ignored many of the social barriers that kept people separate. This breaking down of walls is still a hallmark of the Kingdom of God.

TALKING TO GOD

Praise God for the diversity of your community of believers. Ask God to make you part of his ministry of breaking down the walls that separate people in our contemporary culture.

FAMILY TIES

READING THE WORD

❋ *Mark 3:20-21, 31-35, NLT*
One time Jesus entered a house, and the crowds began to gather again. Soon he and his disciples couldn't even find time to eat.
21When his family heard what was happening, they tried to take him away. "He's out of his mind," they said. . . . 31Then
Jesus' mother and brothers came to see him. They stood outside and sent word for him to come out and talk with them. 32There
was a crowd sitting around Jesus, and someone said, "Your mother and your brothers are outside asking for you." 33Jesus replied,
"Who is my mother? Who are my brothers?" 34Then he looked
at those around him and said, "Look, these are my mother and brothers. 35Anyone who does
God's will is my brother and sister and mother."

TALKING TO GOD

Spend some time thanking God, by name, for members of your family of origin and members of your family of faith. Praise him for his creativity and love that encompasses such a diversity of people.

Setting the Scene

No doubt Jesus' family had heard that huge crowds taxed Jesus to the point of exhaustion. Many of us can identify with the expression of love and exasperation that only a family member could voice: "He's out of his mind!"

Without being contrived, the Gospels weave a story that includes both the strand of Christ's divine nature and his human nature. The results are almost funny at times. Notice, for instance, an earlier family interaction between Jesus and his mother in Luke 2:48-49 (NLT). She approached her twelve-year-old son frantically, having spent three days wondering and worrying about his whereabouts. To her classic motherly statement ("Son, why have you done this to us?"), Jesus' response captures both the guileless confidence of early adolescence ("But why did you need to search?"), as well as the deeper perception of his unique identity ("Didn't you know that I must be in my Father's house?"). Most of us can imagine or remember hearing a young teenager say something like, "Why were you worried? I knew where I was the whole time!" And yet Jesus' divine claim was followed by the actions of an obedient son (see Luke 2:51).

In today's text, Jesus reminded his family that his ultimate role went far beyond the relationship they shared. Jesus taught his disciples, "If you love your father or mother more than you love me, you are not worthy of being mine; or if you love your son or daughter more than me, you are not worthy of being mine" (Matthew 10:37, NLT). Here he simply showed how the teaching applied to him. Jesus used this moment of human family dynamics to point out that the family of faith goes beyond earthly attachments to eternity.

Getting Personal

How has your family helped or hindered your relationship to Christ?

In what ways does "doing God's will" connect you with other believers?

The old saying, "You can't choose your family members" applies to the family of God as well. As Jesus said, "Anyone who does God's will is my brother and sister and mother." God includes all—imperfect though we may be—in his family.

HEALING THE HELPLESS

Setting the Scene

Healing is one of Jesus' most prominent acts of ministry. He healed those with physical needs: lameness, blindness, and so on. He healed some who were troubled by a demonic presence, as in today's passage. And Jesus helped those who needed spiritual healing: forgiveness of sin, cleansing of the soul, restoration of wholeness. Mark 2:1-12 shows Jesus healing people physically to demonstrate that he could also heal people spiritually.

No one talks much about demons today. Talk of demons is interpreted as primitive ignorance combined with a barely hidden fear that such an obvious display of evil would be terrifying. Some people chalk up all reported demonic activity to a simplistic view of reality that explains all natural phenomena in spiritual terms. But insisting that everything can be explained naturalistically eventually strips life of any meaning beyond chemical reactions. The Bible takes a more realistic approach by describing life experiences in real terms. The writers understood demons to be as much of the natural (fallen) order as any one of many items that can't be seen (gases, love, light) but are still real.

In today's passage, we glimpse an encounter between Jesus and demonic powers that had incapacitated a man's sight and speech. This man with normal eyes and vocal cords couldn't use them because a demon prevented him. Jesus' expulsion of the demon freed this man to engage the world. Imagine for a moment the helplessness of blindness and muteness. This man was *brought* to Jesus; he didn't find his own way. His whole experience is a teaching case for us of the incapacitating effects of sin and the wonderful ways God heals us.

Getting Personal

How have your beliefs about healing helped or hindered you from asking for healing?

Are there limits to what you would ask God to do in your life? Why or why not?

Jesus' desire to heal others clearly demonstrated his compassion. His healing helped bring isolated people back into community. He urges us to show compassion toward others by praying for healing or bringing a healing word to those who are hurting.

READING THE WORD

✿ *Matthew 12:22-23, NLT*
Then a demon-possessed man, who was blind and couldn't speak, was brought to Jesus. He healed the man so that he could both speak and see. 23The crowd was amazed and asked, "Could it be that Jesus is the Son of David, the Messiah?"

TALKING TO GOD

Ask God to give you his compassion as you pray by name for those you know who need healing—from physical disorders, from satanic oppression, and from spiritual darkness.

READING THE WORD

❁ *Matthew 12:24-29, NKJV*
Now when the Pharisees heard
it they said, "This fellow does
not cast out demons except
by Beelzebub, the ruler of the
demons." 25But Jesus knew their
thoughts, and said to them:
"Every kingdom divided against
itself is brought to desolation,
and every city or house divided
against itself will not stand.
26If Satan casts out Satan, he
is divided against himself. How
then will his kingdom stand?
27And if I cast out demons by
Beelzebub, by whom do your
sons cast them out? Therefore
they shall be your judges. 28But if
I cast out demons by the Spirit of
God, surely the kingdom of God
has come upon you. 29Or how can
one enter a strong man's house
and plunder his goods, unless he
first binds the strong man? And
then he will plunder his house."

TALKING TO GOD

The Lord fully understands your doubts and reservations. Don't hesitate to pray, "Help my unbelief" or "Show me your truth." God promises to be found by those who seek him earnestly.

CRITICS

Setting the Scene

For those determined not to believe, even a miracle can be a waste of time and effort! When the Pharisees heard about Jesus' power over demons, they didn't doubt the miracle; but they refused to believe what the miracle indicated. They looked diligently for another explanation. *The miracle occurred*, they said, *because Jesus was on the same team as the demons—they were playing along with him rather than being forcibly removed from their victims!*

Their explanation at first certainly seemed to them to fit the observable facts. But Jesus shattered their accusation with two devastating counterarguments. First, what could possibly be accomplished if Satan were casting out Satan? If the demons were being exorcised by friendly fire, then Satan's kingdom was self-destructing. Second, the Pharisees, so eager to discredit Jesus' power, ended up discrediting their own exorcists. By saying that only the demonic can expel the demonic, they had inadvertently offended some of their own group who were involved in confronting demonic powers. Jesus mildly pointed out that those people would not sit idly by and let their ministry be discredited.

But Jesus wasn't finished. He now answered the question originally posed by the crowd that had witnessed the healing: "Could it be that Jesus is the Son of David, the Messiah?" (Matthew 12:23, NLT). He said, "But if I am casting out demons by the Spirit of God, then the Kingdom of God has arrived among you" (v. 28, NLT). The "if" challenged Jesus' listeners to make up their own minds. They had just seen the miracle and heard two widely divergent explanations; which one were they going to believe?

Getting Personal

What questions or doubts keep your commitment to Christ from being wholehearted?

In the quest for faith, would you describe your questions more as tools for searching or weapons for defense? Why?

Even today, we can hardly think about Jesus without asking questions, so it helps that the Bible doesn't forbid questions. But it does press us to use questions on the way to faith rather than using unending questions to put off believing. If we insist that every question must be answered before we believe, we will never get around to believing.

LIMITS OF FORGIVENESS

Setting the Scene

Discussions about forgiveness often get detoured by the question, *Is there a sin God can't forgive?* Once this question has been raised, there is an almost inevitable corollary, *How do I know I haven't committed that sin?* Today's passage certainly seems to declare that there is indeed an unforgivable sin. And blaspheming the Holy Spirit sounds suspiciously like a sin someone might commit simply by thinking about it.

So what does it mean to blaspheme or speak against the Holy Spirit? At the basic, personal level, those who worry about this probably haven't done it! Someone who blasphemes the Holy Spirit isn't interested in forgiveness.

Blaspheming the Holy Spirit involves invalidating or rejecting God's most compelling move toward us. Once the Holy Spirit has appealed to us, God can go no further. If we are hardened against that approach, we have placed ourselves beyond reach of forgiveness, even if it's offered. When Jesus described the Holy Spirit's role in salvation, he said, "When he comes, he will convict the world of its sin, and of God's righteousness, and of the coming judgment. The world's sin is that it refuses to believe in me" (John 16:8-9, NLT). Unbelief in Christ is the sin we all commit and that the Holy Spirit works to convict us about. If we irrevocably turn from that conviction, we're permanently lost.

Knowing what blaspheming the Holy Spirit is doesn't give us the right to declare when anyone (even ourselves!) has done it. Only God ultimately knows about those who have blasphemed his Holy Spirit. Rather than worrying about offending the Spirit, we ought to invest more time in obeying the Spirit!

Getting Personal

What evidences of the Spirit's work can you identify in your life?

How do you respond to the Holy Spirit's leading?

The Holy Spirit is God's indwelling presence in us, starting from the moment of faith (Ephesians 1:13-14). Just as Jesus is Immanuel—"God with us"—the Holy Spirit is "God in us." He is not our conscience, dispensing common sense. He is the eternal wisdom—wholly God.

READING THE WORD

❋ *Matthew 12:30-32, NLT*
Anyone who isn't with me opposes me, and anyone who isn't working with me is actually working against me. 31So I tell you, every sin and blasphemy can be forgiven—except blasphemy against the Holy Spirit, which will never be forgiven. 32Anyone who speaks against the Son of Man can be forgiven, but anyone who speaks against the Holy Spirit will never be forgiven, either in this world or in the world to come.

TALKING TO GOD

God's Holy Spirit is with you as you pray. Thank him for his work in your life, beginning with convicting you of your need for God. If you can, identify specifically other ways the Spirit has been at work in your life.

READING THE WORD

❋ *Matthew 12:33-37, NLT*
A tree is identified by its fruit.
If a tree is good, its fruit will
be good. If a tree is bad, its
fruit will be bad. ³⁴You brood
of snakes! How could evil men
like you speak what is good and
right? For whatever is in your
heart determines what you say.
³⁵A good person produces good
things from the treasury of a
good heart, and an evil person
produces evil things from the
treasury of an evil heart. ³⁶And
I tell you this, you must give an
account on judgment day for
every idle word you speak. ³⁷The
words you say will either acquit
you or condemn you.

TALKING TO GOD

*Thank God for being the master
gardener, in charge of growing
good fruit in your life. Thank
him for the Spirit's power and
presence to make those fruits
appear.*

CONNECTED OR NOT

Setting the Scene

Trees are identified by leaf structure and organization, bark, shape, fruit, and even DNA. Some trees like pecans, hickories, and walnuts produce seeds without fruit—nuts. So what was Jesus' first point? He wasn't talking about identifying a type of tree; he was talking about the qualities within a certain type of tree. He wasn't comparing apple trees and orange trees; he was pointing to the difference between a good apple tree and a bad apple tree, a desirable orange tree and an undesirable orange tree. In that case, the proof is in the fruit.

The kind of fruit Jesus had in mind was words. He was directing his comments to the Pharisees who had mocked the healing of the demon-possessed man by accusing Jesus of operating under the influence of Satan (Matthew 12:24). By this point Jesus had demonstrated that the opposite was actually true—his accusers had revealed that they were producing the fruit of Satan.

In the passage we considered yesterday, we focused briefly on what happens when we resist the work of the Holy Spirit. But the wider teaching of Scripture gives us good clues about the positive side of that process—what happens when we cooperate with the Holy Spirit and let God bring forth fruit in our lives. Paul put it very well in Galatians 5:22-23: "The Holy Spirit produces this kind of fruit in our lives: love, joy, peace, patience, kindness, goodness, faithfulness, gentleness, and self-control. There is no law against these things!" (NLT).

Jesus' words of confrontation in today's Scripture portion may seem harsh to us, but his awareness of the Pharisees' deep-seated unbelief required a kind of shocking language. The Holy Spirit used his words to crack their internal hardness or they simply rejected what he had said. Either way, they could never say they weren't sternly warned.

Getting Personal

What kind of fruit have you been producing lately?

What is contained in the treasury of your heart?

Fruit quantity is not the same as quality. What a disappointment to bite into a beautiful fruit that is mealy or rotten inside. We must go beyond asking for fruit to ask God to grow good fruit.

JESUS DESCRIBES GOD'S KINGDOM
Week 13, Day 1

❋ Matthew 13:1-53; Mark 4:1-34; Luke 8:4-15; 13:18-21

Jesus left the synagogue and began to teach outdoors. He left those opposed to him and reached out to those who were more responsive. This week, we will look at several stories and parables about the Kingdom of Heaven, also called the Kingdom of God. As Jesus said, "Anyone with ears to hear should listen and understand."

BEING GOOD SOIL

Setting the Scene

Jesus had made unmistakable claims about his true identity, and the division was growing between those who accepted and those who rejected them. The religious leaders had already decided Jesus was not the Messiah. The crowds who followed him, listening to his teaching and observing his miracles, wondered if Jesus could be the "Son of David" (Matthew 12:23), but their leaders told them he was not.

Jesus began using stories to get his listeners to think. These "parables" hid the truth from those who had already made up their minds to reject Jesus. Those who truly wanted to know Jesus, however, would understand his words.

This first parable features a farmer, seeds, and soils. In ancient Israel, farmers sowed seeds by hand. Walking across the field, the farmer would plant the seeds by scattering handfuls of seed from a large bag slung across the shoulders.

As the farmer in this story walked along, some scattered seeds fell on the compacted soil of the footpath. That would be like grass seeds falling on the sidewalk. The seeds wouldn't penetrate the earth, so the birds ate them. Other parts of the field were rocky; a shallow layer of soil lay on top of rock. The soil was good, so the seeds sprouted. But with no depth to the soil, the roots couldn't take hold, and the plants soon withered. Some of the seeds fell among weeds ("thorns"), and the young plants were soon choked out.

READING THE WORD

❋ *Matthew 13:3-12, NLT*

"Listen! A farmer went out to plant some seeds. 4As he scattered them across his field, some seeds fell on a footpath, and the birds came and ate them. 5Other seeds fell on shallow soil with underlying rock. The seeds sprouted quickly because the soil was shallow. 6But the plants soon wilted under the hot sun, and since they didn't have deep roots, they died. 7Other seeds fell among thorns that grew up and choked out the tender plants. 8Still other seeds fell on fertile soil, and they produced a crop that was thirty, sixty, and even a hundred times as much as had been planted! 9Anyone with ears to hear should listen and understand." 10His disciples came and asked him, "Why do you use parables when you talk to the people?" 11He replied, "You are permitted to understand the secrets of the Kingdom of Heaven, but others are not. 12To those who listen to my teaching, more understanding will be given, and they will have an abundance of knowledge. But for those who are not listening, even what little understanding they have will be taken away from them."

TALKING TO GOD

Tell the Lord you are willing for him to remove distractions and worries from your life, and any "weeds" that threaten to keep you from being fertile ground for his work in you.

Some of the seeds landed in plowed and readied soil, with the depth, space, and moisture to enable the seeds to produce a large crop.

Jesus told the disciples that the types of soil in his parable represent the ways that people respond to the gospel message. Some have hearts so hard, like the "footpath," that the Word makes no impression. They hear but don't understand, and Satan, like the birds in the story, snatches the seeds.

"Rocky soil" people seem to accept God's Good News, but their faith is shallow, not deep or real, and it doesn't take hold. These people abandon their faith at the first sign of problems or persecution.

The seeds that fall among thorns sprout and take hold but produce no fruit because they are soon crowded out by weeds—the "worries of this life and the lure of wealth" (Matthew 13:22, NLT). These seem to be true believers, but they don't grow in their faith.

Other people are like the "fertile" or "good soil" (Matthew 13:23, NLT)—they hear the Word and accept it. The seeds penetrate, take root, flourish, and produce fruit. These are the true disciples—those who accept Jesus, believe his words, and allow him to make a difference in their lives.

Getting Personal

When have you encountered people who seemed hardened to hearing God's message?

When have you seen people with a "rocky soil" faith experience? What told you their Christianity wasn't real?

What worries and lures threaten to keep you from growing in your faith and producing fruit?

What keeps your "soil" fertile, receptive to God and his work in your life?

Worldly worries, the false sense of security brought on by prosperity, and the desire for material things plagued first-century disciples just as they do us today. Daily routines overcrowd and materialistic pursuits distract believers, choking out God's Word so that it produces no fruit. God wants us to weed out those thorns, to be fertile ground for his seeds planted in us.

SHINING LIGHT

Setting the Scene

There are parallel passages with these same comments of Jesus given in Luke 8:16-18 and at several places in Matthew. Jesus probably was speaking to the disciples with the crowd gathered around them. Here in Mark, the discussion of "a lamp," "a basket," and "understanding" appear immediately after Jesus' explanation of the parable of the farmer, seeds, and soils.

A "lamp" was a lighted wick in a clay bowl full of oil. The lamp would never be lit and then put "under a basket or under a bed." It would be put on its stand in order to illuminate the room. In the same way, the purpose of the parables was not to conceal the truth but to reveal it.

Jesus was telling the disciples that the benefits of knowing him were to be passed on, like light shining in darkness. They should "pay close attention," so they would know the truth and be able to share it with others. Jesus added that those who listen and understand would continue to grow because they let God's Word make a difference in their lives; but those who listen casually would miss the point entirely.

Getting Personal

Often Jesus would say, "Anyone with ears to hear should listen and understand." When have you experienced others who listened to the gospel message without seeming to understand it at all?

How can paying close attention to the gospel teaching about Jesus shine light on your daily priorities?

What can you do to "pay close attention" (v. 24) to Jesus and his teachings?

Christ's message about God's Kingdom is intended for everyone. At times, believers seem to hide their faith from the watching world, as if putting their light under a basket. But Jesus calls us to spread the truth about the Kingdom, scattering seeds, shining light. We can only share what we know, so we should be diligent about listening and learning from the Master. But God will lead us to those whom we can help with what we know.

Regardless of your level of spiritual maturity, "let your good deeds shine out for all to see, so that everyone will praise your heavenly Father" (Matthew 5:16, NLT).

READING THE WORD

❁ *Mark 4:21-25, NLT*

Then Jesus asked them, "Would anyone light a lamp and then put it under a basket or under a bed? Of course not! A lamp is placed on a stand, where its light will shine.
22For everything that is hidden will eventually be brought into the open, and every secret will be brought to light. 23Anyone with ears to hear should listen and understand." 24Then he added, "Pay close attention to what you hear. The closer you listen, the more understanding you will be given—and you will receive even more. 25To those who listen to my teaching, more understanding will be given. But for those who are not listening, even what little understanding they have will be taken away from them."

TALKING TO GOD

When you are tired, stressed, or distracted, it can be hard to "pay close attention" as you read God's Word and listen to God in prayer. Ask God to help you as you focus your attention on him; ask for the Holy Spirit to quicken your understanding and interest.

READING THE WORD

❋ *Mark 4:26-29, NLT*

Jesus also said, "The Kingdom of God is like a farmer who scatters seed on the ground. 27Night and day, while he's asleep or awake, the seed sprouts and grows, but he does not understand how it happens. 28The earth produces the crops on its own. First a leaf blade pushes through, then the heads of wheat are formed, and finally the grain ripens. 29And as soon as the grain is ready, the farmer comes and harvests it with a sickle, for the harvest time has come."

TALKING TO GOD

Ask God to give you such a love for the truths you find in God's Word that your life overflows in living it and sharing it with others. Trust God for the spiritual development of others, even as you share the gospel with them.

Setting the Scene

This Kingdom parable is found only in Mark, and its main point is that spiritual growth is continual, gradual, and totally caused by God. The farmer's faithfully scattered seeds germinate, sprout, and grow. Although the farmer doesn't know how all this happens, he can depend on the process and can be certain of the growth of his crop.

In the same way, God's Kingdom begins in a person's life with a seed of understanding that takes root, through the Holy Spirit, in the good soil of the person's heart. That seed sprouts and grows into strong faith. But how that happens is God's responsibility. While God uses his followers to plant the seeds, he gives the growth. As Paul wrote to the Corinthian believers, "I planted the seed in your hearts, and Apollos watered it, but it was God who made it grow" (1 Corinthians 3:6, NLT).

The disciples must have wondered about the difficult mission ahead of them, so Jesus explained they need not worry about how the Kingdom would grow. That part was up to God alone. Their job was to plant the seeds.

The planting and growing seasons won't last indefinitely, however. Eventually God will intervene and "harvest," separating the grain from the weeds (Matthew 13:30). The weeds (unbelievers) will receive judgment for sin; the good grain (believers) will be ushered into God's eternal Kingdom.

Getting Personal

What has God used (people, crises, conflicts, challenges, insights, etc.) to help you grow in your faith?

In what ways have you matured in your faith over the last few years; that is, how are you a different person than you were three years ago?

What new believers are you encouraging and nurturing?

The two strongest lessons from this passage are the importance of sowing and the necessity of trusting. In talking about the inevitable harvesttime, Jesus was saying that we have a limited time to spread his Word. We should not become complacent or relax; instead, we should continue to live and speak God's truth. At the same time, however, we have to trust God to work in people's lives to produce the desired results.

LIVING WITH WEEDS

Setting the Scene

Jesus explained that the Kingdom grows quietly and abundantly, but evil still exists in the world. Jesus provided the meaning of this parable: Jesus, the "Son of Man," is the farmer; the "field" is the world; the "good seed" symbolizes God's people; the "weeds" are Satan's people; the "enemy" is Satan; the "harvesters" are angels. A common practice in ancient warfare and feuds was to destroy the enemy's agriculture. Thus, the presence of Satan's people among the people of God would weaken them.

At first, the weeds and wheat are indistinguishable; eventually, however, the differences become obvious. At harvesttime, harvesters remove the weeds and get rid of them. The "weeds" may be people in the church who appear to be believers but who never truly believe. Later, the apostles would battle the problem of false teachers who had come from within the ranks of the believers (see, for example, 2 Peter 2:1-3, 13-22).

As new believers begin to mature in faith, their lives begin to reflect the Holy Spirit's work, affecting values, perspectives, priorities, attitudes, and actions. Those who aren't true followers of Christ, however, continue to reflect the values and attitudes of the world.

Eventually, the truth will be revealed, and God will judge and send each group to their right destination. For the "weeds," those who "cause sin" and "do evil" (Matthew 13:41, NLT), that will be terrible. But "the righteous will shine like the sun in their Father's Kingdom" (Matthew 13:43, NLT).

Getting Personal

Jesus said we can tell a lot about people by their "fruit," how they act and what they produce (Matthew 7:20). What "fruit" do you produce that shows you belong to Jesus?

How do your values, perspectives, attitudes, and actions differ from those who don't know Christ?

God is the ultimate judge of who truly belongs to him. We should be slow to judge others, realizing people have different levels of spiritual maturity. Only God knows their hearts. Instead, we can lovingly share the gospel, teach, encourage, and confront and discipline, when necessary, leaving the final judgment to him.

READING THE WORD

❊ *Matthew 13:24-30, 36-39, NLT*
"The Kingdom of Heaven is like a farmer who planted good seed in his field. 25But that night as the workers slept, his enemy came and planted weeds among the wheat, then slipped away. 26When the crop began to grow and produce grain, the weeds also grew. 27The farmer's workers went to him and said, 'Sir, the field where you planted that good seed is full of weeds! Where did they come from?' 28'An enemy has done this!' the farmer exclaimed. 'Should we pull out the weeds?' they asked. 29'No,' he replied, 'you'll uproot the wheat if you do. 30Let both grow together until the harvest. Then I will tell the harvesters to sort out the weeds, tie them into bundles, and burn them, and to put the wheat in the barn.'" . . . 36His disciples said, "Please explain to us the story of the weeds in the field." 37Jesus replied, "The Son of Man is the farmer who plants the good seed. 38The field is the world, and the good seed represents the people of the Kingdom. The weeds are the people who belong to the evil one. 39The enemy who planted the weeds among the wheat is the devil. The harvest is the end of the world, and the harvesters are the angels."

TALKING TO GOD

Express your desire to bring all areas of your life—values, perspectives, attitudes, and actions—under God's authority. Ask God to make you sensitive to areas that still need his healing and instruction.

READING THE WORD

✿ *Luke 13:18-21, NLT*

Then Jesus said, "What is the Kingdom of God like? How can I illustrate it? 19It is like a tiny mustard seed that a man planted in a garden; it grows and becomes a tree, and the birds make nests in its branches." 20He also asked, "What else is the Kingdom of God like? 21It is like the yeast a woman used in making bread. Even though she put only a little yeast in three measures of flour, it permeated every part of the dough."

TALKING TO GOD

Thank God for the faith seed he planted in you. Ask him to help you live out your role in spreading his Kingdom, a part in his wonderful plan to grow the church around the world.

Setting the Scene

Jesus used the parables about the mustard seed and the yeast to explain that his Kingdom would have a small beginning but then grow quickly from there. Most of Jesus' hearers assumed the Messiah would come as a great king and leader, freeing the nation from Rome and restoring Israel's former glory. But Jesus' Kingdom began quietly. The "mustard seed" is so small it would take almost twenty thousand seeds to make one ounce. But one tiny seed can produce the largest shrub among all the herbs in a person's garden, growing ten to twelve feet in a few weeks. Just as the tiny mustard seed becomes a large plant, the Kingdom of God would eventually push outward until the whole world would be changed.

"Yeast" is another symbol of something small producing something much larger. Although yeast looks like a minor ingredient in making bread, it is responsible for the dough's rising. In the same way, God's Kingdom had small beginnings but would grow to have a great impact on the world.

Getting Personal

How can you "water" and "weed" in your faith-garden?

What evidence of growth can you see from when you first gave your life to Jesus?

What stories have you heard recently about the spread of God's Kingdom in other nations?

What can you do to support your brothers and sisters in other lands?

Imagine how encouraging these parables would have been to the disciples, surrounded by hostile religious leaders and living under Roman occupation. How could this insignificant band of Christ-followers dare hope to have any impact? But they did. The mustard seed, the yeast, grew and expanded from tiny Israel to the whole earth. When you trusted Christ with your mustard seed–size faith, the Holy Spirit took up residence in you and began to change you from the inside out. Your growth may be slow and quiet, but it's sprouting and reaching for the sun.

FINDING TREASURE

Setting the Scene

To teach the inestimable value of God's Kingdom, Jesus said it was like a "treasure" and like a "merchant" looking for "choice pearls." To obtain the treasure in the field, the man, excitedly and without hesitation, "sold everything he owned." The same was true with the "pearl of great value"—the merchant "sold everything he owned and bought it."

The Kingdom is also like a "fishing net" filled with fish that are eventually sorted. Like a net pulling in a variety of fish, the gospel message goes out to all kinds of people. But not all will be chosen.

Finally, Jesus says a "teacher of religious law who becomes a disciple" is like someone who owns valuable gems. These teachers (Pharisees and others) already had access to God's truth as revealed in the Law, which they studied.

By mixing these metaphors, Jesus was saying that all types of people gain the Kingdom and eternal life in a wide variety of ways. They can stumble upon it, search for it, be pulled toward it, or realize that it is nearby.

The disciples learned three lessons: Nothing is more important or valuable than God's Kingdom—it's worth everything we have and are. We need to keep casting the net to everyone and let God do the sorting. And no one is beyond God's reach, not even those who oppose us.

Getting Personal

When you found God's Kingdom, did you stumble over it or seek after it or discover it among the truths that had already been given to you?

What did you give up to follow Christ? How do you know that it was worth it?

For the disciples, Jesus' teachings about God's Kingdom must have been confusing, at times, and amazing, almost unbelievable. Today we have the advantage of knowing much more of God's story: the Cross, the Resurrection, the promised return, the Holy Spirit, the church, and the whole Bible. We know Christ established his Kingdom in the hearts of his people, changing the world one person at a time. Possessing the treasure and sharing it with others is worth everything.

READING THE WORD

✦ *Matthew 13:44-53, NLT*

"The Kingdom of Heaven is like a treasure that a man discovered hidden in a field. In his excitement, he hid it again and sold everything he owned to get enough money to buy the field. 45Again, the Kingdom of Heaven is like a merchant on the lookout for choice pearls. 46When he discovered a pearl of great value, he sold everything he owned and bought it! 47Again, the Kingdom of Heaven is like a fishing net that was thrown into the water and caught fish of every kind. 48When the net was full, they dragged it up onto the shore, sat down, and sorted the good fish into crates, but threw the bad ones away. 49That is the way it will be at the end of the world. The angels will come and separate the wicked people from the righteous, 50throwing the wicked into the fiery furnace, where there will be weeping and gnashing of teeth. 51Do you understand all these things?" "Yes," they said, "we do." 52Then he added, "Every teacher of religious law who becomes a disciple in the Kingdom of Heaven is like a homeowner who brings from his storeroom new gems of truth as well as old." 53When Jesus had finished telling these stories and illustrations, he left that part of the country.

TALKING TO GOD

Celebrate the treasure you have in knowing Jesus. Thank God for the love he shows in bringing so many to himself, in the various ways they need for understanding the truth. Thank him for the great gifts of his salvation and his Spirit.

JESUS CALMS THE SEA

Week 14, Day 1

Matthew 8:23-27; Mark 4:35-41; Luke 8:22-25

Jesus and his disciples got into a boat and went out on the Sea of Galilee. The disciples could not have realized when they left the shore that in a matter of hours they would have experienced what we might call "the ultimate paradigm shift." They were soon to realize that Jesus was much, much more than a wise teaching "Master" and was actually Master of the created world. This week, let your vision of who Jesus is be shaken so that you discover that he is truly King over all Creation.

READING THE WORD

Mark 4:35-36, NLT
As evening came, Jesus said to his disciples, "Let's cross to the other side of the lake." 36So they took Jesus in the boat and started out, leaving the crowds behind (although other boats followed).

MEN IN BOATS

Setting the Scene

Our scene for this week opens with Jesus and the disciples embarking for a journey across the lake, and Mark provides us with wonderful details surrounding a miracle in which Jesus displayed his authority over the created order.

It wasn't uncommon for a fishing boat in Jesus' time to be capable of transporting thirteen men. In 1986 a fishing boat dating from the time of Christ was discovered and dug out of the mud on the northwest shore of the Sea of Galilee. Its size is similar to the boat Jesus and his disciples must have used on that stormy evening.

Although it is called a "sea," the Galilee is a freshwater body that teems with fish. The lake is approximately six miles wide and thirteen miles long. The waters are fed by the young Jordan River, which channels water from Mount Hermon and other mountains to the north.

During daylight hours, the shore is visible from any point on the Sea of Galilee. The land rises on most of the north, east, and west sides of the lake so it's difficult to imagine getting lost out there. But at night, the occasional distant flicker of a home fire may have been the only hint of land in any direction. And even those clues would have been absent in the dead of night if a storm blew in.

The geography of the Sea of Galilee makes it possible for violent weather to swoop down on the lake from out of the mountains that surround it. The clashing of climates between air temperature at lake level and at mountain height creates conditions for sudden storms.

But Jesus and his disciples were not worried as they set out during "the calm before the storm." "As evening came" may seem like unusual timing for a boat trip, but night has always been a traditional time for fishing. Jesus suggested the trip, and the disciples immediately got in the boat and set out. Mark even mentions that a small flotilla accompanied them.

They left the crowds, chaos, and noise behind, and the only sounds were the wind in the sails, the water lapping against the boat, and the quiet conversations among the disciples. It was the end of a long day. It was time to think about all that had happened since these men had begun to follow Jesus. They were still in familiar settings, but life for these men was changing. They were in the company of Jesus, and they had already discovered that the unexpected was commonplace around the Teacher.

Getting Personal

The disciples were relating to Jesus on their home turf. Imagine Jesus being at home where you live each day. What difference would his presence make?

If Jesus visibly spent the day with you today, how would your schedule and activities change?

One of the last things Jesus said before he ascended into the clouds was not only a command to go to the world with his message but also to "be sure of this: I am with you always, even to the end of the age" (Matthew 28:20, NLT). Jesus is with us everywhere we go—in times of calm and in times of storm.

TALKING TO GOD

God's Holy Spirit is with you. Ask God to help you "practice" his presence by remembering he is with you throughout the day today.

READING THE WORD

✤ Luke 8:23, NLT
As they sailed across, Jesus settled down for a nap. But soon a fierce storm came down on the lake. The boat was filling with water, and they were in real danger.

TALKING TO GOD

Today in prayer, focus on aspects of God's power, authority, and trustworthiness that emphasize his sovereignty. Then shift your focus to his great love and complete goodness. Put all your fears into the care of this powerful and perfectly loving Lord.

WISE FEAR

Setting the Scene

Jesus chose twelve men to follow him and learn from him. At least five of his disciples had been fishermen who understood winds and waves. But this also means that as many as seven of the Lord's traveling band were "landlubbers."

It's difficult to measure which is greater—fear based on ignorance or fear based on knowledge. If we're in a situation we've never been in before and things begin to look like they are getting out of control, it's natural to check out the reactions of those who are experienced. If they are calm, our worries seem unfounded. But if things look precarious and even people with lots of experience appear scared, we start to fear for our lives.

The account tells us, "Jesus settled down for a nap." Perhaps some of the disciples also nodded off. But the sudden change in the elements put everyone on edge. Once the boat began to fill with water, there was no longer any doubt they were all in danger.

Five of the disciples had good reason to be afraid, and the other seven took their cues from them! The capacity to fear is a God-given ability to sense danger and avoid it. When the danger is real, the fear is wise. It prevents us from doing stupid things and can sharpen our focus for problem solving. If the danger is imagined, fear is wasted effort. The disciples were about to discover that Jesus redefines danger and removes fear. They learned that even wise fear can be set aside by the power of God.

Getting Personal

Is fear more likely to turn you toward God in trust or to turn you away from him, doubting his control? Why?

When was the last time you were truly fearful? How did you handle that occasion?

Fear ought not to have the last word in our lives. Fear can grab our attention and motivate action, but it can also be a reminder that our ultimate trust must be in God, who is greater than our fears.

CONCLUSIONS

Setting the Scene

Most of us struggle with making good decisions, but we seem to have no trouble at all jumping to conclusions. While the disciples were frantically bailing water from the boat, they realized their efforts would not be enough. At that point they jumped to a conclusion: *We're going to drown.* Their conclusion was realistic and depressing.

Then someone noticed Jesus was still asleep. He hadn't stirred when the boat began to buck with the waves, and the shouts of the sailors-turned-bailers hadn't wakened him. Now they jumped to another conclusion: *Jesus must not care about our fate.* After all, he was soundly sleeping while the boat sank!

We might chalk it up to plain terror, but hearing the disciples skip right past the opportunity to ask Jesus for help and move right to accusing Christ of not caring reveals a deep failure to treat Jesus with respect. They didn't give him the benefit of the doubt. Their comments don't indicate that they were resentful because Jesus didn't do something about the storm (they really didn't expect anything like *that* to happen). They were upset that Jesus wasn't up worrying with them. What's the point of drowning if you can't be terrified together? They wanted the fear to be shared by everyone in the boat.

It's hard to keep up appearances under stress. Fear brings out the real *us.* When we are only going through the motions of trusting God with our lives, the least bit of difficulty will shatter that brittle trust. We need to practice trusting God when the seas are calm so that it isn't so hard to trust him when the seas of life are rough!

Getting Personal

When have you felt that God didn't care about a particular situation in your life? What caused you to feel that way?

If the situation has been resolved, what happened to show you that God indeed did care?

Consider where the edge of your trust in God is today. How far are you depending on him? Now take a step beyond that edge. Where can you stretch your faith in a new area?

READING THE WORD

✳ *Mark 4:35-38, NLT*

As evening came, Jesus said to his disciples, "Let's cross to the other side of the lake." 36So they took Jesus in the boat and started out, leaving the crowds behind (although other boats followed). 37But soon a fierce storm came up. High waves were breaking into the boat, and it began to fill with water. 38Jesus was sleeping at the back of the boat with his head on a cushion. The disciples woke him up, shouting, "Teacher, don't you care that we're going to drown?"

TALKING TO GOD

Trust the Lord today with your most pressing problems and stressors. Ask him to develop your confidence in his sovereign control. Ask him to help you think clearly, without panicking or jumping to false conclusions.

THE LORD OF CREATION

❋ *Matthew 8:26, NLT*
Jesus responded, "Why are you afraid? You have so little faith!" Then he got up and rebuked the wind and waves, and suddenly there was a great calm.

❋ *Mark 4:39-40, NLT*
When Jesus woke up, he rebuked the wind and said to the waves, "Silence! Be still!" Suddenly the wind stopped, and there was a great calm. 40Then he asked them, "Why are you afraid? Do you still have no faith?"

TALKING TO GOD

In prayer today, identify areas of worry and fear. Thank God that he is aware of each one and that, in love, he is working to protect and preserve you.

Setting the Scene

Both Mark and Luke record the sequence of Jesus' response to the impassioned plea of the disciples as miracle first, comment after. Matthew tells us Jesus questioned their faith and then spoke to the wind and waves. The order is probably not significant, since Jesus may have spoken with the men before and after the miracle. But Matthew, who was present in the boat, seems to capture more vividly the style Jesus usually used with his disciples. The thinking and the challenge came first, followed by the miracle. As we've already seen in the incident with the lame man lowered through the roof, Jesus said what needed to be said and then confirmed his words with a miracle (see Mark 2:1-12).

Jesus asked a question and then made a statement: "Why are you afraid?" and "You have so little faith!" Fears deserve to be questioned. We ought to ask ourselves regularly, "Why am I afraid?" If we never doubt our fears, they will control us. As we have already learned this week, some fears are legitimate, and some fears are not. Sometimes we don't need to be afraid. When we are with Jesus, we don't have to fear.

When fear is in control, faith is stifled. Acting fearfully is not acting faithfully. Jesus' question wasn't directed toward the disciples' feelings but their actions. The problem arises when we give in to fear and make it the basis of our decisions—which is what the disciples were doing. They needed faith—as Jesus pointed out. Faith doesn't ignore feelings; it simply refuses to obey them.

Getting Personal

What is your usual strategy for handling fear?

To what degree are your choices determined by fear?

When did you last act in faith in the face of fear? What was the outcome?

Acknowledging fears can be an important first step in disabling their influence. The psalm writer had a great thought when he wrote, "When I am afraid, I will put my trust in you" (Psalm 56:3, NLT). What you do before and after you are afraid can be as important as no longer being afraid.

REVISED CONCLUSIONS

Setting the Scene

Jesus' disciples went from terror over almost certain death one moment to stunned awe the next as the boat drifted in the suddenly still waters. There's no indication in this account that the disciples expected Jesus to do something about their predicament other than share it with them. The last thing they anticipated was to hear him address the elements and command them into submission. The significant miracles they had already witnessed had not prepared them for his exercise of power on such a grand scale. No wonder they murmured, "Who is this man?" They had observed Jesus teaching and healing people of diseases and demon possession, but their understanding of the Lord was still stuck at seeing him as a human being with special powers rather than as God of the universe. Their exposure to the power that the wind and waves obeyed left them "terrified and amazed."

We who are used to sin-hobbled efforts and mixed results find it hard to comprehend the wonder of an encounter with a limitless being. We always expect complications and disappointments—not fully accepting that with God all things are possible. So when God answers our prayers, we pinch ourselves in wonder. We want to believe God *could* do something, but we often stop short of trusting that God *will* do something. And so we find ourselves in the sandals of the disciples, continually surprised by God's faithfulness and power. Fortunately, God is not limited by our faith. He is able "to accomplish infinitely more than we might ask or think" (Ephesians 3:20, NLT).

Getting Personal

When has God worked in your life or answered a prayer beyond your expectations?

How would your prayer life be different if, rather than affirming that God could *do something about a situation in your life, you began to affirm that God* will *do something?*

We can be so intent on giving God a way out that we don't fully trust him to provide a way through *for us. Instead of just thinking about leaving things in God's hands, we need to actually leave things in his hands!*

READING THE WORD

❈ *Mark 4:41, NLT*
The disciples were absolutely terrified. "Who is this man?" they asked each other. "Even the wind and waves obey him!"

❈ *Luke 8:25, NLT*
The disciples were terrified and amazed. "Who is this man?" they asked each other. "When he gives a command, even the wind and waves obey him!"

TALKING TO GOD

Anticipate God's powerful work in your future by thanking him, in advance, for the resolution of problems you are facing today.

READING THE WORD

Mark 4:37-41, NLT
But soon a fierce storm came up. High waves were breaking into the boat, and it began to fill with water. 38Jesus was sleeping at the back of the boat with his head on a cushion. The disciples woke him up, shouting, "Teacher, don't you care that we're going to drown?" 39When Jesus woke up, he rebuked the wind and said to the waves, "Silence! Be still!" Suddenly the wind stopped, and there was a great calm. 40Then he asked them, "Why are you afraid? Do you still have no faith?" 41The disciples were absolutely terrified. "Who is this man?" they asked each other. "Even the wind and waves obey him!"

TALKING TO GOD

Tell the Lord that you depend on his patience with you just as much as those first disciples did. Affirm your commitment to the only one who has the words that give eternal life.

EXPECTING THE UNEXPECTED

Setting the Scene

With thorough integrity, Scripture always reveals its heroes' painful flaws. The followers of Jesus were shining examples that the road to growth and learning runs smack through the middle of missteps, mistakes, and downright failures. We can learn plenty from the lives of the disciples—and then go on to make our own mistakes.

The disciples were right where Jesus had led them—and they were still overwhelmed by circumstances beyond their control. Like those men, we know that storms come up suddenly and conditions can change in a heartbeat, yet we're still surprised when troubles come. The real issue is: Are we determined to trust Jesus? As long as we trust Christ, we will find throughout life that each day will contain its share of opportunities to learn something new.

We may think that if we had been in the boat with those disciples and seen, in person, that amazing display of Christ's power, we would never again hesitate to trust Jesus. But such assumptions simply reveal how poorly we appreciate our slowness to learn and remember. We know God has been faithful to us in the past, and yet we fail almost daily to fully trust him with our present or future. At the end of most days, Jesus could rightly ask us, "Why are you afraid? Do you still have no faith?"

We can look to the disciples as fellow strugglers with whom we can identify in our failures and take hope. Like them, as long as we trust in Jesus, we always have more room to grow.

Getting Personal

What have been some recent lessons through failure that Christ has allowed into your life?

How will you show Jesus today that you trust him?

Peter captured the crucial importance of trusting Jesus at a time when many followers were abandoning Christ. When Jesus asked the Twelve about their plans, Peter responded, "Lord, to whom would we go? You have the words that give eternal life" (John 6:68, NLT). It's never about who we are; it's always about the one who is with us.

❋ *Matthew 10:1–11:1; Mark 6:7-13; Luke 9:1-6*

The twelve men chosen as apostles had already joined Jesus (see Mark 3:14-19). This week we will see Jesus sending them out to minister on their own for the first time, giving them authority, power, and specific instructions for their actions and attitudes.

ANNOUNCE AND GIVE

Setting the Scene

Many people followed and listened to Jesus, but the twelve listed here composed the inner circle and received authority and the most intense training. They had authority over the forces of evil, as well as the ability to speak the word to have God's power cast out evil spirits. They also had power "to heal every kind of disease and illness." Verse 1 says they are "disciples," but verses 2 and 5 call them "apostles," meaning "sent ones." The fact that Jesus limited their ministry "to the people of Israel" doesn't mean he opposed evangelizing Gentiles and Samaritans. In fact, Jesus had already ministered to both groups (Matthew 8:28-34; John 4). But the message was to go to "the Jew first" (Romans 1:16, NLT). Another factor may be that the disciples weren't ready to branch out beyond their own people. Eventually Jesus would commission them to go to "all the nations" (Matthew 28:19, NLT).

Jesus gave the apostles two tasks: They were to "announce" and to "give." As Jesus' representatives, they were to spread his message, announcing that "the Kingdom of Heaven is near," letting everyone know that the Messiah had come. Jesus also told them to "give as freely" as they had received, healing the sick, raising the dead, curing those with leprosy, and casting out demons. These four miracles were exactly the ones Jesus had done and would demonstrate that the disciples had Jesus' power.

Jesus had quite a diverse collection of disciples, especially the Twelve—fishermen, tax collector, zealot, and so

READING THE WORD

❋ *Matthew 10:1-8, NLT*

Jesus called his twelve disciples together and gave them authority to cast out evil spirits and to heal every kind of disease and illness. 2Here are the names of the twelve apostles: first, Simon (also called Peter), then Andrew (Peter's brother), James (son of Zebedee), John (James's brother), 3Philip, Bartholomew, Thomas, Matthew (the tax collector), James (son of Alphaeus), Thaddaeus, 4Simon (the zealot), Judas Iscariot (who later betrayed him). 5Jesus sent out the twelve apostles with these instructions: "Don't go to the Gentiles or the Samaritans, 6but only to the people of Israel—God's lost sheep. 7Go and announce to them that the Kingdom of Heaven is near. 8Heal the sick, raise the dead, cure those with leprosy, and cast out demons. Give as freely as you have received!"

TALKING TO GOD

If you feel anxious about what God may be asking of you, confess your worries and intimidation to him. Ask God for the power of his Spirit to enable you to handle any task or relationship he asks of you.

on. Yet he entrusted his message and mission to them. Through this small band, the word would go forth, the Kingdom of Heaven would be introduced, and the world would be changed. Imagine what those men must have thought as Jesus gave his final instructions, especially considering their specific tasks. This was a significant and intimidating assignment, but Jesus had confidence in the apostles as he sent them out.

Getting Personal

What does the fact that you are a "disciple" of Christ mean to you?

When have you felt commissioned or assigned by God to a specific mission? In what ways did God prepare and empower you for that task?

Jesus told the apostles to announce a specific message of hope and salvation. He also told them to act with mercy. And the principle guiding their actions should be, "Give as freely as you have received." The disciples had received salvation and the Kingdom without cost; they were to give their time under the same principle. Because God has showered us with his blessings, we can give generously to others of our time, love, and possessions.

What can you do to give more "freely" of what you have received from God?

WORK WITH OTHERS

Setting the Scene

These instructions seem, at first, to be contrary to normal travel plans, but they simply reveal the urgency of the task and its temporary nature. This was a training mission; the apostles were to leave immediately and travel light, taking along only minimal supplies. Instead of being sent out as isolated individuals, Jesus sent them in pairs (Mark 6:7). Each pair of disciples would enter a city or village and stay in the home of a "worthy person."

The disciples' dependence on others had four good effects: (1) It showed that the Messiah had not come to offer wealth to his followers; (2) it forced the disciples to rely on God's power and not on their own provision; (3) it involved the villagers, making them more eager to hear the message; and (4) it built long-term relationships.

Jesus also had harsh words concerning those who would reject them and their message. Shaking the dust from their feet would demonstrate to the people that the disciples had nothing further to say and would leave the people to answer to God. Jesus was clearly stating that the listeners were responsible for what they did with the gospel. As long as the disciples had faithfully and carefully presented the message, they were not to blame if the townspeople rejected it. Likewise, we have the responsibility to share the gospel clearly, faithfully, and personally, but we are not responsible when others reject Christ's message of salvation.

Getting Personal

In what ways has working with others in ministry enhanced and deepened your ministry?

What can you do to be more relational in ministry?

These days, with instant communication, modern transportation, and other high-tech resources, we can be tempted to maintain our independence or to rely on impersonal ministry methods. But God created us to live in relationship and to do his work with others. This training assignment implies that we have a clear responsibility to care for those who minister among us, especially those who visit from out of town. What can you do to relate more personally to those who minister in your community?

READING THE WORD

❋ *Matthew 10:9-15, NLT*
Don't take any money in your money belts—no gold, silver, or even copper coins. ¹⁰Don't carry a traveler's bag with a change of clothes and sandals or even a walking stick. Don't hesitate to accept hospitality, because those who work deserve to be fed. ¹¹Whenever you enter a city or village, search for a worthy person and stay in his home until you leave town. ¹²When you enter the home, give it your blessing. ¹³If it turns out to be a worthy home, let your blessing stand; if it is not, take back the blessing. ¹⁴If any household or town refuses to welcome you or listen to your message, shake its dust from your feet as you leave. ¹⁵I tell you the truth, the wicked cities of Sodom and Gomorrah will be better off than such a town on the judgment day.

TALKING TO GOD

If you tend to be a "lone ranger," managing your life and spiritual life independently, ask God to help you find others to work with and to hold you accountable. As you pray, listen for the Spirit's prompting with ideas of brothers or sisters in God's family whom you might bring alongside you.

BE READY FOR ANYTHING

✿ *Matthew 10:16-20, NLT*
Look, I am sending you out as sheep among wolves. So be as shrewd as snakes and harmless as doves. 17But beware! For you will be handed over to the courts and will be flogged with whips in the synagogues. 18You will stand trial before governors and kings because you are my followers. But this will be your opportunity to tell the rulers and other unbelievers about me. 19When you are arrested, don't worry about how to respond or what to say. God will give you the right words at the right time. 20For it is not you who will be speaking—it will be the Spirit of your Father speaking through you.

TALKING TO GOD

Express your willingness—or confess your unwillingness—to suffer misunderstanding or outright persecution for the Lord's sake. Ask him for courage to face those difficult times, and thank him in advance for giving you the right words to say and actions to take.

Setting the Scene

The key instruction in this passage is "beware!" Battles lay ahead, and the apostles needed to be prepared—shrewd, harmless, and ready for anything. They would need to be unafraid of conflict but also able to deal with it with integrity. Jesus warned them that the gospel would not be warmly welcomed in all places. At times the disciples would face outright antagonism. This would be more than mere differences of opinion or unfriendly families and communities. The opposition would come from religious and civil authorities. The apostles would be arrested and could face harsh punishment simply for believing in Jesus and telling others about him. But these persecutions would provide opportunities for presenting the gospel. Later, the disciples did experience these hardships (Acts 5:40; 12:1-3; 22:19; 2 Corinthians 11:24). Interestingly, the word *martyr* comes from the Greek word for witness or testimony.

Jesus said, "Don't worry about how to respond or what to say." Some mistakenly think this means believers do not have to prepare to present the gospel because God will take care of everything. The Bible says, however, that we are to make carefully prepared, thoughtful statements (Colossians 4:6). Later one of these commissioned men, Peter, would write, "If someone asks about your Christian hope, always be ready to explain it" (1 Peter 3:15, NLT). Jesus was telling his followers to prepare but not to worry. He promised special inspiration for times of great need.

Getting Personal

When have you encountered opposition for your Christian beliefs?

How have you seen God work in and through you, giving you the right words to say?

Jesus warned the apostles to focus on their mission and turn their defense into a testimony of faith. Such a serious warning would make most people think twice about going! No one welcomes aggressive opposition and physical threats. But we should assume that as we live for Christ and tell others about him, we will face persecution. At those times, we can thank God for the opportunities and remember that Christ has "overcome the world" (John 16:33, NLT).

DON'T FEAR

Setting the Scene

After explaining that the disciples would be opposed and persecuted, Jesus detailed some of the persecutions to come and how the disciples should react. Christ and his message would tear apart families—nothing could be more painful than a brother betraying his brother "to death" or a parent causing his or her child to be killed. In addition, they would be hated by all types of people. Jesus' disciples would share his authority, but they would also share his sufferings. Then Jesus explained that his followers should be patient and faithful throughout the persecution, knowing that they have a reward that is certain.

The key phrase in this section is "Don't be afraid"—of those who threaten and of those who cannot touch the soul. The apostles should boldly proclaim God's truth, shouting it "from the housetops for all to hear!" Christ's followers should be far more fearful of disobeying God than of facing martyrdom. We are not to be afraid of people but in awe of God.

Later, many of the disciples suffered and died for following Christ. Yet their bold witness ignited a fire that spread all over the world.

Getting Personal

How has your family responded to your personal faith and bold witness for Christ?

Of what have you been most afraid as you've followed Christ?

Whether the Bible translation reads "Fear not," "Have no fear," or "Don't be afraid," the message is clear. Yet often we pull back from sharing our faith because of what it might cost us in relationships, income, or social status. Believers in many parts of the world face harsh persecution, living out Jesus' predictions of verse 21. God asks for bold witnesses to his truth, men and women whose actions and words shout the truth about Christ. Hear your Savior's words as he commissions you: "Don't be afraid."

READING THE WORD

❀ *Matthew 10:21-28, NLT*
A brother will betray his brother to death, a father will betray his own child, and children will rebel against their parents and cause them to be killed. 22And all nations will hate you because you are my followers. But everyone who endures to the end will be saved. 23When you are persecuted in one town, flee to the next. I tell you the truth, the Son of Man will return before you have reached all the towns of Israel. 24Students are not greater than their teacher, and slaves are not greater than their master. 25Students are to be like their teacher, and slaves are to be like their master. And since I, the master of the household, have been called the prince of demons, the members of my household will be called by even worse names! 26But don't be afraid of those who threaten you. For the time is coming when everything that is covered will be revealed, and all that is secret will be made known to all. 27What I tell you now in the darkness, shout abroad when daybreak comes. What I whisper in your ear, shout from the housetops for all to hear! 28Don't be afraid of those who want to kill your body; they cannot touch your soul. Fear only God, who can destroy both soul and body in hell.

TALKING TO GOD

Today give the Lord your primary loyalty, and ask him to help you bear it if others criticize or malign that central commitment to him.

READING THE WORD

✤ *Matthew 10:29-31, NLT*
What is the price of two
sparrows—one copper coin?
But not a single sparrow can
fall to the ground without your
Father knowing it. 30And the
very hairs on your head are all
numbered. 31So don't be afraid;
you are more valuable to God
than a whole flock of sparrows.

TALKING TO GOD

*Take a few moments before you
pray to make a quick list of recent
evidences that God cares for you.
Pray with a thankful heart over
this list, rejoicing in the personal
care you receive from the God of
the universe.*

KNOW GOD'S CARE

Setting the Scene

Jesus continued his encouragement for fearless faith by
highlighting how much his followers mean to God. This
awesome God whom we are to fear (Matthew 10:28)
is also the God who cares about the smallest sparrow.
When we fear him, we have nothing to worry about,
because he loves us. God is concerned about all his creatures, even sparrows, and he knows about their lives and
deaths—and we are much more valuable than sparrows.
God also knows about every detail of our lives, even the
number of our hairs.

Sparrows will fall to the ground; God's people die,
sometimes by martyrdom. Yet we are so valuable that
Jesus died for us. Because God places such a high value
on us, we need never fear personal threats or difficult
trials. Our Father is in control. He knows and controls
everything that happens to us: the big problems and the
tiniest details.

Getting Personal

When have you felt as if God didn't care about you?

*How does this passage encourage you and give you
hope?*

*In these words to his apostles, Jesus states what the
Scriptures affirm time and time again, that God
cares for us and is a refuge for us (see Nahum 1:7).
And Peter echoes Jesus' promise of verse 31: "Give
all your worries and cares to God, for he cares about
you" (1 Peter 5:7, NLT). When you feel hemmed in on
every side, remember that God is with you. When you
feel alone, cut off from love, remember he loves you.
When doubts and questions about the future fill your
emotions, remember that Jesus cares.*

COUNT THE COST

Setting the Scene

Here Jesus laid it all out for the disciples: Following him would come with a high cost. Thus all who wished to follow him should consider the cost before signing up.

Jesus' followers would encounter enemies on all sides, even in their own homes. They would feel great pressure to turn back, to deny the truth and their Lord. Christ must be everything to them, more important than any family member or loved one. Jesus was not encouraging disobedience to parents or conflict at home; rather, he was showing that his presence demands a decision. In the early church, Jews who became Christians would be excommunicated from the synagogues and often shunned by their families. Jesus did not come to make such divisions happen, but his coming, his words, and his call inevitably causes conflict between those who accept him and those who reject him.

When Jesus used this picture of his followers taking up their crosses to follow him, the people knew what it meant. Death on a cross was a Roman form of execution. To follow Christ means denying self and carrying one's cross, being prepared to die for him.

Earlier, Jesus had described how the disciples should go about their ministry—staying in homes of worthy people (Matthew 10:11-14). Here he added that even giving "a cup of cold water" (Matthew 10:42, NLT) would be important—serving others, not just preaching.

Getting Personal

What sets you apart from those who don't know Christ? How do your family members and others feel about those differences?

Besides loved ones, what else do you find competing for your loyalty in place of God?

The best way to find life is to loosen your grasp on earthly rewards so that you can be free to follow Christ. You will risk pain, discomfort, conflict, and stress as you acknowledge Christ's claim over your relationships, possessions, and career. But in doing so, you will experience the benefits of following Christ. Do not neglect your family, but remember that living for God should be your first priority.

READING THE WORD

✤ *Matthew 10:32-40, NLT*
Everyone who acknowledges me publicly here on earth, I will also acknowledge before my Father in heaven. 33But everyone who denies me here on earth, I will also deny before my Father in heaven. 34Don't imagine that I came to bring peace to the earth! I came not to bring peace, but a sword. 35"I have come to set a man against his father, a daughter against her mother, and a daughter-in-law against her mother-in-law. 36Your enemies will be right in your own household!" 37If you love your father or mother more than you love me, you are not worthy of being mine; or if you love your son or daughter more than me, you are not worthy of being mine. 38If you refuse to take up your cross and follow me, you are not worthy of being mine. 39If you cling to your life, you will lose it; but if you give up your life for me, you will find it. 40Anyone who receives you receives me, and anyone who receives me receives the Father who sent me.

TALKING TO GOD

Express to the Lord your willingness to give up your life to gain life with him, your willingness to "take up your cross" and follow his way. Ask him for strength to deal with any opposition that might arise.

JESUS FEEDS THE FIVE THOUSAND

Week 16, Day 1

❈ *Matthew 14:13-21; Mark 6:30-44; Luke 9:10-17; John 6:1-15*

Jesus had cast out demons, healed a bleeding woman, and restored a girl to life. And he had given the disciples power to do the same and sent them out. Then they heard that John the Baptist had been executed. These twelve men were learning and experiencing so much, so quickly. Next they would have a huge crowd to feed. This week, together with the disciples, learn how Jesus solved this problem and discover personal life lessons in the process.

READING THE WORD

❈ *Mark 6:30-34, NLT*
The apostles returned to Jesus from their ministry tour and told him all they had done and taught. ³¹Then Jesus said, "Let's go off by ourselves to a quiet place and rest awhile." He said this because there were so many people coming and going that Jesus and his apostles didn't even have time to eat. ³²So they left by boat for a quiet place, where they could be alone. ³³But many people recognized them and saw them leaving, and people from many towns ran ahead along the shore and got there ahead of them. ³⁴Jesus saw the huge crowd as he stepped from the boat, and he had compassion on them because they were like sheep without a shepherd. So he began teaching them many things.

THE SIGHT

Setting the Scene

During Jesus' short time on earth, specifically his three years of public ministry, he focused on choosing and teaching his disciples, while moving steadily toward fulfilling his mission on the Cross. This event was early in Jesus' ministry, so the disciples were just beginning to learn about his amazing teachings, unusual claims, and true identity. The Twelve had decided to follow Jesus for a variety of reasons. We don't know the motives for all of them, but certainly they thought he might be the promised Messiah. But they weren't sure what to expect from him.

Today's passage describes Jesus, after an exhausting day, going off with the disciples across the lake. Beginning near Capernaum, Jesus and the Twelve sailed "to the far side" of the Sea of Galilee (John 6:1, NLT), to a remote area near Bethsaida on the north. Figuring out where Jesus and his party were headed and seeing their boat, the crowd followed them along the shore, hiking the distance on land.

When Jesus he saw the huge crowd, he could have herded the disciples back into the boat and sailed away again, or he could have dismissed the people. After all, they were pestering him, crowding out his time alone with his disciples. Instead, he "had compassion on them" and spent most of the day teaching them and healing their sick.

Jesus saw the "huge crowd" certainly, but he also saw individuals and knew their needs. No one was lost in the crowd. And when Jesus saw these people, he knew each one's deepest needs and felt with them and for them. He had compassion. Jesus ministered with and to ordinary men and women, just as assorted as people today. Some in the crowd were simply curious about this new teacher; some were needy, desperate for a miracle; many had gnawing questions about Jesus' identity and supposed power. Despite the self-centered motives of most of the crowd, Jesus took them seriously and met their needs.

Getting Personal

What did Jesus see and feel when he saw the approaching crowds? (See Matthew 14:14.)

What motives do you think the people in the crowd and the twelve disciples had for coming to Jesus?

What do you want Jesus to do for you?

Jesus sees you in the crowd. He knows you by name. He hurts with you and wants to be with you, to heal your wounded spirit. Don't let anything keep you from Jesus. He doesn't expect you to get your act together before approaching him. He made you; he knows you; he knows your strengths, potential, and weaknesses. He just wants you to come, to allow him to work in you and through you. When you do come, Jesus meets you where you are.

TALKING TO GOD

Talk with the Lord today about anything that keeps you from coming to him in prayer. Thank him for his compassion and for his healing touch. Acknowledge your deep need of him today.

READING THE WORD

✤ *John 6:1-6, NLT*
After this, Jesus crossed over
to the far side of the Sea of
Galilee, also known as the Sea
of Tiberias. 2A huge crowd kept
following him wherever he went,
because they saw his miraculous
signs as he healed the sick. 3Then
Jesus climbed a hill and sat down
with his disciples around him.
4(It was nearly time for the Jewish
Passover celebration.) 5Jesus
soon saw a huge crowd of people
coming to look for him. Turning
to Philip, he asked, "Where can
we buy bread to feed all these
people?" 6He was testing Philip,
for he already knew what he was
going to do.

TALKING TO GOD

*Ask the Lord to help you trust
him with every area of your life,
even with relationships, tasks, or
problems that seem impossible.*

THE TEST

Setting the Scene

Jesus didn't seem to be bothered about the pressure of the crowd (Luke 9:11 says, "He welcomed them"), his workload, and the hours consumed by teaching and healing. The disciples asked Jesus to stop, to send the crowds away (Luke 9:12). They may have been genuinely concerned for the people—at least that's what they expressed. On the other hand, they may have been tired, wanting to resume their close fellowship with just Jesus. Still, they did not see the crowd as Jesus did.

Philip would have known where to get food, if anyone had, because he was from Bethsaida (John 1:44), a town about nine miles away. Jesus was testing Philip to strengthen his faith. By asking for a human solution (knowing that there was none), Jesus highlighted the powerful and miraculous act he was about to perform.

As in other tests, God allowed the test to occur, not expecting failure, but placing the person in a situation in which his or her faith might grow stronger. Jesus did not want Philip and the others to miss what he was about to do.

So Jesus tested them. Jesus knew the people were hungry; he knew the disciples' resources were scarce and that they were far from any places for buying bread, even if they had the money. Did Philip and the others believe Jesus could actually feed all these people? Did they believe he could solve this problem? Or did they believe only in what they could see and touch—the physical realities of their situation? After administering the test, Jesus gave the answers.

Getting Personal

When have you felt overwhelmed by the apparent needs around you? Which, if any, were you yourself able to meet?

In what ways was Jesus' question about the bread a test for Philip and the other disciples?

We can limit what God does in us by assuming what is and what is not possible. Remember who Jesus is, his power and resources.

THE DONATION

Setting the Scene

The disciples were shocked by Jesus' response. They didn't understand what he was saying. How could they possibly feed this huge crowd? Thus they gave him the typical reasons his request seemed impossible: too many people, no stores, no money. So Jesus told them to find out what they actually had (see Mark 6:38). A check of the resources yielded just a boy with five loaves of bread and two fish, a small boy's lunch that he was willing to share for Jesus' use.

The Bible doesn't tell us what the boy was thinking or even where his parents were, for that matter. Was he the only one who had thought ahead? He was risking a lot, turning over his lunch to Jesus. We don't know the interchange between the boy and the disciples, but they brought the food to Jesus.

In all the accounts of this incident, we read nothing about the disciples giving of their resources to Jesus. Instead, they expressed their grave concerns about the problem and their doubts about any possible solutions. In contrast, the boy gave Jesus everything he had, even though it wasn't much in light of the huge need. The boy's faith in Jesus, expressed by turning over his meager resources, made all the difference.

Getting Personal

What holds you back from giving something to God?

What resources can you submit to Jesus for his use?

Because we are painfully aware of our weaknesses and limitations, we can easily think we have nothing to offer God. After all, we might think, I'm only a housewife, or I'm only a layperson, or I haven't been a Christian very long, or I'm poor. We and our resources are meager, but our God is infinite and omnipotent, with unlimited resources. He wants us to release control, to turn everything over to him.

READING THE WORD

❋ *Luke 9:12-14, NLT*
Late in the afternoon the twelve disciples came to him and said, "Send the crowds away to the nearby villages and farms, so they can find food and lodging for the night. There is nothing to eat here in this remote place." 13But Jesus said, "You feed them." "But we have only five loaves of bread and two fish," they answered. "Or are you expecting us to go and buy enough food for this whole crowd?" 14For there were about 5,000 men there.

❋ *Mark 6:37, NLT*
Jesus said, "You feed them." "With what?" they asked. "We'd have to work for months to earn enough money to buy food for all these people!"

❋ *John 6:8-9, NLT*
Then Andrew, Simon Peter's brother, spoke up. 9"There's a young boy here with five barley loaves and two fish. But what good is that with this huge crowd?"

TALKING TO GOD

If you feel ready, offer the Lord everything you have for his use—your money, time, talents, relationships, and possessions. If you feel reluctant, ask the Lord to help you grow in your faith and confidence in him.

READING THE WORD

❋ *Luke 9:14-15, NLT*
For there were about 5,000 men there. Jesus replied, "Tell them to sit down in groups of about fifty each." 15So the people all sat down.

TALKING TO GOD

Ask God to give you strength of conviction and purpose as you seek to do whatever he requires of you. Thank him for the power of his Holy Spirit, which leads you in the paths God wants you to take—and then enables you each step of the way.

THE RESPONSE

Setting the Scene

Jesus had just told the disciples to find out how much food they had in the large crowd. They returned with a boy and his five loaves of bread and two fish. Certainly they must have wondered how that meager amount could feed the five thousand–plus gathered on the hillside. Then Jesus told them to organize the people into smaller groups.

The disciples didn't understand what Jesus wanted them to do, so he gave them a job and prepared to show them what he could do. The disciples followed Jesus' instructions to have everyone "sit down in groups of about fifty each." We don't know why Jesus organized the people this way—perhaps to make food distribution more efficient. The men were probably separated from the women and children for the meal according to Jewish custom. So the disciples went through the crowd, organizing them and having them all take a seat. "The people," perhaps realizing that this would be worth staying for, "all sat down."

At this point the disciples didn't express their opinions about what Jesus had just asked them to do. Certainly they must have had their doubts. To their credit, they did what Jesus told them to do.

Getting Personal

When have you taken a step of faith, doing something you knew God wanted you to do, even though it didn't make much sense at the time?

What are you certain God wants you to do in the next day or two?

What's holding you back?

God speaks to us today through his Word and through the nudging of the Holy Spirit in us. When we read a passage about feeding the hungry and then see or learn of a hungry person, we know what we must do. When we read the story of the Good Samaritan and then encounter a hurting "neighbor," we know what Jesus wants us to do. Each time the Holy Spirit prompts us to act, we need to obey, to take those steps in doing God's will.

THE MIRACLE

Setting the Scene

Jesus, acting as the host of the soon-to-be banquet, took the loaves and fish, thanked God beforehand for the provision he was about to give, and then broke the loaves—and the miracle occurred in Jesus' hands. He gave the bread to his disciples to then give "to the people." He did the same thing with the fish. The disciples acted as waiters, taking bread and fish, distributing it, and then returning to Jesus to get more. They continued to serve the crowd until everyone had had enough to eat.

What an amazing miracle. Before the eyes of the disciples and the gathered crowd, the small offering of food had somehow multiplied so that everyone had more than enough to eat.

Through this miracle, God was authenticating Jesus as his Son and portraying the generous blessings of the Kingdom. Just as God had provided manna to the Hebrews in the wilderness (Exodus 16) and had multiplied oil and flour for Elijah and the widow at Zarephath (1 Kings 17:7-16) and oil for Elisha (2 Kings 4:1-7), he was providing bread for the people on this day.

The people, especially those on the fringe, probably couldn't see Jesus multiply the loaves and fish. On the other hand, they had been watching Jesus perform miracles all day. The disciples had also seen the healings, yet even they wondered about Jesus' ability to provide food for them and the crowd. Jesus took that small donation and increased it to an incredible amount, plus leftovers! God can do anything. He can, and will, multiply what we give to him—beyond our wildest expectations.

Getting Personal

When have you witnessed a "miracle" of multiplication?

What resources do you have that can be invested in God's work?

God gives in abundance. If we take the first step in making our time, abilities, and other resources available to God, he will show us how greatly we can be used to advance his work.

READING THE WORD

✤ *Matthew 14:19-21, NLT*
Jesus took the five loaves and two fish, looked up toward heaven, and blessed them. Then, breaking the loaves into pieces, he gave the bread to the disciples, who distributed it to the people. 20They all ate as much as they wanted, and afterward, the disciples picked up twelve baskets of leftovers. 21About 5,000 men were fed that day, in addition to all the women and children!

TALKING TO GOD

Praise God for this display of Christ's glorious power. If you are willing, express to the Lord your readiness for him to use your time, your talents, your relationships, and your possessions for his purposes.

READING THE WORD

✤ *John 6:14-15, NLT*
When the people saw him do this miraculous sign, they exclaimed, "Surely, he is the Prophet we have been expecting!" 15When Jesus saw that they were ready to force him to be their king, he slipped away into the hills by himself.

TALKING TO GOD

Ask God to give you increased realization of his character and holiness and power. Thank God for revealing himself to you through his Word and especially through the divine-human person, Jesus.

THE DISCOVERY

Setting the Scene

The people were impressed. What Jesus had done in multiplying the loaves and fish was a sign that Jesus was not a mere mortal. At the very least he was the prophesied Prophet to come. The people saw and filled their stomachs as a result of this sign—who could have missed it?—and this led them to believe that Jesus was "the Prophet" Moses had predicted (Deuteronomy 18:15-18). John does not say the people were wrong to think of Jesus as "the Prophet," but the next verse shows they thought this Prophet should be a political leader. In this they were wrong.

Elisha foreshadowed this Prophet (who was one and the same as the Messiah) to come. According to 2 Kings 4:42-44, Elisha fed one hundred men with twenty loaves (a 5:1 ratio), but Jesus fed five thousand with five loaves (a 1,000:1 ratio)! Isaiah 25:6-9 says the Messiah will prepare a great feast for all people, Jews and Gentiles. This miracle showed Jesus to be the Messiah.

The people wanted a king, a leader who would free Israel from Rome. The people expected this of the coming Messiah-King. When Jesus realized their intentions, he left. Jesus' Kingdom would not be an earthly one established by a groundswell of popularity. In the wilderness, Satan had already offered Jesus this same opportunity for political power (Matthew 4:1-11). Jesus knew the immediate opportunity was nothing compared to what God had planned.

Later we find that the people may have been more interested in Jesus' meeting their physical needs than anything else (see John 6:22-40).

Getting Personal

As you see Jesus in action in the pages of Scripture and especially in this incident, what are you noticing about his identity and his power?

How does what you're learning about Christ change your relationship with him?

As the disciples watched Jesus, they began to discover his person and purpose. More than feeding hungry people on a hillside, Jesus was revealing his true identity and limitless power. In each incident, each interaction with their Lord, the disciples understood a bit more.

JESUS CHALLENGES THE PHARISEES
Week 17, Day 1

❋ *Matthew 15:1-20; Mark 7:1-23*

Jesus' dramatic actions were met by determined resistance from groups identified as "Pharisees and teachers of religious law." Unable to overcome Jesus directly, they shifted to the disciples. But Jesus confronted them with their hypocrisy and used the confrontation as a teaching opportunity. This week, he'll teach us, too.

SEEING JESUS

Setting the Scene

Mark simply states that these religious leaders came "to see Jesus." Matthew wrote the same thing (Matthew 15:1). Then verse 2 says, "they noticed." "Seeing Jesus" and "noticing" what he did sound innocent enough. In fact, John wrote that one time some Greeks came to Jerusalem and asked Philip if they could see Jesus (John 12:20-22). The expression is used to describe one person about to meet another or the actions of a curious person. Many were coming to "see" Jesus because they thought he might be the promised Messiah; these honest seekers truly wanted to know him. Others weren't quite as involved, but they came with good motives, too, wanting to see the one who was teaching, healing, and changing lives.

Yet these Jewish religious leaders were neither seeking information nor merely satisfying their curiosity. When they came "to see Jesus," they came to scrutinize him as they tried to find fault in order to judge and silence him. Unable to discover anything wrong with Jesus' actions, they turned to his followers and "noticed that some of his disciples" hadn't washed their hands before eating. In an aside, Mark explains the Jewish tradition to his Gentile readers.

After seeing the nontraditional actions, the religious leaders asked Jesus, "Why don't your disciples follow our age-old tradition?" At least they were honest about the fact that this was their tradition, not a divine command, although they often gave their traditions and interpretations of Scripture almost the same authority as God's Word.

READING THE WORD

❋ *Mark 7:1-5, NLT*

One day some Pharisees and teachers of religious law arrived from Jerusalem to see Jesus. ²They noticed that some of his disciples failed to follow the Jewish ritual of hand washing before eating. ³(The Jews, especially the Pharisees, do not eat until they have poured water over their cupped hands, as required by their ancient traditions. ⁴Similarly, they don't eat anything from the market until they immerse their hands in water. This is but one of many traditions they have clung to—such as their ceremonial washing of cups, pitchers, and kettles.) ⁵So the Pharisees and teachers of religious law asked him, "Why don't your disciples follow our age-old tradition? They eat without first performing the hand-washing ceremony."

During the centuries since the Jews' return from Babylonian captivity, Jewish religious leaders had added hundreds of religious traditions to God's laws, regulating every part of Jewish life. The Pharisees and scribes considered these traditions to be as binding as God's law itself. They were wrong, of course, as Jesus pointed out.

Since the common people did not follow all of the extra restrictions and rituals of the Pharisees, the religious leaders considered them ignorant. The fact that Jesus' disciples did not follow all of the laws of the Pharisees' oral tradition led this Jerusalem delegation to resent Jesus' teaching and try to discredit him. According to the Pharisees, if Jesus were truly a rabbi, he and his disciples would follow all of the traditions. The Pharisees had religious blinders on their eyes, seeing only their own rituals and traditions.

Getting Personal

What drew you to Jesus? How did you first come "to see" him?

Today, people still come "to see Jesus" with a variety of motives. Some sincerely seek the Savior. Many look with curiosity. But we still have cynics and critics who try to pick apart Jesus and his followers, looking for problems and negative evidence. When have you felt that certain people were looking at your behavior with a critical eye? How did you respond?

What opinion of Jesus do you think people might form just by watching you?

Although the religious leaders' attitudes and actions toward Jesus and the disciples were wrong, we know that people often form their opinions about Jesus by watching his followers. As those called "Christians" ("Christ-ones"), we bear his name and enhance or detract from his reputation. Some Christians act carelessly; others go to the Pharisee extreme and give their personal rules, policies, and applications of Scripture the same authority as God's Word (and judge others who differ). Instead, we need to humbly follow our Leader and treat others with love.

TALKING TO GOD

Ask the Lord to help you approach others with love and not with a hidden objective of criticizing or judging. Thank him for the way he fully accepted you, even while you were still a sinner.

HONORING TRUTH

Setting the Scene

Instead of directly answering the question of these religious leaders, Jesus asked them a question, pointing out their hypocrisy. They had so honored their traditions that they had elevated their authority above the direct commands of God. In effect, they had broken God's law for the sake of their tradition. So zealous for the traditions, they lost their perspective and had missed the point of God's law entirely. Authority was the issue: their traditions versus what "God says."

Jesus first quoted Moses because the "teachers of religious law" (Mark 7:1, NLT) traced the oral law back to him, and Jesus highlighted one of the Ten Commandments, "Honor your father and your mother" (Exodus 20:12; Deuteronomy 5:16, NIV). The commandment applied to anyone whose parents were living, not just to young children. "Honor" includes speaking respectfully and showing care and consideration. Then Jesus showed how they were dishonoring God's Word and their parents by following their traditions. These religious leaders knew Moses' words, but as Jesus pointed out, they were actually breaking them. In fact, some of the Pharisees had found a way to sidestep God's command completely in their handling of money and property. Unscrupulous people would use this vow to keep from paying debts. Others, as Jesus noted, used it to circumvent their responsibility to their parents. Their devotion to God had stripped them of their compassion for people.

Jesus blasted these self-righteous leaders, calling them "hypocrites," or "actors." The Pharisees were pretending to be holy and close to God, but what they pretended on the outside was not true on the inside.

Getting Personal

What strong religious traditions do you observe or are in your background? How have you responded when those traditions seemed to conflict with what God is telling you in his Word?

What steps can you take to better know and honor God's truth?

In their devotion to the law and tradition, the religious leaders' rules and rituals obscured the true intent of God's Word. We must beware of the same error and constantly evaluate our own traditions. God's truth always trumps traditions, no matter how old and revered.

READING THE WORD

❊ *Matthew 15:3-9, NLT*
Jesus replied, "And why do you, by your traditions, violate the direct commandments of God? 4For instance, God says, 'Honor your father and mother,' and 'Anyone who speaks disrespectfully of father or mother must be put to death.' 5But you say it is all right for people to say to their parents, 'Sorry, I can't help you. For I have vowed to give to God what I would have given to you.' 6In this way, you say they don't need to honor their parents. And so you cancel the word of God for the sake of your own tradition. 7You hypocrites! Isaiah was right when he prophesied about you, for he wrote, 8'These people honor me with their lips, but their hearts are far from me. 9Their worship is a farce, for they teach man-made ideas as commands from God.'"

TALKING TO GOD

Ask the Lord to help you be sensitive to any religious practice or "spiritual" activity that may actually be less than the best way to obey and worship him. Ask him to give you a love for his Word that will help you pursue its truth.

READING THE WORD

❋ *Mark 7:14-15, NLT*
Then Jesus called to the crowd to come and hear. "All of you listen," he said, "and try to understand. 15It's not what goes into your body that defiles you; you are defiled by what comes from your heart."

TALKING TO GOD

Ask the Lord to help you find any trace of the "Pharisee" in yourself. Consider what you may unconsciously hold as a list of spiritual or nonspiritual qualities by which you criticize others. Ask God to help you keep your focus on personally submitting to him.

LIVING INSIDE OUT

Setting the Scene

Jesus called out to the crowd, wanting them to beware of those who would lead them astray and to be careful to get their values and priorities straight. The Pharisees taught that eating with unclean or defiled hands would defile a person before God (Mark 7:5). Jesus explained that they had it backwards. Defilement is an internal matter, not an external one.

Certainly God is concerned about our actions, but focusing on outward actions can pull us away from the more important issue—the condition of the heart. Just as the Pharisees' emphasis on traditions had caused them to ignore God's commands, emphasis on external issues can cause us to neglect internal ones.

Conversely, a person who is right on the inside will reflect that reality with how he or she looks at life, speaks, acts, and relates to others. The Pharisees should have known this. Often God had told his people that he valued mercy and obedience based on love more than merely observing rules and rituals (see 1 Samuel 15:22-23; Psalms 40:6-8; 51:16-19; Jeremiah 7:21-23; Hosea 6:6; Amos 5:21-24; Micah 6:6-8).

Concern about the inside, the "heart," should come first and then outward actions.

Getting Personal

When have you felt pressured to live up to a set standard of Christian behavior?

What external activities, behaviors, etc., tend to make your list of what a good Christian should not do?

When have you judged someone based on his or her actions (negative or positive) only to find out you were totally wrong about that person?

While we don't have a long list of ceremonial rituals and regulations like the Pharisees, we make our own lists. These may involve food and drink, clothes, entertainment, worship styles, and more. Some believers go even further, adding their own behavior tests of a person's commitment to Christ. Yet we are painfully aware of people we've known who looked good on the outside but were far from God. Instead, God wants us to live from the inside out.

FOLLOWING THE RIGHT LEADERS

Setting the Scene

By confronting the Pharisees this way, Jesus was establishing himself as the right interpreter of Scripture. God had given Israel numerous dietary laws, but these laws and the leaders' interpretations of them had become more important than the meaning behind them, leading to the idea that people could be clean before God because of what they refused to eat. And because the Pharisees had become the religious authorities of the day, they naturally became offended by what Jesus said. The disciples pointed out this offense, the implication being that Jesus had taken on the religious establishment at great risk.

The Pharisees were offended, but Jesus explained that they were being rejected as leaders of God's people and, like weeds in the garden, would be "uprooted." Then Jesus told the disciples to "ignore them." They shouldn't follow, listen to, or regard the hypocritical Pharisees.

The Pharisees claimed to be leaders of the people, but Jesus turned this around to show that, in reality, they were "blind guides," who would lead people the wrong way.

Getting Personal

Who are your spiritual leaders?

What can you do to make sure you're not following a "blind guide"?

When have you seen a "leader" go beyond the teachings of the Bible or assume too much authority for him- or herself?

What can you do to make sure that your *teaching stays true to Christ and the Bible?*

Today many claim to be religious authorities. Some teachers, preachers, pastors, and others draw large crowds and have huge followings in churches, special events, seminars, online, and in publishing. Although they may sound and look good, we must be careful whom we follow. Our earthly spiritual leaders should affirm Jesus as fully God and fully human, the only way to salvation and the Bible as God's written and inspired Word, our only rule for faith and practice. Any leader who is offended by those beliefs and values should be left behind. As soon as we know that the true intent of a teacher or preacher is not God's glory, we should stop listening to him or her.

READING THE WORD

❀ *Matthew 15:12-14, NLT*
Then the disciples came to him and asked, "Do you realize you offended the Pharisees by what you just said?" 13Jesus replied, "Every plant not planted by my heavenly Father will be uprooted, 14so ignore them. They are blind guides leading the blind, and if one blind person guides another, they will both fall into a ditch."

TALKING TO GOD

Thank God for the Bible, written authority that helps us know what truly pleases him. Pray for those in spiritual leadership over you, asking for God's truth and wisdom to guide them—and to guide you as you listen and learn from them.

UNDERSTANDING THE WORD

READING THE WORD

❊ *Matthew 15:15-20, NLT*
Then Peter said to Jesus, "Explain to us the parable that says people aren't defiled by what they eat." 16"Don't you understand yet?" Jesus asked. 17"Anything you eat passes through the stomach and then goes into the sewer. 18But the words you speak come from the heart—that's what defiles you. 19For from the heart come evil thoughts, murder, adultery, all sexual immorality, theft, lying, and slander. 20These are what defile you. Eating with unwashed hands will never defile you."

❊ *Mark 7:17-19, NLT*
Then Jesus went into a house to get away from the crowd, and his disciples asked him what he meant by the parable he had just used. 18"Don't you understand either?" he asked. "Can't you see that the food you put into your body cannot defile you? 19Food doesn't go into your heart, but only passes through the stomach and then goes into the sewer." (By saying this, he declared that every kind of food is acceptable in God's eyes.)

TALKING TO GOD

Thank God for his patience with the process of discipleship. Ask that God's Holy Spirit would illuminate the Scriptures for you as you study.

Setting the Scene

Jesus went into a house (probably in Capernaum) to get away from the crowd and to spend time with the Twelve. Often Peter would act as spokesman for the disciples, and he always seemed to speak honestly. In this passage, Peter was saying, in effect, "Hey, I still don't get it." In a couple of years Peter would be confronted directly with this issue of clean and unclean food (see Acts 10:9-15), where he would learn that nothing should be a barrier to proclaiming the gospel to non-Jews. Here he was simply expressing the confusion that all the disciples were experiencing.

Jesus knew the crowd didn't understand but seemed disappointed that his disciples had also failed to comprehend. Jesus' question "Don't you understand yet?" shows that discipleship is a process of growth. Although the disciples knew much about Jesus, they still had more to learn.

Then Jesus explained that what comes out of a person—evil thoughts and deeds—are what defile that person, not what goes in the mouth. Moral defilement has nothing to do with food, but with sin in the heart. Jesus wasn't simply teaching theology or showing he could out-argue the Pharisees. He wanted the disciples to understand this important truth. The more time they spent with Jesus, the more they would understand and put into practice.

Getting Personal

How often do you study the Bible? What do you do when you come to a passage that you don't understand?

If you could ask Jesus one question about something he said, what would you ask?

What can you do to better understand and apply God's Word?

The disciples may not have heard everything or they may have been overly concerned about offending the religious leaders. Whatever the reason, they didn't understand Jesus' words about clean and unclean foods and defilement. Although we don't have Jesus sitting physically with us and explaining his teachings, we have God's written Word—and a wide range of Bible study resources. God gave his Word to reveal himself and his plan to us, to tell us how to believe and how to live. What an amazing gift!

GUARDING YOUR HEART

Setting the Scene

In this confrontation with the Pharisees and his discussion with the disciples, Jesus clearly stated the problem—sin in a person's heart. That's where sin begins, and what is inside a person comes out in words and actions. Jesus' list of these sins is representative of common human conflicts and struggles. Daily we hear reports of these sinful acts. The good news of the gospel offers the only cure for humanity's natural defilement. Cleansing can only come by the blood of Jesus Christ offered on our behalf. Only then can we become pure before God.

Believers aren't immune to sinful actions, however. We also struggle with heart issues—but we have the power to resist, to change, and to choose to do right, through the Holy Spirit who lives in us. Paul explained how this happens (see Romans 6–8). Unless the Holy Spirit controls our sinful nature, we will experience continual outbursts of the "flesh." We need to guard our hearts.

Getting Personal

What evidence do you see in your life of this inward struggle to resist sin? When is this struggle more intense?

What steps can you take to guard your heart?

God promised his people, "I will give you a new heart, and I will put a new spirit in you. I will take out your stony, stubborn heart and give you a tender, responsive heart" (Ezekiel 36:26, NLT). The "heart" is the basic core of a person, home to his or her true motives, thoughts, desires, and values. When we trust in Christ, the Holy Spirit begins living in us, changing us to be more like Christ as we yield to him. As Jesus told his disciples, the heart is what matters. Guard your heart.

READING THE WORD

❋ *Mark 7:20-23, NLT*

And then he added, "It is what comes from inside that defiles you. 21For from within, out of a person's heart, come evil thoughts, sexual immorality, theft, murder, 22adultery, greed, wickedness, deceit, lustful desires, envy, slander, pride, and foolishness. 23All these vile things come from within; they are what defile you."

TALKING TO GOD

Check out Psalm 51:10-12 and pray along with David that God would create in you a "clean heart" and a "loyal spirit." God will honor your longing to please him—from the inside out.

JESUS REVEALS HIS IDENTITY

Week 18, Day 1

❋ *Matthew 16:13-20; Mark 8:27-30; Luke 9:18-21*

Some questions are timely; some are timeless. During the next days we will consider a two-part question that Jesus asks every succeeding generation—"Who do people say the Son of Man is?" and "Who do you say I am?" Our eternity hinges on our answer.

READING THE WORD

❋ *Matthew 16:13, NIV*
When Jesus came to the region of Caesarea Philippi, he asked his disciples, "Who do people say the Son of Man is?"

LOCATION MATTERS

Setting the Scene

Jesus was an equal opportunity visitor. No neighborhood was off limits to him. He visited the forbidden areas of the Samaritans and ministered along the seashore near the Gentile cities of Tyre and Sidon. Our passage for this week records his travels north from his home base into the region of Caesarea Philippi, a cosmopolitan area about twenty-five miles from Bethsaida on the upper end of the Sea of Galilee. This city was part of the territory ruled on behalf of the Romans by Philip, the brother of Herod Antipas. Its setting on the lower slopes of Mount Hermon made it an attractive site. Philip chose the city as his capital. Today, the ancient ruins are known as Banias, a slightly altered form of its most ancient name Panias, related to the Greek god Pan.

Caesarea Philippi and its surrounding area were known as a center for pagan worship. Both Philip and his father, Herod the Great, sponsored the construction of temples and public works. The population of the area was mostly Gentile, so the trip took Jesus and the Twelve out of their usual circumstances. Shrines and other reminders of pagan practices would have been all around them. This was the setting for Jesus' crucial question for the disciples.

The trip to a new region took place at the height of Jesus' ministry. It followed swiftly on the heels of the second large feeding miracle. Jesus had become the focal point of a religious/political power struggle in Israel. The structure of power represented by the Sadducees and

Pharisees had rejected Jesus as Messiah. Plans were now afoot behind the scenes to trick or pressure Jesus into a fatal failure that would make it possible to remove him from the scene.

Throughout these days, Jesus seemed to remain deliberate but never desperate. He was not campaigning for popularity but intent on practicing compassion. He fed four thousand (Matthew 15:32-38), not to increase or even solidify his following, but because, "I have compassion for these people; they have already been with me three days and have nothing to eat. I do not want to send them away hungry, or they may collapse on the way" (Matthew 15:32, NIV). His words to and about those who were the recognized spiritual authorities make it clear that he never angled for their approval.

Jesus asked his question when he was alone with his disciples. Because so few of these private exchanges are recorded, each of them takes on added significance. These were instances in which Jesus communicated with his intimate followers certain truths they wouldn't understand until later. He was preparing them for his eventual departure long before they were ready to consider the fact that Jesus had to die and rise again in order to accomplish God's plan. He was about to give them the jewel that included all the facets of his life and ministry. He would ask them to hold this jewel in confidence until the time was right to share it with the world.

Getting Personal

What settings do you find most conducive for listening to God?

At what age did you first answer Jesus' question, "Who do people say the Son of Man is?"

Not every principle we read or story we study in Scripture has an immediate personal application. Some lessons are preparatory. We may understand a concept like God's ownership of the church but not recognize the personal importance of God's sovereign work through his church until we have been Christ-followers for years.

TALKING TO GOD

Thank God for his constant presence with you that makes it possible for you to have times apart from distractions to be alone with him. Praise God for the teaching of his Word, which can bear fruit in your life immediately and also in years to come.

READING THE WORD

✸ *Matthew 16:13, NKJV*
When Jesus came into the region of Caesarea Philippi, He asked His disciples, saying, "Who do men say that I, the Son of Man, am?"

TALKING TO GOD

Answer the question Jesus poses in Matthew 16:13 before the Lord today, confessing your understanding of who Jesus really is. Ask God to give you opportunities for speaking this truth about him to others.

WHO AM I?

Setting the Scene

The term "Son of Man" was Jesus' most frequent way of speaking about himself (thirty-two times in Matthew alone). There are two major Old Testament sources for this title: the books of Ezekiel and Daniel. In Ezekiel, God uses the term repeatedly to address his prophet. Jesus applied the term to himself as a thought-provoking way of pointing beyond the obvious. No one else ever addressed Jesus as the Son of Man, but on his lips the name has a way of hinting at the fact of Jesus' choice to live among us as one of us. By becoming the Son of Man, Jesus made himself our Savior.

Jesus did not use questions in a quest for knowledge he didn't have. His inquiries were informational for his audience. People considering Jesus' questions always found that formulating a response would require them to discover something about themselves. Jesus was already aware of the various conclusions being reached by the crowds, but he wanted his disciples to take note of those conclusions and be able to answer them. He also wanted them to be aware that others would not have the same view they had of Jesus, but that the view mattered. Even today, what others say about Jesus tells us a lot more about them than it does about Christ. We must be willing to question those ideas about Jesus that don't match the reality of who he is—the Son of God.

Getting Personal

What have been some of the views of Jesus that you have heard recently? How did you respond to those perspectives?

How would you summarize the main weakness of any description of Jesus that falls short of his true identity?

The problem with any view of Jesus other than that he is the Son of God is that it fails to take into account the scope of evidence about Jesus. Both negative and halfhearted descriptions of Jesus are always shattered by the reality of the person who steps from the pages of Scripture.

POSSIBLE IDENTITIES

Setting the Scene

Comparisons are an almost inevitable part of life. People compare a baby's features with those of his parents as they note genetic connections. A rising politician is compared with earlier leaders to demonstrate the influences that have molded the new public servant. In Jesus' day, spiritual notoriety usually led to identification with previous heroes of faith.

Contemporary readers might assume the disciples were responding based on some accepted possibility of reincarnation. They were not. The disciples were not suggesting that famous people relived their lives in the present, but there were rumors that resurrection might be possible.

Some people did speculate that the late John the Baptist was back. No sooner had John the Baptist been murdered by Herod (Matthew 14:1-12) than the guilt-ridden king suggested that reports he was getting about Jesus were indications that John had come back to life. Actually, as John the Baptist had predicted, Jesus was fully engaged in the ministry for which John had been the forerunner.

For those seeking to describe someone with unusual godly presence, common comparisons included Elijah (see 1 Kings 17–21; 2 Kings 1–2), Jeremiah (see 2 Chronicles 35–36 and the book of Jeremiah), and other prophets. People were saying, "This Jesus does things that remind us so much of Elijah that maybe the old prophet has come back to life!"

It is good for people to try to understand Jesus' identity, but it is an error simply to equate Jesus with someone else. He is unique. Others may remind us of him, but Jesus himself is without equal. We're destined to be like him, but there will never be any doubt about who is the original and who are the copies.

Getting Personal

When you think of someone being like Jesus today, what characteristics come to mind?

How has God been changing you to be more like Jesus?

Jesus is the ultimate standard of comparison. We haven't figured out who Jesus is if we never get beyond comparing him with others.

READING THE WORD

✤ *Matthew 16:13-14, NIV*
When Jesus came to the region of Caesarea Philippi, he asked his disciples, "Who do people say the Son of Man is?" 14They replied, "Some say John the Baptist; others say Elijah; and still others, Jeremiah or one of the prophets."

TALKING TO GOD

Thank God for the people in your life who remind you of Jesus or who have showed you some aspect of Jesus by living in a Christlike way. Don't hold back from asking God to work in you to make you more and more like Jesus as the days go by.

READING THE WORD

❈ *Matthew 16:13-15, NLT*
When Jesus came to the region of Caesarea Philippi, he asked his disciples, "Who do people say that the Son of Man is?" 14"Well," they replied, "some say John the Baptist, some say Elijah, and others say Jeremiah or one of the other prophets." 15Then he asked them, "But who do you say I am?"

TALKING TO GOD

If you feel less than confident about your own response to this important question posed by Jesus, ask the Lord to give you wisdom and to show you clearly from his Word who he really is. When you have settled this question before the Lord, ask him to give you opportunities to share with others what you've discovered.

Setting the Scene

We might quickly move on to examine what the disciples said in answer to Jesus rather than stop and listen to the question. We want to keep a safe distance; we would rather Jesus ask someone else his question.

When we realize we must answer this question, we immediately face at least three different responses. The first is evasive. We avoid the question by begging ignorance (*I don't know*) or uncertainty (*I'm not sure yet; can you get back to me later?*), or even deflection (*Would you mind asking someone else?*). We have avoided the question but not voided it. Jesus' words continue to haunt us: "Who do you say I am?"

The second answer is the safe answer. We take a quick poll of the surrounding opinions. *What is everyone else saying? What is the consensus?* Our response is calculated to match what most people say. The answer may be very positive (great teacher, wise man, miracle-worker, even Lord) or negative (liar, lunatic, charlatan). We haven't actually given *our* answer; we've tried to give the majority answer. But that wasn't the point of the question, was it?

The third answer is the truth. This answer may actually involve some of the same responses we just looked at, but instead of being calculated to dodge the question, our answer comes from integrity. Perhaps we really *don't* know. Or we have honestly assumed that his fame must be because he was either a great teacher or an effective con man. Or we blurt out our faith in Peter-like fashion.

God can work with a truthful response.

Getting Personal

What is your truthful, personal answer to Jesus' question: "Who do you say I am?"

With whom have you talked recently about your view of Jesus?

When Jesus asks us who we say that he is, he is not just asking so that we will answer him; he's also asking about how we are sharing the news about him with others. The question assumes we're telling. If we aren't letting anyone know that we know him, maybe we don't.

TRUE CONFESSION

Setting the Scene

We can sense the sudden tension in the air. They had been brainstorming the different ways the crowds were identifying Jesus. Now he was asking them for their own view. First there was silence. Then Peter spoke: "You are the Messiah, the Son of the living God."

Jesus did not ask Peter what he meant. Depending on the Bible translation, the first title in Peter's declaration may be "Christ" or "Messiah." "Christ" comes from transliterating the Greek term *Khristos*, which along with *Messiah* (Hebrew) means "the Anointed One." Peter was placing Jesus in the singular category of the Promised One from the Old Testament prophecies. The disciple got the title right, even if he didn't fully understand what it meant. Peter would have to discover what each of us eventually discovers—we can have the right answers about God, but there will always be more to God than our answers. Even our right answers are only a glimpse of all God has to reveal.

Jesus affirmed Peter and his answer, using his formal name—Simon, son of John. He declared Peter "blessed," not because he had given the right answer but because that right answer had been given to him. God had demonstrated his favor on Peter's life by giving him the insight to speak the right answer.

Getting Personal

You have you been given the same insight from God's Holy Spirit, so that you can acknowledge Jesus as the Promised One, the Son of God. Jesus said Peter was blessed because he had been given this knowledge. What blessing do you think you have because you have acknowledged Jesus as Christ?

God's Word makes it clear that we can't claim to generate the faith it takes to believe in Jesus. The apostle Paul wrote in Ephesians 2:8, "By grace you have been saved through faith, and that not of yourselves; it is the gift of God" (NKJV). *When it comes to receiving credit for our salvation, we get none—all of it goes to Christ. In that moment when we believe, that simple act of faith is itself a gift from God.*

READING THE WORD

❋ *Matthew 16:15-17, NLT*

Then he asked them, "But who do you say I am?" 16Simon Peter answered, "You are the Messiah, the Son of the living God." 17Jesus replied, "You are blessed, Simon son of John, because my Father in heaven has revealed this to you. You did not learn this from any human being."

TALKING TO GOD

Thank God for the combination of gifts that may have brought you to him: the drawing of the Holy Spirit, others to testify to the truth about Jesus, compelling reasons, and simple ability to trust him.

THE CHURCH TRIUMPHANT

READING THE WORD

❊ *Matthew 16:18-20, NIV*

"And I tell you that you are Peter, and on this rock I will build my church, and the gates of Hades will not overcome it. ¹⁹I will give you the keys of the kingdom of heaven; whatever you bind on earth will be bound in heaven, and whatever you loose on earth will be loosed in heaven." ²⁰Then he ordered his disciples not to tell anyone that he was the Messiah.

TALKING TO GOD

Ask the Lord to connect you purposefully to his work in a local body of believers, one that acknowledges Jesus as Lord and Head of the church.

Setting the Scene

Jesus had apparently noticed enough granite in Peter's character to nickname him *Cephas* in Aramaic, which became *Petros* in Greek, meaning "rock" (John 1:42). He returns to that name as part of his response to Simon's declaration of faith.

The play on words has given rise to several possible explanations for the meaning of "rock": (1) Jesus himself; (2) Peter, the first leader of the church and recipient of special authority; (3) the confession of faith Peter made; or (4) Peter, simply the leader among the disciples. The first interpretation parallels other New Testament teaching about Jesus as the cornerstone (see Ephesians 2:20; 1 Peter 2:4-8), but that connection doesn't seem to hold in this context. While the second interpretation underlies much of the Roman Catholic teaching on the authority of those who claim Peter's mantle, there's no mention of succession of power. While Peter himself served in a leadership role in the early church, there's no indication he was viewed as the final authority. The third interpretation was first promoted during the Reformation as a correction on the excesses related to the second one. The fourth explanation simply highlights Peter's role as a leader among the disciples. One way or another, Peter and his companions became the foundation of the church (see 1 Corinthians 3:11; 1 Peter 2:4-8).

Jesus went on to refer to "binding and loosing," as the purpose for the "keys" the disciples would receive—authority to promote both the earthly and heavenly aspects of the church.

Getting Personal

How would you characterize your personal role in the church today?

Even if your role does not seem influential or foundational to others, how is your faithfulness one of the building stones of God's work in his church?

Jesus is the one who owns and develops the church. He said, "I will build my church." You can trace your spiritual heritage back to this moment. Generation after generation, the church as the body of Christ has rescued from Satan's power those who would otherwise be destined for an eternity apart from God (see Colossians 1:13).

JESUS TELLS WHAT FOLLOWING HIM WILL MEAN

Week 19, Day 1

❋ *Matthew 16:21-28; Mark 8:31–9:1; Luke 9:22-27*

Peter made his profound declaration of Jesus' true identity: "You are the Messiah, the Son of the living God" (Matthew 16:16, NLT), and the disciples seemed to grasp the importance of Christ's ministry. But then Jesus told them what would happen to him and what being his followers would entail. This week we discover what Jesus told the Twelve and the gathered crowd—and what he would say to us, his followers, two thousand years later.

THE MESSAGE

Setting the Scene

The phrase "from then on" marks a turning point in Jesus' ministry. In Matthew 4:17, the same phrase signaled the beginning of Jesus' preaching that the Kingdom of Heaven was near. Here it points to Jesus' new emphasis on his death and resurrection. At this time in their association with Jesus, the disciples hadn't understood Jesus' true purpose because of their ideas of what the Messiah should be and do. Although they acknowledged Jesus as Messiah—Peter had just proclaimed him as such (Matthew 16:16)—they still thought this meant Jesus would free Israel from Rome and set up an earthly kingdom. In reality, far from conquering, in the world's view he and they would be conquered.

So Jesus began teaching "plainly" and specifically about what would happen. Jesus would not be the dominating and powerful Messiah because he first had to "suffer many terrible things . . . and . . . be killed." For any human king, death would be the end. Not so for Jesus. Death would be only the beginning, for "on the third day he would be raised from the dead."

Jesus couldn't have said it more clearly. Yet we'll soon see that the disciples still didn't understand, either because they weren't listening very closely or because what Jesus was saying didn't make sense to them.

Getting Personal

Why do we struggle with doing what we know God wants us to do? In what areas is that a problem for you?

READING THE WORD

❋ *Matthew 16:21, NLT*
From then on Jesus began to tell his disciples plainly that it was necessary for him to go to Jerusalem, and that he would suffer many terrible things at the hands of the elders, the leading priests, and the teachers of religious law. He would be killed, but on the third day he would be raised from the dead.

TALKING TO GOD

If there is some plain teaching from God's Word that you have been neglecting, confess that to the Lord right now. Ask him to enable you to obey the truth that you have understood. Thank him for holding your future in his sovereign hands.

THE MESSAGE *continued*

What can you do to better listen to what God is saying, to hear his "plain" message?

People often say they can't understand the Bible—that they get confused by various sections. Even longtime believers can have trouble interpreting certain parts. But God has plainly spoken to us through his Word— we just have to be listening. Certainly some passages can be more difficult to understand than others, but most people have trouble obeying what they know God is saying. The Ten Commandments and Jesus' statement about being the only way to the Father (John 14:6), for example, are quite clear. As you read Scripture, ask the Holy Spirit to prepare your heart and open your eyes; then look for the plain teachings you can believe and obey.

THE SURPRISE

Setting the Scene

Jesus told his disciples "not to tell anyone" that he was the Messiah (Luke 9:21, NLT) because at that point they clearly hadn't understood Peter's confession of faith. So Jesus began to spell it out for them.

He started by saying he would have to suffer greatly at the hands of "the elders, the leading priests, and the teachers of religious law"—in effect, the Jewish supreme court—and that would lead to his death. Those plain statements must have shocked the disciples, especially the part about his dying. And evidently they didn't comprehend the next part, the good news, that "on the third day," he would "be raised from the dead." If they had actually heard what Jesus said about coming back to life, they probably would have pressed him on that issue, saying something like, "Wait a minute! How is that possible?" Instead, Matthew and Mark report that Peter "began to reprimand him for saying such things" (Matthew 16:22; see Mark 8:32). Jesus predicted the Resurrection at least two more times (see Matthew 17:23; 20:19), yet the disciples were shocked when it actually occurred.

Getting Personal

Just as he predicted, Jesus did suffer and die. What difference does this suffering and death make in your life?

Just as he predicted, Jesus was raised from the dead. How does this resurrection make possible your resurrection?

We live on the other side of these predicted events and know the story of Jesus' being rejected, accused, and convicted by the religious authorities and tortured and crucified by the Romans. We also know the truth of the Resurrection—that on "the third day" Jesus was "raised from the dead." Centuries after those facts, people still have misconceptions about Jesus' identity and they are still surprised that Jesus arose from the dead. The Good News is that instead of struggling under the weight of sin, guilt, and worldly issues and conflicts, we can live in the joy of the Resurrection. Because he rose, we know he is the Way, the Truth, and the Life. And because he lives, we too shall live.

READING THE WORD

✹ *Luke 9:22, NLT*
"The Son of Man must suffer many terrible things," he said. "He will be rejected by the elders, the leading priests, and the teachers of religious law. He will be killed, but on the third day he will be raised from the dead."

TALKING TO GOD

Confess to the Lord the many times you have "tuned out" rather than listening with attention to the conviction of scriptural teaching. Ask for the help of the Holy Spirit to overcome this human weakness and become sensitive to God's guidance and teaching.

READING THE WORD

❊ *Matthew 16:22-23, NLT*
But Peter took him aside and began to reprimand him for saying such things. "Heaven forbid, Lord," he said. "This will never happen to you!" 23Jesus turned to Peter and said, "Get away from me, Satan! You are a dangerous trap to me. You are seeing things merely from a human point of view, not from God's."

TALKING TO GOD

Thank God for the blessings of this beautiful world he gave you to live in—rich with delights for the senses. But also ask God to make unseen truths and his invisible presence just as real and important to you. Ask God to help you see all that he has made with a godly perspective.

THE PERSPECTIVE

Setting the Scene

Having just confessed his heartfelt belief in Jesus as "the Messiah, the Son of the living God" (Matthew 16:16, NLT) and having been given great authority in the Kingdom of Heaven (Matthew 16:18-19), Peter was shaken to hear Jesus predict these terrible events. He must have wondered what Jesus' death would mean for the disciples, specifically for him. So Peter began to "reprimand" or rebuke Jesus. The word translated "reprimand" is a strong term meaning that Peter was rejecting Jesus' interpretation of the Messiah as a suffering figure. In effect, Peter was trying to talk Jesus out of going to the Cross. But if Jesus hadn't suffered and died, Peter would have died in his sins.

Shortly before this interaction, Jesus had told Peter, "You are blessed, Simon son of John" (Matthew 16:17, NLT). But at this point Jesus told him, "Get away from me, Satan!" Peter had quickly turned from God's perspective to evaluating the situation from a human one. In the process, he was using one of Satan's tactics in trying to protect his beloved Master.

Peter and the other disciples were motivated by love and admiration for Jesus; nevertheless, their job was not to guide and protect him but to follow him. Unknowingly, the disciples were trying to prevent Jesus from going to the Cross and fulfilling his mission. Only after Jesus' death and resurrection would they fully understand why he had to die.

Getting Personal

When do you slip into viewing life from an earthly, human perspective?

In what ways does seeing life from God's perspective affect your relationships? Your work and career? Your view of success? Your plans for the future?

When he tempted Jesus in the wilderness (see Matthew 4), Satan tried to get him to look at his life and the world from a human point of view. Why endure a cross when you can have an earthly crown? But God's perspective changes everything. Way more important than any earthly fame, fortune, relationships, or power is doing what God wants. This life is but a prelude to eternal life with him.

THE TURN

Setting the Scene

Recognizing and confessing belief in Jesus as the Messiah is only the beginning of discipleship. Jesus invites every person, but those who want to follow him must be willing to "turn from," "take up," and "follow." Jesus didn't make being his disciple sound easy. To those who were hoping to have special positions in Jesus' earthly kingdom (see Luke 22:24), these statements would have been tough to hear. Denying their personal desires and taking up a cross in order to follow this man was not the life they had imagined.

To "turn from your selfish ways" means rejecting the "me first" attitude. Our normal, sinful human tendency is to take care of ourselves, focusing on personal desires and security. Jesus was saying that anyone who wanted to follow him first had to turn away from those selfish desires and earthly security and put him in charge. This attitude transforms self-centeredness to God-centeredness. It means dying to self and living for Christ, putting personal desires and life itself into his hands.

Jesus went on to say that those who willingly "give up" their lives will "save" them. This statement was as jarring to people in Jesus' day as it is today. The Greek word for "life" is *psyche*, referring to the soul, the part of the person that includes the personality with all its dreams, hopes, and goals. Those who "hang on to" their lives in order to satisfy desires and goals apart from God ultimately "lose" life. Those who willingly "give up" or "lose" their lives for the sake of Christ, however, actually "save" them.

Getting Personal

When are you most aware of your tendency to focus on yourself? How does that interfere with your relationship with God?

What makes submission to Christ so difficult? Why must you do this continually, daily?

Nothing we can gain on our own can compare to what we gain with Christ. Jesus wants us to choose to follow him, to turn all that we are and have over to his disposal. Instead of letting us foolishly try to control our futures, he wisely wants to be in control.

READING THE WORD

✿ *Matthew 16:24-26, NLT*
Then Jesus said to his disciples, "If any of you wants to be my follower, you must turn from your selfish ways, take up your cross, and follow me. 25If you try to hang on to your life, you will lose it. But if you give up your life for my sake, you will save it. 26And what do you benefit if you gain the whole world but lose your own soul? Is anything worth more than your soul?"

TALKING TO GOD

Recognize before the Lord your continual, human struggle with the issue of self-centeredness. Ask for God's leadership in every area of your life. Make a conscious turn away from selfish pursuits.

THE CROSS

READING THE WORD

❋ *Mark 8:34-38, NLT*

Then, calling the crowd to join his disciples, he said, "If any of you wants to be my follower, you must turn from your selfish ways, take up your cross, and follow me. 35If you try to hang on to your life, you will lose it. But if you give up your life for my sake and for the sake of the Good News, you will save it. 36And what do you benefit if you gain the whole world but lose your own soul? 37Is anything worth more than your soul? 38If anyone is ashamed of me and my message in these adulterous and sinful days, the Son of Man will be ashamed of that person when he returns in the glory of his Father with the holy angels."

TALKING TO GOD

Admit your justifiable anxieties about what being a follower of Christ might cost you. Ask the Lord to help you find joy in having Christ live in you, whether here on earth or in heaven with him.

Setting the Scene

When Jesus said, "take up your cross," his listeners knew what he meant. Death on a cross was a brutal and public form of Roman capital punishment. A prisoner was required to carry the cross to the place of execution, signifying submission to Rome's power. Jesus was saying that he wanted that kind of humility and submission, a complete break from life as they had known it. Jesus also was implying that identifying with him would lead to social and political oppression and ostracism, and there would be no turning back. Jesus was speaking prophetically as well, for in a few months, he would take up his own cross and walk to Calvary.

Jesus had just said that he would have to suffer and die (Matthew 16:21). Now he was explaining that his followers must be willing to do the same. To lose one's life for Christ's sake refers to a person refusing to renounce Christ, even if the punishment were death. To lose one's life for the Good News implies that the person would be on trial for preaching and circulating the Christian message.

Getting Personal

Following Christ begins with turning from self and turning to him. What makes this so difficult?

The prospect of crucifixion must have deterred many from following Christ—that was too big a price to pay. What has being a Christian cost you?

Paul wrote, "For to me, living means living for Christ, and dying is even better" (Philippians 1:21, NLT). How might that work out in your life?

Those who would follow Christ must count the cost and be prepared to pay it. If we try to save our physical lives from death, pain, or discomfort, we may risk losing our true eternal lives. When we give our lives in service to Christ, however, we discover the real purpose of living. Paul wrote, "My old self has been crucified with Christ. It is no longer I who live, but Christ lives in me. So I live in this earthly body by trusting in the Son of God, who loved me and gave himself for me" (Galatians 2:20, NLT). Are you willing to pay the price of true discipleship?

THE JOURNEY

Setting the Scene

Jesus told the crowd that being his disciple would mean turning away from self, taking up a cross, and then following him. The initial decision to "follow" Jesus is an eternal life-changing decision. From that point, the believer is no longer his or her own; that person belongs to Christ. But recognizing and confessing belief in Jesus as the Messiah is only the beginning of discipleship. True disciples actively follow Jesus "daily." This means taking his road of self-denial and self-sacrifice. Jesus walks ahead, providing an example, and he stands with his followers as encourager, guide, and friend.

Believers must be willing to make the pursuit of God more important than the selfish pursuit of pleasure, giving up the goal of gaining "the whole world." Those who follow Jesus will discover what it means to live abundantly now and to have eternal life later.

Getting Personal

How does a person "follow" Jesus?

How is this walk with Christ a daily process and a lifelong pursuit?

Giving up the "world" to gain Christ is like exchanging deadly poison for an around-the-world cruise. Yet many prefer the bad deal, trading the pleasures of this life for their souls. No amount of money, power, or status can buy back a lost soul. Believers must be willing to make the pursuit of God more important than the selfish pursuit of pleasure. Following Christ means turning from self, taking up the cross, and staying close to the Savior.

READING THE WORD

❁ *Luke 9:23-25, NLT*

Then he said to the crowd, "If any of you wants to be my follower, you must turn from your selfish ways, take up your cross daily, and follow me. 24If you try to hang on to your life, you will lose it. But if you give up your life for my sake, you will save it. 25And what do you benefit if you gain the whole world but are yourself lost or destroyed?"

TALKING TO GOD

Tell God of your longing to follow Jesus closely today, this week, this month, this year. Ask the Lord to inspire and inform your moment-by-moment choices so they reflect his priorities.

JESUS IS TRANSFIGURED
Week 20, Day 1

✸ *Matthew 17:1-13; Mark 9:2-13; Luke 9:27-36*

Peter hit the heights with his "Son of the living God" confession, but then suddenly dropped to the depths with Jesus' reprimand, "Get behind Me, Satan!" (Matthew 16:23, NKJV). Jesus had explained that some of the men standing with him would soon see the Son of Man in his Kingdom. This week we'll watch Jesus take these men to the next level of understanding. In the process we'll discover, with them, more about Jesus' true identity and how that must influence how we think and live.

THEN THERE WERE THREE

Setting the Scene
When Luke mentions "eight days" passing, he connects Jesus' previous statement in verse 27 that foreshadows the Transfiguration. Although Luke has the shortest account of Jesus' revealed glory, he is the only one of the three synoptic Gospel writers who links Jesus' first public words about his death (Luke 9:22) with this foreshadowing. Since the original manuscripts of the New Testament do not include chapter, verse, or paragraph breaks, some translations will even include Luke 9:27 as part of the account of Jesus' trip to the mountaintop. This is partly because there seems to be a shift in perspective after Luke 9:26, where Jesus first makes a broad "whoever is ashamed of Me" statement that points to all those throughout history who refuse to recognize Christ. Then Jesus' next words in 9:27 sound much more immediate and directed, not at the course of history but to the anticipated experience of his audience that day: "But I tell you truly, there are some standing here . . ." The three disciples Jesus took with him up the mountain were certainly standing "there" that day.

Peter, James, and John emerge as a core group within the twelve disciples. Matthew points out that two of the men were brothers. Earlier in Luke 8:51, and later on the night when he was betrayed, Jesus singled out these three to be special witnesses. As we will see, both Peter and John indicate that they had unforgettable firsthand knowledge of Jesus' glory—2 Peter 1:16-18 and John 1:14 obviously refer back to this event on the mountaintop.

Because these three are mentioned by name, we might conclude that they were receiving special privileges. Did Peter, James, and John exhibit greater character so that Jesus decided to give them special attention? We have plenty of evidence throughout the Gospels that a pecking order was on the minds of all the disciples (see Mark 9:33-41). Given the actual track record of these three disciples, however, it might be equally fair to say that Jesus singled them out for remedial work! The special experiences Peter, James, and John shared with Jesus were not rewards but additional responsibilities. Jesus chose them to bear an added weight.

With hindsight we see that each of these "works in progress" grew into a particular role in God's plan. Peter eventually became the leader of the Twelve. John became the scribe of the Twelve, second only to Paul in the quantity of writings included in the New Testament. And James became the first of the apostolic martyrs, dying during the early days of the church. It is interesting that one of Jesus' postresurrection experiences includes a conversation between Jesus, Peter, and John (John 21:15-23). Part of that discussion involved the ongoing roles of Peter and John. James's absence is highlighted by Jesus' words about John, "If I will that he remain till I come, what is that to you? You follow Me" (John 21:22, NKJV). Jesus took these three up the mountain, but he had a particular role in mind for each. Likewise, we can count on his purposeful plans for our lives.

Getting Personal

In hindsight, what experiences in your past clearly show that God was at work in your life?

What relationships have had significant long-term effects in the direction of your life?

God's plans may seem clearer (and even enviable) in other people's lives, but his Word makes it clear that his plans for us are personal. We must faithfully follow as Jesus leads the way.

TALKING TO GOD

The Father knows where you are and who you are—even more clearly than you do. Thank him for that personal care and for his plan for your life, which he has chosen with care for you. Ask God for his wisdom as you move ahead, step by step.

READING THE WORD

❖ *Matthew 17:1-3, NKJV*
Now after six days Jesus took Peter, James, and John his brother, led them up on a high mountain by themselves; 2and He was transfigured before them. His face shone like the sun, and His clothes became as white as the light. 3And behold, Moses and Elijah appeared to them, talking with Him.

TALKING TO GOD

Thank God for mountaintop experiences as well as the certainty of his presence in the valleys. Ask him to help you focus your attention so that you can give him your best in worship and obedience.

WHERE HE LEADS

Setting the Scene

A number of mountains have been suggested for the location Jesus used as a retreat with Peter, James, and John. From the lowlands around the Sea of Galilee, "high mountains" can be seen in almost every direction. The three primary choices are Mount Tabor, Mount Hermon, and Mount Meron, with the latter being slightly favored, given its height and geographical location between Capernaum and Caesarea Philippi.

The tradition of describing positive spiritual events as "mountaintop experiences" is rooted in some of the earliest accounts of God's dealing with people. Abraham took his son Isaac to a mountaintop. Moses encountered the burning bush somewhere on Mount Sinai. Later, he was called up that mountain to meet with God. Before Moses died, God led him up Mount Nebo, where he was able to see the Promised Land. The Psalms are filled with mountain imagery that reminds the writers of God's presence: "I will lift up my eyes to the hills—from whence comes my help? My help comes from the LORD" (Psalm 121:1-2, NKJV).

Going up the mountain alone with Jesus had to have been significant for those three disciples. We don't know what Jesus told them beforehand, but Luke indicates that the immediate purpose was to pray (Luke 9:28). From Luke's account, it appears the disciples got to the top of the mountain and decided it was time for a nap. The transfiguration of Jesus began as the disciples slept.

Being with Jesus requires attentiveness. Even mountaintop experiences can be missed or only partially appreciated if we are not awake enough to note what is going on.

Getting Personal

When have you "awakened" during a significant event in your life and realized that you were partly "asleep at the wheel" while God was working?

What helps you avoid lethargy in your prayer times?

There's a time to sleep and a time to pray. Both are important, and both are gifts from God. We appreciate them most when we learn to practice them in the right ways.

TRANSFIGURED

Setting the Scene

Jesus' power was revealed both in his appearance and in his transcendence over time and space. He looked different, and suddenly he was talking with Moses and Elijah. His brightness ("his face shone like the sun") was not reflected but flowed from within. He wasn't standing in a divine spotlight; he was the source of the light. Jesus was joined by two great Old Testament figures, indicating further glory in Jesus' authority.

Those moments on the mountain were a glimpse into timelessness. Two figures who lived hundreds of years apart—and had long been dead—conversed together with Jesus. We're not told how the disciples identified those two figures, but their presence indicated a realm where life goes on in ways we can hardly imagine. Nor do we know the content of the conversation.

Although most translations use the term "transfigured" when describing what happened to Jesus on the mountaintop, that particular Greek word is also used in Romans 12:2 to describe what needs to happen to those who desire to be living sacrifices: "Do not be conformed to this world, but be transformed [transfigured] by the renewing of your mind, that you may prove what is that good and acceptable and perfect will of God" (NKJV). We've borrowed the Greek term *metamorphosis* to describe the kind of change that happens when a caterpillar becomes a butterfly. In Jesus' case, the metamorphosis revealed his glory in ways that were not usually apparent as he moved through the world. And yet his glory was evident in less remarkable ways as he communicated his grace and truth to those he met. The effects of Jesus' presence in our lives ought to result in the kind of transformation that reveals God's glory in the world. Our "transfiguration" won't be the same as Christ's, but transformation is part of his intention for us.

Getting Personal

What are some of the conversations you want to have with Jesus in eternity?

How is God transforming you these days?

Although our transfiguration may seem to proceed at a snail's pace in this life, we can trust that God is working out his plans for us, for our good and for his glory.

READING THE WORD

✱ *Matthew 17:2-4, NKJV*
And He was transfigured before them. His face shone like the sun, and His clothes became as white as the light. ³And behold, Moses and Elijah appeared to them, talking with Him. ⁴Then Peter answered and said to Jesus, "Lord, it is good for us to be here; if You wish, let us make here three tabernacles: one for You, one for Moses, and one for Elijah."

TALKING TO GOD

Submit to the transformation God wants to bring about in your life. Ask God to "renew your mind" as he accomplishes his purposes for you.

HERITAGE OF FAITH

Setting the Scene

Faced with the figures before them, the disciples must have been astounded. They were suddenly in the company of some of the most revered people in Jewish history. The two men talking comfortably with Jesus had been used by God at crucial moments in the life of his chosen people to bring them to a deeper understanding of himself. Part of Israel's heritage of faith was standing right in front of these disciples.

The crucible of slavery had forged a people that Moses would lead across the desert to the Promised Land. In the process, Moses received the law from God. He wrote the Pentateuch—the first five books of the Bible. Elijah represented the prophets God had sent his people, particularly those who announced the coming Messiah (see Malachi 4:5-6). Both Moses and Elijah shared similar experiences of having had personal appearances (theophanies) from God. The appearance of these two with Jesus removed any confusion over Jesus' identity or his superiority. He was not either of these figures returned to life. He was the ultimate reality, authority, and power about which they had cried out in their own times.

The Bible presents us with an amazing gallery of people whose words and lives point us to Jesus. Others who have followed Jesus before us have also left us examples of faith. These lives offer what could be called our heritage conversation with Jesus. We are privileged to witness and respond to this "conversation." We may be able to point to poor examples of faith in our lives, but the most compelling examples will ultimately be the chorus of voices whispering, speaking, and crying out to us the truth and praises of Jesus.

Getting Personal

Who figures prominently in your personal gallery of voices of faith?

In what ways are your current habits of faith shaped by your heritage of faith?

Good examples of faithfulness are wonderful gifts from God. As often as possible, we should echo Paul's words about the encouragement he received from the lives of even younger believers, "Every time I think of you, I give thanks to my God" (see Philippians 1:2-4, NLT).

READING THE WORD

❀ *Matthew 17:3-7, NKJV*
And behold, Moses and Elijah appeared to them, talking with Him. 4Then Peter answered and said to Jesus, "Lord, it is good for us to be here; if You wish, let us make here three tabernacles: one for You, one for Moses, and one for Elijah." 5While he was still speaking, behold, a bright cloud overshadowed them; and suddenly a voice came out of the cloud, saying, "This is My beloved Son, in whom I am well pleased. Hear Him!" 6And when the disciples heard it, they fell on their faces and were greatly afraid. 7But Jesus came and touched them and said, "Arise, and do not be afraid."

TALKING TO GOD

Pray with thanks over your list of favorite biblical, historical, and living examples of faith. Thank God for providing so many great confirmations of the way he works in this world. Ask God to help you learn from the wisdom of people who have so much to teach you about him.

MOUNTAINTOP EXPERIENCE

Setting the Scene

The three disciples watched in wonder as three astounding figures chatted on the threshold of eternity. Impulsive Peter, always eager to speak what came to mind, announced a possible way to memorialize the moment for himself and others. Basically he said, "Lord, we're so honored that you brought us up here, and we don't want to lose this amazing moment. Say the word and we'll put up three shrines as a memorial to this historic event!" This was more than coming up with a way to remember a moment; it was an attempt to snare eternity for display. Today, he might have pulled out a camera and begun to ask Jesus, Moses, and Elijah to pose so he could get memorable shots to post on Facebook. Sometimes we're so busy trying to capture the moments in our lives that we miss experiencing them fully.

Peter was trying to express his response to an overwhelming experience by suggesting a way to stay in the moment. *Lord, it is good for us to be here—here's a way we can remain here.* But being with Jesus is not nearly as much about *where* we are as about *who* is with us. Jesus brought those three disciples to that special place on the mountain, but it was special primarily because they were with him. Their real privilege wasn't just being there; it was being with him the week before and the week after. Their privilege eventually became the same as ours; hearing Jesus say, "I am with you always, even to the end of the age" (Matthew 28:20, NKJV).

Getting Personal

How do you remember important spiritual events in your life?

What can you do to keep Jesus more important every day, and not just in your "mountaintop" experiences?

The capacity to remember is a great gift God has given us. We can enjoy, remember, and learn from the unexpected experiences God gives us without falling prey to the error that we must hang on to a moment because God can't do better or differently. God always has more in store!

READING THE WORD

❋ *Matthew 17:4-7, NKJV*
Then Peter answered and said to Jesus, "Lord, it is good for us to be here; if You wish, let us make here three tabernacles: one for You, one for Moses, and one for Elijah." 5While he was still speaking, behold, a bright cloud overshadowed them; and suddenly a voice came out of the cloud, saying, "This is My beloved Son, in whom I am well pleased. Hear Him!" 6And when the disciples heard it, they fell on their faces and were greatly afraid. 7But Jesus came and touched them and said, "Arise, and do not be afraid."

TALKING TO GOD

Thank the Lord for the priceless gift of unforgettable moments. Ask him to help you enjoy those memories even while you look expectantly for his presence in your life in ordinary moments and ordinary days.

AFTER THE MOUNTAINTOP

READING THE WORD

✤ *Matthew 17:8-13, NKJV*
When they had lifted up their eyes, they saw no one but Jesus only. 9Now as they came down from the mountain, Jesus commanded them, saying, "Tell the vision to no one until the Son of Man is risen from the dead." 10And His disciples asked Him, saying, "Why then do the scribes say that Elijah must come first?" 11Jesus answered and said to them, "Indeed, Elijah is coming first and will restore all things. 12But I say to you that Elijah has come already, and they did not know him but did to him whatever they wished. Likewise the Son of Man is also about to suffer at their hands." 13Then the disciples understood that He spoke to them of John the Baptist.

TALKING TO GOD

Say thank you again for the hope of promised transformation—gradual and persistent in this life and gloriously complete in the next. Thank God for his leading, during spiritual high points and during everyday experiences of obedience.

Setting the Scene

When the journey of life takes us to the mountaintop, we can be sure the pathway will also lead us down the other side. The disciples may have wished for a few moments to stay at the top, but life was waiting down in the valley.

As they picked their way down the path, Jesus told them, "Tell the vision to no one until the Son of Man is risen from the dead." As the Gospel writers put this account to paper, they were carrying out Jesus' command. However, the disciples seem to have missed the implication of Jesus' statement. If he was going to rise from the dead, he was going to have to die first. They were still not comfortable with that idea, so they deflected with a more immediate question: "Why then do the scribes say that Elijah must come first?" They had just seen Jesus talking with Elijah, so they were trying to work out the sequence of events.

Jesus responded with a double reference to Elijah. This is a classic example of the big picture/little picture aspects of prophecy. The big picture is, "Elijah is coming first and will restore all things"; the little, immediate picture is, "Elijah has come already." The prophetic Elijah-like voice of John the Baptist had been heard and rejected. John had fulfilled his role as the forerunner of the Messiah who would himself be rejected in the process of obtaining salvation.

The Transfiguration was over, but transformation was continuing. The disciples were descending into the world where God's glory was not as easy to see as on the mountaintop but where God's work went on in people.

Getting Personal

When was your last mountaintop experience?

How has that high point affected your response to the flatland or the valley today?

Coming down from a mountaintop is often more an experience of loss than a realization of refreshment and resources for life in the lowlands. The mountaintops let us see transformation, but daily living allows transformation to take root and be seen by others.

❋ *Matthew 18:1-10; Mark 9:33-50; Luke 9:46-50; 17:1-4*

Jesus spoke plainly to the disciples about his death and resurrection, and the costs of following him. Then Peter, James, and John realized Jesus' true identity as they watched him talk with Moses and Elijah. After that incredible event, Jesus continued to teach, highlighting the nature of Kingdom living. This week we'll look at those principles. They apply to us just as much as they were directed to first-century followers.

BEING THE GREATEST

Setting the Scene

When Jesus and the Twelve returned to Capernaum, they went into a house, probably Peter's home, where they often stayed (Mark 1:21, 29). Evidently some of the men had been having a discussion, a short distance from Jesus, as they walked along. When Jesus asked what they had been talking about, they didn't answer. Jesus, however, knew: They had been arguing about who was the greatest and probably wondering who would have positions of prominence in the Kingdom. In Jewish culture, a person's rank was of considerable importance (see Luke 14:7-11 for an example), so the disciples would have wondered about where they would fit in the new order. The argument may have been fueled by the special privileges given to Peter, James, and John at various times.

In the house, when Jesus sat (as a Jewish teacher would), he was signaling that he had something important to tell his listeners. After everyone gathered around, Jesus gave them, in a single sentence, the essence of true greatness: "Whoever wants to be first must take last place and be the servant of everyone else." In other words, greatness is determined by serving. Being a "servant of everyone else" means choosing to meet others' needs without demanding or expecting anything in return. Seeking to be honored, respected, and the center of attention runs contrary to Jesus' requirements for his followers. An attitude of service brings true greatness in God's Kingdom.

READING THE WORD

❋ *Mark 9:33-35, NLT*

After they arrived at Capernaum and settled in a house, Jesus asked his disciples, "What were you discussing out on the road?" 34But they didn't answer, because they had been arguing about which of them was the greatest. 35He sat down, called the twelve disciples over to him, and said, "Whoever wants to be first must take last place and be the servant of everyone else."

Getting Personal

When recently have you felt overlooked and unappreciated because your achievements weren't recognized or you weren't the center of attention?

What makes serving others so difficult?

How can you serve others' needs without expecting anything in return?

Modern Western society seems to be obsessed with social ranking, status, and recognition. In sports, we have "world" championships; in entertainment, we have a constant stream of awards shows; in business we employ a wide range of creative titles. In every field of human endeavor, we note winners and losers. Being labeled "great" or "the greatest" makes us feel important and seems to give our lives significance. So Jesus' statement about the "first" being "last" sounds like crazy talk, overturning our world's values.

All of us, even Christ-followers, are susceptible to the pull of wanting to be better than everyone else, to be first, the champion, the winner. We love to be lauded and served. But if we truly want to follow Christ, we need to take last place, to humble ourselves and serve just as Jesus did. That's the path to greatness.

TALKING TO GOD

Admit to the Lord that you are often concerned about yourself or your image. Ask him to grow in you a strong desire for his glory and a joy in serving others.

WATCHING OUT FOR CHILDREN

Setting the Scene

When Jesus took the child "in his arms," he clarified his explanation of greatness. The way into God's Kingdom is to turn from sin and to Christ in the spirit of humility that a child exhibits when showing simple trust in someone he or she loves. When the disciples were arguing, they were missing the point; such an attitude was enough to keep someone from ever finding and entering the Kingdom. Matthew's account includes more of Jesus' words: "I tell you the truth, unless you turn from your sins and become like little children, you will never get into the Kingdom of Heaven. So anyone who becomes as humble as this little child is the greatest in the Kingdom of Heaven" (Matthew 18:3-4, NLT).

Jesus was teaching the disciples to welcome children, who usually were treated poorly in this society. He emphasized this teaching in the strongest possible terms: "But if you cause one of these little ones who trusts in me to fall into sin, it would be better for you to be thrown into the sea with a large millstone hung around your neck." And later Jesus would say, "Let the little children come to me, and do not hinder them, for the kingdom of heaven belongs to such as these" (Matthew 19:14, NIV). Clearly Jesus valued children.

Getting Personal

When do you come in regular contact with small children in addition to your family members?

What can you do to welcome them on Jesus' behalf?

How can you become more involved in the nurture, guidance, and protection of children?

God expects his people to protect and care for little ones, certainly included in "the least of these" (Matthew 25:40, NLT). Today children seem to be viewed as expensive inconveniences. Killing an unborn child is sanctioned by the state, and reports of child abuse or neglect fill the headlines. The Kingdom should be a safe place for children, and Christ's followers should protect children physically, emotionally, and spiritually. This isn't limited to parents and grandparents; every member of God's family has this responsibility. We do this to obey and serve Christ and to model honesty and humility for children.

READING THE WORD

✤ *Mark 9:36-37, 42, NLT*
Then he put a little child among them. Taking the child in his arms, he said to them, 37"Anyone who welcomes a little child like this on my behalf welcomes me, and anyone who welcomes me welcomes not only me but also my Father who sent me. . . . 42But if you cause one of these little ones who trusts in me to fall into sin, it would be better for you to be thrown into the sea with a large millstone hung around your neck."

TALKING TO GOD

Ask the Lord to help you cultivate childlike humility, dependence, and trust in your relationship with him, your Father. Ask him to improve your willingness to serve others, especially children, in Jesus' name and for his glory.

SERVING WITH OTHERS

Setting the Scene

These minor conflicts over leadership and discussions about being "the greatest" had implications beyond the Twelve. Here we see John and the others wanting to keep Jesus to themselves, to be a closed group as they challenged the credentials of an outsider. John, one of the inner circle of three among the disciples, was the disciple who brought up the matter. He may have been sincerely concerned about the man and his actions, or he may have felt threatened by this person who could do something that he could not—"cast out demons." Whatever John's motives, Jesus rebuked the disciples' attempt to be exclusive. The disciples were wrong to assume they alone would have access to Jesus' power. Jesus' followers would not all look and act alike; they would be quite a diverse collection from all nations and walks of life.

Not only did the man who cast out demons serve Christ's Kingdom in his stand against Satan, but someone doing a humble act such as offering a cup of water to a person in the name of Christ also would be serving the Kingdom. Certainly the Twelve had a special calling, but God uses all people and all gifts for furthering his Kingdom.

Getting Personal

When have you felt competitive with other churches or Christian groups?

What steps can you take to partner with other believers to serve your community in Jesus' name?

After two thousand years of church history, Jesus' followers seem more splintered than ever, with numerous Christian denominations and hundreds of divisive theological distinctions. And while we debate among ourselves the finer points of faith and practice, the world is going to hell. Clearly Jesus wants us to reach beyond our closed circles and work with other men and women who also follow Christ. We serve the same Savior and have a common mission. Just as the man in the story did not have to belong to the select group of disciples to be God's servant, so people today do not have to be just like us to follow Jesus.

READING THE WORD

✤ *Mark 9:38-41, NLT*
John said to Jesus, "Teacher, we saw someone using your name to cast out demons, but we told him to stop because he wasn't in our group." 39"Don't stop him!" Jesus said. "No one who performs a miracle in my name will soon be able to speak evil of me. 40Anyone who is not against us is for us. 41If anyone gives you even a cup of water because you belong to the Messiah, I tell you the truth, that person will surely be rewarded."

TALKING TO GOD

Admit your occasional desire to keep what you have with God all to yourself. Ask the Lord to help you accept others whose beliefs differ from yours but who also love and serve God. Thank him for building his church with such a variety of personalities, experiences, and spiritual traditions.

RESISTING TEMPTATION

Setting the Scene

This teaching ties closely to the two preceding ones. Jesus emphasized the need for continual self-appraisal. Temptation can come from various sources. In the Bible, feet are often associated with deliberately traveling to do wrong, hands with the acts themselves, and eyes with what we see and think about. Those who desire to follow Jesus must remove the stumbling blocks that cause sin—any relationship, routine, or activity (not literally to cut off a body part). As a person would submit to losing a diseased hand, foot, or eye to save his or her life, so believers should be just as willing to "cut off" any temptation, habit, or relationship that could lead them into sin.

In describing hell, Jesus spoke of a place, like the garbage dump in the valley outside of Jerusalem, where worms infested the garbage and fires burned constantly. With these strange words, picked up from Isaiah 66:24, Jesus pictured the serious and eternal consequences of sin and the absolute destruction of God's enemies.

Getting Personal

When are you tempted to go where you shouldn't—either by habit or deliberate choice? What can you do to "cut off" that temptation?

In what situations are you tempted to sin with your eyes or hands? What steps can you take to "cut off" those temptations?

Jesus was describing true, radical discipleship. No one will ever be completely sin-free until heaven, but God wants an attitude that renounces sin instead of one that rationalizes and holds on to sin. Unfortunately the excuses flow easily, even for believers: "It was just once," "No one got hurt," "Everyone's doing it," "I could have done a lot worse," "Look at the good that came because of what I did," and so forth. Pornography, gluttony, petty theft, gossip, lying, and other socially acceptable sins can be very tempting for those who claim to follow Jesus.

Jesus wasn't being tough with his followers to spoil their fun. Our Lord loves us too much to let us walk down destructive paths. We need to take sin as seriously as he does, to walk his way, trusting he wants only the best for us.

READING THE WORD

❁ *Mark 9:43-48, NLT*

If your hand causes you to sin, cut it off. It's better to enter eternal life with only one hand than to go into the unquenchable fires of hell with two hands. 45If your foot causes you to sin, cut it off. It's better to enter eternal life with only one foot than to be thrown into hell with two feet. 47And if your eye causes you to sin, gouge it out. It's better to enter the Kingdom of God with only one eye than to have two eyes and be thrown into hell, 48"where the maggots never die and the fire never goes out."

TALKING TO GOD

Identify areas of going, doing, or looking that you may have rationalized to yourself. Confess these to God today; his forgiveness is already yours in Christ. Ask him for courage and strength to be totally dedicated to living God's way.

READING THE WORD

❋ *Luke 17:3-4, NLT*
So watch yourselves! If another believer sins, rebuke that person; then if there is repentance, forgive. 4Even if that person wrongs you seven times a day and each time turns again and asks forgiveness, you must forgive.

TALKING TO GOD

Ask God to give you a spirit of love and humility as you attempt to give or receive correction. Ask him for his grace to help you forgive those who may have deeply offended or hurt you.

FORGIVING BELIEVERS

Setting the Scene

As leaders, the disciples would have had the responsibility to confront others if they were heading in the wrong direction or involved in sin. But this must be done in love, with a concern for the erring person. Jesus' disciples must be marked by forgiveness. This would have contrasted with the Pharisees and their approach to anyone's missteps. The Pharisees had no problem with the "rebuke" side of Jesus' statement. In fact, they seem to have made that a regular part of their daily routine—looking for anyone who wasn't observing their strict interpretations of and additions to the law. Jesus and the Twelve certainly ran afoul of them several times.

To rebuke does not mean to point out every sin—Jesus also warned against being judgmental (Luke 6:37). Rebuking in love means to bring sin to a person's attention with the purpose of restoring that person to God and to others. And rebuking must be tied to forgiveness, or it would not help the sinning person. Jesus said, in fact, that the disciples "must forgive." The use of the number seven means, in effect, "all the time," just the way that God deals with every person.

Getting Personal

When have you been rebuked? In what ways did the attitude of the confronting person affect your response?

When have you had to confront or correct a fellow Christ-follower for what he or she has done? What can you do to make sure your motives are right in this kind of situation?

"Rebuke" and "forgive"—those two actions have a built-in tension, since they stand at opposite ends of the relational spectrum. But both are by-products of love. If we truly love our brothers and sisters in Christ, we want what's best for them and will do all we can to keep them on the right path. But we shouldn't do this in a judgmental way. Our goal should always be correction, and we should be ready to forgive, even if the sin has been against us.

When you think you must rebuke another Christian for a sin, first check your own attitudes and motivations. Realizing how completely Christ has forgiven you should produce a free and generous attitude of forgiveness toward others.

LIVING IN PEACE

Setting the Scene

In mentioning salt, Jesus was continuing his metaphor about being "tested with fire" ("tested" is also translated "salted" or "seasoned"). The disciples would be tested and purified; here the salt symbolized the disciples and the work they had been called to do.

In the first century, salt was a condiment and a preservative for food. Jesus had told the disciples, "You are the salt of the earth" (Matthew 5:13, NLT), making the point that they were to be life-producing agents in a dying world and life-preserving agents in a sin-spoiled world. Salt had commercial value, but the impure salt taken from the sea was susceptible to deterioration, leaving only flavorless crystals. When that happened, the flavor could not be returned, rendering it worthless.

The disciples had the responsibility to maintain their saltiness (usefulness) by staying close to Jesus. As the disciples allowed God to purify them, they, in turn, would be purifying agents in the world, resulting in "peace with each other." Instead of arguing among themselves, as they had on the road, they would serve others and remain at peace with each other. This peace among the disciples would be of vital importance after Jesus' return to heaven (see 1 Thessalonians 5:13). The future of the church would be left in their hands.

Getting Personal

Think of two or three church disputes in your past. What were the issues? How were they resolved?

When have you been upset about something that happened at church (perhaps something a leader said or did)? How did you respond? How should you have responded?

What can you do to "live in peace" with difficult brothers and sisters in Christ?

Salt can preserve food; it also can enhance flavor. Jesus used those qualities to highlight the importance of his followers living in peace. We need to work together to reach the world, to bring life and healing to men and women instead of allowing petty disputes to divide us. Many churches split over issues as trivial as music choices, worship times, and minor budget items. Living in peace is one way the watching world can see Christ at work in us. He wants his body to be unified.

READING THE WORD

❀ *Mark 9:49-50, NLT*
For everyone will be tested with fire. 50Salt is good for seasoning. But if it loses its flavor, how do you make it salty again? You must have the qualities of salt among yourselves and live in peace with each other.

TALKING TO GOD

Call on your Father to help you with issues that arise among your brothers and sisters in your church family. Ask him to help you be slow to anger and quick to forgive and be a peacemaker.

JESUS DESCRIBES DISCIPLESHIP
Week 22, Day 1

❋ *Matthew 8:18-22; Luke 9:57-62*

Throughout Jesus' years of ministry, he attracted a following. Participants in his entourage came and went. Some he specifically invited to follow; others volunteered. This week we will look at a sampling of these followers beyond the designated twelve. There were certainly others who fit the pattern of disciples or who wanted to have that kind of relationship with Jesus. We will see how Jesus "read" their responses and challenged them to authentic discipleship in ways that can still be applied to our lives today.

❋ *Luke 9:57, NIV*
As they were walking along the road, a man said to him, "I will follow you wherever you go."

WALKING THE WALK

Setting the Scene

Both Matthew and Luke tell us of brief exchanges between Jesus and potential followers. In Matthew's account (8:18-22), Jesus creates some separation between himself and the crowds by taking a boat across the lake. But it is immediately clear there are others around besides the twelve disciples. The relative calm of the moment gives certain individuals an opportunity to approach Jesus. Luke, however, includes these exchanges among the events as Jesus was on his final journey toward Jerusalem, where God's great plan of salvation would be accomplished at the Cross.

We may only remember how Jesus called the Twelve to follow him, but there are hints throughout the Gospels that people were continually offering themselves as willing followers. This passage shows how often people came to Jesus with conditions—just as we do. These conversations indicate that Jesus was approachable. We may wish we had detailed descriptions of more conversations Jesus had, but the Holy Spirit always gives us what is most helpful to communicate to us God's purposes.

People felt comfortable with Jesus. Even those who hated him didn't hesitate to approach him. And those who wanted to follow him were not prevented by his demeanor from speaking to him. We see that to follow Jesus, we must grasp the results and consequences of following. Jesus welcomed people who followed him for the right reasons, and even those who would grow in faith while they experienced the benefits, bumps, and bruises of following Jesus.

Jesus was very direct with those who wanted to be his disciples. In each of these three cases, Jesus' comments helped them realize that following him was not to be undertaken lightly. Jesus often emphasized the necessity of counting the cost in following him (see Luke 14:25-33).

When we turn to the three individuals we're told spoke with Jesus, a certain pattern emerges from the group. Each man expressed a condition for following. In a sense, they were claiming to make a step they were clearly not ready to take. Even the first potential disciple, as we shall see, was making too broad a commitment. His words make us recall Peter's later declaration, "Lord, I am ready to go with you to prison and to death" (Luke 22:33, NIV)—right before Peter denied knowing Jesus. These men were overstating their commitment. Jesus helped them be realistic.

Jesus isn't looking for people who profess what great disciples they will be; he is looking for people who know how difficult it will be to follow him and do it anyway. He is looking for those whose attitude is "Lord, I believe; help my unbelief!" (Mark 9:24, NKJV).

Getting Personal

If you had been there, what conditions might you have made for following Jesus?

When do you feel unequipped or unprepared to be a strong disciple of Jesus? Why?

Our commitment to Christ doesn't need conditions, qualifications, or limitations. These addendums try to shape our relationship to the one who is without limits. Any commitment short of simple trust will prove inadequate and short-lived before the realities of following Jesus.

TALKING TO GOD

Petition the Lord to forgive any attempts you've made to provide conditions for following him. Ask him to help you develop unqualified trust in him as he shows you the way to serve and please him.

WHEREVER

READING THE WORD

❀ *Matthew 8:19-20, NLT*
Then one of the teachers of religious law said to him, "Teacher, I will follow you wherever you go." 20But Jesus replied, "Foxes have dens to live in, and birds have nests, but the Son of Man has no place even to lay his head."

TALKING TO GOD

Praise God for the lasting security he promises, and don't depend on any temporary securities you may be enjoying. Thank God for his faithful presence—wherever you go.

Setting the Scene

Luke describes this volunteer as "a man," but Matthew gives him a distinct position as a teacher of religious law (a *grammateus*, or scribe). There are a couple of attitudes this man possibly used in his approach to requesting to be a disciple. One may have been the "I am someone worth having as a disciple because of my status" attitude. Another might have been the "These common folk will fall away, but I'm the kind of person who is capable of following you wherever" attitude. The scribes had an intimate connection with God's Word because they were charged with the task of copying the scrolls of God's Word. Before printed books, the personal effort involved in the careful reproduction of holy texts not only gave a certain status to those who did the work, it also led to the assumption that those who copied the Law might be the best to interpret it.

Jesus was not impressed by the offer, and he responded with what sounds very much like an Old Testament proverb. This potential disciple wasn't rejected; he was simply challenged to think again about what he was saying. Eventually, people would reject Jesus and his disciples. The expectation of physical comfort or material advantage should not be taken for granted.

This is Jesus' first use of the Son of Man title in Matthew. The term claimed Jesus' messianic role, which at the time had become almost exclusively a description for a hoped-for political leader to throw out the Romans.

Two cautions come to us from this brief encounter: It's easy to align ourselves to a caricature of Jesus, and it's hard to embrace the cost of following the real Jesus.

Getting Personal

This man called Jesus "Teacher." What is your preferred term for Jesus, and what do you mean by it?

What have you discovered about the cost of following Jesus?

For those of us who live in a society that claims religious tolerance, persecution often takes the form of rejection for those who actually take Jesus seriously. But such "tolerance" means little if it isn't based on a firmly held personal worldview.

BURIAL DUTIES

Setting the Scene

Matthew tells us that a "disciple" approached Jesus with a complication; Luke tells us that the exchange was initiated by Jesus. By calling him a "disciple," Matthew may simply be acknowledging that Jesus had already invited him to follow.

The man's immediate response to the invitation to follow Jesus was a qualified yes, but there was something else important he wanted to do first—bury his father. Our first impression might be that the man's father had just died and he was asking for a brief delay, but the circumstances indicate the man's father was still alive, and he was actually asking for an indefinite delay. Once the man's duty to his father was fulfilled at some point in the future, then he would follow Jesus.

This potential disciple may have had legitimate reasons to hesitate making his commitment to Jesus. If he was the oldest son, he had multiple duties and privileges. Jesus' response to his conditional allegiance is not license to disobey the commandment to honor our parents or to ignore our responsibilities as their children. Rather, Jesus' words challenged the man's use of "first" in a way that placed commitment to Christ somewhere farther down on the list.

At first glance, we may think Jesus sounds harsh in saying, "Let the dead bury their own dead," but his expression can also mean *let the dying bury the dead.* In other words, "I'm calling you to a life that is a higher priority; others can take care of the details of death because they are not called to that life." The life-giving task to "proclaim the kingdom of God" takes precedence over all other responsibilities.

Getting Personal

What responsibilities and circumstances in your life challenge you in keeping your commitment to Christ as first priority? Why?

What might you be putting "first" in your life ahead of what Christ has told you to do?

Circumstances will always arise to challenge our commitment to Christ. When they do, our allegiance must be clear. The temptation of the qualified yes is that it allows us to feel like we have responded positively when we have actually just put off the decision. Jesus asks for nothing less than first place.

✳ *Matthew 8:21-22, NIV*
Another disciple said to him, "Lord, first let me go and bury my father." 22But Jesus told him, "Follow me, and let the dead bury their own dead."

✳ *Luke 9:59-60, NIV*
He said to another man, "Follow me." But he replied, "Lord, first let me go and bury my father." 60Jesus said to him, "Let the dead bury their own dead, but you go and proclaim the kingdom of God."

TALKING TO GOD

Confess to the Lord the interests and concerns that occasionally take over first place in your priorities. Thank him for faithfully drawing your heart and mind back to him.

READING THE WORD

❈ *Luke 9:61-62, NIV*
Still another said, "I will follow you, Lord; but first let me go back and say goodbye to my family." 62Jesus replied, "No one who puts a hand to the plow and looks back is fit for service in the kingdom of God."

TALKING TO GOD

Tell the Father that he is Lord of your life. Ask him to fix himself as your unmoving objective, so that everything else can fall into place as he allows it.

GOOD-BYES

Setting the Scene

Of the four Gospel writers, only Luke includes this third brief encounter. Compared with the previous delay of waiting to bury a parent, the postponement for farewells seems reasonable. However, it is clear that this person's conditional "but first" undermines the seriousness of his commitment.

Jesus never said, "If you follow me, you can't say good-bye to loved ones and you can't bury them when they die." In fact, Jesus elsewhere made it a point that a serious disciple counts the cost before he or she decides to follow (see Luke 14:25-33). Jesus certainly cared for his loved ones and attended a funeral or two.

Jesus was objecting to the built-in exception that allowed someone to claim discipleship while pursuing other priorities. In this case, if the good-byes are not a delaying tactic, get them over with and then follow. Following Jesus reorients all other priorities. There is no parallel life for a disciple. Every decision is made based on the deeper commitment to Christ. Saying good-bye to or burying parents are not forbidden; instead, they become actions done only as they are consistent with following Jesus, which is now the guiding principle.

Jesus' response requires that we understand a practical matter in plowing, a task which cannot be accomplished while looking over one's shoulder. A straight furrow depends on the farmer keeping a fixed point on the far side of the field in sight. Otherwise, the plow wanders. Serving in the Kingdom of God is like plowing; it cannot be done effectively with our attention distracted by other things we treat as first in our lives.

Getting Personal

What choices or decisions have you deliberately made "against the grain" simply because of the deeper priority of the Kingdom of God in your life?

What makes you a true disciple even though you are not a full-time teacher, preacher, or evangelist?

When we allow people or circumstances to overrule our decision to follow Christ, our lives take on the look of a field that has been plowed by a distracted farmer. The results are a confusion of conflicting priorities.

JESUS' WORDS

Setting the Scene

At one point in their months together, John tells us, "Many of his disciples turned back and no longer followed him" (John 6:66, NIV). Jesus then asked the Twelve: "You do not want to leave too, do you?" (John 6:67, NIV). Peter's response on behalf of the disciples helps us understand the three statements by Jesus to the potential disciples: "Lord, to whom shall we go? You have the words of eternal life" (John 6:68, NKJV).

To these uncertain disciples, Jesus also offered words of eternal life. In the first case, Jesus offered the man a picture of the Son of Man without a place to lay his head. "If you are following the Son of Man, who has no place to lay his head, don't expect to have a place for your head either." The words of eternal life for this man pointed to Kingdom values that make the pleasures and privileges of this world incidental rather than guaranteed. When we say, "I will follow you anywhere, Jesus," do we really mean *anywhere*?

In the second exchange, Jesus pointed out that death cannot demand a higher priority than eternal life. "I am calling you to the only life that can put death into its true place. Instead of burying your father, I want you to preach the Kingdom of God to him while he lives!"

The third man learned that the Kingdom of God must take precedence over everything else. Eternal life invalidates good-byes. "I'm calling you to a life where you will never have to say good-bye. If you insist on treating life as a time-bound existence, you are not fit for my Kingdom."

Getting Personal

When you consider the various familiar statements Jesus made, which ones come to you most clearly as "words of eternal life"?

How do Jesus' words of eternal life challenge your own commitment to him?

In a world that devalues words, Jesus makes an uncompromising call to commitment. We can't be disciples when we're giving attention to both the world and to Jesus. He doesn't share first place with anyone or anything else.

READING THE WORD

❊ *Luke 9:58, NKJV*
Jesus said to him, "Foxes have holes and birds of the air have nests, but the Son of Man has nowhere to lay His head."

❊ *Luke 9:60, NKJV*
Jesus said to him, "Let the dead bury their own dead, but you go and preach the kingdom of God."

❊ *Luke 9:62, NKJV*
But Jesus said to him, "No one, having put his hand to the plow, and looking back, is fit for the kingdom of God."

TALKING TO GOD

Respond to Jesus' teaching by thanking the Lord for helping you to discover who has the words of eternal life. Ask for God's guidance in shaping your plans so that they fall under the essential primacy of his lordship.

READING THE WORD

✤ *Luke 9:59-60, NIV*
He said to another man, "Follow me." But he replied, "Lord, first let me go and bury my father." 60Jesus said to him, "Let the dead bury their own dead, but you go and proclaim the kingdom of God."

TALKING TO GOD

It's God's great love that persistently demands your wholehearted obedience. Thank him that he loves you enough to keep drawing you closer to him.

THE CALL TO DISCIPLESHIP

Setting the Scene

It's one thing to experience that heady moment when we sense our lives touched by God and realize we are being called to follow. It's another thing to consider the cost of discipleship. Whether Jesus was responding to eager volunteers or approaching people with an invitation to follow, his concern was always that only those who recognized the cost actually became genuine disciples.

The farmer Jesus referred to in Luke 9:62 reminds us of one of the most compelling stories Jesus told about discipleship—the parable of the four soils (see Matthew 13:3-9). In the cases of the three men who interacted with Jesus in Luke 9:57-62, we don't know what kind of "soil" they turned out to be. Their initial responses place them squarely in the rocky or weedy soil categories. Their responses to Jesus may have had little root so that their faith quickly withered, or they may have had conflicting loyalties (weeds) that quickly choked out a commitment to Christ. We do not know the outcome.

We are aware of Jesus' call in our lives. Any response other than an unqualified yes turns out to be a stark or veiled no. Millennia have passed since these men held brief exchanges with Jesus, yet the basic issues remain the same for us. Have we considered the cost of discipleship, and have we answered the call?

Several times this week we have considered Jesus' response to the second man, "Let the dead bury their own dead, but you go and proclaim the kingdom of God." Ultimately the choice for each of us is between life and death. Because Jesus is life, following him is making a choice for life. Any other choice turns out to be a choice for death.

Getting Personal

Which, if any, of the responses of these three men most closely parallels your own initial response to Jesus?

What is your current condition as a follower of Jesus? What changes need to be made?

Jesus will not settle for mere good intentions—not then and not now.

❈ *Luke 10:25-37*

To the disciples, Jesus had explained the realities of what being his follower would entail, what he expected of them. In this passage an "expert in religious law" interrupted Jesus' teaching to ask an important question. This week as we take a close look at Jesus' interaction with this lawyer and Jesus' answer to his question, we'll find several lessons that apply to us as well.

ASKING GOOD QUESTIONS

Setting the Scene

Luke reports that the man "stood up," implying that his question came during a time that Jesus was teaching. As an "expert in religious law," this man had studied the Scriptures (the Law, the Psalms, and the Prophets). He also knew all the traditions. Yet he asked Jesus, "What should I do to inherit eternal life?" Although Luke writes that he asked the question as a "test," this doesn't mean the man was asking with a pharisaical attitude, trying to trip up Jesus. He probably was asking out of curiosity, wondering what kind of answer Jesus would give. The man called Jesus "Teacher," showing his respect. For this lawyer, "eternal life" would have meant life in God's Kingdom, but he would not have understood it as a spiritual Kingdom. Obviously he thought he had to "do" something and would not have understood divine grace.

Jesus responded with a question, framing it in such a way that he accepted the man's question as a valid one. Then, when the lawyer answered by quoting from Deuteronomy 6:5 and Leviticus 19:18 respectively, Jesus affirmed that the man had answered correctly, and Jesus urged the man to do exactly what he had just quoted.

To "love the LORD your God with all your heart, all your soul, all your strength, and all your mind" means holding nothing back, being totally devoted to God. The Greek word for "love" used here (*agape*) means totally unselfish love. We can only love that way through the Holy Spirit working in us. But the law also said, "Love your neighbor as yourself." People tend to look out for

READING THE WORD

❈ *Luke 10:25-28, NLT*

One day an expert in religious law stood up to test Jesus by asking him this question: "Teacher, what should I do to inherit eternal life?" 26Jesus replied, "What does the law of Moses say? How do you read it?" 27The man answered, "'You must love the LORD your God with all your heart, all your soul, all your strength, and all your mind.' And, 'Love your neighbor as yourself.'" 28"Right!" Jesus told him. "Do this and you will live!"

TALKING TO GOD

Whatever questions or doubts you have been wrestling with, bring them all to God without reluctance. Ask him to give you understanding and an openness to learn from him.

themselves—to care about their safety, health, comfort, and security. God expects his people to do that for others.

"Do this and you will live" sounds simple—in reality, however, those commands are impossible to keep in our human strength alone. Kingdom people are saved and then enabled by the Holy Spirit to obey these impossible demands.

Getting Personal

If you could ask God one question, what would it be?

How do you love God with your mind? With your strength?

We don't know much about this "expert in religious law," except that he asked Jesus an important question. The man may already have had an idea of what Jesus should answer and was testing Jesus' orthodoxy. Or the man may have asked out of a deep yearning to know the real answer, to be sure that he would gain eternal life. In either case, Jesus took the lawyer's question seriously and answered him. One fact is clear from this story and from several other places in Scripture: God isn't afraid of our questions and wants us to be totally honest with him. He's not waiting to judge us for having doubts or making a wrong request. He loves us; he's our Father.

LOOKING FOR LOOPHOLES

Setting the Scene

After Jesus answered the expert's question (actually, the man had answered it himself), Luke says the man "wanted to justify his actions." We know the question was a good one and that the lawyer probably had known the answer, even as he was asking it. But hearing God's requirements from his own lips must have caused him to think, "If I take this literally, I'm doomed!" After all, how can anyone *totally* devoted to God, and how can anyone possibly show that kind of love to others? This man may have taken a quick mental inventory of his attitudes and actions and realized he had fallen woefully short. We don't know whether the man wanted to justify his question by asking Jesus to delve deeper into the topic, or whether he wanted his own actions justified. So he pressed Jesus further, asking, "And who is my neighbor?"

Getting Personal

What teachings of Scripture do you find most difficult to obey? In what ways have you rationalized disobedience or shortcomings?

What do you sense God telling you to stop or start doing?

As we read Scripture, the Holy Spirit often convicts us of our sins and challenges us to action. At times we know exactly what God is saying to us about what we need to change and do. Yet like the legal expert in this story, we look for loopholes. We may think, for example, that a teaching applies to someone else, or we may try to interpret it to make it less demanding. Rationalizations come in many forms. Instead, we need to take seriously God's Word, especially when Jesus says, "Do this and you will live!" (Luke 10:28, NLT).

It's human nature to look for loopholes in the law, even God's law, and to justify our actions. We can easily find "good" reasons for doing what we shouldn't do or not doing what we should. The most difficult step to take in following God is that first one when we admit, "I was wrong" or "I'm headed in the wrong direction." But that's where life begins.

READING THE WORD

❀ *Luke 10:29, NLT*
The man wanted to justify his actions, so he asked Jesus, "And who is my neighbor?"

TALKING TO GOD

Request the Lord's forgiveness for times when you have rationalized less-than-total obedience to one of his commands. Ask for his Spirit to work in you to give you "the desire and the power to do what pleases him" (Philippians 2:13, NLT).

IGNORING WOUNDS (PASSING BY)

READING THE WORD

✤ *Luke 10:30-32, NLT*
Jesus replied with a story: "A Jewish man was traveling from Jerusalem down to Jericho, and he was attacked by bandits. They stripped him of his clothes, beat him up, and left him half dead beside the road. 31By chance a priest came along. But when he saw the man lying there, he crossed to the other side of the road and passed him by. 32A Temple assistant walked over and looked at him lying there, but he also passed by on the other side."

TALKING TO GOD

As you tell the Lord that you are willing to help those in need, pray specifically about practical ways that might happen—in real time, with real resources.

Setting the Scene

Jesus began answering the legal expert by telling a story. All of his listeners would have easily pictured the man in the story traveling "from Jerusalem down to Jericho." The seventeen-mile stretch of road was dangerous because it curved through rocky and desolate terrain with many hiding places for thieves. The robbers in the parable did more than just take their victim's money, however; they left him half dead on the road.

The first person to encounter the victim was a "priest." The second was a "Temple assistant." Both clearly saw the wounded man by the side of the road, yet they ignored him and continued their respective journeys "on the other side."

Priests and Temple assistants had different jobs in and around the Temple. Priests performed the sacrifices. The assistants would help the priests, doing the work of today's elders, deacons, custodians, assistants, musicians, movers, and other support staff. Temple worship could not have taken place without the combined efforts of these two groups. The Old Testament law demanded good deeds and caring for those who were hurt. Jesus' story highlighted the shortcomings of the priest and the Temple assistant because they were required to provide care. Jesus didn't say *why* these men ignored the man, just that they refused to help.

Getting Personal

In what ways have you "passed by on the other side" rather than getting involved in some complicated but compassionate action?

In the last couple of days, when have you seen someone in need? How did you respond?

In Jesus' story, religious people went out of their way to ignore a person in need. Whether we are ministry professionals or laypeople, God expects us, his people, to be sensitive to others in need and to reach out. Yet often we act as if we haven't seen the person's need or decide that we're too busy to stop. The world and our neighborhoods are filled with hurting people who need a touch, a bandage, a meal, a friend—and the words of eternal life.

SEEING WITH COMPASSION

Setting the Scene

Everyone listening to Jesus would have expected the priest or Temple assistant to come to the aid of the hurt and helpless man. But in Jesus' story, they kept moving. The next person to come along was the last person the listeners would have expected to help a wounded Jew—a "despised Samaritan." Jews and Samaritans hated each other (see Week 7). So when Jesus introduced this Samaritan man into the story, the Jewish listeners would not have expected him to help a Jewish man. In fact, if Jesus had stopped after "then a despised Samaritan came along" and asked the audience what they thought happened next, none of their answers would have been positive. But when *this* Samaritan saw the man at the roadside, "he felt compassion for him." The Samaritan bandaged the man's wounds, perhaps with strips of cloth from his own clothing, and "took him to an inn, where he took care of him."

The priest, Temple assistant, and Samaritan all "saw" the man by the side of the road, but they responded much differently. The Samaritan saw with *compassion*. Apparently, this Samaritan understood the meaning of helping someone in need, regardless of differences and issues, including racial tensions, and despite the inconvenience and interruption to his personal schedule.

Getting Personal

When has someone been a "good Samaritan" to you?

When have you misread someone's attitude or actions, only to discover later that the person was actually hurting?

What excuses have you used for not helping someone in need?

The term Good Samaritan *is used to describe a person who helps a stranger in trouble. Many factors can keep us from acts of kindness: busyness; unpreparedness or inadequacy to help; fear for our own safety; preoccupation with our own problems. But the root cause for our inaction is the failure to see with compassion. God expects his people to see others as he sees them—as his valued creations for whom Christ died. When we look past our schedules, issues, and prejudices and see real people with real needs, we will stop, reach out, and bandage their wounds.*

READING THE WORD

❀ *Luke 10:33-34, NLT*
Then a despised Samaritan came along, and when he saw the man, he felt compassion for him. 34Going over to him, the Samaritan soothed his wounds with olive oil and wine and bandaged them. Then he put the man on his own donkey and took him to an inn, where he took care of him.

TALKING TO GOD

Anticipate opportunities to meet the needs of others by asking God today to equip you with eyes that see with compassion, and words and deeds that bring a healing touch.

READING THE WORD

❊ *Luke 10:35, NLT*
The next day he handed the innkeeper two silver coins, telling him, "Take care of this man. If his bill runs higher than this, I'll pay you the next time I'm here."

TALKING TO GOD

Admit to the Lord that sometimes the cost in time and resources has kept you from meeting others' needs. Ask the Lord to help you be creative in seeing how much you have to share.

PAYING THE PRICE

Setting the Scene

This act of mercy by the Samaritan in Jesus' parable cost him the time and resources to soothe the man's wounds. He could have thought, *Well, I've done what I could* and left the man there, bandaged but alone. Instead, he took the man to an inn, where he cared for him through the night. The next day the Samaritan had to be on his way, but the wounded man was still in poor shape. The Samaritan gave the innkeeper money for the bill and promised to pay for additional expenses. The "two silver coins" probably would have paid for a few weeks' lodging. He wanted the wounded man to be looked after carefully. And all of this was done anonymously; as far as we know, the Samaritan wasn't even paid with a thank-you note. His compassion cost him quite a bit.

Getting Personal

What might helping someone in your neighborhood cost you? What about a need you hear about in another country?

When has cost been a factor in whether or not you help someone?

Often we think compassion is merely an emotion, feeling sorry or bad for a person in need. Certainly feelings are involved, but true compassion translates into actions. And those actions will cost us something. But think of what Jesus' compassion cost him: He gave everything to reach his people—to reach you and meet your most profound needs. This kind of unselfish sacrifice was Jesus' answer for what it means to "love your neighbor as yourself" (Luke 10:27, NLT).

FINDING NEIGHBORS

Setting the Scene

Upon finishing his story, Jesus came right to the point, asking the expert in religious law to say which of the three men in the story had loved his neighbor. That is, which of the three—the priest, the Temple assistant, or the Samaritan—had kept the law? The legal expert spoke clearly and truthfully when he said, "The one who showed him mercy."

Jesus responded with a pointed application: "Go and do the same."

Go and see people as God sees them.

Go and be ready to serve.

Go and show mercy.

Go and be a neighbor.

Getting Personal

As you have considered this familiar story, in what ways have you identified with the man who asked Jesus, "Who is my neighbor?"

Putting yourself in that man's place, in what ways do you think your life would change after hearing Jesus say, "Go and do the same"?

Usually we think of neighbors as those who live next door or at least in the same neighborhood. But through his story, Jesus shows that neighbors are everywhere, even on the side of a road away from our homes and familiar surroundings. We may see them or hear about them from other neighbors. We may learn about them from news reports or missionaries' stories. Clearly loving our neighbors as we love ourselves means always being ready to serve, to give, to meet needs.

READING THE WORD

❊ *Luke 10:36-37, NLT*
"Now which of these three would you say was a neighbor to the man who was attacked by bandits?" Jesus asked. 37The man replied, "The one who showed him mercy." Then Jesus said, "Yes, now go and do the same."

TALKING TO GOD

Jesus has met your most desperate need, your need to be reconciled to God. Thank him for his awareness of all your needs, and ask him to grow a godly desire in you to be like him in meeting others' needs as you become aware of them.

JESUS TALKS ABOUT HIS RETURN
Week 24, Day 1

❄ *Luke 12:35-59*

Most of us struggle with the idea of active waiting. We assume that waiting is passive—doing nothing means we are waiting well. This week we will listen to Jesus' explanation of the kind of waiting he desires from us in the time period before his return. The picture involves active anticipation. We are waiting while doing and preparing. Jesus said that the timing of his return would be a surprise, but he expected those who were waiting for him not only to be busy up to that moment, but to overcome their surprise with a heartfelt welcome! During these days, consider carefully how you are waiting for Christ's return.

READING THE WORD

❄ *Luke 12:35-36, NKJV*
Let your waist be girded and your lamps burning; 36and you yourselves be like men who wait for their master, when he will return from the wedding, that when he comes and knocks they may open to him immediately.

UNEXPECTED ARRIVAL

Setting the Scene

Luke places this teaching from Jesus about the end times immediately following his account of Jesus' words about worry (Luke 12:22-31) and the relationship his followers were to have toward the poor (Luke 12:32-34). Jesus confronted the usual unhealthy ways we handle the future: by worrying and hoarding. With verse 35, Jesus teaches about the attitudes we ought to have each day as we anticipate his future return.

Unlike other passages in the New Testament about the return of Christ, which include a number of telltale signs, here Jesus' teaching ignores the clues leading up to his impending arrival. Jesus did not want his followers to spend time trying to figure out exactly when he was going to return. Instead, he pointed out that even when we try to predict what will happen, the event will catch everyone by surprise. The difference, Jesus says, will be between those who are morally and spiritually prepared and those who are careless and unbelieving.

In every generation, people have tried to predict the moment of Christ's return—and have been consistently wrong. Rather than being drawn into current debates, our task is to obey Christ, knowing that God is working out his plan in history. Jesus will return and everyone will be held accountable.

Jesus pictures a household anticipating the arrival of the master who has been away at a wedding. A servant was expected to be on call continuously, around the clock, whether the master was home or not. When the master left for the evening or an extended trip, those who served the household had ongoing duties to perform as well as anticipating the master's return.

The master did not expect to return to a dark or slumbering house. The phrase "let your waist be girded" refers to an adjustment of typical clothing in anticipation of action. A person gathered his long outer robe and tucked it into his belt or sash, freeing the lower extremities to work, walk, or run. It implies "dressed for action."

Homes in Jesus' day were occupied spaces. Even the owner returning from the banquet "knocks" to gain admission. His servants must be ready to open the door. The house is humming with life, and the light streaming from the windows provides a beacon in the dark streets and a welcome for the master. That wasn't the time to scramble to light a lamp or dress for action.

Jesus described watchful busyness—servants who are carrying out their duties in anticipation of the master's arrival. His mention of the wedding adds a hint of joy to this picture. The master is returning with joy to his household, signaling the shift of festivities from elsewhere to home. For those eagerly anticipating the Lord's return, the unavoidable surprise is a delight. Authentic disciples are ready to welcome Jesus back—even today.

Getting Personal

When do you feel the tension between anticipating Jesus' return and occupying yourself with his instructions until then?

In what ways can you keep your "lamp lit" (Matthew 5:14-16) today?

There are some unacceptable ways to resolve the tension between waiting and working. Jesus never apologized for asking his disciples to live faithfully in that tension. He promised to make it worth our while.

TALKING TO GOD

Thank God for the promised return of the Master, Jesus. Ask him to help you use your time well while you wait for his return in glad anticipation.

THE SERVING MASTER AND THE THIEF

READING THE WORD

❧ *Luke 12:35-40, NIV*
Be dressed ready for service and keep your lamps burning, 36like servants waiting for their master to return from a wedding banquet, so that when he comes and knocks they can immediately open the door for him. 37It will be good for those servants whose master finds them watching when he comes. Truly I tell you, he will dress himself to serve, will have them recline at the table and will come and wait on them. 38It will be good for those servants whose master finds them ready, even if he comes in the middle of the night or toward daybreak. 39But understand this: If the owner of the house had known at what hour the thief was coming, he would not have let his house be broken into. 40You also must be ready, because the Son of Man will come at an hour when you do not expect him.

TALKING TO GOD

Acknowledge the love of the Lord that provides advance warning of his return. Ask him to keep you prepared so that his coming will be a great joy to you, his servant. Ask him to help you pray, with excitement for that day, "Come, Lord Jesus!" (Revelation 22:20, NKJV).

Setting the Scene

Yesterday we focused on the overall tone of Jesus' teaching about how we should anticipate his return. Today we see two contrasting pictures Jesus added to his opening illustration of the watchful servants waiting for the master's return.

In the first picture, the master serves the servants he finds eagerly awaiting him. Servants were expected to place themselves at the master's disposal, but Jesus turns the tables and informs us that the delighted master will serve his servants. The reversal of roles was not only countercultural, it was consistent with the way Jesus related to his disciples. The first moments of the Last Supper (John 13:1-11) provide us with an unforgettable picture of the master "girding" himself and washing his disciples' feet as they reclined at the table. Jesus was picturing life in God's Kingdom, where worldly expectations related to power and position are turned on their heads. We enjoy partial glimpses of these Kingdom values as we take Jesus' instructions seriously, but we won't see the full scope fulfilled until Jesus returns as he promised.

In the second picture, the scene is still a household. The homeowner is in residence and is about to have a burglar visit. Instead of the tone of joy that permeates the first picture, a note of caution and even fear colors the second one. The purpose in this illustration is not to identify the thief but to focus on the unexpected arrival of the Son of Man. Will we be like the homeowner who has no concerns or inkling that he is about to be robbed? The sudden coming of the Son of Man will shatter that brittle security.

Getting Personal

How might we be like the blissfully ignorant homeowner today?

Which role most closely fits your life: the waiting servants or the clueless homeowner? Why?

Jesus didn't hesitate to use jarring illustrations to focus people's attention. As we will see tomorrow, it is this second picture that provoked a response. Jesus made it clear that his return would not be good news for everyone.

THE TARGET AUDIENCE

Setting the Scene

The passage you just read is part of a longer question and response that includes verses 41 to 48. Peter asks Jesus a question related to the illustrations Jesus had just given. Although there are two parables in the previous five verses, Peter mentions only one. He may have been referring to the theme in all that Jesus had just said, or he may have been somewhat troubled by the second of Jesus' pictures, the household about to be robbed. Peter's question assumes understanding. He simply asks Jesus to whom he is addressing his warning, "to us, or to everyone?"

First, Jesus answered Peter's question with a question. There are four possibilities for the person Jesus called "that slave/servant" (Luke 12:43, 45, 47, and 48). Before the Lord comes, his servants might fall into any of those roles. Jesus' response shifted the focus of Peter's question from "Who gets to be in charge?" to "How will you perform in whatever situation you find yourself?" Three of the possible servant responses are undesirable; only one receives Jesus' promise, "It will be good for that servant." The faithful servant will be rewarded with special responsibilities. Meanwhile, the abusive servant (Luke 12:45-46), the deliberately disobedient servant (Luke 12:47), and the careless servant (Luke 12:48) will receive appropriate punishments.

In Jesus' previous illustration (Luke 12:35-38), the household was populated by servants who were challenged to be ready together; here, the focus is on how individual servants will faithfully anticipate the master's return. Whether we fill a leadership role or a supportive role, we will answer to the Master directly when he returns.

Getting Personal

What are you doing to be a faithful and wise servant?

What might hinder you from wanting Jesus to return today?

Your access to God's Word makes you a highly privileged individual. Consider Jesus' closing words in this section: "From everyone who has been given much, much will be demanded; and from the one who has been entrusted with much, much more will be asked" (Luke 12:48, NIV). The short answer to Peter's question to Jesus is "Yes." Jesus was speaking to everyone.

READING THE WORD

✤ *Luke 12:41-43, NIV*
Peter asked, "Lord, are you telling this parable to us, or to everyone?" 42The Lord answered, "Who then is the faithful and wise manager, whom the master puts in charge of his servants to give them their food allowance at the proper time? 43It will be good for that servant whom the master finds doing so when he returns."

TALKING TO GOD

Ask the Lord to show you any ways you may resemble the three unsatisfactory servants. Thank God for his Word and for his Holy Spirit to help you live for him as a faithful servant.

DIVISIONS

Setting the Scene

These words of warning begin a section (12:49–13:8) in which Jesus urgently invites his fellow Jews to recognize him while there is time. Jesus had just been referring to the relationships between servants and their master; now Jesus talks about how regarding him as master will affect relationships within families. Because many will not choose Christ, painful divisions will develop between people. Jesus offered no middle ground in belief about him (see Luke 11:23). He warned that conflict and division would develop between those who choose him and those who reject him.

When confronted with opposition because of your Christian faith, make sure the conflict is caused by the person's rejection of core truth in the faith and not a personality difference or surface issue. If the problem is over the truth of Jesus, compromise isn't an option; stand firm.

Jesus declared that he came to bring fire and division. John the Baptist had announced that the Messiah would "baptize you with the Holy Spirit and fire" (Luke 3:16, NKJV). By "fire" Jesus was referring both to God's judgment and to the coming of the Holy Spirit. His own baptism would be to experience the wrath of God's judgment as our substitute on the cross. But Jesus was also looking at the long view of God's plan, and when he said, "how I wish it were already kindled," he was expressing a longing for God's purposes to be accomplished on earth. He knew that, in God's timing, his own coming to earth had set the stage for the ultimate division of humanity.

Getting Personal

How has the decision you have made about Jesus affected your closest relationships?

What have you learned about living with divisions that can't be bridged?

Once we are convinced of the truth, it is difficult to see those we love continue to reject it. We can't decide for them, however. We must pray that they may yet come to see the truth in Jesus.

READING THE WORD

✤ *Luke 12:49-53, NKJV*
I came to send fire on the earth, and how I wish it were already kindled! 50But I have a baptism to be baptized with, and how distressed I am till it is accomplished! 51Do you suppose that I came to give peace on earth? I tell you, not at all, but rather division. 52For from now on five in one house will be divided: three against two, and two against three. 53Father will be divided against son and son against father, mother against daughter and daughter against mother, mother-in-law against her daughter-in-law and daughter-in-law against her mother-in-law.

TALKING TO GOD

Pray that you might live peaceably with those who have rejected the Lord, even when those differences create a large divide between you. Ask the Lord to bring about the salvation of those you love, so that you can belong to him together.

NO PEACE

Setting the Scene

Besides declaring that he had come to bring fire and division to earth, Jesus also asked a provocative question: "Do you think I came to bring peace on earth?" Then he answered with an unqualified no. And he was specific about the place where the lack of peace would be felt most deeply—the family.

What are we to make of Jesus, the Prince of Peace, whose birth was heralded by angels proclaiming, "Glory to God in the highest heaven, and on earth peace to those on whom his favor rests" (Luke 2:14, NIV), insisting he did *not* come to bring peace? Did Jesus contradict himself when he told the disciples, "Peace I leave with you, My peace I give to you; not as the world gives do I give to you" (John 14:27, NKJV)?

The apparent contradiction may be created by familiarity and distortion of Bible passages that point to Jesus as the source of peace. For example, we recall the Christmas language "peace on earth, goodwill toward men" and conclude that God was declaring unconditional concord within humanity. But the peace declared by God will come only to people "on whom his favor rests."

The world has not been a peaceful place since the fall of humanity. It will not be a place of peace until God renews it after the final judgment. The divisions are a necessary means to set apart a group who will receive the peace only Jesus can provide—peace with God. He told his disciples that his peace has no equal, "I have told you these things, so that in me you may have peace. In this world you will have trouble. But take heart! I have overcome the world" (John 16:33, NIV).

Getting Personal

What surprises you about the way people divide over the subject of Christ?

In what specific ways are you experiencing the peace that can be found only in Christ?

We often seek peace from objects and relationships apart from Christ. When we do that, we are "dividing" ourselves from Jesus and experiencing the consequences—lack of peace.

READING THE WORD

❁ *Luke 12:51, NIV*
Do you think I came to bring peace on earth? No, I tell you, but division.

TALKING TO GOD

Turn to the only true source of peace in a world where there is no lasting peace. Thank God for his peace, which is not like the peace the world has to offer.

THE SPIRITUAL WEATHER CHANNEL

READING THE WORD

�֍ *Luke 12:54-59, NIV*

He said to the crowd: "When you see a cloud rising in the west, immediately you say, 'It's going to rain,' and it does. 55And when the south wind blows, you say, 'It's going to be hot,' and it is. 56Hypocrites! You know how to interpret the appearance of the earth and the sky. How is it that you don't know how to interpret this present time? 57Why don't you judge for yourselves what is right? 58As you are going with your adversary to the magistrate, try hard to be reconciled on the way, or your adversary may drag you off to the judge, and the judge turn you over to the officer, and the officer throw you into prison. 59I tell you, you will not get out until you have paid the last penny."

TALKING TO GOD

Even as you understand how you will escape God's judgment because of Christ, ask the Lord to help you be aware of how you might help others understand the freedom and forgiveness that are found in him.

Setting the Scene

Progress in meteorology helps us predict the weather, but those who live in various regions eventually recognize certain weather patterns that help them guess what will happen next. Jesus reminded his audience that they regularly used clouds and wind to "interpret the appearance of the earth and the sky." Then he added, "Since you can read these conditions so well, why is it that you cannot read what's happening in time and history that is even more important than the weather?" The word "hypocrites" highlights his point that the problem wasn't an inability to discern the spiritual times but an unwillingness to do so.

Throughout the Old Testament, God provided sign after sign pointing to the coming Kingdom. Those indications were as sure as wind forecasting heat or clouds announcing rain. But the people were ignoring the present signs, rejecting God's Kingdom in favor of the dream of a kingdom of their own making—an earthly Israel freed from Rome.

Today we spend more time talking about the weather, sports, or entertainment than we do the words of Christ. As believers, a passage like this can create a powerful conviction about our responsibility to urge others to settle things with God. We can't force them to recognize Jesus any more than Jesus himself was able to force belief in people. But we have been given the privilege to share with others their opportunity to avoid God's judgment while there is still time.

Getting Personal

Who are the people in your life you can readily see are on the way to judgment before God?

What specific efforts have you made to offer them the gracious alternative of the out-of-court settlement in Christ?

If you spend more time with news, sports, and weather than you do pursuing your understanding of Christ, how might you change your priorities?

Some people imagine they can come up with a plausible defense for their lives when they stand before God. Such thinking is demonic trickery. God's judgment is perfect and irreversible. Each person must decide what to do about Jesus. And the decision must be made before we stand before God.

✸ *John 10:1-42*

As Jesus ministered to the crowds, individuals, and the Twelve, he continued to reveal his true identity and the character of his true followers. This week we will explore another of Jesus' parables, this one about a sheepfold, a gate, thieves, sheep, and a shepherd. Each word picture holds a valuable promise and life lesson.

THE GATE

Setting the Scene

When Jesus began talking about the sheepfold and sheep, his listeners would have paid attention and understood the situation, because shepherds and sheep were common in ancient Palestine.

A "sheepfold" was a cave, shed, or open area surrounded by a wall eight to ten feet high and made of stones or branches. Often the top of the wall would be lined with thorns to discourage predators and thieves. Having a single entrance made guarding the flock at night easier for the shepherd. At times several shepherds, each with his own sheep, would use a single fold and take turns guarding the entrance. Mingling the animals posed no problem, because each flock would respond to its shepherd's voice. The shepherd standing or sitting in the entrance was, in effect, the "gate."

The shepherd in the story calls together his flock and takes them to the pasture. Later, back at the sheepfold, the shepherd sits in the doorway, acting as the gate. In Jesus' parable, the "gate" is the only entrance and probably represents the position of Messiah because Jesus explained that "the one who enters through the gate is the shepherd of the sheep."

Realizing that his listeners hadn't grasped what he was teaching, Jesus stated clearly, "I am the gate for the sheep." In other words, he was the *only* way to salvation and eternal life—"Those who come in through me will be saved." Later, Jesus would emphasize this truth with the Twelve,

READING THE WORD

✸ *JOHN 10:1-9, NLT*

"I tell you the truth, anyone who sneaks over the wall of a sheepfold, rather than going through the gate, must surely be a thief and a robber! 2But the one who enters through the gate is the shepherd of the sheep. 3The gatekeeper opens the gate for him, and the sheep recognize his voice and come to him. He calls his own sheep by name and leads them out. 4After he has gathered his own flock, he walks ahead of them, and they follow him because they know his voice. 5They won't follow a stranger; they will run from him because they don't know his voice." 6Those who heard Jesus use this illustration didn't understand what he meant, 7so he explained it to them: "I tell you the truth, I am the gate for the sheep. 8All who came before me were thieves and robbers. But the true sheep did not listen to them. 9Yes, I am the gate. Those who come in through me will be saved. They will come and go freely and will find good pastures."

THE GATE *continued*

stating, "I am the way, the truth, and the life. No one can come to the Father except through me" (John 14:6, NLT).

Getting Personal

Why do you think people resist the exclusive claim of Jesus—that he is the only *way to salvation?*

When have you heard someone say or imply that people can come to God and get to heaven by many paths? How do you answer that?

Who are the "robbers" today?

In what ways has Jesus being the "gate" for the "sheepfold" affected your life?

Jesus asserted that he was the true and only Messiah for the Jews. As such, his people could find salvation, security, and nourishment only through him. At that time, the Jews knew they would have only one Messiah, so the question for them was, "Is this the one?" Today, the questions seem to center more on the issue of Jesus' exclusive statement to be the only *way. Jesus claimed and proved to be God in the flesh and the only source of salvation. Without him, all people are lost in their sins and bound for destruction. But because of Jesus and through him, we can have eternal life. Instead of wondering why only one way is available, we can be profoundly grateful that God has provided this way.*

Focus your worship today on the uniqueness of Jesus, the only way anyone can come to the Father. Thank him for the protection and the promise of eternal life, which are yours because he is your Shepherd.

THE THIEVES

Setting the Scene

Jesus' statement about all those who had come before him did not refer to Old Testament prophets and other spiritual leaders but to those who had claimed to be the Messiah or who had led the people astray. Many of the Pharisees and religious leaders could be included in that second group. They invented their own gateway (the keeping of numerous traditions and rules) and appointed themselves as gatekeepers. Jesus reminded them that any other supposed way to salvation was false.

The "thieves" (false messiahs) and the "hired hands" (corrupt religious leaders, John 10:12, NLT) had evil intentions. They cared only about feeding themselves or making money off of the flock. Israel had suffered through numerous evil leaders, false prophets, and false messiahs (see, for example, Jeremiah 10:21-22; 12:10; Zechariah 11:4-17).

"Thieves" don't care for the sheep and are only interested in themselves and what they can gain from the flock. For "hired hands," working with the sheep is only a job—at the first sign of trouble they take off, abandoning the vulnerable sheep.

The early church would struggle with false teachers motivated by ego, power, and money. Their heretical teachings always tried to diminish Jesus' identity in some way. But he is humanity's *only* hope. All other ways lead to destruction.

Getting Personal

Which false teachers or false teachings are you most familiar with?

What can you do to make sure you won't be taken in by a spiritual "thief"?

We continue to be plagued by spiritual "thieves and robbers"—false religions and cults, self-serving speakers, and religious leaders demanding allegiance and financial commitment. The one common denominator is that they diminish Jesus. Often the message is subtle and enticing as they offer Jesus-minus or Jesus-plus. Sadly, many of these false teachers can be found in houses of worship with "Jesus," "Christ," or "Christian" in their name.

"And who is a liar? Anyone who says that Jesus is not the Christ. Anyone who denies the Father and the Son is an antichrist" (1 John 2:22, NLT).

READING THE WORD

✣ *John 10:8-10, NLT*
All who came before me were thieves and robbers. But the true sheep did not listen to them. 9Yes, I am the gate. Those who come in through me will be saved. They will come and go freely and will find good pastures. 10The thief's purpose is to steal and kill and destroy. My purpose is to give them a rich and satisfying life.

TALKING TO GOD

Thank God for what he is teaching you about Jesus through the Gospels. Focusing on who Jesus really is prevents confusion when it comes to confronting false teaching. Praise God for the trustworthiness of his Word!

READING THE WORD

❈ *John 10:3-5, 14-16, NLT*

The gatekeeper opens the gate for him, and the sheep recognize his voice and come to him. He calls his own sheep by name and leads them out. 4After he has gathered his own flock, he walks ahead of them, and they follow him because they know his voice. 5They won't follow a stranger; they will run from him because they don't know his voice. . . . 14I am the good shepherd; I know my own sheep, and they know me, 15just as my Father knows me and I know the Father. So I sacrifice my life for the sheep. 16I have other sheep, too, that are not in this sheepfold. I must bring them also. They will listen to my voice, and there will be one flock with one shepherd.

TALKING TO GOD

In comparison to God's omnipotence and omniscience, our ability and reasoning seem very small. Admit to the Lord your great need for his protection and guidance. Ask him to draw you close and keep you there.

THE SHEEP

Setting the Scene

A shepherd would call his sheep; the sheep, recognizing their shepherd's voice, would follow him to the pasture. Shepherds could name each sheep, and each sheep would respond to the shepherd calling its name. True believers, belonging to the true Shepherd, would never follow someone pretending to be their shepherd. The shepherd knows his sheep, and he loves them, so much that he would die for them. The sheep also know the shepherd and trust him.

Jesus added that he had "other sheep . . . not in this sheepfold." Jesus' audience for this parable was Jewish, and they would have understood the "sheepfold" to be made up of Jews who were following the Messiah. Jesus' reference to "other sheep" means that he would save Gentiles as well as Jews. Jesus had come to die for sinful people all over the world, not just in Palestine. Eventually the Jewish believers and the Gentile believers would form one flock.

Getting Personal

What can you do to "listen" to the Good Shepherd? What, if anything, keeps you from fully hearing his voice today?

The difference between listening and hearing is that hearing involves understanding. How can you distinguish his voice from your own reflective thinking?

What can you do to better understand what God wants you to do?

Even if we hear the Shepherd, we still must choose to follow where he leads. Where does he want to lead you? Will you follow?

In this parable, the sheep "listen," they hear the shepherd, and they "follow." The result is that these sheep find good pasture and are protected. The Bible often uses the word sheep to describe people—and not always positively. Isaiah 53:6, for example, says, "All of us, like sheep, have strayed away. We have left God's paths to follow our own" (NLT). How foolish—yet how often we stray away from the Shepherd. Just like sheep, we are weak and vulnerable. We need our Shepherd and dare not follow our own path.

THE SHEPHERD

Setting the Scene

Jesus is not just the shepherd; he's the "good shepherd." In Jesus' conversation with a young man often described as the "rich young ruler," Jesus asked the man, "Why do you call me good? . . . Only God is truly good" (Luke 18:19, NLT). Thus, when Jesus added "good" to shepherd, he was making a significant point. Jesus wasn't just another shepherd—a well-meaning and competent one. He was "the *good* shepherd." In being truly good, Jesus could be trusted to want only the best for his sheep, never to lead them astray. Then Jesus pointed out that the most important trait of the Good Shepherd is that he "sacrifices his life for the sheep." What a difference between the Good Shepherd and the others mentioned in the story. The thief steals, kills, and destroys; the hired hand watches the sheep only for money and abandons the flock at the first hint of trouble or danger. The Good Shepherd, however, is committed to the sheep. Then Jesus compared his relationship with his followers to the relationship he enjoyed with the Father.

Concerning his willingness to give his life for the sheep, when Jesus said, "I have the authority to lay [my life] down when I want to and also to take it up again," he was claiming authority to control his life and beyond, hinting at the Resurrection. Jesus obeyed his Father and voluntarily laid down his life. It was not taken from him.

Getting Personal

When have you doubted God's goodness? When has other advice made you doubt Jesus' words?

What makes following Jesus all the time so difficult at times?

What evidence might others see in you to show that Jesus is your Good Shepherd?

Many people who call themselves Christians profess to believe that God is good, but they hedge their bets. They follow the Shepherd but question whether they are headed in the right direction. They may trust God and *something (money, mental ability, advice of friends, and so forth). But trusting in the Savior means following him wholeheartedly—no additions or corrections. And this begins by believing that he is truly* good *all the time.*

READING THE WORD

❋ *John 10:11-18, NLT*

I am the good shepherd. The good shepherd sacrifices his life for the sheep. 12A hired hand will run when he sees a wolf coming. He will abandon the sheep because they don't belong to him and he isn't their shepherd. And so the wolf attacks them and scatters the flock. 13The hired hand runs away because he's working only for the money and doesn't really care about the sheep. 14I am the good shepherd; I know my own sheep, and they know me, 15just as my Father knows me and I know the Father. So I sacrifice my life for the sheep. 16I have other sheep, too, that are not in this sheepfold. I must bring them also. They will listen to my voice, and there will be one flock with one shepherd. 17The Father loves me because I sacrifice my life so I may take it back again. 18No one can take my life from me. I sacrifice it voluntarily. For I have the authority to lay it down when I want to and also to take it up again. For this is what my Father has commanded.

TALKING TO GOD

Forgive me, dear Shepherd, for my doubts and fears and for wandering off on my own way, thinking that I know better. I do believe you and trust you. I know you are good and that you love me. Help me trust you more.

READING THE WORD

❀ *John 10:19, 24-33, NLT*
When he said these things, the people were again divided in their opinions about him. . . . 24The people surrounded him and asked, "How long are you going to keep us in suspense? If you are the Messiah, tell us plainly." 25Jesus replied, "I have already told you, and you don't believe me. The proof is the work I do in my Father's name. 26But you don't believe me because you are not my sheep. 27My sheep listen to my voice; I know them, and they follow me. 28I give them eternal life, and they will never perish. No one can snatch them away from me, 29for my Father has given them to me, and he is more powerful than anyone else. No one can snatch them from the Father's hand. 30The Father and I are one." 31Once again the people picked up stones to kill him. 32Jesus said, "At my Father's direction I have done many good works. For which one are you going to stone me?" 33They replied, "We're stoning you not for any good work, but for blasphemy! You, a mere man, claim to be God."

TALKING TO GOD

In your worship today, affirm that Jesus is God. Praise him for his incredible sacrifice of becoming like you in order to save you. Ascribe to him the glory due his name (1 Chronicles 16:29, NIV).

THE CLAIM

Setting the Scene

With all that Jesus was teaching and doing, the Jews were divided in their ideas about his identity. So they gathered around and asked Jesus to clear up the controversy—was he the Messiah or not? A straightforward declaration probably would not have convinced them, however, because they had already made up their minds. So Jesus said, in effect, "What I say won't make a difference because you won't hear it. And that's because you don't believe in me—you're not my sheep." Next, Jesus stated who he was by summarizing the effects of the gospel. Those who know him personally have eternal life, will "never perish," and are secure in his care. Then Jesus closed by giving one of the clearest affirmations of his divinity in the whole Bible, saying, "The Father and I are one."

The Jews who were against Jesus got the point—his claim to be God was unmistakable. The religious leaders wanted to kill Jesus because their laws said that anyone claiming to be God should die. Nothing could persuade them that Jesus' claim was true. So as they picked up stones to kill him, they asserted, "We're stoning you . . . for blasphemy! You, a mere man, claim to be God."

Getting Personal

What difference does Christ's divinity make in how you think? In how you act?

What could you say to someone who says, "I believe Jesus was a great moral example and teacher, but he was just a man"?

How do you know that Jesus is more than a man—that he is, in fact, God?

The Jews in Jesus' audience understood what Jesus' words meant. Though they didn't believe him, they knew he asserted equality with God. Jesus' greatest critics have considered him to be nothing more than a man and say that he never claimed to be divine—the idea of his divinity was added later. Yet the greatest enemies of Jesus' time recognized that he was definitely claiming to be God.

THE EVIDENCE

Setting the Scene

Jesus answered his accusers by challenging them to check the facts. At least three different kinds of evidence had been given to convince people about Jesus: (1) Verbal proof convinced some, such as the people who said, "No man has ever taught like this one!" (See, for example, Mark 1:22.) (2) Character proofs convinced others who spent time with Jesus and observed his life. (3) Signs and miracles demonstrated his power over time, space, and the laws of nature. Jesus recognized that some who might not be convinced one way might be open to other evidence. He invited his listeners to consider his miracles if they found his words too difficult to believe. After all, the prophets said the Messiah would do great works (Isaiah 35:4-6). The purpose of all this evidence was to help people "know and understand" that he and the Father are one.

On those with minds already made up, the evidence had no effect. But many considered the evidence and "believed in Jesus."

Getting Personal

When do you tend to doubt what you've been taught about Jesus and God?

What evidence is most helpful to your faith?

In what ways do the facts about Jesus help you as you share the truth about him with others?

Although salvation comes by faith alone, having faith does not mean leaping into the dark or believing despite the facts. Jesus told his accusers to use their minds and to consider the evidence. Today, we have the advantage of even more evidence for the truth of Jesus' claims—the Resurrection, the eyewitness accounts in the New Testament, and twenty centuries of changed lives. God wants us to renew our minds (Romans 12:2), not close them. He wants us to study and know his Word (2 Timothy 2:15), and to compare Bible teachings with what the Bible says (Acts 17:11). The evidence is there. We can know and trust our Savior (2 Timothy 1:12).

READING THE WORD

✦ *John 10:34-42, NLT*

Jesus replied, "It is written in your own Scriptures that God said to certain leaders of the people, 'I say, you are gods!' 35And you know that the Scriptures cannot be altered. So if those people who received God's message were called 'gods,' 36why do you call it blasphemy when I say, 'I am the Son of God'? After all, the Father set me apart and sent me into the world. 37Don't believe me unless I carry out my Father's work. 38But if I do his work, believe in the evidence of the miraculous works I have done, even if you don't believe me. Then you will know and understand that the Father is in me, and I am in the Father." 39Once again they tried to arrest him, but he got away and left them. 40He went beyond the Jordan River near the place where John was first baptizing and stayed there awhile. 41And many followed him. "John didn't perform miraculous signs," they remarked to one another, "but everything he said about this man has come true." 42And many who were there believed in Jesus.

TALKING TO GOD

Thank God for all you are learning about Jesus through his Word. Ask God to strengthen your devotion to Christ as you study his clear teachings and claims, his amazing works, his sinless life, his death in your place, his resurrection, and his work in countless lives.

JESUS ATTENDS A BANQUET

✤ Luke 14:1-24

Jesus was invited to parties and special events—think of the wedding at Cana, the block party Matthew gave the evening after he quit his job at the tax office to become a disciple of Jesus, or his meals with Mary, Martha, and Lazarus in Bethany. When Jesus attended these functions, he clearly felt at home. And he often said or did things that made what might have otherwise been a ho-hum event into a memorable occasion. Jesus was the master of the teachable moment, and gatherings always presented a target-rich environment. As we explore this week's passage, we will observe Jesus using a meal at a Pharisee's house to teach several important lessons.

READING THE WORD

✤ Luke 14:1, NIV
One Sabbath, when Jesus went to eat in the house of a prominent Pharisee, he was being carefully watched.

MAKING AN IMPRESSION

Setting the Scene

Jesus lived under constant scrutiny. People approached him intending to trip him up and possibly arrange for his death. Invitations came with strings attached, and open doors were also possible traps. Jesus' response to these dangerous circumstances was fearless but not careless. He made decisions based on a sense of timing. Beginning back at Luke 9:51, Jesus had been intent on moving toward Jerusalem, where he knew all the elements of God's plan would come together at the Cross. So he accepted these invitations knowing full well that his enemies were trying to build a case against him that they could use to remove him from the scene.

Luke tells us that this event occurred on a Sabbath. Why were the Pharisees having a banquet on the Sabbath? Could Jesus have turned the Pharisees' own behavior against them on this occasion as he did on others? They were adept at going to great lengths to keep a distorted view of the law of the Sabbath that nevertheless allowed them to do what they desired. The preparation of food for this meal would have been carried out the day before.

We are told that the host for this occasion was a "prominent" Pharisee (meaning "leader" or "ruler" among the Pharisees). This term of authority is the same one John used in his account of Jesus' encounter with Nicodemus (John 3:1). It is possible that the invitation to Jesus was genuine and that the prominent Pharisee, someone like Nicodemus, wanted to interact with Jesus, even though his companions had ulterior motives for their presence. Jesus' later words directed to the host (Luke 14:12-14) were more instructive than harsh. The Lord may well have been giving priceless direction to one of his undercover disciples.

But the tone for the occasion is set by the phrase "he was being carefully watched." Lines were being drawn. Strategies were being devised. The religious leaders felt threatened by Jesus as someone who might tip the balance of power among competing Jewish groups or create instability in the tense stalemate with the Romans. But Jesus came to resolve the eternal problem between God and the human race.

Getting Personal

How many of your social activities allow you to make a difference for God?

What opportunities do you have to hang out with those who don't believe in Christ?

Jesus didn't hesitate to show up despite the expectations of a mixed welcome. His decisions weren't based on what would make him look or feel good; they were based on how he could best serve his Father's plans. Our lives will take a different course if we are open to motives other than self-service when we decide where to spend our time.

TALKING TO GOD

Thank God for sending Jesus to inhospitable places—like our world, where we desperately needed to be rescued. Ask him to broaden your own ideas of where you might go, or whom you might invite into your home. Ask him to help you focus on seeking the Father's pleasure over your own.

READING THE WORD

�֍ *Luke 14:1-5, NKJV*

Now it happened, as He went into the house of one of the rulers of the Pharisees to eat bread on the Sabbath, that they watched Him closely. 2And behold, there was a certain man before Him who had dropsy. 3And Jesus, answering, spoke to the lawyers and Pharisees, saying, "Is it lawful to heal on the Sabbath?" 4But they kept silent. And He took him and healed him, and let him go. 5Then He answered them, saying, "Which of you, having a donkey or an ox that has fallen into a pit, will not immediately pull him out on the Sabbath day?"

TALKING TO GOD

Ask the Lord for his wisdom and help in establishing good guidelines and rules of thumb for your everyday life. And then ask God also to help you recognize when others' needs are more important than that good structure.

SET UP

Setting the Scene

No sooner had Jesus arrived at the Pharisee's house than he met a man who was obviously suffering. Luke calls the man's condition *hydropikos* (dropsy), the primary symptom being swelling due to accumulation of fluids. The leaders may have stationed the man just outside the doorway where they could closely observe Jesus' response to his need. The timing of this incident (the Sabbath) makes it probable that he was set up to trap Jesus. Those who "watched Him closely" knew Jesus had a history of violating their interpretation of Sabbath rules.

Today we can hardly appreciate the level of Sabbath-consciousness that was part of life in Jesus' day. Rather than being truly honoring to God or even beneficial for people, the Sabbath had become a day of scrupulous observance of controlling and often arbitrary rules put in place to avoid "work." Yet even within such a high degree of control, there were agreed-upon exceptions to the rules, which Jesus pointed out. Part of Jesus' argument here parallels Luke 13:15-16. If it made sense to practice compassion with one's family or animals on the Sabbath, how could we fail to treat hurting people on the Sabbath? The observers' refusal to answer Jesus' question reveals that their true purpose was to use the law to trap Jesus.

Note the three parts of Jesus' action. He "took him," "healed him," and "let him go." Jesus not only confronted the callous disregard for real suffering, he also treated those he healed with a wholesome compassion that conveyed his power to heal at the spiritual as well as at the physical level. He continues to treat us in the same fashion today.

Getting Personal

When have you practiced compassion in the face of potential conflict?

What might you do to help people even when it may bring opposition?

Routines and rules of thumb get entrenched in our lives because they seem to work—most of the time. But life often conspires to create exceptions that challenge our higher commitment to compassion. Compassion is often measured by our willingness to break our own rules.

HUMILITY

Setting the Scene

After the minor flap over Jesus' healing the sick man, the seating of the guests quickly got under way. Jesus immediately saw a teachable moment as the people jostled for places of honor in the seating arrangement. Luke describes Jesus' next comments as a "parable," though it certainly reads more like direct teaching. The term *parable* is used in the New Testament in a broader sense than the word has come to mean today. Luke 14:8-11 is not included in the usual lists of Jesus' parables. The incisive power of Jesus' statement was that it contrasted sharply with the immediate behavior of those at the gathering. He was saying, "The next time you're in a situation like this, take a different, wiser approach than you have taken today."

Jesus' description contains a touch of humor based on a potentially embarrassing social *faux pas*. The failure to practice humility can easily lead to humiliation. Jesus' use of the proverb, "For all those who exalt themselves will be humbled, and those who humble themselves will be exalted" is echoed by James later in the New Testament and given its deepest application: "Humble yourselves before the Lord, and he will lift you up" (James 4:10, NIV).

We're not told where Jesus sat on this occasion, but it appears he did not participate in the dash for the seats. When we gather in his name today, do we deliberately invite him into the place of honor and give him undivided attention? This is a question we answer both as individuals and congregations every time we gather for worship.

Getting Personal

What situations can you think of in the near future that would allow you to take a humble position?

How do you differentiate between true and false humility?

The idea of Jesus occupying a seat to one side, inconspicuous in a worship service, ought to cause us to think again about our awareness of his presence in worship. It is quite possible that we are more attuned to what we are doing or feeling than to the one we claim to be worshiping.

READING THE WORD

❋ *Luke 14:7-11, NIV*

When he noticed how the guests picked the places of honor at the table, he told them this parable: 8"When someone invites you to a wedding feast, do not take the place of honor, for a person more distinguished than you may have been invited. 9If so, the host who invited both of you will come and say to you, 'Give this person your seat.' Then, humiliated, you will have to take the least important place. 10But when you are invited, take the lowest place, so that when your host comes, he will say to you, 'Friend, move up to a better place.' Then you will be honored in the presence of all the other guests. 11For all those who exalt themselves will be humbled, and those who humble themselves will be exalted."

TALKING TO GOD

Make the subtle distinction between focusing on the actions or forms of your worship and focusing on Christ himself. Ask the Lord to show you his glory and goodness, which will assure your own humility in his presence. Give him your honor.

READING THE WORD

❊ *Luke 14:12-14, NKJV*
Then He also said to him who invited Him, "When you give a dinner or a supper, do not ask your friends, your brothers, your relatives, nor rich neighbors, lest they also invite you back, and you be repaid. 13But when you give a feast, invite the poor, the maimed, the lame, the blind. 14And you will be blessed, because they cannot repay you; for you shall be repaid at the resurrection of the just."

TALKING TO GOD

Allow God to reshape your ideas about what hospitality really is. Thank him for his ultimate hospitality—adoption into his family!—which offered you protection you can never repay. Ask him to develop a family resemblance in you as you practice similar generosity toward others.

JUST HOSPITALITY

Setting the Scene

Much that passes for hospitality is actually an entertainment exchange. We invite friends over, and they return the favor by remembering us the next time they throw a party. With the exception of the sick man who was present early in the affair, it would appear this was a gathering of peers—people in all likelihood capable of reciprocating the meal they were enjoying.

Jesus' counsel makes it clear there were no poor, maimed, lame, or blind at the party. Otherwise, there would have been no need for his comment. While those at the event were presuming to judge Jesus for healing on the Sabbath, he pointed out that they weren't even being hospitable on the day of rest.

The point wasn't to condone an attitude of superiority or even to avoid entertaining friends. Jesus was pointing out the difference between hospitality and mutual entertainment. The latter kind of neighborliness has its place and benefits, but they are restricted to this life's experiences. Entertainment may enrich our lives but rarely stretches us in ways that matter for eternity.

Hospitality, however, is the offer of food, lodging, and protection without expectation of repayment. Hospitality combines practical assistance with generosity. God approves the practice of hospitality because it mirrors his constant treatment of us, supplying in every way what we cannot possibly repay. God has demonstrated hospitality ultimately by offering his Kingdom to all, and even though none of us deserve that privilege nor can we earn it, only those who realize their spiritual poverty truly accept God's hospitality.

The rewards for hospitality are promised by Jesus "at the resurrection of the just," indicating God's plan to express special favor to those who have obeyed him. God accounts for our efforts of hospitality "on his tab," which he will settle.

Getting Personal

When was the last time you practiced hospitality by Jesus' definition?

What do you find most challenging about obeying Jesus' command?

Genuine hospitality flows from someone who is confident in God's plan to settle all accounts at the resurrection of the just—who live by faith.

THE GREAT BANQUET

Setting the Scene

Apparently, one guest who overheard Jesus felt compelled to participate in the conversation. The man's response literally means "Blessed is the one who will eat bread in the kingdom of God." He picked up on two aspects of Jesus' previous words: "feast" and "kingdom of God," and combined them without mentioning the crucial point of immediate obedience to the rule of hospitality Jesus was teaching. But the statement was profoundly true. So rather than correct the man, Jesus responded with a parable that describes just how one might come to experience this blessing of eating at the great feast in the Kingdom of God.

This man, probably a Pharisee, shared an underlying view with Jesus about the reality of the Resurrection. But he was assuming that he and his Pharisee friends would certainly be counted among the righteous (Luke 14:14). The profound and volatile disagreement between Jesus and the Pharisees was *not* over the Resurrection and eternal life; it was over what made someone eligible for that privilege. Just as people today sometimes equate membership in a certain church with citizenship in the Kingdom of God, so the Pharisees assumed their ancestry and familiarity with God's law automatically gave them standing with God. Jesus showed that this was not the case.

Jesus will end his parable with a devastating reference back to the man's statement about those blessed to eat bread in the Kingdom of God: "I tell you, not one of those who were invited will get a taste of my banquet" (14:24, NIV).

Getting Personal

How often do you daydream about heaven? When you think about living in God's presence, what kinds of images pass through your mind?

How confident are you that you will experience the blessing of sharing bread with Christ in God's Kingdom?

One theme in the Gospel of Luke is the reversal of assumed outcomes. Jesus expressed it when he said, "For all those who exalt themselves will be humbled, and those who humble themselves will be exalted" (14:11, NIV). Even humility is not a way to earn heaven; humility simply rejects self-exaltation long enough to receive heaven's blessings as a gift.

READING THE WORD

❊ *Luke 14:15-17, NIV*
When one of those at the table with him heard this, he said to Jesus, "Blessed is the one who will eat at the feast in the kingdom of God." [16]Jesus replied: "A certain man was preparing a great banquet and invited many guests. [17]At the time of the banquet he sent his servant to tell those who had been invited, 'Come, for everything is now ready.'"

TALKING TO GOD

Your invitation to the table in heaven comes by God's grace, not your own merit. Thank him again for his loving goodness that reaches out to you continually with generosity. Ask God to give you glimpses of what it might be like to live eternally in his presence.

OPEN INVITATION

READING THE WORD

✤ *Luke 14:18-24, NKJV*

But they all with one accord began to make excuses. The first said to him, "I have bought a piece of ground, and I must go and see it. I ask you to have me excused." 19And another said, "I have bought five yoke of oxen, and I am going to test them. I ask you to have me excused." 20Still another said, "I have married a wife, and therefore I cannot come." 21So that servant came and reported these things to his master. Then the master of the house, being angry, said to his servant, "Go out quickly into the streets and lanes of the city, and bring in here the poor and the maimed and the lame and the blind." 22And the servant said, "Master, it is done as you commanded, and still there is room." 23Then the master said to the servant, "Go out into the highways and hedges, and compel them to come in, that my house may be filled. 24For I say to you that none of those men who were invited shall taste my supper."

TALKING TO GOD

It's important to be a good steward of your possessions and your relationships, but be sure to bring them all before the Lord, asking him to help you undertake these joyful responsibilities as part of your relationship with him. Affirm your desire to keep him as the informing center of all your decisions and activity.

Setting the Scene

Luke's account of the banquet at the Pharisee's home ends with Jesus' parable of the great banquet. The parable is based on the protocol for such events in first-century Israel. The location of the banquet was accessible—the guest list was made up of local people. The invitation came in two parts: the initial announcement of the banquet to the invitees and the gathering announcement that preceded the beginning of the feast. When the meal was ready, the servants were dispatched to gather the guests, who had presumably notified the host that they planned to attend.

Submitting an RSVP is not quite the same as actually attending an event. The servants in Jesus' story discovered that all the prospective guests had made other plans. Jesus specifies three categories of excuse: a possession that must be inspected (a field), a possession that must be tested (five yoke of oxen), and a new marriage that required attention. The negative responses of the invitees cheapen the value of the invitation. Jesus was speaking to his own people. Israel's history had been marked by a great privilege and invitation extended by God that generation after generation of Israelites rebuffed.

The neighbors' boycott led to an open invitation in the alleys of town. The "poor and the maimed and the lame and the blind" were welcomed to the banquet. And when there was still room, the host issued an even broader invitation to the "highways and hedges." Those who began the day unaware of the feast ended up as guests, while those who were originally invited never even came. Their excuses indicated their true intent regarding the banquet—they were not interested in coming.

Getting Personal

If you have submitted an RSVP to God regarding his invitation to spend eternity with him, how are you occupying yourself in the time leading up to the opening of the banquet hall?

How are you passing on the invitation you received from God?

Those who treated the invitation lightly found out what it was like not to be invited at all. The point isn't the invitation but what we do with it.

JESUS TALKS ABOUT BEING LOST AND FOUND

Week 27, Day 1

❊ *Matthew 18:12-14; Luke 15:1-32*

As the Pharisees grumbled about his spending time with notorious sinners, Jesus answered with parables about being lost and found. This week, if we listen carefully, we can learn profound lessons about God and his seeking and saving love.

THE PRESENCE

Setting the Scene

Jesus had gained a reputation for being associated with those on the outs with the religious establishment. In fact, he chose a despised tax collector to be one of his disciples: "Later, as Jesus left the town, he saw a tax collector named Levi sitting at his tax collector's booth. 'Follow me and be my disciple,' Jesus said to him. So Levi got up, left everything, and followed him" (Luke 5:27-28, NLT). A bit later, after Jesus attended a dinner party in Levi's home, the Pharisees complained, "Why do you eat and drink with such scum?" (Luke 5:30, NLT).

Because Jewish tax collectors worked for the Roman Empire, often charging more than was required and enriching themselves, they were considered traitors. The other "notorious sinners" mentioned probably were people with questionable lifestyles who also had become outcasts. Yet these people "often came to listen to Jesus teach." Jesus had come to reach people like this—those who needed help and knew it. In that previous encounter with the Pharisees over this issue, Jesus had responded to their question by saying, "Healthy people don't need a doctor—sick people do. I have come to call not those who think they are righteous, but those who know they are sinners and need to repent" (Luke 5:31-32, NLT). The self-righteous Pharisees and other religious leaders thought they had their spiritual act together and didn't need to be forgiven. They also thought they were the ultimate authorities on faith and practice.

Having a meal with a person shows that we identify

READING THE WORD

❊ *Luke 15:1-2, NLT*
Tax collectors and other notorious sinners often came to listen to Jesus teach. ²This made the Pharisees and teachers of religious law complain that he was associating with such sinful people—even eating with them!

TALKING TO GOD

Ask the Lord Jesus to give you the sensitivity and courage to reach out to all kinds of people in his name. Spend some time in quietness before him, listening for his prompting regarding people who might need your attention or the truth you have to offer.

with that person and accept him or her. Thus, because Jesus ate with such "sinful people," he was guilty by association. The Pharisees who were always careful to stay "clean" according to the law would not go near such people, not even to point them to God. In contrast, Jesus intentionally risked defilement by touching lepers, not washing the way the Pharisees prescribed, and reaching out to social and religious outcasts, such as Samaritans and tax collectors.

Getting Personal

When, if ever, have you felt as if you were a religious or social outcast?

How did you sense Jesus coming close to you, meeting your need?

What types of people are considered outcasts in your social and religious circles?

What can you do to be Jesus' presence to those who need him?

Jesus expects those who call him Lord and carry his name ("Christian") to follow his example. This means being present with all types of people, especially those who desperately need the Savior. Jesus came to offer salvation to sinners, to show that God loves them. Despite the hits to his reputation, Jesus loved the unlovable—hanging out with them, seeing their real needs, touching, healing, and forgiving. To bring salvation to people, Jesus lived among them. He was not distant, but close and present. He still is.

THE PERSISTENT

Setting the Scene

Jesus told three parables about loss, two of which appear in today's reading. The first one features a shepherd and his sheep. Typically, each shepherd would count the sheep every night to make sure that all were accounted for. When the shepherd in Jesus' story discovers a sheep is missing, he searches until he finds it, and then joyfully returns with the lost lamb. Each sheep is highly valued to this shepherd.

Jesus' next story features a woman who loses a coin. Palestinian women would often receive ten silver coins as a wedding gift. These coins held monetary and sentimental value, much like a wedding ring; to lose one would be extremely distressing. In Jesus' story, when the woman discovers one of the coins is missing, she lights a lamp and sweeps every part of the dirt-packed floor in hope of finding it. Although the woman still would have nine coins, she continues to look for the tenth. When she finds the missing coin, like the shepherd, she shares her joy with "her friends and neighbors."

In these two stories, the items represent men and women who are "lost"; they do not know God and his salvation. The shepherd and the woman both represent God. Clearly God loves lost people so much that he seeks them and rejoices when they are "found."

Jesus wanted to bring the good news of God's Kingdom to people considered beyond hope. Just as the shepherd and the woman took the initiative to search, so Jesus actively seeks lost souls.

Getting Personal

When did you feel that you were "lost" or far rom God? Looking back, what evidence do you see of God's seeking you?

How should the fact that God doesn't give up on people affect your attitudes and actions toward the lost?

What an amazing promise: The Creator of the universe doesn't give up on people. He compassionately searches for them, freely offering them forgiveness through his Son. God's outreach to sinners went so far as to involve Jesus coming to earth as a human being and taking our sins on himself. "The Son of Man came to seek and save those who are lost" (Luke 19:10, NLT).

READING THE WORD

❋ *Luke 15:3-10, NLT*

So Jesus told them this story: 4"If a man has a hundred sheep and one of them gets lost, what will he do? Won't he leave the ninety-nine others in the wilderness and go to search for the one that is lost until he finds it? 5And when he has found it, he will joyfully carry it home on his shoulders. 6When he arrives, he will call together his friends and neighbors, saying, 'Rejoice with me because I have found my lost sheep.' 7In the same way, there is more joy in heaven over one lost sinner who repents and returns to God than over ninety-nine others who are righteous and haven't strayed away! 8Or suppose a woman has ten silver coins and loses one. Won't she light a lamp and sweep the entire house and search carefully until she finds it? 9And when she finds it, she will call in her friends and neighbors and say, 'Rejoice with me because I have found my lost coin.' 10In the same way, there is joy in the presence of God's angels when even one sinner repents."

TALKING TO GOD

Remember God's great love for you that sought you out and drew you to him. Thank him specifically for the people and circumstances he used to help you learn about the Savior. Thank him that Christ died for us, "while we were still sinners" (Romans 5:8, NLT).

THE PRODIGAL

READING THE WORD

✿ *Luke 15:11-19, NLT*

To illustrate the point further, Jesus told them this story: "A man had two sons. 12The younger son told his father, 'I want my share of your estate now before you die.' So his father agreed to divide his wealth between his sons. 13A few days later this younger son packed all his belongings and moved to a distant land, and there he wasted all his money in wild living. 14About the time his money ran out, a great famine swept over the land, and he began to starve. 15He persuaded a local farmer to hire him, and the man sent him into his fields to feed the pigs. 16The young man became so hungry that even the pods he was feeding the pigs looked good to him. But no one gave him anything. 17When he finally came to his senses, he said to himself, 'At home even the hired servants have food enough to spare, and here I am dying of hunger! 18I will go home to my father and say, "Father, I have sinned against both heaven and you, 19and I am no longer worthy of being called your son. Please take me on as a hired servant."'"

TALKING TO GOD

Our sin made us no longer worthy to be God's children. Thank the Father for Christ's sacrifice that makes it possible to be his dearly loved child (1 John 3:1).

Setting the Scene

In Jesus' third parable of Luke 15, the younger of two sons asked his father for his share of the inheritance. This would have been one-third of the total estate, with the older son receiving two-thirds, a double portion as prescribed by the law (Deuteronomy 21:17). In making this request, the younger son showed disrespect for the father. But the father agreed and gave the younger son his inheritance. That was all he needed to travel to a "distant land."

Soon the young man had "wasted all his money in wild living," just when a famine hit the land. So he "finally came to his senses" and decided to return home. Note the words that he planned to say to his father: "I have sinned against both heaven and you." He wanted to tell his father he was sorry. He wanted to repent of the selfishness that had sent him away and used up all the money his father had set aside for his future. Even if the result meant becoming a hired hand in his own home, he would return there in order to say these things to his father.

Getting Personal

At one time or another, each person has been a "prodigal." In what ways does your story parallel the younger son's?

Where are you in the story right now? What's your next move?

Jesus said that the young man "came to his senses" and admitted he had sinned. What caused you to come to your senses?

In this story, the father gave his younger son the opportunity to make his own mistakes and to suffer the consequences. Jesus didn't say anything about the conversation between father and son as the boy left home; if they had one, the father would have spoken with love and probably through tears as he said goodbye. The story describes the son at home, thinking about leaving; the journey away; the "wild living" in a distant land; the desperation and regret; the return; and the reunion.

THE PATH

Setting the Scene

For the father to see his son "still a long way off," he must have been looking every day, hoping to see the boy returning. The same path the son had traveled away from home, he now used to return. And on that same path the Father *ran*, "filled with love and compassion." Typically in the first century a father would wait until a son showed some sign of respect before addressing him. In Jesus' story, the father threw all social conventions aside and ran, opened his arms, and pulled his son tightly to himself. Then, thrilled in this joyous reunion, the Father interrupted his son's prepared statement to proclaim a celebration.

In the two preceding stories, the seekers actively looked for the sheep and the coin, neither of which could return on their own. In this story, the father watched and waited. He was dealing with a human being with a will, but he was ready to greet his son if he returned.

Getting Personal

When did you realize that your heavenly Father was waiting for you to come to him?

In what ways have you experienced his loving embrace?

How has God's love for you put you on track again and kept you there?

This father's love and compassion picture the love God has always shown to his wayward people. Psalm 103:13 says, "The LORD is like a father to his children, tender and compassionate to those who fear him" (NLT). And he always welcomes his children home.

God gives opportunities to respond, but he doesn't force his children to come to him. Like the father in this story, God waits patiently for them to come to their senses. He wants to welcome sinners back home with open arms. What compassion! What love! What grace!

READING THE WORD

❈ *Luke 15:20-24, NLT*

So he returned home to his father. And while he was still a long way off, his father saw him coming. Filled with love and compassion, he ran to his son, embraced him, and kissed him. 21His son said to him, "Father, I have sinned against both heaven and you, and I am no longer worthy of being called your son." 22But his father said to the servants, "Quick! Bring the finest robe in the house and put it on him. Get a ring for his finger and sandals for his feet. 23And kill the calf we have been fattening. We must celebrate with a feast, 24for this son of mine was dead and has now returned to life. He was lost, but now he is found." So the party began.

TALKING TO GOD

Express your gratitude for the Father's love that never gave up on you and never turns away from you.

THE POUTING

READING THE WORD

✤ *Luke 15:25-30, NLT*

Meanwhile, the older son was in the fields working. When he returned home, he heard music and dancing in the house, 26and he asked one of the servants what was going on. 27"Your brother is back," he was told, "and your father has killed the fattened calf. We are celebrating because of his safe return." 28The older brother was angry and wouldn't go in. His father came out and begged him, 29but he replied, "All these years I've slaved for you and never once refused to do a single thing you told me to. And in all that time you never gave me even one young goat for a feast with my friends. 30Yet when this son of yours comes back after squandering your money on prostitutes, you celebrate by killing the fattened calf!"

TALKING TO GOD

Search your own heart before the Lord and admit to him the times you have been self-righteous and resentful, conveniently forgetting your own sins and judging others. Thank him for his forgiveness and join in the rejoicing for every sinner who comes home.

Setting the Scene

During the joyous reunion of father and son, the older brother was "in the fields working," being responsible and contributing to the well-being of the family. When he returned from his hard work, probably dirty and sweaty, he encountered a grand celebration at the house; so he asked a servant "what was going on."

Upon learning that his reprobate brother had returned and that the party was for *him*, the older son was enraged and refused to join the celebration or even to greet his brother. Jesus contrasted the father's response with the older brother's. The father forgave because he was filled with love. The older son refused to forgive because he was bitter about what he perceived as injustice.

In this story, the older brother represents the "Pharisees and teachers of religious law" of Luke 15:2; the younger brother represents the "tax collectors and other notorious sinners" of 15:1; the father represents God. The religious leaders, ever claiming how hard they "slaved" for God, were attempting to keep myriad rules and regulations. They had the Father's love but had rejected it in favor of hard work and self-denial. So when God eagerly welcomed the sinful, common people into the Kingdom, the religious leaders refused to join the celebration. Notice that in the story, the father loves *both* sons. He welcomes home the penitent, wayward son and pleads with his loyal son to join the party.

Getting Personal

What characteristics of the older brother do you see in yourself (positive and negative)?

When have you felt resentment that a "notorious sinner" or prodigal received lots of attention? How did you deal with those feelings?

What would help you remember that your heavenly Father loves you just as much as any of your brothers and sisters in Christ?

In this story, the older son explained that he had been slaving away for his father and accused his father of "never" acknowledging his loyalty and hard work. Bitterness works that way—we selectively remember and build evidence for our case. Wallowing in self-pity and anger, this son ignored his father's obvious love for him and the wonderful news about his brother. He preferred to pout rather than party.

THE PARTY

Setting the Scene

The father immediately restored the destitute and humbled young man as his son. The calf had been fattened for a special feast—and the time for celebrating had come. The son who had been as good as dead to the father was now alive and found. And immediately, the party began.

Just as the shepherd celebrated upon finding his lost sheep, and the woman upon finding her lost coin, so this father celebrated at finding his lost son. The father wanted his elder son also to rejoice at getting his brother back. This was truly a joyful time in the life of this family.

The language Jesus used in these parables is full of joy and celebration: "There is more joy in heaven over one lost sinner who repents and returns to God than over ninety-nine others who are righteous and haven't strayed away!" and "There is joy in the presence of God's angels when even one sinner repents" (Luke 15:7, 10, NLT).

These stories aren't simply about a sheep being brought back to the safety of the fold, a woman finding her valuable coin, or a reunion between father and son. They are all about lost people being found. No wonder those in heaven rejoice!

Getting Personal

Who celebrated when you were "found" by God?

What will help you feel the urgency of sharing the good news about Jesus with others?

What can you do to join in the heavenly celebration when someone comes to Christ?

Often the people who are most grateful for their salvation are those who have lived far from God and have sinned openly. They know that they've come from a "distant land" and are now home. Many believers are like the older brother and think they haven't been so bad compared to some. Yet a sinner who repents and turns to Christ is brought from death to life (see Ephesians 2:5). This is why we celebrate.

READING THE WORD

❂ *Luke 15:31-32, NLT*
His father said to him, "Look, dear son, you have always stayed by me, and everything I have is yours. 32We had to celebrate this happy day. For your brother was dead and has come back to life! He was lost, but now he is found!"

TALKING TO GOD

Make a quick list of those you love who have also come to believe in Jesus as their Savior. In prayer, celebrate in praise to the Father for his welcoming love that makes you a family.

JESUS RAISES LAZARUS

❊ *John 11:1-57*

Chapter 11 of the Gospel of John brings us to the threshold of Jesus' final week before the Cross. At the center of these events is a man named Lazarus who was sick, then died, and then was brought back to life by Jesus. This chapter includes one of the memorable and crucial statements Jesus made about himself: "I am the resurrection and the life. The one who believes in me will live, even though they die; and whoever lives by believing in me will never die. Do you believe this?" (John 11:25-26, NIV). Jesus' question is one each of us must answer.

READING THE WORD

❊ *John 11:1, 3-6, NIV*

Now a man named Lazarus was sick. He was from Bethany, the village of Mary and her sister Martha. . . . ³So the sisters sent word to Jesus, "Lord, the one you love is sick." ⁴When he heard this, Jesus said, "This sickness will not end in death. No, it is for God's glory so that God's Son may be glorified through it." ⁵Now Jesus loved Martha and her sister and Lazarus. ⁶So when he heard that Lazarus was sick, he stayed where he was two more days.

DELIBERATE DELAY

Setting the Scene

John 11 opens with an individual named Lazarus who was sick. We learn Lazarus is from Bethany and that he has two sisters (Mary and Martha). Luke has already introduced Mary and Martha (Luke 10:38-42), creating the impression that Jesus was a frequent guest in their home. Now the sisters send word to Jesus that "the one you love is sick."

Jesus treated family units in ways that allowed them to learn significant spiritual lessons about themselves and about him. He treated them as individuals, but he also spoke into their relationships with one another—most notably with Mary and Martha in handling Martha's complaint that her sister was not playing the part of hostess (Luke 10:38-41). Jesus recognized the needs presented to him, but he also saw underlying needs that were even more important. Even though we might consider keeping someone from dying as the highest priority for action, Jesus clearly made decisions based on his authority even over life and death. This is apparent in his actions related to the sisters' urgent message that their brother was sick.

Jesus declared that the events about to unfold were not about dying but about the glory of God. Since it is likely that Lazarus was already dead by the time the messenger found Jesus, it seems ironic that Jesus could say, "This sickness will not end in death." Lazarus did die, so what was Jesus saying? Jesus rejected the understanding that "death" and "end" were synonymous, even in casual conversation. He knew better. Death for Lazarus would come, but it wouldn't be the end of the story. Jesus would make sure of that.

John heightened the tension for his readers by pointing out that Jesus "loved Martha and her sister and Lazarus," but he remained where he was for "two more days." By mentioning both aspects of Jesus' actions, John shows that Jesus' response did not alter his love for these three siblings. This deliberate delay is directly connected with the purpose of this event: "for God's glory so that God's Son may be glorified through it."

Words related to the Greek expression *doxa* are used for "glory" and "glorified," a term we also use directly in *doxology*—meaning "words of praise or glory to God." Jesus could see that what would happen in the lives of his friends would bring a heightened awareness (glory) to others about God. This incident demonstrates how both delightful and difficult times can point others to God. God's glory can be described as anything that makes God more difficult to ignore. The more we are exposed to the truth, divinity, and power of God's character, the more we find our attention drawn to him; and the more we become aware of God's glory.

Getting Personal

How do you tend to respond when you ask God for help and he seems to delay?

In what ways are you most aware of God's love for you?

We see three values at work in this incident with Lazarus: what God does about our needs in the short term, what God does regarding his plans, and what God does for us in the long term. We tend to expect God to act based on our immediate needs, but he repeatedly teaches us that he has a much larger picture in mind.

TALKING TO GOD

Praise God that his plans and his means are always greater and better than your own. Ask him to help you trust him in confusing circumstances and long periods of waiting. Ask him to show you his glory, even in your derailed expectations.

TIME TO GO

READING THE WORD

✤ *John 11:7-16, NKJV*
Then after this He said to the disciples, "Let us go to Judea again." 8The disciples said to Him, "Rabbi, lately the Jews sought to stone You, and are You going there again?" 9Jesus answered, "Are there not twelve hours in the day? If anyone walks in the day, he does not stumble, because he sees the light of this world. 10But if one walks in the night, he stumbles, because the light is not in him." 11These things He said, and after that He said to them, "Our friend Lazarus sleeps, but I go that I may wake him up." 12Then His disciples said, "Lord, if he sleeps he will get well." 13However, Jesus spoke of his death, but they thought that He was speaking about taking rest in sleep. 14Then Jesus said to them plainly, "Lazarus is dead. 15And I am glad for your sakes that I was not there, that you may believe. Nevertheless let us go to him." 16Then Thomas, who is called the Twin, said to his fellow disciples, "Let us also go, that we may die with Him."

TALKING TO GOD

Thank God that he is more powerful, more wonderful than you are able to imagine. Ask him to give you faith to follow where he leads, no matter how uncertain the future may seem.

Setting the Scene

As far as the disciples were concerned, Jesus' announcement that he wanted to return to Judea came as an unwelcome development. They raised the specter of a hostile welcome for Jesus in that territory.

Jesus responded by telling them his main purpose was to "wake up" Lazarus. But he also included a somewhat cryptic statement about the hours of the day and the difference between walking by light or in darkness. Jesus was using the observation about natural light to point to the significance of supernatural light and the specific time frame by which his "day" was unfolding on earth. As long as the disciples were walking in the light of Christ, they would not stumble like those in the world who had no real light.

When the disciples realized Jesus was finally answering the call to help Lazarus, they were puzzled by what they thought was Jesus' unnecessary visit to a friend recovering from an illness. So Jesus clarified by telling them his friend was dead and that there would be a benefit for them because of Jesus' absence during Lazarus's sickness and death. His purpose was that they "may believe." Jesus intended to bring his friend back to life, and part of his purpose was to bolster the faith of the disciples.

When Jesus then said, "Let us go to him," Thomas voiced what must have been the general thought among the disciples: "Let us also go, that we may die with Him." The mixed faith revealed by Thomas was precisely the reason Lazarus was raised.

Getting Personal

In what ways might following Christ open you up to new areas and therefore new fears?

What incidents in your life with Christ have particularly increased your faith?

God knows our faith is always a work in progress. We believe, and yet we struggle with unbelief. Even though Thomas couldn't imagine a good outcome, he was still willing to go. We often won't take even that first important step of faith to follow Jesus wherever he leads.

THE RESURRECTION AND THE LIFE

Setting the Scene

The math behind these events isn't difficult: one day for the messenger to find Jesus (during which Lazarus died), two days of intentional delay, and one more day of travel to Bethany for Jesus and his disciples. Burials in the Middle East were not delayed since conditions led to quick deterioration of a body. Once the body was interred, the grieving went on for days.

Exchanges with people in deep grief are usually awkward. Martha got word Jesus was approaching and felt compelled to share both her frustration and faith. Her greeting is difficult to understand fully. It is possible she hoped God would give Jesus whatever he asked and raise her brother to life, but her later comments don't seem to reflect that expectation. She may have been saying something like, "I know my brother would have been healed if you had been here, and even though he died, I continue to believe in your special relationship with God." In that case, she would have been speaking about her own relationship with Jesus, not what she hoped he might still do for Lazarus.

Jesus said to Martha, "I am the resurrection and the life," declaring himself Lord over both life and death. Any believer in Jesus will live—even those who experience physical death. Life in Jesus is eternal, and not even death can prevent it!

Jesus' gentle confrontation, "Do you believe this?" echoes across the generations to the twenty-first century. Martha's simple, direct response was unconditional faith. She didn't make her brother's situation a factor in her allegiance to Jesus.

Getting Personal

How do you apply Jesus' claim of resurrection and life to your own thoughts about death?

What would have been the outcome of this story if Martha's last statement had been, "I will believe if you raise my brother back to life"?

Martha's declaration to Jesus—"You are the Messiah, the Son of God"—puts Jesus forever beyond the company of wise men and profound teachers. The Son of God can demand our ultimate response because he is the only one worthy of our trust.

READING THE WORD

✤ *John 11:17-27, NIV*

On his arrival, Jesus found that Lazarus had already been in the tomb for four days. [18]Now Bethany was less than two miles from Jerusalem, [19]and many Jews had come to Martha and Mary to comfort them in the loss of their brother. [20]When Martha heard that Jesus was coming, she went out to meet him, but Mary stayed at home. [21]"Lord," Martha said to Jesus, "if you had been here, my brother would not have died. [22]But I know that even now God will give you whatever you ask." [23]Jesus said to her, "Your brother will rise again." [24]Martha answered, "I know he will rise again in the resurrection at the last day." [25]Jesus said to her, "I am the resurrection and the life. The one who believes in me will live, even though they die; [26]and whoever lives by believing in me will never die. Do you believe this?" [27]"Yes, Lord," she replied, "I believe that you are the Messiah, the Son of God, who is to come into the world."

TALKING TO GOD

Echo Martha's simple declaration in your own prayer time: "You are the Messiah, the Son of God." Thank God that every prophetic word of Scripture was true: The promised Messiah did come into the world to be your Savior.

THE OTHER SISTER

READING THE WORD

✤ *John 11:28-37, NIV*

After she had said this, she went back and called her sister Mary aside. "The Teacher is here," she said, "and is asking for you." 29When Mary heard this, she got up quickly and went to him. 30Now Jesus had not yet entered the village, but was still at the place where Martha had met him. 31When the Jews who had been with Mary in the house, comforting her, noticed how quickly she got up and went out, they followed her, supposing she was going to the tomb to mourn there. 32When Mary reached the place where Jesus was and saw him, she fell at his feet and said, "Lord, if you had been here, my brother would not have died." 33When Jesus saw her weeping, and the Jews who had come along with her also weeping, he was deeply moved in spirit and troubled. 34"Where have you laid him?" he asked. "Come and see, Lord," they replied. 35Jesus wept. 36Then the Jews said, "See how he loved him!" 37But some of them said, "Could not he who opened the eyes of the blind man have kept this man from dying?"

TALKING TO GOD

Jesus completely understands your emotional responses to him as you pray. Even when words fail you in prayer, he understands your heart. So pray freely and honestly.

Setting the Scene

After her declaration of faith, Martha abruptly returned to her sister, exhibiting the busy character that we see in her elsewhere (Luke 10:38-42). Ever the manager, she informed her sister Mary that Jesus was asking for her, though the account doesn't record Jesus making that request.

The encounter earlier between Martha and Jesus was initiated with Martha's blunt verbal affirmation. Mary's approach was subtly but significantly different. She humbly fell at Jesus' feet before she spoke. The first words uttered by both sisters were identical. But Mary had already acted on her faith, though neither sister expected what was about to happen.

John tells us that seeing Mary and those following her weeping "deeply moved" and "troubled" Jesus. Various explanations have been considered regarding Jesus' tears. Some read the tears as signs of Jesus' care for Lazarus; others questioned Jesus' motive for withholding healing. We are left with the fact of Jesus' tears—signs of humanity and engagement, evidence of emotional vulnerability. We who often cannot explain our own tears are touched by Jesus' demonstration that "we do not have a high priest who is unable to empathize with our weaknesses, but we have one who has been tempted in every way, just as we are—yet he did not sin" (Hebrews 4:15, NIV).

Martha and Mary didn't know what Jesus would do, but they did know Jesus. That was enough.

Getting Personal

Jesus knew what he was going to do (11:11), so why do you think John made a note of his tears in the prelude to a great miracle?

What does it mean to you that Jesus understands your tears—even the ones that go unshed?

Jesus' tears confirm our permission to grieve, as long as we are not "uninformed about those who sleep in death, so that [we] do not grieve like the rest of mankind, who have no hope" (1 Thessalonians 4:13, NIV). Tears don't have to be hopeless. Jesus isn't ashamed to cry with us, even before he intervenes miraculously.

PARTICIPATION

Setting the Scene

Martha couldn't help but be practical—inside that tomb was a mess she didn't want to clean up. And she knew she would probably be the one to have to do it! How often we forget that Jesus' power to intervene isn't sidetracked by complications or "stench." How often does Jesus have to remind us, "Did I not say to you that if you would believe you would see the glory of God?"

Once the stone was rolled away, Jesus prayed aloud in the same intimate format he taught his disciples, addressing God as Father (see Matthew 6:9-13). He meant his prayer to be overheard, referring to his listeners as he thanked God for having "heard Me," indicating the Father's agreement and blessing over what Jesus was about to do. Then he called to Lazarus by name, not only confirming what he had previously declared, "Very truly I tell you, a time is coming and has now come when the dead will hear the voice of the Son of God and those who hear will live" (John 5:25, NIV), but also narrowing his summons to a specific person. Who knows how many people might have sprung to life if Jesus had simply commanded, "Come out!"

Lazarus's raised and restored body appeared in the cave entrance, awkwardly moving while still bound by cloth graveclothes.

Getting Personal

Since you have been brought into eternal life in Christ, what former habits or troubles has Christ removed, like graveclothes, from around your life?

When were you last surprised to see the glory of God?

The belief that leads to seeing the glory of God often manifests itself in a willingness to remove obstacles, like stones and wrappings. These are preliminaries and follow-ups to the real miracles, but they allow us to see better what we might not otherwise see at all— God's glory.

READING THE WORD

❈ *John 11:38-44, NKJV*
Then Jesus, again groaning in Himself, came to the tomb. It was a cave, and a stone lay against it. 39Jesus said, "Take away the stone." Martha, the sister of him who was dead, said to Him, "Lord, by this time there is a stench, for he has been dead four days." 40Jesus said to her, "Did I not say to you that if you would believe you would see the glory of God?" 41Then they took away the stone from the place where the dead man was lying. And Jesus lifted up His eyes and said, "Father, I thank You that You have heard Me. 42And I know that You always hear Me, but because of the people who are standing by I said this, that they may believe that You sent Me." 43Now when He had said these things, He cried with a loud voice, "Lazarus, come forth!" 44And he who had died came out bound hand and foot with graveclothes, and his face was wrapped with a cloth. Jesus said to them, "Loose him, and let him go."

TALKING TO GOD

No matter how old you were when you came to Christ, you can imagine how your life might have been without his love and grace. Thank God for giving you abundant, eternal life. Thank him for being "the resurrection and the life."

THE GRANDER SCHEME

Therefore many of the Jews who had come to visit Mary, and had seen what Jesus did, believed in him. 46But some of them went to the Pharisees and told them what Jesus had done. 47Then the chief priests and the Pharisees called a meeting of the Sanhedrin. "What are we accomplishing?" they asked. "Here is this man performing many signs. 48If we let him go on like this, everyone will believe in him, and then the Romans will come and take away both our temple and our nation." 49Then one of them, named Caiaphas, who was high priest that year, spoke up, "You know nothing at all! 50You do not realize that it is better for you that one man die for the people than that the whole nation perish." 51He did not say this on his own, but as high priest that year he prophesied that Jesus would die for the Jewish nation, 52and not only for that nation but also for the scattered children of God, to bring them together and make them one. 53So from that day on they plotted to take his life.

TALKING TO GOD

Ask God to teach you again today the harmony between living in obedience to him and desiring to see his will be done. Pray that you will always stay open to doing his will.

Setting the Scene

After Lazarus's resurrection, "many . . . believed in" Jesus, but certainly not all. Some saw and reported the event as an action worthy of suspicion and perhaps condemnation.

As John describes it, the problem for those who rejected Jesus wasn't that they disbelieved the miracles; the problem was that their view of reality included fears, desires, and obstacles they assumed were somehow greater than someone's ability to work miracles. The perspective of the negative conclusion in 11:47-48 states the issue exactly and gets the conclusion exactly wrong: "Then the chief priests and the Pharisees called a meeting of the Sanhedrin. 'What are we accomplishing?' they asked. 'Here is this man performing many signs. If we let him go on like this, everyone will believe in him, and then the Romans will come and take away both our temple and our nation'" (NIV). They feared for their "temple" (their place of distinction) and their "nation."

John provides us with Caiaphas's pronouncement and then highlights the stunning hidden prophecy it stated. The high priest was acting as a practical power broker, equating one man's life with beneficial collateral damage. He did not realize he was verbalizing the very decision God had made regarding the fate of humanity. The prophetic irony in Caiaphas's statement makes the case for substitutionary sacrifice—it really was better in God's grander scheme that Jesus' solitary, innocent, willing death would spare Israel and God's scattered children from destruction and unite them as one. We were included in the high priest's prophecy. The evil plot against Jesus turned out to accomplish part of God's plan for our salvation.

Getting Personal

What practices have you found most beneficial in staying awake and alert to the wonders of a God-centered life?

How does talking about Jesus with others affect your sense of intimacy with him?

God's grander scheme is neither advanced by our deliberate efforts nor delayed by our shortsighted plans. His will is ultimately accomplished. But the benefits we experience are more immediate and positive when we are seeking to cooperate fully with what God wants to do.

JESUS SPEAKS TO THE RICH YOUNG MAN

Week 29, Day 1

❋ *Matthew 19:16-30; Mark 10:17-31; Luke 18:18-30*

Jesus and his disciples were traveling toward Jerusalem when they encountered a young man on a mission. His question, Jesus' answer, and the disciples' reactions provide provocative challenges for us this week.

THE RIGHT WORDS

Setting the Scene

Matthew describes the man who ran up to Jesus as "young" (19:22, NLT), and Luke says he was a "religious leader" (18:18, NLT). We know that this young man was both wealthy (Mark 10:22) and of prominent social standing. Considering the man's position, the fact that he knelt down reveals his respect for Jesus. Then he addressed Jesus as "good Teacher," not the more common "rabbi." Both of these actions indicate that the young man was sincere with his inquiry, unlike many of the other religious leaders who had interviewed Jesus. And the man's question concerned eternal life, the most important issue for anyone.

Instead of responding directly to the question asked, Jesus turned the conversation to God by pointing out that "only God is truly good." Jesus wanted the man to take his attention off himself and Jesus, whom he probably thought was merely a "good teacher," and instead to think about God's absolute goodness. If the young man truly did this, he would conclude that he could do nothing to obtain eternal life.

Jesus was also saying, "Do you really know the one to whom you're talking?" In effect the young man confirmed Jesus' deity. Probably without realizing what he was saying, the man was calling Jesus "God" because only God is truly good.

The man's question contains a contradiction in his use of the two verbs "do" and "inherit." An inheritance comes to members of a family (and, in our culture, to

READING THE WORD

❋ *Mark 10:17-18, NLT*
As Jesus was starting out on his way to Jerusalem, a man came running up to him, knelt down, and asked, "Good Teacher, what must I do to inherit eternal life?" [18]"Why do you call me good?" Jesus asked. "Only God is truly good."

TALKING TO GOD

In our world where so much seems to depend on our actions and our control, it is hard for us to accept that we can do nothing to earn salvation or God's favor. But praise God today for this truth! Your salvation is purchased fully by Jesus, and God has complete control of your days.

others named in a will). A person doesn't normally "do" anything in order to inherit. Yet most people, this man included, expect that certain good works or a compilation of them must be necessary in order to become right with God and live forever. But salvation is by grace alone, which Jesus would explain a bit later in the story.

Getting Personal

What makes you believe that Jesus is more than just a good religious teacher, that he is fully God?

Knowing that Jesus is God, what claims of his on your life must you take more seriously?

This rich and young religious leader wanted to be sure he would live forever after he died, so he asked what he should do, *viewing eternal life as something that one achieves. Although this man had been a meticulous commandment-keeper (Mark 10:20), he still had concerns about his eternal destiny and thought Jesus could help him. He was correct about Jesus (more than he knew), and he came with the right attitude. We don't know the young man's heart; his question seems to be sincere. But he may have wanted to add Jesus to his résumé or to make sure he had considered all his options. Instead, Jesus wants total allegiance, total commitment, from all of us; he's not an add-on. And as we'll soon see, this young man was unable to accept that truth as Jesus answered his question.*

THE TEST

Setting the Scene

These six commandments Jesus mentioned focus on behavior, and this man's obedience could have been easily verified. The first four of the Ten Commandments, especially number one ("You must not have any other god but me" [Exodus 20:3, NLT]) all have more to do with *being* than doing and probably would have elicited a different response from the young man. But how he was keeping the first commandment was the crucial question. What was most important to this young man?

Upon hearing Jesus' list, the young man replied that he had kept them all since youth. We don't know whether he answered with pride or confusion, but Jesus lovingly explained, "There is still one thing you haven't done," and told him, "Go and sell all your possessions and give the money to the poor, and you will have treasure in heaven. Then come, follow me." Immediately Jesus exposed the problem: Money and possessions were most important to this young man; they occupied God's rightful place in his life.

This young man's wealth gave him power and prestige. In telling him to sell everything he owned, Jesus was touching the very basis of the young man's security and identity. This man did not understand that he would be even more secure if he followed Jesus than he was with all his wealth. He could not meet the one requirement Jesus gave—to turn his whole heart and life over to God.

Only by putting his treasure in heaven and following Jesus could the man be assured of his eternal destiny. But he failed the test and "went away sad."

Getting Personal

Usually our personal idols are good pursuits or desires that we elevate. What, if anything, competes for God's place in your life?

Why is idol removal so difficult? What can you do daily to make God the center of your life?

The human heart is an idol factory. We continually elevate or invent a wide variety of God-substitutes: career, relationship, status, power, prized possession, financial security, and so on. Even after a person embraces Christ as Savior and Lord, the factory remains in business. But God demands total allegiance. We must continually remove those idols—repenting and believing.

READING THE WORD

✸ *Mark 10:19-22, NLT*

"But to answer your question, you know the commandments: 'You must not murder. You must not commit adultery. You must not steal. You must not testify falsely. You must not cheat anyone. Honor your father and mother.'" 20"Teacher," the man replied, "I've obeyed all these commandments since I was young." 21Looking at the man, Jesus felt genuine love for him. "There is still one thing you haven't done," he told him. "Go and sell all your possessions and give the money to the poor, and you will have treasure in heaven. Then come, follow me." 22At this the man's face fell, and he went away sad, for he had many possessions.

TALKING TO GOD

Confess to the Lord your struggles to keep him central and first in your priorities. Name the issues that compete for your loyalty and attention. Ask the Lord to show you how you should handle these "other gods" in order to keep your affections in an order that pleases him.

✤ *Mark 10:21, NLT*
Looking at the man, Jesus felt genuine love for him. "There is still one thing you haven't done," he told him. "Go and sell all your possessions and give the money to the poor, and you will have treasure in heaven. Then come, follow me."

TALKING TO GOD

Thank the Lord that he loves your friends and acquaintances just as much as he loves you. Ask him to fill you with his love for these people, so that you can live his love for them, in your words and in your actions.

THE LOOK

Setting the Scene

Mark reports with a simple statement that when Jesus looked at the young man he "felt genuine love for him." We've seen Jesus "looking" at people this way several times: the widow at Nain whose only son had died (Luke 7:13), the suffering woman who touched the fringe of his robe (Matthew 9:22), the crowd of five thousand–plus that had followed him (Mark 6:34), the lame man at the pool of Bethesda (John 5:6), and more. Jesus had great compassion and love for the young man kneeling before him.

We have already read facts about the man that could have put a barrier between him and Jesus. He was young and wealthy (Matthew 19:22), a combination that can cause a person to be self-assured and self-absorbed. He was also a "religious leader" (Luke 18:18), and Jesus had experienced mostly opposition from the Pharisees and other Jewish religious leaders. Yet Jesus looked past those outward appearances and saw a needy person who sincerely wanted an answer to life's most important question. So Jesus treated the young man with respect and answered him truthfully.

Getting Personal

What example(s) can you remember of someone who heard the gospel from an unlikely source?

When have you avoided talking to someone about your faith because of a potential communication gap?

Think about someone in your circle of acquaintances you've assumed wouldn't be interested in hearing about Christ. What can you do to see that person the way Jesus does?

Jesus showed genuine love for this man, even though he knew the man might not follow him. And Jesus loved the man enough to give him the hard truth about what he needed to do. As we strive to be more like Christ, we can see people the way he sees them. Too often our assumptions keep us from reaching out to others and cause us to write off people who are different from us. Jesus sees them with compassion. We can too.

THE SHOCK

Setting the Scene

Jesus loved the young man enough to tell him the truth: He had to remove the wealth idol. Mark reports, "At this the man's face fell, and he went away sad, for he had many possessions" (10:22, NLT). Jesus turned to the Twelve and explained that for a rich person, getting into heaven was virtually impossible. And to make sure they understood, he used the extreme example of a camel trying to navigate a needle's eye.

The disciples were "amazed" and "astounded." Like most Jews, they regarded wealth as a sign of God's blessing. This rich young man may have seemed like perfect Kingdom material, so they must have wondered, *What kind of Kingdom is this if those most blessed have difficulty entering? If the rich have a hard time, we will never make it.* So they exclaimed, "Then who in the world can be saved?"

The answer is *no one*—and *everyone.* That is, no person can be forgiven, made right with God, and have eternal life on his or her own. Good works cannot earn God's approval. Status and achievement cannot claim the Kingdom. Riches cannot buy salvation. It's all God's grace. The first point of the gospel message is that all people are totally, absolutely lost in their sins and without hope . . . but for God's mercy. Jesus was teaching the disciples this lesson. But the Kingdom is open to *all* who put their trust in Christ.

Getting Personal

When are you most susceptible to the allure of wealth?

When have money and possessions, or the lack of them, hindered your relationship with God?

What does Jesus' statement to the rich young man to give up all his money and possessions mean to you?

Money is an insidious idol. We don't have to be rich to be pulled in. Because money allows us a degree of comfort and pleasure, we can be trapped into thinking, If I had just a little bit more . . . But money can never fill the emptiness in our lives, bring joy, or buy eternal life. "A little bit more" is never enough.

READING THE WORD

❋ *Mark 10:23-26, NLT*
Jesus looked around and said to his disciples, "How hard it is for the rich to enter the Kingdom of God!" 24This amazed them. But Jesus said again, "Dear children, it is very hard to enter the Kingdom of God. 25In fact, it is easier for a camel to go through the eye of a needle than for a rich person to enter the Kingdom of God!" 26The disciples were astounded. "Then who in the world can be saved?" they asked.

TALKING TO GOD

Before the Lord, admit the tension between contentment and desire for more, and the difficulty of coping with present financial needs or pressures even while you try to trust God with this area of your life. Affirm the truth that everything you have comes from God and belongs to him.

TALKING TO GOD

Rejoice in your prayer time today in the freedom of knowing you don't have to earn or deserve God's love. Let his grace overwhelm you with gratitude, joy, and praise.

THE IMPOSSIBLE

Setting the Scene

The answer to the question, "Who in the world can be saved?" (Mark 10:26, NLT), turns out to be quite simple. From a human point of view, salvation is not possible for *anyone*. No one can be saved by his or her wealth (or lack of it) or achievements or talents or good deeds: "Humanly speaking, it is impossible." But here's the good news: "Everything is possible with God." Salvation cannot be earned; it is a gift from God, available to people regardless of financial portfolio, social status, ethical track record, moral reputation, race, religion, political affiliation, nationality, or other identifying characteristics. *No one* is saved on merit; but *all* are saved who humbly repent and follow Jesus—by grace through faith. As Paul wrote, "God saved you by his grace when you believed. And you can't take credit for this; it is a gift from God. Salvation is not a reward for the good things we have done, so none of us can boast about it" (Ephesians 2:8-9, NLT).

Getting Personal

When did you realize that you were a sinner and could not save yourself?

How do you know that you have eternal life?

How do you respond when you consider all that God has done for you through Christ?

Two basic attitudes can hinder people from following Christ. Some people might think they are good enough and somehow deserve God's forgiveness and rewards. Their pride keeps them from repenting and following. Others, at the opposite end of the spectrum, might think that they have nothing to offer God or that they are too bad, what they have done is too great to be forgiven. The truth is that God can and does save all kinds of people. The Bible records a diverse and unlikely collection of individuals God chose to serve him: Abraham, Jacob, Moses, Rahab, Ruth, David, Josiah, Esther, Amos, Peter, Mary Magdalene, Zacchaeus, Paul, Luke, and Lydia—to name a few. None of them deserved anything from God. God still uses unlikely people to change the world—people like you.

THE TRADE

Setting the Scene

In contrasting the disciples with the young man and the interaction he had just observed, Peter exclaimed that they had "given up everything" to follow Jesus. Jesus reminded Peter and the others that following him has its benefits as well as its sacrifices. Yes, they had to leave "everything" to follow him, but they would be paid back "now" (the time period between Jesus' first and second comings) as well as "in the world to come" (after Jesus' second coming). Anyone who gave up something valuable for Jesus' sake would be repaid a hundred times over, although not necessarily in the same form. Along with the rewards, however, would come "persecution."

This was the answer to the rich young man's question about how to obtain eternal life (Mark 10:17). Jesus explained that by submitting to his authority and rule, making him top priority over all else and giving up anything that hinders following him, each person can have "eternal life." In the future, the values of this world will be reversed. Those who have much and seem important now will be "least important then" and vice versa. Jesus may have been speaking to the disciples' mixed motives. Some were hoping for victory over the Romans; some wanted status in God's Kingdom. Yet rewards in heaven are not given on the basis of merit or other earthly standards. All that matters in heaven is a person's commitment to Christ.

Getting Personal

What have you given up to follow Christ?

In what ways have you experienced persecution because of your faith?

How does Jesus' promise to the disciples (Mark 10:29-31) encourage you? Motivate you?

Persecution comes in many forms: social ostracism, public ridicule, financial deprivation, physical abuse, loss of employment, and even rejection by family and friends. In some parts of the world, this persecution is severe, including torture and death. During such times, many wonder if what they gave up to follow Christ was worth it. Jesus answers with a resounding "Yes!" He promises his presence—to be with us now during our difficult times—and a glorious eternity after this life ends.

READING THE WORD

✤ *Mark 10:28-31, NLT*
Then Peter began to speak up. "We've given up everything to follow you," he said. ²⁹"Yes," Jesus replied, "and I assure you that everyone who has given up house or brothers or sisters or mother or father or children or property, for my sake and for the Good News, ³⁰will receive now in return a hundred times as many houses, brothers, sisters, mothers, children, and property— along with persecution. And in the world to come that person will have eternal life. ³¹But many who are the greatest now will be least important then, and those who seem least important now will be the greatest then."

TALKING TO GOD

Pray today about any discomfort you may be experiencing because of the gospel. Then take time to pray for persecuted brothers and sisters in great pain and danger around the world because of the cause of Christ.

❋ *Matthew 20:1-16*

As the parables of Jesus go, the one we will be considering this week is among the longest. Only Jesus' parable of the nobleman's servants (Luke 19:11-27) equals this one in length. Interestingly, both are about the experience of candidates for citizenship in the Kingdom of God. At first reading, this story may appear to focus on rewards, but we will discover that the ultimate lesson from this story has to do with admission to the Kingdom.

READING THE WORD

❋ *Matthew 20:1, NIV*
For the kingdom of heaven is like a landowner who went out early in the morning to hire workers for his vineyard.

GOING ON TO JERUSALEM

Setting the Scene

Matthew 20 opens without a transition from the previous chapter, when Jesus was responding to Peter's question about who can get into the Kingdom of God. The use of "for" (*gar* in Greek) indicates an ongoing thought. Chapter 19 ends with Jesus' statement, "But many who are first will be last, and many who are last will be first" (Matthew 19:30, NIV). He repeats the statement, almost verbatim, after the parable about the vineyard workers: "So the last will be first, and the first will be last" (Matthew 20:16, NIV).

In this parable, Jesus' subject is the "kingdom of heaven," and the word *like* sets up the comparison. The Kingdom is represented by the landowner; believers are compared with workers hired at various times during the day; the vineyard is the world; the harvest is the work God wants done between belief and eventual reward; and the wages represent what believers receive "at the renewal of all things, when the Son of Man sits on his glorious throne" (Matthew 19:28, NIV). The foreman plays a representative role as the deliverer of the wages according to the landowner's instructions.

As the story unfolds, group after group of workers is hired for the harvest although the available time for work continually becomes shorter. The time frame of the parable has the action occurring during a single day, but the day can as easily represent a lifetime or an age. Peter had just inquired about the Kingdom reward of the disciples who have given up "everything" (Matthew 19:27, NIV) to follow Jesus. They were among the first and they gave up a lot. Jesus indicated that the disciples will have responsibilities in the Kingdom but that everyone who has left behind anything will eventually receive a hundred-fold reward as well as eternal life. In other words, all the believers will receive much more than they deserve, apart from how they, in their human understanding, might be measuring or valuing sacrifices made for the Kingdom.

Jesus' parable expands on his teaching that "many who are first will be last, and many who are last will be first" (Matthew 19:30, NIV). The first hired in the parable are the last paid. The landowner/employer had agreed to pay a specified amount to the first group hired but hired the rest without wage negotiations. In the economy of the parable, the first workers received every cent they were promised. The potential fairness argument arises from the fact that the landowner paid everyone the same amount, which made the early workers assume they should receive more.

What God has given us in Christ is far beyond anything we have done to deserve it. This parable challenges how ready we are to see others be given that same priceless privilege entirely apart from anything they have done to deserve it. If we desire more, have we really understood how privileged we are to receive anything at all?

Getting Personal

As you serve the Lord, when do you find yourself slipping into a feeling of smug satisfaction, as if you are really earning your place in the Kingdom after all?

What really was the price paid for your gift of eternal life?

In what ways would you characterize your life right now as an example of work in the vineyard?

While Jesus' illustration made use of the work patterns in the ancient world, he was, in reality, describing God's grace. Any interpretation of this parable that leads to the idea of earning something regarding eternal life woefully misses the point. Eternal life is the more-than-adequate and undeserved gift apart from the time and effort one has devoted to the Kingdom in this life.

TALKING TO GOD

Ask the Lord to help you get rid of the persistent human tendency to take some credit for what he has graciously done for you. Ask him to help you be diligent out of gratitude and desire to please him because you love him.

THE ORIGINAL CREW

✸ *Matthew 20:1-2, NKJV*
For the kingdom of heaven is like a landowner who went out early in the morning to hire laborers for his vineyard. ²Now when he had agreed with the laborers for a denarius a day, he sent them into his vineyard.

TALKING TO GOD

Spend some time today valuing the gift of eternal life by praising God for his great love, for his sacrifice, for his perfect plan. Thank him for bringing you into his vineyard, where the landowner provides what his workers can never earn.

Setting the Scene

There are two vineyard parables in Matthew's Gospel. Matthew, Mark, and Luke all record the parable of the unworthy tenants, which Jesus told to the religious leaders in Jerusalem during his final week, but only Matthew includes this parable of the payment to the workers.

The setting and details would have been immediately familiar to Jesus' listeners. In a typical Middle Eastern agricultural village surrounded by fields, orchards, and vineyards, the laborers would gather in the marketplace or at the gate where landowners would come to hire those needed for the day. This landowner arrived at the break of day and found the early risers—those motivated or driven to work. They agreed with the landowner on a standard one-day contract for work.

The potential laborers were looking for work, but it was the landowner who found them. Their diligence in showing up at the "employment office" didn't guarantee them a job. It put them in the right place, but without the landowner and his offer, their efforts would have been in vain. If the landowner is the Lord of the Kingdom of Heaven and the hired men are those who are saved, then this first group of workers could be called the early believers. These are the "lifers" who meet God shortly after they realize their need for him and live out their time on earth in God's service.

Getting Personal

How long have you been a believer? Were you brought in "early" or "later"?

How has your appreciation of the gift of eternal life changed over time as you've served the Lord?

It's easy to focus on the privilege of being first rather than taking seriously the responsibility that comes with that privilege. One of the spiritual challenges for "lifers" is what might be called "pride of longevity." However, this parable makes it clear that length of service has nothing to do with the value of the gift.

ENLISTING BACKUP

Setting the Scene

There were twelve hours in the Middle Eastern workday, roughly measured from sunup to sundown, or about six in the morning to six in the evening. Here the landowner in the parable hired four other shifts of workers throughout the day, in addition to those he had hired early in the morning. In each case, quitting time remained the same.

When the landowner hired the original crew, he negotiated a day's wage. With the second crew, he promised to pay "whatever is right," an agreement which seems to have carried over into each of the remaining three groups hired. With the sun an hour from setting, the landowner approached the last group. The previous three crews he hired with little discussion. But he asks this final group why they have been "standing here all day long doing nothing." We are not told why this group was overlooked during the previous three trips by the landowner. Their answer is a helpless "because no one has hired us" that drives home the point that a day or a life can be wasted if a relationship to the landowner is never established.

Harvests maintain their own timetable. Ripening fruit will not wait until the workers get around to it. A harvest delayed becomes decay. The landowner sees value in the work of the final group even though they will be employed only an hour. In the economy of the parable, the landowner is committed to getting the harvest; the cost is secondary. In the meaning of the parable, God sees value in our lives even if commitment comes at the final hour.

Getting Personal

What were you doing when the landowner found you, and how has your life changed since then?

How are you working today for your landowner?

Almost invariably, adult believers express regrets over the time wasted before they knew the Lord. Jesus' parable makes it very clear that surrender is ultimately more significant than the timing of surrender, as long as there is daylight left.

READING THE WORD

✤ *Matthew 20:3-7, NIV*
About nine in the morning he went out and saw others standing in the marketplace doing nothing. 4He told them, "You also go and work in my vineyard, and I will pay you whatever is right." 5So they went. He went out again about noon and about three in the afternoon and did the same thing. 6About five in the afternoon he went out and found still others standing around. He asked them, "Why have you been standing here all day long doing nothing?" 7"Because no one has hired us," they answered. He said to them, "You also go and work in my vineyard."

TALKING TO GOD

Pray for those you know who, in the eleventh hour of their lives, still have not accepted the gift of salvation. Pray that the Lord of the harvest will bring them in to serve him too.

READING THE WORD

✤ *Matthew 20:8, NIV*
When evening came, the owner of the vineyard said to his foreman, "Call the workers and pay them their wages, beginning with the last ones hired and going on to the first."

TALKING TO GOD

As you come to the Lord in prayer, remember that you are his child and not a worker who labors to earn his place in God's family. Thank God for his persistent grace that brought you into the Kingdom.

WAGES

Setting the Scene

In Jesus' day, sundown was quitting time and pay time. According to Leviticus 19:13 and Deuteronomy 24:14-15, payment for day labor was to be made at sundown in order to give the poor the best chance to benefit from their labors.

The owner in the parable deliberately organized the payment sequence to reverse the order of hiring. This was the first significant alteration of normal business practices. Staggered hiring throughout the day might have been unusual, but it made some sense if the pressure of harvest was great enough. But the first expected to be paid first. Although not mentioned in the parable itself, this development definitely set the tone for what followed. From a worldly perspective, things were suddenly out of order.

In Jesus' parables that begin, "The kingdom of heaven is like," the story line is understandable and familiar. But each contains a point of departure when we suddenly remember that this isn't a description of earthly events but a reflection of a heavenly pattern. The landowner who did the hiring took control of the order of payment. There was a purposeful tone to this arrangement that will unfold the key lesson of this parable. In the Kingdom of Heaven, people are "hired" throughout the day, and when the work is done, the latecomers will be first in line, because this is not about the kingdom of earth. In the Kingdom of Heaven, the Lord even decides when it's quitting time!

Getting Personal

When it comes to being a worker for God in the harvest, how would you evaluate your work ethic?

How do you maintain the difference between working out *your salvation (Philippians 2:12) and* working for *salvation (Ephesians 2:8-10)?*

Believers may struggle to understand this parable, since it appears to foster salvation by effort. But the original finding and hiring of the workers is always the originating act of grace by the landowner. The work we do as believers is measured by how well it expresses our gratitude for the gift of life we could otherwise never afford or receive.

COMPLAINTS

Setting the Scene

Two things happen as the workers are paid. The last workers hired receive their wages and express delight over the unexpected windfall. They get a full portion even though they joined the crew at the end of the day. Meanwhile, those in the earlier crews begin to refigure their pay upward. In the kingdom of earth, that makes perfect sense. It's only fair. It doesn't matter what the earlier agreement was—things have changed.

As each crew receives the same payment, things are subdued until the last group realizes they are getting only what they had agreed to that morning. They "expected to receive more." If the landowner is foolish enough to pay a full day's wages for an hour of work, he ought to be fair enough to increase the wages for everyone else. This would be expected in the kingdom of earth. But not in the Kingdom of Heaven, which is what this story is all about!

It's interesting that the grumbling workers are not only upset about the amount of the pay, they are also angry because the landowner "made them equal to us." For them, this is unacceptable equality. In the fallen kingdom of this world, fairness usually means "more for me."

In the Kingdom of Heaven, as it should be on earth, the landowner keeps his word. He gives what he promised. In the case of God the landowner, the gift is eternal life. How could anyone expect more than everything?

Getting Personal

What examples have you observed of this tendency to translate a worldly sliding scale into our expectations of eternal life?

How do you respond to the idea that God has the same unimaginably great gift in store for each of us that simply could not be improved?

When we allow this parable to inform our thoughts about heaven, we may find ourselves in the position of the man who said he expected to have three initial experiences upon arrival in heaven: first, amazement at who is there; second, amazement at who isn't there; and third, profound amazement that he is there!

READING THE WORD

❋ *Matthew 20:9-15, NIV*

The workers who were hired about five in the afternoon came and each received a denarius. 10So when those came who were hired first, they expected to receive more. But each one of them also received a denarius. 11When they received it, they began to grumble against the landowner. 12"These who were hired last worked only one hour," they said, "and you have made them equal to us who have borne the burden of the work and the heat of the day." 13But he answered one of them, "I am not being unfair to you, friend. Didn't you agree to work for a denarius? 14Take your pay and go. I want to give the one who was hired last the same as I gave you. 15Don't I have the right to do what I want with my own money? Or are you envious because I am generous?"

TALKING TO GOD

Ask the Lord to help you stay away from sinful comparisons with other believers, or from assuming greater importance than any other believer. Focus on the joyful expectation of the glories of heaven and of being with the Lord forever, which is your gift of eternal life.

KINGDOM ORDER

READING THE WORD

✤ *Matthew 20:16, NIV*
So the last will be first, and the first will be last.

TALKING TO GOD

As you focus on the holiness and goodness of the Lord, your focus will shift away from others and what they are doing or not doing for the Kingdom. Thank God for his "unfair" generosity to every person who comes to him for salvation.

Setting the Scene

At the end of this week's parable, Jesus, as the landowner, asks two unsettling questions: "Don't I have the right to do what I want with my own money? Or are you envious because I am generous?" (Matthew 20:15, NIV). When God poses questions like those, we are most likely to answer, "You can do whatever you want with your money as long as it benefits me" and "I'm not envious when you are generous as long as you are generous with me"—which was precisely the problem of the first workers in the parable: They couldn't see beyond themselves far enough to appreciate all that they had been given.

The order of things in the Kingdom of Heaven consistently reverses the worldly order. Those who are first here or demand to be first will be content with last place in the Kingdom of Heaven, or they perhaps will not even be there.

Our response to Jesus' echoed statement "The last will be first and the first will be last" (Matthew 20:16, NIV; see also 19:30) will depend on whether we see ourselves primarily as first or last in this life. Unfortunately, this doesn't prepare us for a healthy translation into Kingdom values. In the Kingdom of Heaven, the last discover that being first is really no different from being last, so it doesn't matter. Heaven isn't payback; heaven is an order of existence that never steps on someone else to get ahead or to feel greater.

Getting Personal

How has this parable given you a new anticipation of what it means to work for God now and be with God later?

How might learning to be content with "last" in this world be good preparation for heaven?

If our overwhelming reason to reach for heaven is so that we can demand justice, we will be disappointed (and we may not even get there). Everything lacking in this world because of sin will be settled in heaven, but grace, mercy, and access to God will make everything else fade to insignificance.

JESUS HEALS A BLIND BEGGAR
Week 31, Day 1

❁ *Matthew 20:29-34; Mark 10:46-52; Luke 18:35-43*

Continuing on their way to Jerusalem and nearing Jericho, Jesus and the Twelve were confronted by a man. Earlier another man had approached Jesus, asking how to inherit eternal life. The man we meet this week differs greatly from the rich young religious leader in an earlier encounter, but we can be encouraged and challenged from his approach to Jesus and Jesus' response.

THE SHOUT

Setting the Scene

As usual, a "crowd" was accompanying Jesus and his disciples, probably mostly Jews on their way to Jerusalem for the Passover. Matthew writes that two blind men were begging, while Mark and Luke mention only one. Actually, *more* than two may have been in that area, but of the two who called out to Jesus, Mark and Luke singled out the more vocal one. Mark gives his name, Bartimaeus (Mark 10:46). In ancient times, blind people and others with debilitating infirmities had no other option but to beg, waiting along the roads near cities. There they would be able to contact the most people. Jericho, with its fairly wealthy inhabitants, was a popular location for beggars. Bartimaeus could not see the approaching crowd, of course, but he and the other beggar heard them and asked what was happening. When they were told that "Jesus the Nazarene" was passing by, they began shouting. They had undoubtedly heard that Jesus had healed many, including blind people (see Matthew 9:29-31). They called Jesus "Lord" (Matthew 20:31) and "Son of David," acknowledging that Jesus was the Messiah. This was an opportunity not to be missed, so Bartimaeus shamelessly cried out for Jesus' attention.

Getting Personal

When have you felt a desperate need for God's intervention?

When have you been reluctant to bring your needs to Jesus? What keeps you from calling out to him?

READING THE WORD

❁ *Luke 18:35-43, NLT*

As Jesus approached Jericho, a blind beggar was sitting beside the road. 36When he heard the noise of a crowd going past, he asked what was happening. 37They told him that Jesus the Nazarene was going by. 38So he began shouting, "Jesus, Son of David, have mercy on me!" 39"Be quiet!" the people in front yelled at him. But he only shouted louder, "Son of David, have mercy on me!" 40When Jesus heard him, he stopped and ordered that the man be brought to him. As the man came near, Jesus asked him, 41"What do you want me to do for you?" "Lord," he said, "I want to see!" 42And Jesus said, "All right, receive your sight! Your faith has healed you." 43Instantly the man could see, and he followed Jesus, praising God. And all who saw it praised God, too.

TALKING TO GOD

Capture Bartimaeus's urgency as you pray his prayer: "Have mercy on me!" The Lord understands your great need and the "blindness" that comes from an imperfect view of his Kingdom. His love and forgiveness are already prepared for you.

THE SHOUT *continued*

Bartimaeus and his friend were desperate. The fact that Mark knew this blind man's name suggests that Bartimaeus had been a regular at that spot, so he probably wasn't young. And being dependent on donations from people means he must have been poor—quite a contrast to the rich young religious leader we met earlier in the chapter (Luke 18:18-23). He had no social standing, no resources, and no religious credentials. But he knew who Jesus was and that Jesus could meet his need, so Bartimaeus began shouting to Jesus. And what was he asking? "Have mercy on me!"

Jesus loves us, and he wants us to bring our needs to him. Like blind Bartimaeus, we shouldn't be deterred by our state in life or the crowds. We don't even have to shout—a simple prayer will do, asking for mercy, for our Savior's presence and touch.

THE REBUKE

Setting the Scene

The people standing near Bartimaeus tried to keep him quiet. We don't know why—perhaps because Bartimaeus had been blind for so long, they considered him a lost cause. Perhaps they thought the dirty and noisy man would cause Jesus to turn away. Maybe they wanted to hear what Jesus was saying to his disciples, and the noise was making that impossible. They may have been embarrassed by the man's actions. Or perhaps they were trying to keep Jesus from being harassed by beggars. Presumably these people knew Bartimaeus and may even have responded to his begging from time to time, giving him money. Whatever their reasons, they didn't appreciate his causing a ruckus, and they tried to silence him. But Bartimaeus shouted even louder, risking an angry response from the crowd. He would not miss this opportunity to receive mercy and healing from Jesus. His blindness meant he could not find his way through the crowd to touch Jesus' cloak, as the sick woman had done (Mark 5:27-28). So he kept on shouting in an attempt to gain Jesus' attention. And it worked.

Getting Personal

When have you felt uncomfortable or embarrassed by a person's expressions of faith or of need?

When have you been the one "shouting," only to have people say or imply that you should be quiet? How did you feel? What did you do?

If we've ever stood in the crowd's place in a situation like this, we can identify with the crowd's feelings and reaction. A misfit—perhaps a child, a teenager, someone with a severe physical or mental need, or a stranger—gets a bit too enthusiastic in worship, doesn't use the religiously correct language in a testimony, dares speak up in Bible study, or confesses a desperate, embarrassing prayer request. Our internal impulse is to tell them to be quiet, to keep their thoughts and needs to themselves.

God wants to hear our sincere questions, requests, and exclamations, whether whispered, sung, or shouted. He welcomes sinners, seekers, and saints of every type—even you.

READING THE WORD

❈ *Luke 18:39, NLT*
"Be quiet!" the people in front yelled at him. But he only shouted louder, "Son of David, have mercy on me!"

TALKING TO GOD

Admit to the Lord that some expressions of need or worship make you feel uncomfortable. Ask him to help you react like Jesus would to people who are difficult for you. Ask him to improve your level of truth and candor about your own deepest needs.

THE QUESTION

✳ *Mark 10:49-51, NLT*
When Jesus heard him, he stopped and said, "Tell him to come here." So they called the blind man. "Cheer up," they said. "Come on, he's calling you!" ⁵⁰Bartimaeus threw aside his coat, jumped up, and came to Jesus. ⁵¹"What do you want me to do for you?" Jesus asked. "My rabbi," the blind man said, "I want to see!"

TALKING TO GOD

Thank God that he is all-knowing and present everywhere. Thank him that he loves you enough to know and love you personally. Praise God for the wonderful juxtaposition of his glorious might in close relationship with his human creation.

Setting the Scene

As Jesus made his way toward Jerusalem, he was on a mission and knew that he was heading toward certain death; yet he stopped and took time with a blind beggar at the side of the road. Blindness was considered a curse from God (see John 9:2 when Jesus healed another blind man), but Jesus refuted that idea when he told the people to tell the man to come to him. At first the crowd had sternly rebuked Bartimaeus, but after Jesus called him, their tone changed to friendly encouragement.

Jesus did not ignore Bartimaeus or reject him as the crowd had done. He "heard" the man's shouts, "stopped," and invited the man to come to him, taking personal interest in this poor beggar. Jesus knew what Bartimaeus needed and wanted, but he asked Bartimaeus to make his request. "What do you want me to do for you?" Jesus asked. The man replied unhesitatingly, "My rabbi . . . I want to see!" He probably had considered that desire thousands of times. But now he stood before the one person who could actually make his desire a reality. And he would not have asked if he had not believed that it could be so.

Getting Personal

When have you felt separated from Jesus, almost lost in the crowd?

How does knowing that Jesus hears and sees you affect your relationship with him?

If Jesus asked you personally, "What do you want me to do for you?" what would you answer?

With the crowd moving down the road and the people gathered at the edges, probably jostling to get close or gain a view of Jesus, the scene would have been busy, borderline chaotic—noisy and dusty. Yet Jesus "heard," "stopped," and called a man to come to him. This was an individual and personal encounter. Jesus asked, "What do you want me to do for you?"

THE FAITH

Setting the Scene

Jesus recognized the man's faith. A poor and blind beggar could see that Jesus was the Messiah, and the crowds understood that God was to be praised for such miracles. But the religious leaders who saw his miracles were blind to his identity and refused to recognize Jesus as the Messiah. Bartimaeus believed in Jesus as the Messiah and as his healer. He also put that faith into action: He shouted to Jesus, he came to him, and he publicly acknowledged Jesus as "Lord." This wasn't a long shot for Bartimaeus—he believed Jesus could heal him. His clear expression of his need proved it.

Biblical faith involves the whole person. We believe in our minds that Jesus is the God-man, our Lord and Savior; we trust in our hearts that he loves us and wants only good for us; we commit our lives to him through our actions, taking those steps toward him, following him closely, and doing what he says. Clearly Bartimaeus had faith in Jesus.

Getting Personal

In what ways have you demonstrated your faith in Christ lately, moving beyond words to action?

How do you respond to someone who is spiritually blind but doesn't know it?

What real questions of need are people around you expressing?

What can you do to help people "see" the Savior?

Some people don't realize they are spiritually blind; some don't realize they need Jesus at all. Some believe facts about Jesus, even acknowledging him as the Son of God, but that's where the believing stops. Others struggle with the trust issue, wondering if they really can commit themselves wholly to him.

READING THE WORD

❀ *Luke 18:41-42, NLT*

"What do you want me to do for you?" "Lord," he said, "I want to see!" 42And Jesus said, "All right, receive your sight! Your faith has healed you."

TALKING TO GOD

Ask the Lord to give you courage and strength to make what you believe in your mind and heart real in your words and actions. Ask with confident faith, as Bartimaeus did.

THE HEALING

READING THE WORD

❧ *Matthew 20:34*, NLT
Jesus felt sorry for them and
touched their eyes. Instantly
they could see! Then they
followed him.

TALKING TO GOD

*Praise God for his amazing works
in the world and in your life. Thank
him for life, sustenance, shelter,
relationships, forgiveness, eternal
life, and the miracle of transformation going on inside you.*

Setting the Scene

Jesus had compassion on the blind men, knowing their
need and their faith. The result was that Bartimaeus and
the other blind man received their sight—"Instantly they
could see!" They could see Jesus, the one who had healed
them, each other, the onlooking crowd, their hands, the
trees, the clouds—Jesus had made them well! Unlike
Matthew, Mark mentions no healing touch of Jesus. His
emphasis is not on the miracle but on the faith that led to
it. Jesus just had to touch the men and speak the words,
and they could see. Everyone was amazed because the
Old Testament records no healings of blind people. Jesus
was unique. Thus the Jews believed that such a miracle
would be a sign that the messianic age had begun (see
Isaiah 29:18; 35:5). Jesus had healed other blind people,
so the crowd knew they were witnessing something
extraordinary.

Getting Personal

*Why should we expect that God will heal people
today? In what other ways have you seen God's direct
intervention?*

*How do you usually respond when you pray and God
doesn't heal "instantly"? How should you respond?*

What daily "miracles" of God do you see?

*In considering miracles, we usually think of examples
such as blind Bartimaeus receiving his sight, a lame
man walking again, a leper brought back to full
health, or even a dead person coming alive. So our
requests to God for something "big" usually involve
physical healing. God can heal any broken bone, cure
any disease, and fully restore our senses—and Jesus did,
many times. But he didn't heal all the sick, lame, deaf,
and blind people in Palestine. He did, however, offer
his greatest miracle to everyone who would believe—
forgiveness of sins and eternal life. God still performs
miracles, changing lives every day because of Christ
and through the power of his Spirit.*

THE RESPONSE

Setting the Scene

As soon as the beggars received their sight, they began following Jesus—down the road to Jerusalem and throughout their lives as new disciples. Bartimaeus had been healed physically and spiritually; thus as he followed Jesus, he praised God along the way. This would be a natural response for someone whose life had been turned around so dramatically. When Jesus healed the paralyzed man who had been brought by his friends and lowered through the roof, the man "jumped up, picked up his mat, and went home praising God" (Luke 5:25, NLT). And the one leper of the ten whom Jesus had healed "came back to Jesus, shouting, 'Praise God!'" (Luke 17:15, NLT). All those who had witnessed this miracle also praised the Lord. Many probably began following Jesus because of the signs and wonders, perhaps hoping for healing themselves. Most of those people would leave the parade when they didn't gain what they expected or when times of persecution came. Those who stayed were following Jesus for who he was—God's Son, the Messiah, and their only hope of salvation.

Getting Personal

What happens when you forget that you're forgiven, when you take God's work for granted?

What does a praise-filled life look like?

In addition to singing in church, how can you make praise a more integral part of your life?

This was a remarkable event, an amazing, life-changing miracle, so we can understand the spontaneous praise by the crowd of witnesses. But God is always at work in the world. He allows the earth to keep spinning and the sun to continue to shine. He calls his people and holds Satan at bay. He gives life—and he gives new life. And we see these miracles daily. Certainly our lives should be filled with praise for what God has done and is doing and, most important, for who he is.

READING THE WORD

✽ *Luke 18:43, NLT*
Instantly the man could see, and he followed Jesus, praising God. And all who saw it praised God, too.

TALKING TO GOD

Praise him, praise him! Praise him for being the all-powerful, all-knowing, all-loving Creator and Sustainer. Praise him for his wonderful works, past, present, and future. Praise the Father for knowing you before the foundations of the world. Praise Jesus, who died in your place. Praise the Spirit, whose power to change your perspective, attitudes, and motives is transforming you day by day.

JESUS CONFRONTS ZACCHAEUS
Week 32, Day 1

☀ *Luke 19:1-10*

Some of the most fascinating events in Jesus' life have to do with his individual encounters with people. Jesus' words and actions had transformative power. Whatever needs people brought to Jesus, he showed them their deeper needs, which he also met. That was the case when Zacchaeus of Jericho observed Jesus as he passed through town on his final trip to Jerusalem.

READING THE WORD

✤ *Luke 19:1-2, NKJV*
Then Jesus entered and passed through Jericho. ²Now behold, there was a man named Zacchaeus who was a chief tax collector, and he was rich.

JERICHO

Setting the Scene

Matthew, Mark, and Luke all record that Jesus passed through Jericho on his final journey to Jerusalem. But only Luke includes the encounter with Zacchaeus that took place there. This is the only instance mentioned in the Gospels when Jesus spent time in Jericho. The ten-mile road from Jerusalem descended to the wide Jordan valley and Jericho. Jesus mentioned the dangers of the desolate, mountainous area of the route in his parable of the Good Samaritan (Luke 10:30-37).

It was Herod the Great who had rebuilt Jericho in one of his grand architectural projects. Rather than add another layer to the traditional site of Jericho, the workers constructed a model city south of the old location. In Jesus' day, the area around the city was known for its dates and balsam. As an agricultural and trade center, Jericho was a notable source of revenue for the Romans.

If Jesus had not approached Jericho with a traveling crowd, one certainly would have formed on the outskirts of town as he healed the blind man (Luke 18:35-43). Three years into his ministry, Jesus was widely known. His arrival and passage through Jericho may have caused almost as much excitement as the parade that erupted days later when the crowds of Jerusalem welcomed him as a king.

Luke introduces Zacchaeus as a "chief tax collector" who was "rich," two descriptive points that would have put him on the unwanted list of many people. Zacchaeus would have been widely recognized and resented in

Jericho. Not only was he a collaborator with the occupying Romans and therefore a betrayer of his own people, but he also compounded the offense by holding a supervisory role as chief collector. Mention of Zacchaeus's economic status indicates that he had used his position to enlarge his wealth. Tax collecting under the Roman system was an entrepreneurial playground. Those collecting the tariffs, fees, and taxes kept a percentage for themselves. The larger the take, the more the agent kept for himself. Zacchaeus amassed a fortune and a reputation.

The people of Jericho would have despised Zacchaeus and seen him as a person who had put himself beyond God's mercy. It would have been as difficult for his fellow residents to see Zacchaeus as an uncertain and terrified searcher after God as it is difficult for us to see certain people as candidates for genuine conversion. It is as easy today as it was in Jesus' day to relegate certain people to a theologically untouchable category—too rich, too happy, too occupied, too successful, or too evil to reach with the gospel. The fact that we are all sinners means each of us has to deal with God's visitations in our lives. For Zacchaeus, that moment began when he heard Jesus was coming through Jericho.

Getting Personal

At what points in your life have you experienced a jarring interruption by God?

What were the results of those encounters?

The structures of our lives—possessions, relationships, positions—can be our primary source of security. Sooner or later, we discover that whatever we have amassed, legally or otherwise, isn't enough. It can be destroyed, lost, or taken away. We are all left looking for something we cannot lose. That quest should lead us to God.

TALKING TO GOD

The Lord knows how much we human beings want to depend on security we can see and touch, like money in the bank account. Come to him empty-handed, not depending on any of your earthly bulwarks or foundations, and accept the righteousness of Christ as your only hope for lasting security. Praise him that your life, present and future, is secure in him.

DESPERATE MEASURES

Setting the Scene

Zacchaeus set out on a mission. He "sought to see who Jesus was," to find out for himself if what he had heard about Jesus was true. He was simply curious.

Zacchaeus had two problems: He was short and he had alienated almost everyone he met on the street. Imagine a short person showing up at a parade, discovering that the whole crowd lining the streets is made up of people he has offended. The spectators that day in Jericho were in no mood to let Zacchaeus see anything other than their backs. His height disadvantage insured that unless he was allowed close to the road, he would not be able to see Jesus' passage.

In that moment when curiosity was battling with rejection, Zacchaeus came up with a creative alternative. If he couldn't get *through* the crowd, maybe he could get *above* it! The overhanging branches of a sycamore tree along the road offered a tempting view if only he could climb up. Those who fail to find humor in the Bible haven't paused long enough to consider the sight of a middle-aged man awkwardly ascending a tree and gingerly crawling out on a limb to a precarious perch above the road. Zacchaeus probably expected nothing except to see Jesus pass by. But God had other plans for him.

Getting Personal

What personal shortcoming have you faced as you have sought Jesus?

When has pursuing knowledge about the Lord put you in a somewhat precarious situation? What happened?

Zacchaeus set out to see Jesus, not necessarily to know him. Given his current status in the city, he would not have expected anything except rejection from Christ. It would be fascinating to know what was going through his mind as he hung on to that branch!

READING THE WORD

✸ *Luke 19:2-4, NKJV*
Now behold, there was a man named Zacchaeus who was a chief tax collector, and he was rich. 3And he sought to see who Jesus was, but could not because of the crowd, for he was of short stature. 4So he ran ahead and climbed up into a sycamore tree to see Him, for He was going to pass that way.

TALKING TO GOD

There is always more to the Lord than we have already understood. Ask him to open your eyes to truths about him and his character, especially as you study Jesus' life and teachings.

INTERRUPTIONS

Setting the Scene

We don't know who was more surprised in those moments on Main Street in Jericho: the crowd whose attention was suddenly drawn to the despised chief tax collector up high on a sycamore branch, or Zacchaeus himself at having Jesus call him by name. The parade came to a sudden halt when Jesus stopped under the tree and looked up.

Jesus singled out Zacchaeus, requested his presence, and insisted on his extended company. What an amazing glimpse of Jesus' approach with each of us. He knows us and calls us by name. He invites us to come to him and know him, and then he goes with us. Jesus always personalizes his invitations.

Verse 6 can be read several different ways. It either describes the immediate events, or it summarizes what occurred for several hours. The phrase "welcomed him gladly" would seem to indicate that Zacchaeus took Jesus home with him. They spent time together. The tax collector got to see and *hear* who Jesus was. Three things contributed to Zacchaeus's "gladly" (literally "with joy"): Jesus acknowledged him, Jesus accepted his hospitality, and Jesus (as we will see) radically altered the tax collector's view of himself. Jesus stepped into Zacchaeus's life where he was, as he was, and left him changed forever. The details may change, but the work Jesus offers to do in any life is the same work he accomplished for Zacchaeus.

Getting Personal

What does it mean to you to know that Jesus knows you personally, by name?

When was the last time you sensed yourself singled out for his attention?

We have no record that gives us a hint of the tone of voice used by Jesus as he began to speak to Zacchaeus. Did he burst into laughter as he looked up? Was there a smile on his face as he spoke? Was there an unrecorded humorous caution for Zacchaeus, urging him to climb down carefully rather than fall out of the tree? However he shaped his voice and tone, Jesus was connecting with Zacchaeus, person to person. Pondering these possibilities promotes within us a deeper intimacy with Jesus, who knows us just as well as he knew Zacchaeus.

READING THE WORD

✤ *Luke 19:5-6, NIV*
When Jesus reached the spot, he looked up and said to him, "Zacchaeus, come down immediately. I must stay at your house today." 6So he came down at once and welcomed him gladly.

TALKING TO GOD

Being with Jesus changed Zacchaeus forever. Your quiet time with God, apart from distractions, has the potential of being just as life changing. Come to God today with mind and spirit open for the Lord's conviction and encouragement.

CHANGES

READING THE WORD

❧ *Luke 19:7-8, NKJV*
But when they saw it, they all complained, saying, "He has gone to be a guest with a man who is a sinner." 8Then Zacchaeus stood and said to the Lord, "Look, Lord, I give half of my goods to the poor; and if I have taken anything from anyone by false accusation, I restore fourfold."

TALKING TO GOD

Seek a transformation as complete as the change in Zacchaeus, no matter what the cost. Offer the Lord all you are and all you have for his purposes and his glory.

Setting the Scene

There can be little doubt that the crowd was not pleased with Jesus for interacting with Zacchaeus. The little chief tax collector had gone from being their intended outcast to suddenly being the center of attention. Verse 7 is often read as an immediate response to Jesus' words, but it is more likely that there is a time gap between verses 6 and 7, during which Jesus was at Zacchaeus's house. We can only guess at the content of the conversation at Zacchaeus's table. The fact of Jesus' presence may well have been more transformative for the tax collector than anything he said.

The grumbling of the crowd may have begun immediately, but the consensus of criticism about Jesus' lack of judgment in accepting a sinner's hospitality would have taken a little time. In response to the complaints of the crowd, however, Zacchaeus rose to the occasion. He "stood," as a host would get up from the table in order to give a toast. The chief tax collector was about to make a public announcement. He would definitely be held to his next words. Zacchaeus immediately gave half his wealth away to the poor. With the other half, he promised to pay back 400 percent to anyone he had cheated. The crowd must have been shocked into silence as some of them began to do the math in their heads.

Zacchaeus didn't make this stunning announcement as a way to gain God's acceptance; this unexpected radical change in his behavior was *evidence* of God's acceptance and transformation of his life.

Getting Personal

What clues might people discover in you that indicate your ultimate commitment to God?

How do you think acceptance from God alters a person's understanding of righteous behavior?

We can get lost in comparing Zacchaeus's sudden generosity with our own paltry giving, and losing ourselves there for a while might be healthy. But the crucial lesson to remember is that true generosity is always an expression of how much we value what we ourselves have been given by God. For those who realize they have received a priceless gift, all other artificial values become disposable.

TRIUMPHAL PRE-ENTRY

Setting the Scene

Days before Jesus arrived in Jerusalem for what has become known as the Triumphal Entry, he made a remarkable entry into one man's life—the life of the chief tax collector Zacchaeus from Jericho. Salvation in the person of Jesus came to Zacchaeus's house. The tax collector went from being a lost, rejected, and despised Jew to being a restored son of Abraham who was saved by the Son of Man.

Earlier, under the sycamore tree, Jesus had told Zacchaeus, "I must stay at your house today" (Luke 19:5, NIV). We can see immediately that Jesus invited himself for a visit—and that Zacchaeus responded to that idea with joy. But the word *stay* is also literally "remain," and while the use of the word *today* seems to imply a limited duration, it can also be taken to mean something like, "Zacchaeus, today is the day I take up residency in your house." Jesus uses the same word *oikos* for "house" in both verses 5 and 9. The word can be used to describe a physical residence, but it is also used to indicate a household or family. When Jesus announced that "salvation has come to this house," he was describing at the least the arrival in Zacchaeus's home of the transformative power of the gospel.

Jesus continues to "seek and to save the lost." This brief account begins with a man setting out to seek and observe "who Jesus was" (Luke 19:3, NIV). By the time the account ends, that man himself has been found and restored. God wants our lives to fit that pattern.

Getting Personal

How did you discover at some point that you were lost?

In what sense have you found your relationship with Jesus to be restorative?

Zacchaeus reminds us that very successful people can be hopelessly lost. We may have found ourselves in that very state at some point. The artificial means we use to give us a feeling of location and place can actually become barriers to perceiving how lost we really are. It takes the arrival of Jesus to help us see our condition and the only remedy for it—the Savior.

READING THE WORD

✴ *Luke 19:9-10, NIV*
Jesus said to him, "Today salvation has come to this house, because this man, too, is a son of Abraham. 10For the Son of Man came to seek and to save the lost."

TALKING TO GOD

Thank God for coming to seek and save what was lost, including yourself. Thank him that his Holy Spirit has taken up residence in you. Welcome the changes that come from having the Savior at home in your heart.

READING THE WORD

✤ *Luke 19:8-10, NKJV*
Then Zacchaeus stood and said to the Lord, "Look, Lord, I give half of my goods to the poor; and if I have taken anything from anyone by false accusation, I restore fourfold." 9And Jesus said to him, "Today salvation has come to this house, because he also is a son of Abraham; 10for the Son of Man has come to seek and to save that which was lost."

TALKING TO GOD

Take a minute to think of friends or family members whose lives have been transformed because of their relationship with Jesus. Thank God for those people by name, and praise him for his power that is at work in such personal ways.

AFTERMATH

Setting the Scene

The brief scene in Luke 19:1-8 is the only time Zacchaeus is named in the New Testament. He is mentioned by one of the early church fathers, Clement of Alexandria, who indicates the former chief tax collector eventually became the bishop of Caesarea. So much happens in this short account that we arrive somewhat breathless at Jesus' closing words.

Few of us can identify with the spontaneous clarity of Zacchaeus's response to Christ's acceptance. We can remember promises we have made to God, often much broader promises than the ones made by the newly converted tax man, but which we haven't made good. Perhaps our efforts at impressive sacrifice were doomed from the outset because we assumed our grandiose commitment would impress Jesus. Jesus didn't comment on the content of Zacchaeus's commitment; he declared again what God had done for Zacchaeus.

Zacchaeus made a specific public commitment. We might expect that his example made a deep impression on other lost sons and daughters of Abraham, even as it does on us, centuries later. Commitment to Christ is rooted in a private encounter, but the reality of that encounter will always be questionable without an external, public expression. This is why Paul tells us, "If you declare with your mouth, 'Jesus is Lord,' and believe in your heart that God raised him from the dead, you will be saved. For it is with your heart that you believe and are justified, and it is with your mouth that you profess your faith and are saved" (Romans 10:9-10, NIV). Zacchaeus got it right.

Getting Personal

Even if you've been familiar with this story since childhood, what strikes or convicts you now about the encounter between Zacchaeus and Jesus?

When was the last time you were able to speak publicly about your commitment to Christ?

Zacchaeus declared his changed life while he was surrounded by his closest enemies. He didn't argue with those who had just called him a sinner. But he showed them what could happen in a sinner's life after meeting Jesus. The world takes notice of such changes.

JESUS IS ANOINTED BY MARY

Week 33, Day 1

Matthew 26:6-13; Mark 14:3-9; John 12:1-11

As Jesus continued on his journey to Jerusalem, his final destination before his death, he had dinner with dear friends in Bethany. This week, we'll discover significant interactions with Jesus and an invitation to walk with him.

MOVING

Setting the Scene

Less than a week before Passover, Jesus stopped in Bethany on the way to Jerusalem. According to John, Jesus had been in Ephraim, where he had gone to be alone with his disciples (John 11:54). From there, they had returned to Galilee for a while. Then they had begun traveling from Galilee to Jerusalem for this Passover. Along the way, Jesus had healed ten lepers (Luke 17:11-19); traveled and taught in Judea, beyond the Jordan (Matthew 19:1-2; Mark 10:1-2); warned his disciples that this trip to Jerusalem would result in him being crucified—but he would rise from the dead (Matthew 20:17-19; Mark 10:32-34; Luke 18:31-34); healed blind Bartimaeus near Jericho (Matthew 20:29-34; Mark 10:46-52; Luke 18:35-43); and transformed Zacchaeus, a tax collector in Jericho (Luke 19:1-10).

From Jericho, Jesus traveled to Bethany, the hometown of Mary, Martha, and Lazarus (see Matthew 21:17; Luke 10:38). Bethany is near the Mount of Olives. This would be Jesus' final visit with these dear friends because he was en route to Jerusalem where, as he had told his disciples, "the Son of Man will be betrayed to the leading priests and the teachers of religious law. They will sentence him to die. Then they will hand him over to the Romans to be mocked, flogged with a whip, and crucified. But on the third day he will be raised from the dead" (Matthew 20:18-19, NLT).

Jesus knew he was traveling to his death. He predicted it, and at this dinner he explained that Mary's anointing

READING THE WORD

John 12:1, 3, 7-8, NLT

Six days before the Passover celebration began, Jesus arrived in Bethany, the home of Lazarus—the man he had raised from the dead. . . . 3Then Mary took a twelve-ounce jar of expensive perfume made from essence of nard, and she anointed Jesus' feet with it, wiping his feet with her hair. . . . 7Jesus replied, "Leave her alone. She did this in preparation for my burial. 8You will always have the poor among you, but you will not always have me."

MOVING *continued*

was preparing him for his "burial." Yet knowing what lay ahead, he moved steadily onward. Spending time in Bethany to fellowship with friends, Jesus gave no indication that he was dreading what lay ahead in Jerusalem. And clearly his host and other guests had no idea, even though he had told them what would occur.

Getting Personal

How does Jesus' willingness to fulfill this plan help you to understand God's character?

When do you think you might be persecuted because of your stand for Christ? How can remembering Jesus' walk toward Jerusalem motivate you to do what you know you should?

Why do many Christians seem to forget what Jesus did, or at least take it for granted?

Soon Jesus would suffer excruciating physical torture and a horrible death. Most painful of all, however, would be his spiritual pain, taking our sins on himself and being punished in our place, separated from his Father. Yet Jesus moved forward without hesitation and ministered along the way to those he loved.

Most people do everything they can to avoid pain. If we had been facing political and religious intrigue and the prospect of crucifixion, we probably would have taken a different path or gone into hiding. But Jesus chose to walk this road for us . . . for you.

TALKING TO GOD

Marvel at Jesus' wholehearted commitment to doing his Father's will, even though that meant ultimate suffering and personal sacrifice. Praise him for this incredible act of obedience that changed the whole world and is changing you, too.

HONORING

Setting the Scene

One evening, Simon, a former leper who had been healed by Jesus, hosted a dinner in Jesus' honor. The Gospel accounts reveal that in addition to Simon, those in attendance included Mary, Martha, Lazarus, and the Twelve. All those named would have had great reasons for honoring Jesus.

Each person in this story expressed a particular attitude toward Jesus through specific actions. Martha was practicing her gift of hospitality (see Luke 10:38-42), though apparently with a new attitude of meekness. She honored her Lord with hospitality and refreshment. Lazarus was reclining at the table with his Lord, who had brought him back to life. The tender attention given to Jesus by his friends in Bethany contrasts sharply with the treachery Judas planned to commit in just a few days.

Getting Personal

Why do you go to a worship service? How would visitors to your worship service know that it was given "in Jesus' honor"?

What can you do to make sure that you're not simply going through the motions?

Guests at this dinner party had major differences in background and social status: a former leper (the lowest element in society); fishermen; a former tax collector (considered a traitor by fellow Jews); a zealot hoping to overthrow the Romans; a man whom Jesus had brought back to life; and more. What brought them together was Jesus. Lazarus, Mary, Martha, and Judas were all in Jesus' close circle of friends, but their relationships and motives for following him differed greatly. What a contrast between Mary and Judas: Mary expressed her great love for and faith in Jesus by offering a very special gift, and Judas betrayed his true character by disapproving Mary's extravagance.

Today, Christian churches have similar collections of attendees: a wide range of people from all walks of life and social strata and with a variety of motives. These disparate groups gather ostensibly to honor Jesus. But some are simply going through the motions, reducing the life of faith to a brief semiannual (Christmas and Easter) or weekly appearance at their local church. Being close to Jesus is not enough if we don't have heartfelt trust and obedience.

READING THE WORD

✤ *Matthew 26:6, NLT*
Meanwhile, Jesus was in Bethany at the home of Simon, a man who had previously had leprosy.

✤ *John 12:2, NLT*
A dinner was prepared in Jesus' honor. Martha served, and Lazarus was among those who ate with him.

TALKING TO GOD

All believers occasionally come to a worship service casually or with a bad attitude. Confess this weakness to the Lord, and ask him to make his presence real to you in the company of your church family, as you make his person, his work, and his Word the center of attention.

✤ *Mark 14:3, 6-9, NLT*

Meanwhile, Jesus was in Bethany at the home of Simon, a man who had previously had leprosy. While he was eating, a woman came in with a beautiful alabaster jar of expensive perfume made from essence of nard. She broke open the jar and poured the perfume over his head. . . . 6But Jesus replied, "Leave her alone. Why criticize her for doing such a good thing to me? 7You will always have the poor among you, and you can help them whenever you want to. But you will not always have me. 8She has done what she could and has anointed my body for burial ahead of time. 9I tell you the truth, wherever the Good News is preached throughout the world, this woman's deed will be remembered and discussed."

✤ *John 12:3, NLT*

Then Mary took a twelve-ounce jar of expensive perfume made from essence of nard, and she anointed Jesus' feet with it, wiping his feet with her hair. The house was filled with the fragrance.

TALKING TO GOD

Let your gratitude overwhelm you as you thank God for how much he loves you, what he has done for you, and what he has planned for you. Ask him to help you not to hold back in your private and public expressions of love and praise for him.

WORSHIPING

Setting the Scene

During the meal, Mary poured an expensive bottle of perfume on Jesus' head and feet. (This is a different event than the one recorded in Luke 7:36-50.)

This ointment or perfume was made from an aromatic herb (also called spikenard) from the mountains of India and imported in alabaster bottles. This item was so valuable that people would invest in it, much like gold today. According to John 12:5, this bottle was worth "a year's wages" (NLT). Nard was used to anoint kings, so Mary may have been "anointing" Jesus as her kingly Messiah. When the disciples criticized Mary for her act of worship, Jesus reprimanded them, explaining that this was a unique act for a specific occasion—an anointing that anticipated Jesus' burial and a public declaration of faith in him as Messiah. Jesus was not saying that his followers should neglect or be indifferent to the poor.

Jesus said Mary had prepared his body "for burial." In this culture, fragrant ointments would be used for anointing dead bodies to prepare them for burial. Embalming was not the Jewish custom, and perfume would cover the odor of the dead body. Mary probably did not understand Jesus' approaching death any more than the disciples. She may have realized that something was going to happen, so she sympathized with him and did "what she could" by honoring him with the greatest gift she could give.

Jesus said Mary's unselfish act would be remembered forever. This has come true because we read about it today.

Getting Personal

What holds you back from being fully engaged in worship (for example, being preoccupied, distracted, fearful of what others might think, etc.)?

In what ways does your devotion to Christ cost you something? For you, what would be an "extravagant" act of love for Jesus?

While the disciples misunderstood Jesus' mission and constantly fought about places of honor in the Kingdom, and the religious leaders stubbornly refused to believe in Jesus and plotted his death, this one quiet woman considered no sacrifice too great for her beloved Master. Jesus wants our total devotion—heart, soul, mind, and strength (Mark 12:30).

PRETENDING

Setting the Scene

According to Matthew's account, "the disciples were indignant" at Mary's act, but John names Judas as the disciple who spoke up. The disciples had mixed reactions about what Mary was doing and exclaimed that the perfume could have been sold and the money given to the poor. That seems like a good point, especially considering the desperate plight of poor people and that Passover was the time of special giving to the poor (see John 13:27-29). But John points out that Judas didn't actually care about poor people; instead, his reaction was based on greed. Because Judas served as the disciples' treasurer, the proceeds for such a sale, if given to the disciples for distribution to the poor, would have been placed in Judas's care. The book of John notes that Judas "was a thief" who would often help himself to the disciples' funds.

Undoubtedly, Jesus would have known what Judas was doing—that Judas had a weakness for money and soon would betray him for thirty silver coins—but Jesus never did or said anything about it. When we see what kind of person Judas was, we cannot regard him as a tragic hero for his role in bringing Jesus to the Cross. No, he was a man with base motives who was living a lie.

Getting Personal

When have you been unfairly criticized for not being spiritual enough? How did you feel?

When have you been critical of a fellow believer's words, actions, or dress? What were your true motives?

When have you pretended to be more spiritual than you are? How should you have acted differently?

In Christian circles, pious phrases and clichés come easily, especially when we want to enhance our spiritual image. We may want to give the impression we are prayer warriors, serious Bible students, protectors of righteous moral standards, or, like the disciples in this story, champions of the disenfranchised and oppressed— while the reality of our lives is quite different. But God knows the real person behind the facade. He knows our thoughts and intentions and isn't fooled by feigned outrage or spirituality. He wants actions, not words. The disciples talked while Mary worshiped.

READING THE WORD

❊ *Matthew 26:8-9, NLT*
The disciples were indignant when they saw this. "What a waste!" they said. 9"It could have been sold for a high price and the money given to the poor."

❊ *John 12:4-6, NLT*
But Judas Iscariot, the disciple who would soon betray him, said, 5"That perfume was worth a year's wages. It should have been sold and the money given to the poor." 6Not that he cared for the poor—he was a thief, and since he was in charge of the disciples' money, he often stole some for himself.

TALKING TO GOD

Give up any pretense as you come to the Lord in prayer, using the words of Psalm 139:23-24: "Search me, O God, and know my heart; test me and know my anxious thoughts. Point out anything in me that offends you, and lead me along the path of everlasting life" (NLT).

READING THE WORD

✸ *John 12:9-11, NLT*

When all the people heard of Jesus' arrival, they flocked to see him and also to see Lazarus, the man Jesus had raised from the dead. 10Then the leading priests decided to kill Lazarus, too, 11for it was because of him that many of the people had deserted them and believed in Jesus.

TALKING TO GOD

Before the Lord, humbly remember your hopelessness and helplessness to save yourself. Thank him again for his love that sought you, his mercy that forgave you, his grace that pours out on your life, and eternal life with him. Ask him to give you the words and courage to share how your life has been changed.

BELIEVING

Setting the Scene

When Jesus called Lazarus from the tomb, it wasn't a private or secret event. John reports, "Bethany was only a few miles down the road from Jerusalem, and many of the people had come to console Martha and Mary in their loss" (John 11:18-19, NLT). Later we read, "Many of the people who were with Mary believed in Jesus when they saw this happen" (John 11:45, NLT). Word would have spread throughout the community about this amazing miracle. Certainly many of the Jews who were coming to Jerusalem from all over the world for the Passover celebration would have heard of Jesus bringing Lazarus back to life. When they discovered Jesus had returned to be with Lazarus in Bethany, they came to see both of them.

Lazarus must have been a powerful witness, since he could testify to the truth that he had been dead for days when Jesus gave him life again. No wonder many people "deserted" the priests "and believed in Jesus."

Getting Personal

What was your life like before you met Jesus?

In what ways has Jesus changed your life?

What can you do to share your story with others? Who can you tell? How can you point people to the Savior?

Lazarus must have been as famous as a rock star in the small town of Bethany and the surrounding area. We can imagine people pointing and saying, "There he is—the one who died and Jesus brought him back to life!" Lazarus knew he had done nothing to deserve the attention; the situation had been hopeless, and he had been helpless; then everything had changed—all because of Jesus. He pointed everyone to the Savior.

Although your story isn't quite that dramatic, it does have definite similarities to that of Lazarus. You were dead in your sins—totally hopeless and helpless. Then Jesus called you from death to eternal life. You did nothing to deserve or cause what Jesus did. In his grace, God called you and saved you. Many came to Jesus because of Lazarus; many may come to him because of you. Tell your story.

PLOTTING

Setting the Scene

Only a few weeks had gone by since Jesus had raised Lazarus from the dead. The fact that this miracle had caused many Jews to believe in Jesus had angered the leading priests so much that they were plotting to have both Jesus and Lazarus killed. From the Jewish leaders' point of view, they could accuse Jesus of blasphemy because he was claiming equality with God. But Lazarus had done nothing of the kind. They wanted Lazarus dead simply because he was a living witness to Jesus' power.

Note the contrast between the crowd (wanting to see Jesus and Lazarus) and the leading priests (wanting to kill both). The religious leaders, not the people, were actually guilty of Jesus' death. The chief priests had already formulated a plan to kill Jesus (John 11:50-53); then they added Lazarus to their hit list. As someone who had been brought back to life by the person they wanted to kill, Lazarus was embarrassing to them.

Getting Personal

Who may feel threatened because of your faith in Christ?

What believers do you know or know of, here or in other countries, who have suffered severe persecution because they follow Jesus? What can you do to encourage them?

We might assume that everyone would be thrilled at Lazarus's story—a person who had been dead was alive again! Instead, Lazarus was targeted by the leading priests for death because he was a powerful witness for Jesus and the power of God to transform lives. Lazarus was the ultimate before-and-after story; no one who knew him could doubt that Jesus had performed an amazing miracle in his life. Thus, jealous for their power and influence, the religious leaders felt threatened by Lazarus's popularity and influence, so they decided to take him out.

Those who stand for Christ, honoring him as the sovereign Lord, often threaten existing power structures and undermine many worldly values. It happens in families, schools, and communities. We don't know what happened to Lazarus, but we know Jesus' story. And Christians throughout the world are following in his steps (Acts 5:40-42).

READING THE WORD

❃ *John 12:10-11, NLT*

Then the leading priests decided to kill Lazarus, too, 11for it was because of him that many of the people had deserted them and believed in Jesus.

TALKING TO GOD

Spend some time today praying for your Christian brothers and sisters around the world who are being persecuted, some experiencing torture and death, just because they faithfully follow Christ. Pray that they will be filled with a strong sense of God's presence and renewed courage and grace.

JESUS ENTERS JERUSALEM
Week 34, Day 1

❁ *Matthew 21:1-11; Mark 11:1-11; Luke 19:29-44; John 12:12-19*

Up to this point in the Gospel accounts, the four writers have made unique contributions to the story of Jesus' life. With Jesus' arrival in Jerusalem at the beginning of what we now call Holy Week, the accounts become much more parallel and detailed. A quarter of Matthew's Gospel is devoted to the final week, and almost half of the Gospel of John covers the same time period. Those who recorded Jesus' life and ministry knew that an understanding of Jesus' final week would be a significant contribution to faith. Everything Jesus taught about his purpose came into sharp focus during those last days.

READING THE WORD

❁ *Matthew 21:1-3, NIV*
As they approached Jerusalem and came to Bethphage on the Mount of Olives, Jesus sent two disciples, ²saying to them, "Go to the village ahead of you, and at once you will find a donkey tied there, with her colt by her. Untie them and bring them to me. ³If anyone says anything to you, say that the Lord needs them, and he will send them right away."

❁ *Luke 19:29-34, NIV*
As he approached Bethphage and Bethany at the hill called the Mount of Olives, he sent two of his disciples, saying to them, ³⁰"Go to the village ahead of you, and as you enter it, you will find a colt tied there, which no one has ever ridden. Untie it and bring it here. ³¹If anyone asks you, 'Why are you untying it?' say, 'The Lord needs it.'" ³²Those who were sent ahead went and found it just as he had told them. ³³As they were untying the colt, its owners asked them, "Why are you untying the colt?" ³⁴They replied, "The Lord needs it."

APPROACHING JERUSALEM

Setting the Scene

Luke's account of the Triumphal Entry begins with the final reference to Jesus' impending arrival in Jerusalem, which has been mentioned several times since Luke 9:51 (see also 13:22; 17:11; 18:31; 19:28). Jesus had this trip to Jerusalem on his mind for a long time before he arrived. All four Gospels mention the fact that Jesus rode the last leg of his journey into Jerusalem on the colt of a donkey. For John, the mode of transportation Jesus used is fairly secondary to the response of the people to his presence. But the other three biographers give details that help us see the significance of Jesus' actions. He was not riding the last few miles because he was tired; he was riding a colt because that was the most appropriate way someone with his credentials and purpose should arrive in David's city.

Traveling the road from Jericho meant Jesus approached Jerusalem from the east. The mountainous terrain makes it impossible to see the city until only a valley separates the traveler on the ridge of the Mount of Olives from the magnificent city. Jesus' route took him by or through Bethphage and Bethany, which were part of a ring of villages around the capital, which also featured Bethlehem on the south.

The instructions Jesus gave to the two disciples were explicit, so it strikes readers as somewhat odd that Mark and Luke only mention one donkey, but Matthew describes two—a female donkey and her colt. The reason for Matthew's inclusion of both animals can be seen in his immediate mention of Zechariah's prophecy announcing the arrival of the Messiah. True to form, Matthew addressed his Jewish audience, who would take significance from the Son of David deliberately entering the ancient capital of the kingdom, but unexpectedly "gentle and riding on a donkey, and on a colt, the foal of a donkey" (Matthew 21:5; Zechariah 9:9, NIV).

The signal given to the owner of the colt ("the Lord needs it") requires us to ask ourselves how available for the Lord's use is everything we own. Jesus exercised a right of usage that had been in some way established previously. When we acknowledge Jesus as Lord, we are also acknowledging his rightful claim over our lives, our possessions, our plans, and our future. We were never more than stewards, but believing in Jesus makes that role of mere stewards all the more immediate. Discipleship means we learn to release unhesitatingly anything God claims. If "the Lord needs it," it's his to use. Like the colt owners, we may experience a temporary loss of usage or access (a lost job, separation of friends, a possession needed by someone else), or it may mean permanent loss (to rust, thieves, destruction, death), but we are ultimately experiencing God's choice to deprive us of something that was never ours to begin with. It may be easy to say to God, "All that I am and have is yours, Lord," but we may well feel intense loss when God takes us at our word and removes something from us with only a hint, "The Lord needs it."

Getting Personal

When have you been deprived of something and you now realize the Lord had a higher purpose?

What would be difficult for you to give to him today?

Hundreds of people participated in Jesus' ministry in one way or another. Many we can only guess about—like the owners of this particular donkey. Part of eternity will include filling in the details. In the meantime, these unsung participants remind us that our participation in God's work may not be recognized in this life, but God will take note.

TALKING TO GOD

Since everything you have really came from God and belongs to him, ask God to help you hold these possessions loosely, so that you are ready to relinquish them if he asks it. Though it may be difficult, stretch to increase your availability to God.

SPONTANEITY AND INTENT

READING THE WORD

✤ *Matthew 21:4-9, NKJV*
All this was done that it might
be fulfilled which was spoken by
the prophet, saying: 5"Tell the
daughter of Zion, 'Behold, your
King is coming to you, Lowly,
and sitting on a donkey, A colt,
the foal of a donkey.'" 6So the
disciples went and did as Jesus
commanded them. 7They brought
the donkey and the colt, laid their
clothes on them, and set Him on
them. 8And a very great multitude
spread their clothes on the road;
others cut down branches from
the trees and spread them on
the road. 9Then the multitudes
who went before and those
who followed cried out, saying:
"Hosanna to the Son of David!
'Blessed is He who comes in the
name of the LORD!' Hosanna in
the highest!"

TALKING TO GOD

*Ask the Lord to develop in you
the humility of knowing and
understanding that leads to
genuine, exuberant praise.*

Setting the Scene

The crowd that enveloped Jesus during the Triumphal
Entry was, for the most part, not present because of Jesus
but because of the Passover. There would have been thousands of pilgrims in the capital for this grandest of the
Jewish religious celebrations, remembering God's great
act in liberating his people from captivity in Egypt. This
would have been on many troubled minds regarding
their current subjection under Roman rule. The possibility that Jesus could be the long-awaited king who would
return the glory of David's kingdom to Israel fueled praise
from the multitude.

John 12:12-13 tells us that as news of Jesus' approach
reached Jerusalem, people left the city to meet him. Taking their cue from the disciples' seating Jesus on the colt,
others spread their coats on the road in front of the donkey, a tradition mentioned in 2 Kings 9:12-13.

Jesus' actions fulfill Zechariah's prophecy (Zechariah 9:9). The response of the crowd confirmed that the
people were looking for some kind of king who would
come "in the name of the LORD." Each of the Gospel
writers captured a little different flavor of the crowd's response, but all of them include that phrase. Although fif-
teen psalms are traditionally associated with the pilgrims'
arrival in Jerusalem (Psalms 120–134), the phrases and
actions used by the crowd in relation to Jesus are found
in Psalm 118:26-27: "Blessed is he who comes in the
name of the LORD. From the house of the LORD we bless
you. The LORD is God, and he has made his light shine
on us. With boughs in hand, join in the festal procession
up to the horns of the altar" (NIV).

Getting Personal

*What are some of the ways you publicly acknowledge
Jesus' presence in your life?*

*From what kinds of "captivity" have you been delivered
because of Jesus?*

*The crowd's understanding of Jesus was woefully
shortsighted and narrow. That disconnect between
expression and understanding ought to continually
remind us that God is not distracted or fooled by
external acts; he reads our hearts.*

TAKING OFFENSE

Setting the Scene

Here we catch a glimpse of the undercurrent of resistance that was inevitably part of the Triumphal Entry. Our impression of an event may be that *everyone* is praising God or that people are *of one mind*, but in reality, this world is hostile territory, and even in the most welcoming environment there may be those whose hearts oppose him. The Triumphal Entry was a great declaration of God's intention, but it represented the ongoing struggle between God's purposes and a world intent on rebellion.

In an effort to maintain control, Pharisees in the crowd urged Jesus to quieten and even "rebuke" those who were praising him. The crowd was shouting the truth, but some heard only trouble. Jesus' approach to Jerusalem was clearly too humble and too human to be a significant threat to Roman rule. However, these leaders had the most to lose if Jesus started a rebellion that would receive harsh smothering by the Empire. They wanted Jesus to realize there was a lot more at stake than his own popularity.

Jesus' response that the rocks would cry out if the crowd was silenced not only reminds us of Psalm 19:1, "The heavens declare the glory of God; And the firmament shows His handiwork" (NKJV), it also makes it clear that Jesus was publicly presenting himself to his people as the Messiah. The moment had come for acceptance or rejection.

Getting Personal

When do you find yourself embarrassed by the exuberance of some Christians? Could their energetic praise be a challenge to your own lethargy or sense of decorum?

How do you determine when the appropriate worshipful response requires silence and when it requires shouting?

We are less likely to consider what the situation demands and more likely to consider what makes us comfortable. We tend toward self-centeredness. The question we ought to ask ourselves in worship more often is, "Since the rocks are silent, why don't we cry out?"

READING THE WORD

❧ *Luke 19:39-40, NKJV*
And some of the Pharisees called to Him from the crowd, "Teacher, rebuke Your disciples." 40But He answered and said to them, "I tell you that if these should keep silent, the stones would immediately cry out."

TALKING TO GOD

Combine thoughtful silence and joyful noise in your personal worship time today. Ask the Lord to take away your inhibitions in private worship, so that you may express the full range of your human response to his goodness and glory.

READING THE WORD

✷ *Luke 19:41-44, NKJV*

Now as He drew near, He saw the city and wept over it, ⁴²saying, "If you had known, even you, especially in this your day, the things that make for your peace! But now they are hidden from your eyes. ⁴³For days will come upon you when your enemies will build an embankment around you, surround you and close you in on every side, ⁴⁴and level you, and your children within you, to the ground; and they will not leave in you one stone upon another, because you did not know the time of your visitation."

TALKING TO GOD

Remind yourself, as you come to God in prayer, that the Lord is not cold and distant or mechanical in his responses to you. Remember his tears for those he came to save, and praise him for his ability to empathize with the full range of human emotion.

Setting the Scene

It seems that, as the time of his sacrifice approached, Jesus' emotions were close to the surface. As he reached the crest of the Mount of Olives, the city came into view and Jesus began weeping.

Jesus' words help us understand his tears. Others might cry tears of joy and wonder over the sight of Jerusalem; Jesus looked at the city with eyes that saw her fate. He saw how he would be received, with a welcome that served as a prelude to crucifixion. His tears were not for himself but for the city that represented his objective. He came to save her, whether she knew it or not.

Where others saw a proud and impregnable city, Jesus saw broken walls and broken people. The one who could bring them peace was arriving in Jerusalem that day, but Jesus knew he was "hidden" from their eyes. God's purposes would be worked out in his death and they would also be worked out in the tragic unfolding of events for Jerusalem. Jesus' tearful prophecy was fulfilled in AD 70, when the Romans utterly destroyed the city.

The picture of Jesus weeping over people, over us, has a powerfully sobering effect. How could we not conclude that the one who would die for us would also cry for us? He cries over us because we are lost like Jerusalem or because we have been saved from certain death.

Getting Personal

What do you take from the real tenderness of Jesus' emotions at this point, on the brink of his crucifixion?

When have you felt sorrow for the lost people God loves?

Most of the heresies regarding the person of Jesus in church history have had to do with his humanity (see Arianism, Appolinarianism, Gnosticism). Confining Jesus in some form of godhood is easier than dealing with him as also fully human. Moments like these in Jesus' life are the evidence to back up Hebrews 4:15, "For we do not have a High Priest who cannot sympathize with our weaknesses, but was in all points tempted as we are, yet without sin" (NKJV).

RECEPTION

Setting the Scene

Matthew's account makes it seem as if the first thing Jesus did on reaching Jerusalem was the cleansing of the Temple (20:10-13), but Mark's version of events provides a more reasonable sequence, saving the confrontation with the sellers and money changers for the following day. Matthew does make it clear that Jesus was the talk of the town. Those who had accompanied Jesus into town described him as the "prophet from Nazareth in Galilee," but not as the Messiah or the King.

Jesus entered Jerusalem and didn't stop until he reached the heart of the city—the Temple. This would have been the masterpiece of Herod the Great, still under construction at that time. It was the second replacement for Solomon's grand structure that had been razed by the Babylonians in 586 BC. A much smaller and simpler Temple had been rebuilt by Zerubbabel and the first exiles who returned from Babylon. Herod was creating a legacy for himself. Mark tells us that Jesus walked through the Temple and "looked around at everything."

Since the city was filled beyond capacity with pilgrims, Jesus and the disciples returned to Bethany for the night, presumably staying with Mary, Martha, and Lazarus.

Jesus entered this world just outside Jerusalem to the south, in Bethlehem. He spent his final week commuting between the city and the outlying village of Bethany. He narrowly escaped death as a child in Bethlehem; he wouldn't escape death as the Savior in Jerusalem. His words and actions throughout this week confront us with the same question that echoed in the streets of Jerusalem: "Who is this?"

Getting Personal

Jesus went first to the center of worship in Jerusalem and looked around at the Temple. What would please or displease Jesus if he inspected your personal center of worship, your heart?

Who is Jesus—to you?

Jesus' actions must have puzzled the disciples. He didn't take advantage of the momentum of the Triumphal Entry. They may have expected him to declare his role as king, but instead he let the excitement of the parade die away to lingering questions about his identity. They were learning the same lesson we learn: Jesus doesn't accomplish his purposes by our timetables, agendas, or priorities.

READING THE WORD

❊ *Matthew 21:10-11, NIV*
When Jesus entered Jerusalem, the whole city was stirred and asked, "Who is this?" 11The crowds answered, "This is Jesus, the prophet from Nazareth in Galilee."

❊ *Mark 11:11, NIV*
Jesus entered Jerusalem and went into the temple courts. He looked around at everything, but since it was already late, he went out to Bethany with the Twelve.

TALKING TO GOD

You can't lay your coat on the ground for Jesus to walk over, but you can prepare your mind for worship by laying your life— possessions, relationships, time, values—before him and inviting him to be King.

FLASHBACK

READING THE WORD

✼ *John 12:16-19, NKJV*
His disciples did not understand these things at first; but when Jesus was glorified, then they remembered that these things were written about Him and that they had done these things to Him. 17Therefore the people, who were with Him when He called Lazarus out of his tomb and raised him from the dead, bore witness. 18For this reason the people also met Him, because they heard that He had done this sign. 19The Pharisees therefore said among themselves, "You see that you are accomplishing nothing. Look, the world has gone after Him!"

TALKING TO GOD

Thank God for his Word, the truth (John 17:17). Thank him for its richness and the blessing of the Holy Spirit to quicken your understanding and teach you from day to day.

Setting the Scene

In his Gospel, John frequently reminds us that he was recording Jesus' biography after decades of reflection of the events that had so radically altered his life. He couldn't help but include in various places explanatory notes like we find in 12:16, "His disciples did not understand these things at first" (see also 2:22; 6:60; 8:27; 10:6). Later the disciples experienced what Jesus promised during the Last Supper: "But when the Father sends the Advocate as my representative—that is, the Holy Spirit—he will teach you everything and will remind you of everything I have told you" (John 14:26, NLT). If those who were eyewitnesses to all that Jesus taught found it hard to understand fully, we can take comfort when we also find it difficult. Fortunately, we have not only the record of the events but also the enlightenment of the Holy Spirit.

The story of Jesus raising Lazarus from the dead was all over Jerusalem, and people were curious to find out more about Jesus. John gives this as the primary reason why Jesus received such a welcome during the Triumphal Entry. This was tabloid curiosity, a fascination with the incredible, odd, and sensational.

Meanwhile the Pharisees were becoming desperate in their frustration. They exaggerated Jesus' popularity as a way of justifying the actions they were about to take. They resorted to bribery, treachery, deceit, and conspiracy to eliminate Jesus.

All people face a choice. Jesus approaches people in the way most likely to get their attention and gives them a clear opportunity to consider his claims. If they reject him, it is because they have chosen to do so.

Getting Personal

How has the Holy Spirit helped you understand Jesus' teachings?

In what ways have you grown in your relationship with Jesus in the past year? What changes have you made?

Sometimes we realize after the fact that God has brought a person into our lives to give us a perspective we might not otherwise have gotten. Other times, we look at a passage of Scripture after long acquaintance and suddenly see a personal application we've never seen before. God has a wide assortment of attention-getting methods to use.

JESUS CLEANSES THE TEMPLE
Week 35, Day 1

✤ *Matthew 21:12-17; Mark 11:15-19; Luke 19:45-48*

Jesus entered Jerusalem for the last time, and he made his entrance in dramatic fashion, beginning with a second Temple "cleansing." What can we learn from this event? That's what we'll discover this week.

OUTBURST

Setting the Scene

The Temple in Jerusalem was rich with history. Three Temples had been constructed on the same site. Solomon's glorious Temple, built in the tenth century BC was the first, but it was destroyed in 586 BC when the Babylonians captured Jerusalem. The second, Zerubbabel's Temple, much smaller, was built on the same site by the exiles who returned from captivity and finished the job in 515 BC. This Temple was enlarged by Herod the Great, construction having begun in 20 BC, and was the one Jesus entered. Actually this project may not have been finished before the Temple was destroyed by the Romans in AD 70 in response to a Jewish revolt.

The Temple was run by the high priest and his associates. When Jesus entered, he would have encountered tremendous chaos. Josephus, an ancient Jewish historian, wrote that 256,500 lambs were sacrificed at the Passover in AD 66. This lack of worshipful atmosphere didn't seem to bother the priests, who were counting their profits. The money changers exchanged international currency for special Temple coins—the only money the merchants would accept. With so many foreign visitors, these money changers would do big business during Passover. The money changers also would exchange Hebrew shekels for Roman drachmas for the Temple tax. Because the drachmas had the stamped image of Caesar (who was an idol worshiper) on them, they were considered blasphemous by the Jews.

In addition to the money changers were those "buying

READING THE WORD

✤ *Mark 11:15-16,* NLT
When they arrived back in Jerusalem, Jesus entered the Temple and began to drive out the people buying and selling animals for sacrifices. He knocked over the tables of the money changers and the chairs of those selling doves, 16and he stopped everyone from using the Temple as a marketplace.

OUTBURST *continued*

TALKING TO GOD

Ask God to align your affections with his own, so that you will be righteously angry at those situations that make him angry and brokenhearted over the issues that break his heart. Ask him to help you discipline yourself to react in love, thinking of others more than yourself.

and selling animals for sacrifices." God had originally instructed the people to bring sacrifices from their own flocks (Deuteronomy 12:5-7), but the religious leadership had established four markets on the Mount of Olives where animals could be purchased. If the priests decided that an animal brought from home was unacceptable, the worshiper was forced to buy another one. "Doves" could be an alternate sacrifice for those too poor to purchase larger animals. Doves were also sacrificed for the cleansing of women and lepers (Leviticus 12:6; 14:19-22).

One of these markets was in the Court of the Gentiles, the only place Gentile converts to Judaism were allowed to worship because they were not pure Jews. But the market filled their worship space.

So Jesus drove them all out. He was angry that God's house of worship had become a secular place of extortion and was preventing Gentiles from worship. Jesus was fully human, so he experienced the broad range of human emotions—joy, sadness, love, and even anger. But in expressing those emotions, he did not sin.

Getting Personal

When has an angry outburst caused harm to yourself and others? What did you do to heal the relationship or make the situation right?

What daily irritations, inconveniences, or personal slights tend to make you angry?

What injustices or sinful acts bring out your righteous indignation? Which ones have you tended to overlook or ignore?

Jesus knew exactly what he was doing and why. His anger was directed at those sellers and buyers. Righteous indignation and uncontrolled rage are quite different, yet both are called "anger." Quoting Psalm 4:4, Paul wrote, "And 'don't sin by letting anger control you'" (Ephesians 4:26, NLT).

We must be careful how we use this powerful emotion. Being angry about injustice and sinful acts is right; being angry over trivial personal offenses is wrong. But even anger for the right reasons can become sinful when we let it control us or push us into an extreme response. We can err on both sides of this issue, not becoming upset over what we should and lashing out when we shouldn't.

REPEAT PERFORMANCE

Setting the Scene

These two passages mark two different times that Jesus cleared the Temple. Early in his public ministry, just after he had turned water into wine in Cana (John 2:1-12) and during the Passover season, Jesus had taken a whip and had chased out the merchants and money changers (John 2:13-17). At that time, Jesus had declared, "Stop turning my Father's house into a marketplace!"

Evidently, keeping the Court of the Gentiles open and accessible didn't last long because just a couple of years later Jesus returned and found the Temple again filled with stalls and the sounds of merchants shouting, sheep bleating, and coins clinking—all with the priests' approval.

Getting Personal

When have you tried to stop or start a specific habit or routine? How long did your reformation last?

What changes has God through his Spirit made in your life since you first believed?

What changes do you want him to make?

Bad habits are difficult to break, especially in our own strength and without true repentance. The merchants and money changers who had been using the Temple court as a religious shopping mall had scattered and fled under Jesus' authority and whip. But they hadn't left because they had seen the error of their ways; neither had the priests. So everyone returned to business as usual, presumably at the first opportunity.

Jesus wants to drive out all sorts of sinful attitudes, motives, and actions from our lives. We may respond by conforming or reforming for a while, making resolutions and trying our best to do better. Unless change occurs on the inside through sincere sorrow and the work of the Holy Spirit, however, we'll return to those bad habits or worse. Make your "temple" God's "house of prayer" (Matthew 21:13, NLT).

READING THE WORD

❀ *Luke 19:45, NLT*
Then Jesus entered the Temple and began to drive out the people selling animals for sacrifices.

❀ *John 2:13-16, NLT*
It was nearly time for the Jewish Passover celebration, so Jesus went to Jerusalem. 14In the Temple area he saw merchants selling cattle, sheep, and doves for sacrifices; he also saw dealers at tables exchanging foreign money. 15Jesus made a whip from some ropes and chased them all out of the Temple. He drove out the sheep and cattle, scattered the money changers' coins over the floor, and turned over their tables. 16Then, going over to the people who sold doves, he told them, "Get these things out of here. Stop turning my Father's house into a marketplace!"

TALKING TO GOD

God already knows your weaknesses, shortcomings, and failures—and he knows when you truly desire to be better and do better. Bring your longing for change before him today, and ask for his Spirit to bring lasting change.

BUYERS AND SELLERS

READING THE WORD

✵ *Matthew 21:12-13, NLT*
Jesus entered the Temple and began to drive out all the people buying and selling animals for sacrifice. He knocked over the tables of the money changers and the chairs of those selling doves. 13He said to them, "The Scriptures declare, 'My Temple will be called a house of prayer,' but you have turned it into a den of thieves!"

TALKING TO GOD

Ask the Lord to prepare you for your times of corporate worship. Ask for help in improving your focus on Christ, in fully engaging in worship, and in ministering to your brothers and sisters at church with love and pure motives.

Setting the Scene

The sacrificial system had been established by God, and making a sacrifice was supposed to be a holy event. The Passover commemorated Israel's deliverance from Egypt when the Angel of Death had passed over homes where blood had been sprinkled on their doorways. The Passover also pictured the final, ultimate sacrifice that would be made by Jesus, the Lamb of God. Yet those involved in the Temple that day—the leaders, the sellers, and the buyers—missed the point of this worship experience through their self-serving attitudes and actions.

The leaders viewed their role as simply a job—with status and perks. And their cut of the merchants' profits helped fill the treasury. The sellers saw Passover as a way to enrich themselves. The buyers were also at fault. The "sacrifices" were meant to be just that—sacrifices; that is, each individual was to think carefully about what he or she was doing, especially in selecting the animal to be sacrificed. If they waited until they arrived at the Temple just for the convenience, their "sacrifice" meant nothing.

Getting Personal

What changes might Jesus make in your church if he were to come at worship time?

With which of the three types of people do you most identify (leaders, sellers, buyers)? How can you be careful not to repeat their mistakes?

Although many centuries have passed since this event and the Old Testament sacrificial system, we still have houses of worship where we regularly gather. The main purpose for our worship services is to express our adoration of God and gratitude for his works and to renew our commitment to serve him. The sacrament of Communion recalls the Last Supper (the Passover meal) and commemorates Jesus' death on the cross, for us. But we still can have hypocritical "priests" (church leaders who just have a job, not a calling), greedy "merchants" (those who attend to enhance their image, make contacts, do business, or other less-than-holy motives), and superficial or casual "buyers" (attendees, even members, who come when it's convenient and then just go through the motions).

HOUSE AND DEN

Setting the Scene

Jesus quoted from Isaiah 56:7 to explain God's purpose for the Temple. It belonged to *God* and was meant to be a "house of prayer" and open "for all nations." But the chaos and the blocking of the Gentiles made this no more than a "den of thieves." The merchants had turned the Temple into their hangout, their "den." This was a horrible desecration. No wonder Jesus was so angry.

Here we see Jesus placing himself in authority above the religious leaders—the high priest (Caiaphas) and all those in the Sanhedrin. Those men were in charge of the Temple, and they would soon have words with Jesus about this episode (Mark 11:27-28).

Getting Personal

What might cause a church to lose sight that their main purpose is to meet God together, to worship?

What Lord's Day activities distract you or your family from worship?

What can you do to prepare to meet God when you go to church?

"House" and "den" refer to places—physical structures with specific purposes. We know that God isn't limited to any human structure, but this text and others call certain places his "house." It can be any place that has been set apart ("sanctified"), dedicated to him, where believers gather for the kind of worship modeled in Acts 2:42, where they "devoted themselves to the apostles' teaching, and to fellowship, and to sharing in meals (including the Lord's Supper), and to prayer" (NLT). Whether a house, storefront, warehouse, modern edifice, or ancient cathedral, God meets his people there. It's only a building, but it's not only a building. Clearly God wants to meet us there, in his "house." A church isn't primarily a social club, cultural center, or coffee bar. First and foremost, it should be a "house of prayer."

Today Jesus probably wouldn't drive out bake sales to fund youth ministries, book tables, or camp and retreat sign-ups from your church foyer. (Yet even these seemingly harmless activities must not distract or upstage true worship.) He wasn't standing against any money changing hands in the building, but he is against treating his house like any other place and altering the purpose for worship.

READING THE WORD

✤ *Mark 11:17, NLT*
He said to them, "The Scriptures declare, 'My Temple will be called a house of prayer for all nations,' but you have turned it into a den of thieves."

TALKING TO GOD

Thank the Lord for your church and your church building, and for your brothers and sisters in Christ who regularly gather there. Ask him to make you good stewards of that facility and to remember that it is his "house" and that he wants to meet you there.

ELITES

READING THE WORD

❧ *Matthew 21:14-16, NLT*
The blind and the lame came to him in the Temple, and he healed them. ¹⁵The leading priests and the teachers of religious law saw these wonderful miracles and heard even the children in the Temple shouting, "Praise God for the Son of David." But the leaders were indignant. ¹⁶They asked Jesus, "Do you hear what these children are saying?" "Yes," Jesus replied. "Haven't you ever read the Scriptures? For they say, 'You have taught children and infants to give you praise.'"

TALKING TO GOD

Seek the Lord's generosity and openness toward all types of people. Ask him to give you his love for others, so that you will avoid the pitfalls of condescending disapproval or easy dismissal of people God loves.

Setting the Scene

That "the blind and the lame" came to Jesus in the Temple is significant. Usually people with those conditions were excluded from Temple worship based on laws stemming from 2 Samuel 5:8. But Jesus, the Messiah, welcomed them there and "healed them." Then some children in the Temple began shouting, "Praise God for the Son of David."

The "leading priests" were mostly Sadducees (the wealthy, upper-class, priestly party among the Jewish political groups). The "teachers of religious law" were usually Pharisees. These two groups had great contempt for each other (see Acts 23:6-10) and seldom agreed on anything. But Jesus' actions in the Temple united the enemies against him.

The exact timing of these events is not clear, but certainly they happened in the same day. Jesus entered the Temple and observed the buying and selling and general chaos, and he drove everyone out. Next, the outcast "blind" and "lame" came to Jesus, certainly stepping around the overturned tables and other clutter, and he healed them. Then some children began shouting. All of these events were observed by the religious leaders. They were supposed to be in charge, yet there was Jesus, encroaching on their territory. Who did he think he was?

The blind and lame knew. But these religious leaders missed the Savior.

Getting Personal

When have you felt on the outside in a religious setting?

In what ways are you part of the "in crowd" at your church?

When have you stood in judgment like those religious leaders in the Temple, feeling disgusted by someone's less-than-kosher actions?

We can wonder how the religious leaders could be so blind to their own Messiah, but we can do the same. Wrapped in our own religious robes (righteous words and actions, biblical knowledge, position in the church), we can easily dismiss or even judge outsiders. It could be a visitor asking a pointed question in Sunday school, a baby crying in a worship service, a family from a different social class, a teenager's clothes and assumed attitude—anyone who might threaten the status quo. We can become the condescending elites.

THE WORD

Setting the Scene

Jesus habitually quoted Scripture—in this case, to the merchants and to the religious leaders. The Old Testament prophecies proved that what he was saying and doing agreed with God's Word and was, therefore, right and true. Jesus had heard what the children were saying, and what they were saying was absolutely true. Jesus affirmed his agreement with their shouts of praise. His question, "Haven't you ever read the Scriptures?" was an insult to these religious leaders who spent much time reading and studying the law. Yes, they read and studied, but they didn't understand, especially those passages that were being fulfilled before their eyes. Jesus was quoting from Psalm 8:2, regarded as messianic by the early church.

Quoting Scripture wasn't merely a technique to be used in debates with religious scholars. Jesus referred to the Bible often, for example, when he was tempted by Satan in the wilderness (Matthew 4:1-11), and even on the cross (Matthew 27:46). The Bible is inspired, authoritative, and true.

Getting Personal

How often do you read the Bible and other resources devotionally?

How often do you study the Bible? What Bible study tools do you use (study Bible, commentaries, Bible studies, Bible dictionary, etc.)?

When do you study the Bible with others (church, Sunday school class, small group, etc.)?

What steps should you take to better understand and apply Scripture?

The religious leaders also valued the Scriptures. But they didn't understand them because of their personal additions and interpretations. We can do the same unless we allow the Bible to speak to us. This involves looking at the whole story—the immediate and wider context—to determine what was going on. Bible study tools are also helpful, and we are blessed to have so many available to us these days. We also can invite more mature Christians to offer their opinions on the passage. But this process all begins by regularly reading God's Word.

READING THE WORD

✶ *Matthew 21:13, 16, NLT*
He said to them, "The Scriptures declare, 'My Temple will be called a house of prayer,' but you have turned it into a den of thieves!" . . . 16They asked Jesus, "Do you hear what these children are saying?" "Yes," Jesus replied. "Haven't you ever read the Scriptures? For they say, 'You have taught children and infants to give you praise.'"

TALKING TO GOD

How wonderful that our Creator God has revealed himself and his will through the Bible, his holy Word. Ask God to open your eyes as you read and study, so that you might understand more of who he is and how he wants you to live.

JESUS' AUTHORITY IS CHALLENGED
Week 36, Day 1

❁ *Matthew 21:23-46; Mark 11:27–12:12; Luke 20:1-19*

The passages from the Gospels for this week capture an extended confrontation Jesus had with the chief priests, teachers of the law, and the elders one day during Holy Week. The strategy of Jesus' opponents was to get him to utter something they could clearly label as blasphemous. They were looking for evidence to convict rather than evidence to believe. Sometimes people who seem to be busy seeking are actually very busy trying their best not to see.

READING THE WORD

❁ *Matthew 21:23-27, NIV*
Jesus entered the temple courts, and, while he was teaching, the chief priests and the elders of the people came to him. "By what authority are you doing these things?" they asked. "And who gave you this authority?" 24Jesus replied, "I will also ask you one question. If you answer me, I will tell you by what authority I am doing these things. 25John's baptism—where did it come from? Was it from heaven, or of human origin?" They discussed it among themselves and said, "If we say, 'From heaven,' he will ask, 'Then why didn't you believe him?' 26But if we say, 'Of human origin'—we are afraid of the people, for they all hold that John was a prophet." 27So they answered Jesus, "We don't know." Then he said, "Neither will I tell you by what authority I am doing these things."

QUESTIONING CREDENTIALS

Setting the Scene

Jesus had entered the city of Jerusalem as a peaceful king, cleansed the Temple as the indignant Son of God, and generally created a buzz around the city about his identity. Each day he was teaching in the Temple, never in want of an audience. During one of these sessions, he was approached by the local authorities, who questioned his authority to be "doing these things" (Matthew 21:23).

Their question was really two questions: "by what authority?" and "who gave you this authority?" Their points were, "How are you doing this?" and "Who told you that you could do it?" If Jesus had declared that he was exercising God's authority, they would have accused him of claiming to be God or God's Messiah—and therefore committing blasphemy. Based on Leviticus 24:10-23, they would have brought him to trial and sentenced him to death. But if Jesus claimed authority in himself, they would have branded him as simply another self-appointed fanatic out to get a following.

Jesus made them the tantalizing offer that he would answer their question directly if they would answer his. He asked them about John the Baptist, who was still a popular figure. John's murder at the hands of Herod remained a sore spot with the people. Jesus' question was, "Let's talk about John's authority: Was it his own or did it come from God?"

Suddenly those who had tried to trick Jesus had a dilemma. Either answer got them in trouble, exactly what they had intended by their question to Jesus. If they accepted John's legitimate authority, they would be admitting their own failure to believe him; if they questioned his authority, they would run afoul of the people's high regard for John. They didn't want to admit publicly that they had rejected John the Baptist as a God-endorsed prophet, because the crowds would not have taken kindly to that confession. So they took the cowardly way out, answering, "We don't know." They avoided giving the answer, but they also lost that opportunity to trap Jesus.

The religious leaders who confronted Jesus might have claimed to be pursuing the truth, but their real objective was to destroy Jesus. They instinctively saw him as a threat because he reminded them how far they were from faithfully discharging the responsibilities they had among God's people. There were a few individual leaders (like Nicodemus) among Jewish religious leaders of the time who became authentic believers, but most of the establishment actively served to lead the people in rejecting Christ. As John put it, "He came to that which was his own, but his own did not receive him" (John 1:11, NIV).

Getting Personal

How do you often rationalize your way out of obedience to Christ rather than submit to his authority?

What makes arguing with God especially pointless?

We can become adept at playing the game of appearances, in which we claim to live in obedience to God but we merely live to pursue our desires. But what would happen if we won that game? "What good is it for someone to gain the whole world, yet forfeit their soul?" (Mark 8:36, NIV).

TALKING TO GOD

Don't hold back in expressing yourself freely to God, who knows and understands you. At the same time, remember God's authority over all he has created, including you. Respecting his power and authority is the beginning of wisdom. Ask him to help you participate gladly in his plans.

READING THE WORD

✤ *Matthew 21:28-32, NKJV*
"But what do you think? A man had two sons, and he came to the first and said, 'Son, go, work today in my vineyard.' 29He answered and said, 'I will not,' but afterward he regretted it and went. 30Then he came to the second and said likewise. And he answered and said, 'I go, sir,' but he did not go. 31Which of the two did the will of his father?" They said to Him, "The first." Jesus said to them, "Assuredly, I say to you that tax collectors and harlots enter the kingdom of God before you. 32For John came to you in the way of righteousness, and you did not believe him; but tax collectors and harlots believed him; and when you saw it, you did not afterward relent and believe him."

TALKING TO GOD

Request that the Lord combine in you the second son's readiness to accept his Father's authority and the first son's determination to obey. Thank God for his ongoing patience with you, as you increasingly understand and do his will.

TWO SONS

Setting the Scene

Jesus wasn't done reminding the chief priests and their allies that they had made a grave error in dismissing John the Baptist. Shortly before John was beheaded, Jesus said, "Truly I tell you, among those born of women there has not risen anyone greater than John the Baptist; yet whoever is least in the kingdom of heaven is greater than he" (Matthew 11:11, NIV). By human standards, John was as good as they come in fulfilling his God-given role. And yet even he couldn't measure up to those who are saved by grace and become citizens of the Kingdom of Heaven.

So Jesus told the story of the two sons, with their different answers to their father and their different actions. Jesus made the point of his story painfully clear: The first son represents the "tax collectors and harlots" who are entering the Kingdom of God ahead of "you," the religious establishment who were like the second son. These tax collectors and prostitutes may have been in rebellion against God initially, but they eventually believed the message of John and repented, while the chief priests and their allies not only rejected the message but rejected the witness of those who were being transformed by it. The privileged faith of the religious leaders turned out to have no root of obedience to sustain it.

Getting Personal

Why doesn't access to spiritual knowledge or information insure that we will be in a right relationship with Christ?

What have you said you would do in obedience to God but have not yet done?

Even in his judgment, Jesus offered a glimpse of hope. He said, "tax collectors and harlots enter the kingdom of God before you." He did not say, "but you don't enter the kingdom." These stubborn leaders still had an opportunity if they would "relent and believe" John's message and accept Jesus.

THE TALE OF THE TERRIBLE TENANTS

Setting the Scene

In this parable, a certain landowner created a fully equipped vineyard. Then he turned it over to tenants under an arrangement where they agreed to give him a share of the produce of the farm in exchange for the privilege of living and working there. The characters in the story are easily identifiable: God is the landowner and his vineyard is Israel (see Isaiah 5:2); the tenants are the religious establishment; the landowner's servants are the prophets and all those who remained faithful to God; the son is Jesus; and the "other tenants" are new spiritual leadership that will include the Gentiles.

At harvesttime, the landowner sent servants to collect his share. The tenants emphatically and cruelly rejected the landowner's right to his share of the products of his land. And when the landowner sent his son to collect, the tenants figured they could claim total ownership of the vineyard if they killed the heir.

Jesus' story ends with a question: "When the owner of the vineyard comes, what will he do to those tenants?" In the book of Matthew his listeners know the answer; in Mark and Luke, Jesus supplies it. The terrible tenants will receive a terrible fate and the vineyard will be turned over to others. The consequences may be delayed, but they are inevitable. When it comes to God, getting away with something is never more than a temporary success. God will not be mocked, ignored, or disobeyed by his creatures without eventual consequences.

Getting Personal

In what ways have you rejected Jesus' advice or control of your life?

Why do we tend to take God's blessings for granted?

Accepting the vineyard of life without humbly acknowledging the Giver is possible. People do it all the time. But their apparent success and, at times, even prosperity must be seen from the perspective of the brevity of life and the length of eternity. Squandering the opportunity to trust God in this life is no way to prepare for eternity.

READING THE WORD

�֍ *Matthew 21:31, 33-41, NIV*
Jesus said to them, ... ³³"Listen to another parable: There was a landowner who planted a vineyard. He put a wall around it, dug a winepress in it and built a watchtower. Then he rented the vineyard to some farmers and moved to another place. ³⁴When the harvest time approached, he sent his servants to the tenants to collect his fruit. ³⁵The tenants seized his servants; they beat one, killed another, and stoned a third. ³⁶Then he sent other servants to them, more than the first time, and the tenants treated them the same way. ³⁷Last of all, he sent his son to them. 'They will respect my son,' he said. ³⁸But when the tenants saw the son, they said to each other, 'This is the heir. Come, let's kill him and take his inheritance.' ³⁹So they took him and threw him out of the vineyard and killed him. ⁴⁰Therefore, when the owner of the vineyard comes, what will he do to those tenants?" ⁴¹"He will bring those wretches to a wretched end," they replied, "and he will rent the vineyard to other tenants, who will give him his share of the crop at harvest time."

TALKING TO GOD

Recall your status as a privileged steward and ask the Lord to make you a faithful one. Ask him to fill your understanding with who he is, as ultimate authority.

READING THE WORD

❀ *Matthew 21:42, NIV*
Jesus said to them, "Have you never read in the Scriptures: 'The stone the builders rejected has become the cornerstone; the Lord has done this, and it is marvelous in our eyes'?"

❀ *Luke 20:16-18, NIV*
When the people heard this, they said, "God forbid!" ¹⁷Jesus looked directly at them and asked, "Then what is the meaning of that which is written: 'The stone the builders rejected has become the cornerstone'? ¹⁸Everyone who falls on that stone will be broken to pieces; anyone on whom it falls will be crushed."

TALKING TO GOD

Affirm that the Lord is the capstone and cornerstone of your life: the capstone holding it together and the cornerstone providing a solid foundation.

UNDERSTANDING

Setting the Scene

We can identify three distinct audiences for this exchange: Jesus' disciples, the priestly delegation, and the mixed crowd in the Temple that day. Jesus had just ended his story in a way that seemed to transition from illustration to reality. The story began in the past; Jesus' closing question, "What then will the owner of the vineyard do to them?" (Luke 20:15, NIV) is present and future. And when Jesus supplies the answer, "He will come and kill those tenants" (20:16, NIV), the crowd's instinctive response is to cry for an alternate ending. In Luke's account, they cry out, "God forbid!"

In Matthew's and Mark's versions, Jesus ends his parable of the tenants and immediately quotes Psalm 118:22-23, referring to a very familiar passage for the Passover pilgrims. The verses about the rejected stone come immediately before the phrases from the same psalm that had been shouted about Jesus during the Triumphal Entry. Apparently the theme of rejection in the psalm had been neglected by the enthusiastic crowd in teaching in favor of the theme of welcome.

Matthew and Luke include Jesus' ominous words, "Everyone who falls on that stone will be broken to pieces; anyone on whom it falls will be crushed" (Luke 20:18, NIV; see Matthew 21:44). The stone remains the same, but people's relation to it may be radically different. It can be the capstone (cornerstone) of life, a stone we trip over, or a stone that crushes. Sooner or later, everyone must encounter the stone. Jesus *was* unmistakably presenting his credentials to that mixed audience, to be taken or rejected, but with eternal consequences riding on the choice.

Getting Personal

Think of someone who rejected Jesus only to turn to him later as Lord. What happened?

What difficult requests of Jesus trip you up today?

In one important sense we must experience the stoniness of Jesus before we can appreciate his foundation and cornerstone role in our lives. In this way, "tripping" over him can have a good result, if our brokenness involves our will, pride, and anything that ought to be broken in us.

JUDGMENT

Setting the Scene

In case there was any doubt, Jesus turned the crucial point of his parable into an explicit judgment on the priestly delegation that had come to question his authority.

Matthew records that Jesus explicitly begins to use the words *the kingdom of God*. The special privileges of awareness and access regarding God's Kingdom will be "taken away from you and given to a people who will produce its fruit." The "you" Jesus was addressing was not all of Israel as a nation, but those in spiritual leadership who had proven themselves unfaithful in the tasks God had entrusted to them. The "people who will produce its fruit" were originally all Jews, the first members of the church. A door was opened here for the Gentiles, but not to the exclusion of Israel (see Romans 11:11-24).

The group to whom Jesus was speaking was clearly guilty of taking the Kingdom of God for granted and treating it as a resource to advance their own kingdom in this world. Their concerns about Jesus might have been couched in the righteous language of spiritual purity and God's holiness, but their intent was to protect their own power, prestige, and position.

Jesus certainly had more in mind than the religious leaders of his day when he pointed out that talking the talk meant little if there was no consistent walk to go with the words. Lip service to God means claiming to be a citizen of his Kingdom with no discernible evidence for the claim.

Getting Personal

What might Jesus say to you or your church about how well you are producing fruit?

What is the fruit that Jesus requires you to produce?

A currently popular but perennial tendency is to substitute pretense for reality in spiritual circles. Sometimes religious talk is used as a tool to manipulate, comfort, and control others even though the user believes that the words are meaningless. Such disregard for the Kingdom of God is yielding a harvest of deep disappointment and unbelief. True believers live what they say they believe.

READING THE WORD

❁ *Matthew 21:43-44,* NIV
Therefore I tell you that the kingdom of God will be taken away from you and given to a people who will produce its fruit. 44 Anyone who falls on this stone will be broken to pieces; anyone on whom it falls will be crushed.

TALKING TO GOD

Let sincerity mark your interaction with the Lord in prayer as well as your conversations among believers and nonbelievers. Ask God to make your life in him increasingly real and significant; that reality and significance will carry into all your dealings with others.

FEAR OF TRUTH

READING THE WORD

❧ *Matthew 21:45-46, NIV*
When the chief priests and the Pharisees heard Jesus' parables, they knew he was talking about them. 46They looked for a way to arrest him, but they were afraid of the crowd because the people held that he was a prophet.

❧ *Luke 20:19, NIV*
The teachers of the law and the chief priests looked for a way to arrest him immediately, because they knew he had spoken this parable against them. But they were afraid of the people.

TALKING TO GOD

Let any reluctance to obey be shattered against "the stone." Ask God to help you seek his Kingdom and his righteousness first, and let other priorities fall into place.

Setting the Scene

This week's readings began with a delegation of priests confronting Jesus about his authority. They end with the confrontation reversed. The chief priests had been out-maneuvered. Jesus had managed to sidestep their trap, provide an answer to their question for those who really wanted to know the source of his authority, and then turn the tables on them using a parable that highlighted their historic failure to be the spiritual leaders God had intended them to be. And they were livid.

Luke tells us that though the chief priests were looking for a "way to arrest him immediately," they didn't because they were "afraid of the people." Matthew helps us understand why they were afraid: "because the people held that he was a prophet." Those trying to destroy Jesus knew they needed to move cautiously and plan carefully.

We may not give the messengers God sends to us the violent treatment given to the landowner's servants, but do we listen and learn from those God sends our way? Or are we sullen, silent, or even prideful, thinking we have nothing new to learn?

Getting Personal

Based on Jesus' parable of the tenants, how do you think we should treat the messengers that God sends into our lives?

What is your relationship like right now with your pastor and other religious leaders in your life?

One of the killers of spiritual vitality is calculated behavior. We want to figure out the minimum standards for pleasing God and then pretend to meet them. This is a game we can't win by trying or by pretending. A halfhearted effort to surrender to God means that the other half of our heart is desperately looking for a way of escape.

❋ *Matthew 24:1-51; Mark 13:1-37; Luke 21:5-37*

While returning with Jesus to Bethany from Jerusalem, a disciple made a casual statement about the Temple. Jesus' response led to questions and to startling predictions about the future. This week we'll hear Jesus' call to action to those first-century followers and what it means to us.

BE SECURE

Setting the Scene

This may have been either Tuesday or Wednesday evening of the week before the Crucifixion. Jesus and the disciples had just left the Temple. This was Jesus' last visit to that area and the end of his public preaching and teaching.

The Temple was a magnificent structure, considered one of the architectural wonders of the ancient world. Built by Ezra after the return from exile in the sixth century BC (Ezra 6:14-15), it had been remodeled, expanded, and beautified under Herod the Great. The impressive edifice covered about one-sixth of the land area of Jerusalem and was a majestic mixture of porches, colonnades, separate small buildings, and courts surrounding the Temple proper. The disciples gazed in wonder at marble pillars forty feet high, carved from a single solid stone. The foundation was so solid that some of the original footings remain to this day. The Jews were convinced of the permanence of the Temple, not only because of the stability of construction but also because it was God's house.

Jesus made a startling statement: This "permanent" wonder of the world would be completely destroyed. This happened in AD 70 when the Romans sacked Jerusalem and fulfilled Jesus' words to the letter. After fire raged through the Temple, Emperor Titus ordered the leveling of the whole area, so no part of the original walls or buildings remained. Titus considered this as punishment for the Jewish rebellion in AD 66.

READING THE WORD

❋ *Mark 13:1-4, NLT*

As Jesus was leaving the Temple that day, one of his disciples said, "Teacher, look at these magnificent buildings! Look at the impressive stones in the walls." [2]Jesus replied, "Yes, look at these great buildings. But they will be completely demolished. Not one stone will be left on top of another!" [3]Later, Jesus sat on the Mount of Olives across the valley from the Temple. Peter, James, John, and Andrew came to him privately and asked him, [4]"Tell us, when will all this happen? What sign will show us that these things are about to be fulfilled?"

BE SECURE *continued*

TALKING TO GOD

Praise God that Jesus is "the same yesterday, today, and forever" (Hebrews 13:8, NLT) and that his Holy Spirit is always with you. Human institutions and endeavors fail you, so go to God and tell him you put your trust totally in him for your security and hope.

The disciples must have had difficulty believing Jesus' words, "Not one stone will be left on top of another!" Because the Temple symbolized God's presence among them, all Jews would be horrified to see it destroyed.

The disciples' question had two parts. They wanted to know *when* all this would happen, and *what sign* would "signal [Jesus'] return and the end of the world" (Matthew 24:3, NLT). The second part of their question refers to the Messiah's reign in God's Kingdom. The disciples expected that one event would occur immediately after the other. They expected the Messiah to inaugurate his Kingdom soon.

Jesus gave them a prophetic picture of that time, including events leading up to it. He also talked about far future events connected with the last days and his second coming, when he would return to earth to judge all people. As many of the Old Testament prophets had done, Jesus predicted both near and distant events without putting them in exact order. The coming destruction of Jerusalem and the Temple only foreshadowed a future destruction that would precede Christ's return.

Getting Personal

When have you put your trust in something or someone only to have it or that person let you down?

What helps you keep your focus on God and his Word instead of the empty promises of the world?

Jesus told his disciples, "I am with you always, even to the end of the age" (Matthew 28:20, NLT). How does that promise affect how you feel? How you live?

Nothing seemed more solid, more permanent than the magnificent Temple. Yet Jesus said it would be destroyed, leveled, with "not one stone . . . left on top of another." No wonder the disciples were shocked. In reality, nothing in this world is permanent. Yet like those ancient Jews, we make assumptions about the future. Often acting as though we have knowledge and control, we put our confidence in human institutions and endeavors: government, investments, career, personal talents and abilities, or a leader. But true security comes from only one source—almighty, eternal God.

BE WARNED

Setting the Scene

The disciples asked about a sign that would signal when these events would occur. Jesus answered by first warning them about false messiahs. Then he warned them about "wars and threats of wars," famines, earthquakes, other human-caused and natural disasters, and rampant sin. He also told them to expect to be "arrested, persecuted, and killed . . . hated all over the world," simply because they were his followers. With these dire predictions, however, Jesus also offered hope, describing the troubles as "birth pains"—that is, these events would signal that the Kingdom was near and that God would prevail.

The disciples probably assumed this end-of-the-age destruction would occur in the not-too-distant future. But much more had to happen first. The disciples may also have assumed that Jesus, the Messiah, would triumph and usher in this Kingdom in their lifetimes. So his words about persecution and death would have been jarring, even though he had warned them previously (see, for example, Matthew 5:11-12).

Not only would the disciples face hatred from religious and civil leaders and their own families, they would be "hated all over the world." The fear and persecution will be so intense that people will betray and hate in order to keep themselves safe. Then, because of the persecution and because of "false prophets," many who claim to follow Christ will abandon their profession of faith.

Getting Personal

At what time in your Christian experience did you believe that your life should be problem free? What brought you back to reality?

How do Jesus' warnings help you plan? In what ways do his words encourage you and give you hope?

Twenty centuries later, we have experienced the events predicted by Jesus—a world torn by disasters, false messiahs and their followers, and true Christ-followers marginalized and punished for their faith. As believers, we should not be shocked or surprised that the world hates us. Christians aren't immune from pain, conflicts, and troubles; in fact, we often get more simply because we follow Christ. But we follow him because he is the Truth and the only way to life.

READING THE WORD

✱ *Matthew 24:4-14, NLT*
Jesus told them, "Don't let anyone mislead you, 5for many will come in my name, claiming, 'I am the Messiah.' They will deceive many. 6And you will hear of wars and threats of wars, but don't panic. Yes, these things must take place, but the end won't follow immediately. 7Nation will go to war against nation, and kingdom against kingdom. There will be famines and earthquakes in many parts of the world. 8But all this is only the first of the birth pains, with more to come. 9Then you will be arrested, persecuted, and killed. You will be hated all over the world because you are my followers. 10And many will turn away from me and betray and hate each other. 11And many false prophets will appear and will deceive many people. 12Sin will be rampant everywhere, and the love of many will grow cold. 13But the one who endures to the end will be saved. 14And the Good News about the Kingdom will be preached throughout the whole world, so that all nations will hear it; and then the end will come."

TALKING TO GOD

Acknowledge the Lord's warnings in your prayer time today. Ask God to help you be strong and stead-fast during times of difficulty, remembering that he is with you— and that he alone has eternal life.

READING THE WORD

✱ *Matthew 24:4-5, 23-26, NLT*
Jesus told them, "Don't let anyone mislead you, 5for many will come in my name, claiming, 'I am the Messiah.' They will deceive many. . . . 23Then if anyone tells you, 'Look, here is the Messiah,' or 'There he is,' don't believe it. 24For false messiahs and false prophets will rise up and perform great signs and wonders so as to deceive, if possible, even God's chosen ones. 25See, I have warned you about this ahead of time. 26So if someone tells you, 'Look, the Messiah is out in the desert,' don't bother to go and look. Or, 'Look, he is hiding here,' don't believe it!"

TALKING TO GOD

Pray for a renewed hunger for God's Word, since knowing biblical truth is your best safeguard against false teaching. Ask the Lord to give you discernment so that you can distinguish good teaching from false teaching. Ask him to help you recognize only the Good Shepherd's voice and to help you follow him only.

BE FOCUSED

Setting the Scene

Jesus said, "Don't let anyone mislead you." Some translations use the word *beware* because Jesus was emphasizing watchfulness and vigilance. He knew that if the disciples were looking for signs, they would be susceptible to deception. Someone with counterfeit signs of spiritual power and bogus claims of authority could deceive eager and sincere believers anxiously looking for Christ.

Throughout the first century, such deceivers did arise (see Acts 5:36-37; 8:9-11; 2 Timothy 3; 2 Peter 2; 1 John 2:18; 4:1-3). Since that time many false messiahs have come and gone, and others have claimed to have inside knowledge about the Second Coming. According to Scripture, the one clear sign of Christ's return will be his unmistakable appearance in the clouds, which will be seen by all people (Matthew 24:30; Revelation 1:7). When Jesus comes back, believers will know beyond a doubt because he will be evident to all.

In times of persecution even strong believers can find it difficult to be loyal. Wanting Christ to return so much, they will grasp at any rumor that he has arrived. Jesus warned his disciples not to be swayed by whatever "signs and wonders" these people might produce. Their "power" will be by trickery or from Satan, not from God. Sometimes the arguments and proofs from deceivers in the end times will be so convincing that being faithful will be difficult. But if we are prepared and focused on the truth, Jesus says, we will stay true.

Getting Personal

Thinking back over your lifetime, what "false messiahs" can you remember? What did they offer? What happened to them and their followers?

Of what false teachings are you aware these days? What makes those teachings so appealing to so many people? How do you know the teachings are false?

What can you do to stay focused on the Truth?

In the centuries following Jesus' warnings to the disciples, numerous false messiahs and religious gurus have led millions astray, and others continue to do so today. We should only listen to teachers and other spiritual leaders whose teachings agree with the Bible, God's inspired Word. We must keep focused on the Truth—on Christ.

BE ENCOURAGED

Setting the Scene

The "sacrilegious object that causes desecration" refers to the desecration of the Temple by God's enemies. Matthew used the phrase "Reader, pay attention!" to urge readers to understand Jesus' words in light of Daniel's prophecies (Daniel 9:27; 11:31; 12:11). The "desecration" (pagan idolatry) that would occur in the Temple would cause the Temple to be desolated and abandoned.

The first fulfillment of Daniel's prophecy occurred in 168 BC when Antiochus Epiphanes sacrificed a pig to Zeus on the sacred Temple altar and made Judaism an outlaw religion, punishable by death. The second fulfillment would occur at the destruction of the Temple in AD 70. Based on verse 21, the third fulfillment is yet to come. The Antichrist will commit the ultimate sacrilege by setting up an image of himself in the Temple and ordering everyone to worship it (2 Thessalonians 2:4; Revelation 13:14-15).

Jesus tempered the news of great suffering by a promise of hope for true believers—the time would be shortened so that the destruction would not wipe out God's people and their mission. God controls world events and will not allow evil to exceed the bounds he has set. Jesus had predicted the Cross for himself; now he was predicting persecution, death, and resurrection for his disciples. The main thrust of Jesus' teaching was to show God's mercy toward the faithful and to show that God is loving and sovereign and will remember his people.

Getting Personal

Currently, thousands of our Christian brothers and sisters all over the world are enduring torture and imprisonment with joy for being counted worthy to suffer for Christ. In what ways does their experience encourage and inspire you?

When have you suffered for being a Christian? How do Jesus' words about God's sovereignty and love encourage you?

According to Jesus, these difficult times will get worse as we approach his return. When the time of suffering comes, the disciples and all believers must remember that God is sovereign. Persecution will occur, but God knows about it and is in control. We should also remember Jesus' promise that "it will be shortened for the sake of God's chosen ones."

READING THE WORD

❋ *Matthew 24:15-22, NLT*
"The day is coming when you will see what Daniel the prophet spoke about—the sacrilegious object that causes desecration standing in the Holy Place." (Reader, pay attention!) 16"Then those in Judea must flee to the hills. 17A person out on the deck of a roof must not go down into the house to pack. 18A person out in the field must not return even to get a coat. 19How terrible it will be for pregnant women and for nursing mothers in those days. 20And pray that your flight will not be in winter or on the Sabbath. 21For there will be greater anguish than at any time since the world began. And it will never be so great again. 22In fact, unless that time of calamity is shortened, not a single person will survive. But it will be shortened for the sake of God's chosen ones."

TALKING TO GOD

Praise God that he is the sovereign ruler of the universe and that nothing happens outside of his will. Thank him that your life is hidden with him, safeguarded for heaven.

BE READY

READING THE WORD

❧ *Matthew 24:30-36, 43-44, NLT*
Then at last, the sign that the Son of Man is coming will appear in the heavens, and there will be deep mourning among all the peoples of the earth. And they will see the Son of Man coming on the clouds of heaven with power and great glory. 31And he will send out his angels with the mighty blast of a trumpet, and they will gather his chosen ones from all over the world— from the farthest ends of the earth and heaven. 32Now learn a lesson from the fig tree. When its branches bud and its leaves begin to sprout, you know that summer is near. 33In the same way, when you see all these things, you can know his return is very near, right at the door. 34I tell you the truth, this generation will not pass from the scene until all these things take place. 35Heaven and earth will disappear, but my words will never disappear. 36However, no one knows the day or hour when these things will happen, not even the angels in heaven or the Son himself. Only the Father knows.... 43Understand this: If a homeowner knew exactly when a burglar was coming, he would keep watch and not permit his house to be broken into. 44You also must be ready all the time, for the Son of Man will come when least expected.

TALKING TO GOD

Ask the Lord to help you steer clear of the tendency to get bogged down in predicting or calculating the time of his return. Instead, ask him to help you be wise in being with him and serving him from day to day, so that you will always be ready for his return.

Setting the Scene

This passage looks to the Second Coming as a time of judgment. When Jesus spoke of the anguish "of those days" (Matthew 24:29, NLT), he was talking specifically about the end times (see similar wording in the Prophets: Isaiah 34:4; Jeremiah 3:16, 18; 31:29; Joel 3:1; Zechariah 8:23).

Coming persecutions and natural disasters will cause great sorrow in the world. When believers see these events, however, they should realize the Second Coming is near and look forward to Christ's reign of justice and peace.

Although Jesus told about events that would precede this time of triumph and judgment, describing in some detail the Coming itself, he said, "No one knows the day or hour when these things will happen." Jesus did not mean to stimulate predictions and calculations about the date of his coming but to warn his people to be ready.

The Second Coming and the angels' gathering "[God's] chosen ones" will happen suddenly, in the blink of an eye. Because no one except the Father knows when Christ will return, believers must be constantly ready for him to come.

Jesus commanded his followers to "keep watch" (Matthew 24:42). This is an Old Testament concept, arising out of the necessity of maintaining a constant vigil on city walls against marauding bands. It also refers to the spiritual vigilance needed to keep people from wandering away from God. This is an active, not a passive, command. Believers are to be ready for Christ's return at any moment.

Getting Personal

If you knew Christ would be returning tomorrow morning, how would you get ready?

What is a healthy balance between focusing on the end times and actively serving God from day to day?

Jesus' disciples fully expected Jesus to return in their lifetimes, so we might be tempted to wonder if he will ever come back. But if we knew the precise date of the Second Coming, we might be tempted to be lazy in our work for Christ. Worse yet, some might plan to keep sinning and then turn to God right at the end. Instead, we must live as if Jesus will return today.

BE FAITHFUL

Setting the Scene

In ancient times, masters often would put one servant in charge of all household business. The "servant" in this story, described as "faithful" and "sensible," parallels the disciples who were given unprecedented authority by Jesus. Clearly how people act reveals what they really believe. True followers of Christ, especially spiritual leaders, will be faithful to him, even during difficult times or when his return seems distant.

Peter worked tirelessly to spread the Good News of the Kingdom. Eventually, responding to what many of the early believers must have wondered about (and reflecting Jesus' words—see Matthew 24:43, 45), Peter wrote, "But you must not forget this one thing, dear friends: A day is like a thousand years to the Lord, and a thousand years is like a day. The Lord isn't really being slow about his promise, as some people think. No, he is being patient for your sake. He does not want anyone to be destroyed, but wants everyone to repent. But the day of the Lord will come as unexpectedly as a thief. Then the heavens will pass away with a terrible noise, and the very elements themselves will disappear in fire, and the earth and everything on it will be found to deserve judgment. Since everything around us is going to be destroyed like this, what holy and godly lives you should live. . . . And so, dear friends, while you are waiting for these things to happen, make every effort to be found living peaceful lives that are pure and blameless in his sight" (2 Peter 3:8-11, 14, NLT).

Getting Personal

How do you know what God wants you to do and how you should live?

What aspects of your calling do you find most difficult to do, especially in difficult times?

What does the phrase "faithful, sensible servant" (v. 45) mean for you? Why?

Although two thousand years have passed since Jesus predicted the events of Matthew 24, he will return. And he expects us to be ready—not idly waiting for the trumpet's blast but faithfully living for him and spreading the good news of the gospel.

READING THE WORD

✣ *Matthew 24:45-51, NLT*

A faithful, sensible servant is one to whom the master can give the responsibility of managing his other household servants and feeding them. 46If the master returns and finds that the servant has done a good job, there will be a reward. 47I tell you the truth, the master will put that servant in charge of all he owns. 48But what if the servant is evil and thinks, "My master won't be back for a while," 49and he begins beating the other servants, partying, and getting drunk? 50The master will return unannounced and unexpected, 51and he will cut the servant to pieces and assign him a place with the hypocrites. In that place there will be weeping and gnashing of teeth.

TALKING TO GOD

Give the Lord all the days of your lifetime. Pray that he will find you faithfully using your talents, abilities, and gifts for him, whether it's on the day of your homegoing to heaven or the day of the Second Coming.

JESUS IS BETRAYED
Week 38, Day 1

✹ *Matthew 26:1-5, 14-16; Mark 14:1-2, 10-11; Luke 22:1-6*

This week's study takes us to one of the tragic events in the final week of Jesus' ministry. One of the Twelve whom he had chosen and led for almost three years sold out and betrayed the Lord. We naturally wonder why and how someone who had a front-row view of all that Jesus said and did would, in the end, willingly cooperate to destroy him. We face the haunting question about what it would take for us to commit a similar betrayal.

READING THE WORD

✹ *Matthew 26:1-2, NKJV*
Now it came to pass, when Jesus had finished all these sayings, that He said to His disciples, 2"You know that after two days is the Passover, and the Son of Man will be delivered up to be crucified."

WHAT JESUS KNEW

Setting the Scene

Long before the final trip to Jerusalem, Jesus had prepared his followers for what would happen to him and why it needed to happen: "From that time Jesus began to show to His disciples that He must go to Jerusalem, and suffer many things from the elders and chief priests and scribes, and be killed, and be raised the third day" (Matthew 16:21, NKJV). Then, shortly after his transfiguration on the mountain, Jesus again told his disciples, "The Son of Man is about to be betrayed into the hands of men, and they will kill Him, and the third day He will be raised up" (Matthew 17:22-23, NKJV). Later, as they made their way toward Jerusalem, Jesus was even more explicit: "We are going up to Jerusalem, and the Son of Man will be betrayed to the chief priests and to the scribes; and they will condemn Him to death, and deliver Him to the Gentiles to mock and to scourge and to crucify. And the third day He will rise again" (Matthew 20:18-19, NKJV).

The disciples could not seem to put together what Jesus was telling them with the authority they saw him exercising over sickness, the demonic, natural forces, and even death. He seemed impervious to threats or danger. It upset them to hear him make such dire predictions when they were witnesses to his supernatural power.

Jesus' final trip to Jerusalem was planned and timed to coincide with Passover. The significance of Jesus' death at this particular time of the year was indirectly included in John the Baptist's great declaration, "Behold! The Lamb of God who takes away the sin of the world!" (John 1:29, NKJV). Every year for millennia, thousands of lambs had been slaughtered at Passover commemorating the historic event in which God had allowed the blood of lambs to secure the safety of Israel's families on that epic night in Egypt (see Exodus 11–12). The temporary atonement for sin that the Passover lambs provided was about to be replaced with the perfect substitute sacrifice—God's Son. As the spotless Lamb of God, Jesus served as the willing recipient of the penalty of death brought about by sin. By him, through him, and in him we have "redemption through His blood, the forgiveness of sins" (Colossians 1:14, NKJV).

In all that Jesus did and said, we see deliberate movement toward the Cross. In the counsels of God, the decision had already been made. Jesus was simply carrying out the plan of salvation because no alternative would do. He went to the Cross because he chose to, because of the "joy that was set before Him" (Hebrews 12:2, NKJV). That week in Jerusalem, when the flocks of perfect lambs were rounded up for the ritual Passover slaughter, a spotless lamb was added to the flock that made all the other sacrificial lambs no longer necessary. The Lamb of God took away the sins of the world.

Getting Personal

What does it mean to you to realize Jesus knew ahead of time exactly what would happen in Jerusalem, yet he resolutely went anyway?

How did the Feast of the Passover parallel what was happening to Jesus?

Romans 10:9 insists, "If you declare with your mouth, 'Jesus is Lord,' and believe in your heart that God raised him from the dead, you will be saved" (NIV). We don't have to understand everything before we can trust that Jesus knew what he was doing for us when he went to the Cross.

TALKING TO GOD

God graciously holds our future in his hands, so we don't have to live with too much knowledge—and anxiety—about the future. Thank him for his sovereign goodness and power that allows you to trust him completely. Thank him for the sacrifice of Jesus, who walked into his future, knowing full well the suffering that was there. Thank him for the spotless Lamb, who has taken away your sin.

THE PLOT

READING THE WORD

❈ *Matthew 26:3-5, NKJV*
Then the chief priests, the scribes, and the elders of the people assembled at the palace of the high priest, who was called Caiaphas, 4and plotted to take Jesus by trickery and kill Him. 5But they said, "Not during the feast, lest there be an uproar among the people."

❈ *Mark 14:1-2, NKJV*
After two days it was the Passover and the Feast of Unleavened Bread. And the chief priests and the scribes sought how they might take Him by trickery and put Him to death. 2But they said, "Not during the feast, lest there be an uproar of the people."

TALKING TO GOD

Confess your relief at knowing you cannot mess up the Lord's plans. Lay your plans before him, knowing he is aware of any internal scheming that has gone on. Ask for his will to be done in every circumstance.

Setting the Scene

God had his plans, and men made theirs. God knew what would happen, and a certain group did everything in its power to make it happen, though they did not foresee or comprehend what was actually at stake behind their plot to arrange Jesus' death.

The principal leaders of the plot gathered at Caiaphas's house. This was the Who's Who of Jewish leadership, at the time assembled in an official capacity to break the law they were pledged to uphold. Apparently they assumed that "Thou shalt not kill" and "Thou shalt not bear false witness" were parts of God's commandments they were exempt from in the pursuit of their duties. Among those gathered in this behind-closed-doors meeting of the Sanhedrin were the "elders of the people," a group Matthew identifies several times in the events surrounding Christ's death (see Matthew 21:23; 26:3, 47; 27:1). This subgroup appears to have been made up of civic rather than religious leaders. Those whom the people had entrusted with leadership were busily betraying that trust as they agreed to find a way to kill Jesus.

The plot specifies that Jesus should be killed after the Passover festival—"not during the feast." But God's plan stipulated an eternal connection between the Passover and the death of the Lamb of God. At this point, the assorted plotters did not have a specific means in mind, but they planned to use "trickery" to create circumstances under which they might arrest Jesus. Once he was out of sight, they would kill him after the Feast. As always, God's plan prevailed.

Getting Personal

Why did the religious leaders hate Jesus so intensely?

What leads people in every era to harden their hearts against God?

The "heart that devises wicked plans" is among the "things the LORD hates" (Proverbs 6:16-19, NKJV). More precisely, "A man's heart plans his way, But the LORD directs his steps" (Proverbs 16:9, NKJV). We are challenged to make plans for the right and good, and trust God to make them better in the doing.

SATAN'S MOVE

Setting the Scene

Luke is the only Gospel writer to include this chilling note describing Satan's direct participation in the events leading up to Jesus' death. Matthew (10:4), Mark (3:19), and Luke (6:16) mention Judas once early on in their list of disciples. Each notes that he was the betrayer. John 6:70-71 refers to one earlier comment by Jesus indicating that he knew beforehand that one of his chosen followers would betray him.

The first clue we get of Judas's less-than-wholehearted devotion to Jesus comes in John 12:4-6 when he voiced an objection to Mary's lavish display of worship in anointing Jesus with costly oil. John notes, "He did not say this because he cared about the poor but because he was a thief; as keeper of the money bag, he used to help himself to what was put into it" (John 12:6, NIV).

Luke's description of Satan's role is confirmed by John 13:2: "The evening meal was in progress, and the devil had already prompted Judas, the son of Simon Iscariot, to betray Jesus" (NIV). The fact that Satan found a willing ally to work through in setting Jesus up doesn't remove any responsibility from Judas. Alongside the human events transpiring around Jesus was also a great spiritual battle. Judas was used, but he made himself available. John's insight into Judas's character as a thief reminds us that we can't accept demonic suggestions and then blame Satan for what we do. If we give ourselves to Satan's influence, we will eventually be shocked (as Judas clearly was) where that influence leads us.

Getting Personal

When are you most aware of demonic suggestions in your life?

How do you respond when you recognize that temptation is from Satan?

Ephesians 6:11-12 includes a warning and instructions regarding Satan's influence: "Put on the whole armor of God, that you may be able to stand against the wiles of the devil. For we do not wrestle against flesh and blood, but against principalities, against powers, against the rulers of the darkness of this age, against spiritual hosts of wickedness in the heavenly places" (NKJV). We can't afford to take spiritual warfare lightly.

READING THE WORD

❊ *Luke 22:3, NIV*
Then Satan entered Judas, called Iscariot, one of the Twelve.

TALKING TO GOD

Learn from the negative example of Judas. Ask the Lord to alert you to attitudes and habits that leave the door open for Satan's influence in your life. Ask him to protect you by the power of his Holy Spirit.

READING THE WORD

✤ *Matthew 26:14-15, NIV*
Then one of the Twelve—the one called Judas Iscariot—went to the chief priests 15and asked, "What are you willing to give me if I deliver him over to you?" So they counted out for him thirty pieces of silver.

✤ *Luke 22:4-5, NIV*
And Judas went to the chief priests and the officers of the temple guard and discussed with them how he might betray Jesus. 5They were delighted and agreed to give him money.

TALKING TO GOD

Don't trust your own assumptions that when things seem to be going all right, everything is fine. Ask God to keep your heart open to his Word and to his Spirit's prompting, so that something that is only temporarily satisfying doesn't distract you from what God is calling you to do or to be.

THE DEAL

Setting the Scene

The group plotting to kill Jesus was "delighted" (Mark 14:11; Luke 22:5, NIV) to be approached by one of Jesus' own disciples with an offer they couldn't refuse. Judas's approach is consistent with John 12:6 as someone who helped himself to the disciples' money bag. Greed and satanic suggestion may be enough to explain Judas's motivation, but we are not given specific insight into his reasoning. He may have also taken personal offense over Jesus' rebuke in John 12:7-8 that Mary should not be chastised for her gesture of worship in anointing him. Having decided on a course of action, Judas approached the one group he knew could afford to fund his betrayal.

The thirty pieces of silver have some interesting biblical connections. Exodus 21:32 informs us that was the fair market value for a slave. One of the startling messianic prophecies written by Zechariah several hundred years earlier actually mentions thirty pieces of silver (Zechariah 11:12-13) and will come up in our discussion of Judas's regrets. The amount turned out to be enough to buy a field, but it was a poor sum for Judas to accept in exchange for his soul.

Getting Personal

Looking back on life, we can usually remember that the turning point in our worst mistakes has often come at the moment when our plans begin to work out. Things suddenly "falling into place" can be a sign they are about to fall apart.

What examples can you apply in your life of Satan's attacks when things seemed to be going well?

When has success in your life not been a good thing? And when has failure been later revealted to have been the best event of all?

Judas's plans were paying off, but success is not a sure measure of what's right. When we ask God for open doors, we ought to ask him for the wisdom to see that an open door may lead us into an elevator shaft. The success of evil plans is always temporary.

OPPORTUNITY

Setting the Scene

Luke tells us that Judas "consented" to participate in betraying Jesus. He accepted money to use his position of trust to violate that trust and put Jesus' life in jeopardy.

Luke also tells us that Judas was instructed to choose a time for the betrayal "when no crowd was present" to complicate or interrupt the arrest. By this point in the week, Jesus and the disciples may have established a routine. Each day was spent in Jerusalem with an evening stop in the garden of Gethsemane on the way out to Bethany, where they spent the nights. Judas's betrayal was premeditated. The disciples' running away when the armed group came for Jesus was an impulsive expression of surprise and fear. Peter's denial was an expression of fear of exposure compounded by shame. Some have suggested that Judas may have been disillusioned over Jesus' talk of death rather than taking advantage of his popularity to set up the Kingdom. He might have been trying to force Jesus' hand by creating the confrontation. But if this was the case, why betray Jesus when he was practically alone? Judas was doing what he had consented and been paid to do.

Because he had time to plan and to consider when would be the ideal time to betray Jesus, Judas also had time to feel the first twinges of regret. Matthew 27:3 tells us Judas didn't exhibit remorse until after Jesus was condemned by the Jewish court and turned over to Pilate. Sometimes, realizing we've made a terrible mistake and expressing remorse over that mistake will not undo the damage we have set in motion. Judas didn't live to see the tragedy or the triumph created out of his actions.

Getting Personal

What is the difference between regret (or remorse) and repentance?

When have you felt stuck at feeling very bad about something without actually repenting? How has that been resolved in your life?

We can confuse regret with repentance. But feeling bad that we got caught or disliking the consequences that flow from wrongdoing is clearly not the same as taking responsibility for the wrongdoing and turning away from it.

READING THE WORD

❀ *Matthew 26:16, NIV*
From then on Judas watched for an opportunity to hand him over.

❀ *Luke 22:6, NIV*
He consented, and watched for an opportunity to hand Jesus over to them when no crowd was present.

TALKING TO GOD

Don't miss the hopeful aspect of repentance. In turning away from your sin, you are turning toward the comfort and joy of the Lord. Ask him to be near you, comforting you as you turn away from sin and submit more and more of your life to him. Thank him for his promise that he is "faithful and just and will forgive us our sins and purify us from all unrighteousness" (1 John 1:9, NIV).

WHY CHOOSE JUDAS?

Setting the Scene

The Gospels, written years after Judas Iscariot's death, consistently list him last among the twelve disciples.

We are stunned that someone who was given so much and had seen so much would turn his back on Jesus and betray him. We have considered possible explanations to help us understand his motivation, but they do not diminish his responsibility for his actions.

Judas made a crucial decision. He turned away from the opportunity to be a faithful disciple and instead looked for an opportunity to hand Jesus over to his enemies. Judas betrayed everything that Jesus stood for and the message he must have heard many, many times. He heard the parables of the Kingdom and everything Jesus taught about the difference between the world's way of doing things and the Father's way. He probably understood as little as the other eleven, but he was the one who turned that lack of understanding into treacherous action.

As we wonder over the tragedy of Judas's actions, we must consider our own attempts at faithfulness. Perhaps we may simply have lacked opportunity—we haven't had the chance (or been faced with the risk) of betraying what we say we believe. We may not even risk letting others know what we believe. Which is the greater betrayal—falling short in following or never giving any real appearance of following at all?

Getting Personal

Which of Jesus' teachings do you imagine was the most difficult for Judas to accept?

In what ways have you demonstrated that your loyalty to Christ is real?

Obedience and loyalty are not the means of salvation, but they demonstrate that we are saved. If we are not intent on actually following Jesus, it makes little sense to claim to be a Christ-follower. Pretending to be something we are not is a form of betrayal.

READING THE WORD

�֍ *Mark 14:10-11, NIV*
Then Judas Iscariot, one of the Twelve, went to the chief priests to betray Jesus to them. 11They were delighted to hear this and promised to give him money. So he watched for an opportunity to hand him over.

TALKING TO GOD

Admit your moments of disloyalty, when what you do doesn't measure up to what you say you believe. Thank God for his patience with you and his great love for you. Ask him to develop your deep loyalty to him.

JESUS CELEBRATES THE PASSOVER
Week 39, Day 1

✣ *Matthew 26:17-30; Mark 14:12-26; Luke 22:14-23; John 13:21-30*

Jesus was moving steadily toward the Cross. He knew what lay ahead and wanted to spend Passover with his disciples. During the meal, he made unsettling comments about death and betrayal. But he also reaffirmed his bond with his disciples and gave them hope for the future. This week, we'll hear Jesus and watch the disciples react, and we'll be challenged by Jesus' directive: "Do this to remember me" (Luke 22:19, NLT) until he returns.

FOLLOWING

Setting the Scene

The Passover took place on one night and at one meal, but the Feast of Unleavened Bread, which was celebrated with it, continued for a week. The first day of the feast was technically the day after Passover, but the two were often seen as the same. Thus, this was either Wednesday night (the day before Passover) or Thursday of Jesus' last week (the night of the Passover meal). The highlight of the festival was the Passover meal, a family feast with lamb as the main course. The sacrifice of a lamb and the spilling of its blood commemorated Israel's escape from Egypt after the blood of a lamb painted on their doorposts had saved their firstborn sons from death. After applying the blood, the Israelites were to prepare the meat for food and eat it in their traveling clothes.

Jesus and his disciples had celebrated Passover together in previous years, so Jesus' disciples assumed they would again have the Passover meal with Jesus. The meal had to be eaten in Jerusalem, however, so the disciples asked Jesus where they should go to make preparations. His response indicates he had made plans in advance.

After being with Jesus for three years, learning from him and learning *about* him, these men were becoming real disciples. The first words of their question "Where do you want us to go?" reveal their willingness to do whatever Jesus said they should do. Notice that after Jesus answered their question, they didn't express doubts or question him further. Instead, after receiving their instructions, "the two disciples went"; or as Matthew

READING THE WORD

✣ *Mark 14:12-16, NLT*
On the first day of the Festival of Unleavened Bread, when the Passover lamb is sacrificed, Jesus' disciples asked him, "Where do you want us to go to prepare the Passover meal for you?" 13So Jesus sent two of them into Jerusalem with these instructions: "As you go into the city, a man carrying a pitcher of water will meet you. Follow him. 14At the house he enters, say to the owner, 'The Teacher asks: Where is the guest room where I can eat the Passover meal with my disciples?' 15He will take you upstairs to a large room that is already set up. That is where you should prepare our meal." 16So the two disciples went into the city and found everything just as Jesus had said, and they prepared the Passover meal there.

TALKING TO GOD

In a culture that celebrates individualism and autonomy, it is increasingly countercultural to submit your own plans and desires to anyone or anything else. But in your prayer time today, submit yourself to the lordship of Christ without fear, because his plans for you are for your ultimate good and for his glory.

wrote, "the disciples did as Jesus told them" (Matthew 26:19, NLT). Then, as they followed Jesus' instructions, the men "found everything just as Jesus had said."

These faithful men could not know what each day would bring, but they were learning to follow Jesus step-by-step. Each step was guided by God's sovereign will. They wouldn't fully understand Jesus' identity and mission until after his resurrection and ascension, but they certainly had progressed far beyond where they had started in their relationship with him. They were coming to understand the partnership of their calling: They go, God provides; they work, God blesses.

Getting Personal

How long have you been following Christ? In what ways has your faith grown over those years?

Which aspect of "following" do you find most difficult: asking for instructions, being willing to do what God instructs, or obeying him? Why?

How can you know what God wants you to do?

The key to following Christ is submission: asking him for instructions, having the attitude of being willing to do whatever he says, and then following through—obeying him. We don't know how God is preparing the way or working out the details of our journey, so we ask in faith, "Where do you want us to go?" Then we go, also in faith, excited about seeing God's plans unfold. Regardless of how long you have been a Jesus-follower, the process is the same. Daily ask him to reveal what he wants you to do (usually that happens through his Word). Then, when you know, do it! That's submission.

EATING

Setting the Scene

The Passover meal was supposed to be eaten in Jerusalem after sunset and finished before midnight. Everyone took their places on the reclining couches around the table.

Jesus had "been very eager" to share this quiet time with his disciples, eating, worshiping together, and preparing. John's Gospel reveals much more that was said during their time together (John 13–16). But Luke tells us that Jesus knew his "suffering" would soon begin and that Passover would not be "fulfilled" until the "Kingdom of God." The mention of fulfillment reveals the complete and ultimate significance of the entire Passover celebration. While Passover commemorated a past event (Israel's escape from Egypt when the blood of a lamb painted on their doorframes saved their firstborn sons from death), it also foreshadowed Jesus' work on the cross.

Knowing what he was about to endure and how the disciples would respond, Jesus wanted to spend these precious hours with his closest friends. Imagine how he must have felt as he looked into their eyes, spoke about his suffering, and gave new meaning to the bread and wine—certainly a mixture of sadness (especially considering Judas's betrayal), resolve, and joy.

Jesus loved these "dear friends" (Luke 12:4, NLT) and was entrusting his work and the advance of the Kingdom to them.

Getting Personal

What activities and interests threaten to keep you from finding personal time to spend with God?

What specific changes would help you carve out time, apart from distractions, for prayer and God's Word?

Jesus wants to spend time with us as well. In a message to complacent believers in Laodicea, he said, "Look! I stand at the door and knock. If you hear my voice and open the door, I will come in, and we will share a meal together as friends" (Revelation 3:20, NLT). At times, life is so noisy that we don't hear his knock. At other times, we're busily occupied with other concerns and don't make room in our schedules to spend time with Jesus. But he loves us and wants to be with us, listening, healing, teaching, preparing, and leading. Will you let him in?

READING THE WORD

❈ *Luke 22:14-16, NLT*
When the time came, Jesus and the apostles sat down together at the table. 15Jesus said, "I have been very eager to eat this Passover meal with you before my suffering begins. 16For I tell you now that I won't eat this meal again until its meaning is fulfilled in the Kingdom of God."

TALKING TO GOD

Admit to the Lord the difficulties you encounter in making time for developing your relationship with him. Ask him to help you be wise so that you don't neglect or rush through your time together with him. Ask him to help you make the best choices about work and leisure, so that Christ remains the top priority.

READING THE WORD

❁ *Matthew 26:20-22, NLT*
When it was evening, Jesus sat down at the table with the twelve disciples. 21While they were eating, he said, "I tell you the truth, one of you will betray me." 22Greatly distressed, each one asked in turn, "Am I the one, Lord?"

TALKING TO GOD

Whether or not your actions were intentional or unintended, confess that you have, at times, denied Christ by your words and actions. Thank the Lord for his patient forgiveness and reaffirm your love for him. Ask him to forgive you and help you be a bold witness for the Truth.

WONDERING

Setting the Scene

The Passover seder followed a traditional pattern. First would come a blessing of the event and the wine, followed by drinking the first cup of wine. After other events would come the eating of the meal, including roasted lamb sacrificed in the Temple.

Jesus and the disciples were at the point of eating the bread with the sauce of herbs and fruit when Jesus declared that someone at the table would betray him. News that one of them was a traitor caused quite a stir among the disciples and saddened them greatly. Apparently Judas was not the obvious choice as the betrayer because he was the one the disciples trusted to keep the money (John 12:4-6). So each disciple asked Jesus for assurance: "Am I the one, Lord?" The Greek form of the question would be rendered, "It is not I, is it?" and implied a negative answer. But the fact that the question was asked indicates that each disciple recognized he was capable of such a betrayal and perhaps had even considered it along the way. Certainly, each must have harbored doubts about Jesus and his mission at some time as they journeyed together. The disciples looked around the table and wondered about the traitor's identity. In asking this question, each one hoped to clear himself while, at the same time, wondering if he would have the courage to remain faithful.

Getting Personal

When do you often feel pressured to keep silent about your feelings about Jesus and your Christian faith?

If you were to ask Jesus, "How do I betray you, Lord?" what do you think he would say?

What helps you stay loyal to your Savior?

Because we're all sinners, every group of human beings contains potential traitors. Each person, even a Christ-follower, has the potential to betray the Lord, as evidenced by Peter's actions just a few hours after this meal (Matthew 26:69-75). We betray or deny Jesus by being silent when we should speak up, by not identifying with him, by being indistinguishable in lifestyle from anyone else in the world, and by turning our backs on him and leaving him to his accusers.

BETRAYING

Setting the Scene

Although Jesus knew Judas was about to betray him, he didn't stop the process. Jesus was committed to completing his mission "to be sin for us" (2 Corinthians 5:21, NKJV). Jesus must have expressed his inner turmoil when he said, "I tell you the truth, one of you will betray me!"

Peter signaled to John to ask Jesus for more information. So John asked, and Jesus identified the betrayer as "the one to whom I give the bread I dip in the bowl." Then Jesus dipped the piece of bread into a dish filled with a sauce (probably made of dates, raisins, and sour wine) and handed it to "Judas, son of Simon Iscariot." With this sign of friendship, Jesus identified his betrayer. Later, in the garden, Judas would identify Jesus to the guards with another sign of friendship—a kiss (Luke 22:47-48). After Judas received the bread, "Satan entered into him," setting the betrayal in motion. Satan assumed that Jesus' death would end his mission and thwart God's plan. Like Judas, Satan did not know that Jesus' death was the most important part of God's plan.

Satan's role in the betrayal does not remove responsibility from Judas. Judas may have been disillusioned because Jesus was talking about dying rather than setting up his Kingdom, and he may have been trying to force Jesus' hand to make him use his power to prove he was the Messiah. Or perhaps Judas didn't understand Jesus' mission and no longer believed Jesus was God's chosen one. Whatever Judas may have thought, clearly Satan used his doubts, fears, and disillusionment to convince him to do the unthinkable.

Getting Personal

When have you felt like an outsider to Jesus and his close followers?

When do you feel impatient with the way God is unfolding his plan?

Three truths emerge from this incident. First, Jesus' love knows no limitation. He loved Judas even with his deceptions, plots, and eventual betrayal. Second, no one is immune from Satan's attacks and manipulations; we should always be on guard. Third, God can use for his glory even the most despicable act.

READING THE WORD

✤ *John 13:21-30, NLT*
Now Jesus was deeply troubled, and he exclaimed, "I tell you the truth, one of you will betray me!" 22The disciples looked at each other, wondering whom he could mean. 23The disciple Jesus loved was sitting next to Jesus at the table. 24Simon Peter motioned to him to ask, "Who's he talking about?" 25So that disciple leaned over to Jesus and asked, "Lord, who is it?" 26Jesus responded, "It is the one to whom I give the bread I dip in the bowl." And when he had dipped it, he gave it to Judas, son of Simon Iscariot. 27When Judas had eaten the bread, Satan entered into him. Then Jesus told him, "Hurry and do what you're going to do." 28None of the others at the table knew what Jesus meant. 29Since Judas was their treasurer, some thought Jesus was telling him to go and pay for the food or to give some money to the poor. 30So Judas left at once, going out into the night.

TALKING TO GOD

Praise God for his sovereign, omniscient control that works even wrongdoing for his own purposes. Thank him, too, for his love that persists despite your sin.

READING THE WORD

❀ *Matthew 26:26-30, NLT*

As they were eating, Jesus took some bread and blessed it. Then he broke it in pieces and gave it to the disciples, saying, "Take this and eat it, for this is my body." 27And he took a cup of wine and gave thanks to God for it. He gave it to them and said, "Each of you drink from it, 28for this is my blood, which confirms the covenant between God and his people. It is poured out as a sacrifice to forgive the sins of many. 29Mark my words—I will not drink wine again until the day I drink it new with you in my Father's Kingdom." 30Then they sang a hymn and went out to the Mount of Olives.

❀ *Mark 14:22-25, NLT*

As they were eating, Jesus took some bread and blessed it. Then he broke it in pieces and gave it to the disciples, saying, "Take it, for this is my body." 23And he took a cup of wine and gave thanks to God for it. He gave it to them, and they all drank from it. 24And he said to them, "This is my blood, which confirms the covenant between God and his people. It is poured out as a sacrifice for many. 25I tell you the truth, I will not drink wine again until the day I drink it new in the Kingdom of God."

TALKING TO GOD

Thank God that he is the ultimate promise keeper. Thank him for fulfilling the covenant through the death of Christ Jesus and for drawing you personally into his family.

CONFIRMING

Setting the Scene

The blessing of the bread refers to the Jewish practice of giving thanks for bread at a meal by saying, "Blessed are you, Lord, our God, who brings forth bread from the earth." Because bread was considered a gift from God, cutting it with a knife seemed irreverent, so Jews would tear ("break") it with their hands. When Jesus gave the bread to his disciples, he gave this Passover practice an entirely new meaning. The Passover celebrated deliverance from slavery in Egypt. The Lord's Supper celebrates deliverance from sin by Christ's death.

The word *covenant* refers to an arrangement established by one party that cannot be altered by the other party. Thus, because God established the covenant, humans can only accept or reject it; they cannot alter it in any way. God made a covenant with Abraham and his descendants (Genesis 12:1-3). He renewed this covenant with Moses (Exodus 20) and with David (2 Samuel 7:8-16). Each time, the covenant looked forward to Jesus. His sacrifice would both fulfill and confirm the covenant.

Jesus' blessing occurred at the drinking of the third cup at the Last Supper, the cup that stands for "I will redeem." Jesus' words recall Exodus 24:6-8, where Moses poured half of the blood of the covenant on the altar and sprinkled the people with the other half to seal the covenant. Jesus understood his death as sacrificial, inaugurating and sealing the new covenant. Under this new covenant, Jesus would die in the place of sinners. Unlike the blood of animals, Jesus' blood would truly remove the sins of all who would put their faith in him.

Getting Personal

Jesus shed his blood to fulfill the covenant, God's promise to Abraham and to his people. What makes you a child of the covenant?

What other promises has God made that directly relate to you?

God has kept and will keep his promises to you. What promises have you made to him?

In Old Testament ("testament" also means "covenant") times, the covenant was personally confirmed through the regular, bloody sacrifices of animals. These sacrifices pictured the final, once-for-all sacrifice of Jesus on the cross (Hebrews 7:27).

REMEMBERING

Setting the Scene

Jesus took the loaf of unleavened bread, gave thanks, and "broke it in pieces." Just as the Passover celebrated deliverance from slavery in Egypt, so this act celebrated deliverance from sin by Christ's death. Jesus told the disciples, "This is my body, which is given for you," using literal terms to describe a figurative truth. The bread symbolized Jesus' work of salvation on behalf of those who trust in him.

Jesus told the disciples to eat the broken bread, saying, "Do this to remember me." He wanted them to remember his sacrifice, the basis for forgiveness of sins, and also his friendship that they would continue to enjoy through the work of the Holy Spirit.

A little later, Jesus took the cup of wine and said it represented his blood that would be "poured out as a sacrifice." In describing this event, Paul later wrote, "On the night when he was betrayed, the Lord Jesus took some bread and gave thanks to God for it. Then he broke it in pieces and said, 'This is my body, which is given for you. Do this to remember me.' In the same way, he took the cup of wine after supper, saying, 'This cup is the new covenant between God and his people—an agreement confirmed with my blood. Do this to remember me as often as you drink it'" (1 Corinthians 11:23-25, NLT).

Whether it is called the Lord's Supper, Communion, or the Eucharist, this sacrament has been observed by Christians since Jesus instituted it.

Getting Personal

How often do you partake in the Lord's Supper?

How do you prepare for this event, before and during the service?

In what ways is Communion a solemn event for you? How is it a celebration?

We can remember Jesus in many ways: reading the Gospels, listening to sermons and teachings about him, and working through studies and devotional books. But Communion is a powerful memorial experience as we join with other believers through the centuries and around the world to "do this to remember" him. It should never be taken casually or as a religious routine.

READING THE WORD

❀ *Luke 22:17-20, NLT*

Then he took a cup of wine and gave thanks to God for it. Then he said, "Take this and share it among yourselves. 18For I will not drink wine again until the Kingdom of God has come." 19He took some bread and gave thanks to God for it. Then he broke it in pieces and gave it to the disciples, saying, "This is my body, which is given for you. Do this to remember me." 20After supper he took another cup of wine and said, "This cup is the new covenant between God and his people—an agreement confirmed with my blood, which is poured out as a sacrifice for you."

TALKING TO GOD

Spend some time over the biblical description of Christ's physical suffering, and thank God for the brokenness he suffered to pay for your sins. Thank God that you are part of the great community of believers stretching across two millennia, who have celebrated his sacrifice to "remember" him.

JESUS WASHES THE DISCIPLES' FEET
Week 40, Day 1

❋ *Matthew 26:31-35; Mark 14:27-31; Luke 22:31-34; John 13:1-20, 33-38*

We are now considering the last day of Jesus' life on earth until after the Resurrection. When John wrote his Gospel, the other three accounts had been in circulation for a while. They had focused on the powerful symbol of Communion that Jesus instituted during the final meal together with his disciples. John gives us a sense of what Jesus communicated during the rest of the meal. This week we will observe the tender practicality of Jesus' love in serving his disciples and the persistence of that love in Jesus' unfolding relationship with Peter.

READING THE WORD

❋ *John 13:1-5, NIV*

It was just before the Passover Festival. Jesus knew that the hour had come for him to leave this world and go to the Father. Having loved his own who were in the world, he loved them to the end. ²The evening meal was in progress, and the devil had already prompted Judas, the son of Simon Iscariot, to betray Jesus. ³Jesus knew that the Father had put all things under his power, and that he had come from God and was returning to God; ⁴so he got up from the meal, took off his outer clothing, and wrapped a towel around his waist. ⁵After that, he poured water into a basin and began to wash his disciples' feet, drying them with the towel that was wrapped around him.

SEE WHAT LOVE

Setting the Scene

John begins his account of the Last Supper with a stirring prelude to all that is to come: Jesus "knew" and he "loved," so he showed the disciples what that meant. The Lord was keenly aware of the shortness of time left in his mission, and he focused his attention on some lasting lessons he wanted to leave with those he loved. As important as it is to communicate love verbally, our actions highlight and communicate love in ways that cannot be fully expressed in words. Jesus would show his disciples the full extent of his love—first with a basin and towel, then on the cross.

The book of John recalls the overwhelming intimacy and life-changing hours the Twelve spent around that Passover table. The aroma of fresh-baked unleavened bread and lamb would have filled the room and awakened appetites. The Twelve gathered at the table with Jesus as the food was being served. Perhaps to one side of the room a basin had been placed along with water, and the men would have washed their hands in the ceremonial way required before the Passover meal. This had nothing to do with physical hygiene but with long-established rituals of cleanliness. Everyone and everything was in place for the meal.

John 13:3 shows that not only did Jesus know what time it was, he also knew who he was. Jesus was not confused about his identity or compelled to prove himself in that moment: "Jesus knew that the Father had put all things under his power, and that he had come from

God and was returning to God." The betrayal, suffering, humiliation, and death he would soon experience were merely part of "returning" to God. Unless we stop to ponder the divinity of Jesus, we will not appreciate the profound gesture of humility expressed in what he did next. Jesus took off his outer cloak and wrapped a wiping cloth around his waist. His surprised men must have exchanged questioning glances as he poured water into the basin and then knelt at the feet of each disciple. He gently lifted their feet into the water, washed them, and then wiped them dry. The disciples were shocked; their Master was washing their feet!

Somehow this simple act of hospitality had been overlooked in the preparations. If they had been eating in Bethany, Martha would probably have seen to that detail and had a servant ready to wash the men's feet as they stepped into the room. While the unintentional oversight showed a sense of equality among the disciples, it also revealed a lack of servant attitudes. The disciples had been known to spar verbally over who was the greatest, but there's little evidence that they jostled one another for opportunities to serve. This faux pas provided Jesus with teachable moments he used to lasting effect. He demonstrated loving servanthood—seeing a need others missed or ignored and taking steps without being asked to meet that need. Loving servanthood in its highest expressions always does the unexpected.

Getting Personal

When was the last time you did something unexpected for others?

In what areas of your life have you learned what serving means? How do you practice those lessons?

Love as a feeling is simple, uncomplicated, and terribly fragile. It can be ignored or acted on, but the feelings themselves are not subject to our will. They come and go on a whim. Love as service is hard, complicated, and sometimes messy. Love as service is not always understood or necessarily appreciated. But serving love is an act of the will, a decision we make to express our value of others into action.

TALKING TO GOD

Look to Jesus for the perfect example of service that is extreme and unexpected. Ask the Lord to forgive your halfhearted gestures of service or for hidden longings for the thanks and praise of others for your acts of service. Ask him to help you follow him in serving creatively, even when no one notices.

CLEAN

READING THE WORD

❀ *John 13:6-11, NIV*

He came to Simon Peter, who said to him, "Lord, are you going to wash my feet?" 7Jesus replied, "You do not realize now what I am doing, but later you will understand." 8"No," said Peter, "you shall never wash my feet." Jesus answered, "Unless I wash you, you have no part with me." 9"Then, Lord," Simon Peter replied, "not just my feet but my hands and my head as well!" 10Jesus answered, "Those who have had a bath need only to wash their feet; their whole body is clean. And you are clean, though not every one of you." 11For he knew who was going to betray him, and that was why he said not every one was clean.

TALKING TO GOD

Thank God for the amazing juxtaposition of his almighty power and authority and the role of crucified Savior. Thank him for coming to make you clean.

Setting the Scene

Simon Peter is disturbed by seeing the Master stoop to such menial duties as foot washing. Typical of Peter, he wasn't sure what to say, so he said the first thing that came to mind: "Lord, are you going to wash my feet?" Jesus was right there, towel and basin ready, so the tone in Peter's question must have conveyed something like, "Not my feet, you're not!" Jesus' answer refers to both a short-term and a long-term understanding. After he is done with this task, Jesus plans to explain it to the disciples so they will immediately have a certain level of understanding. But life in the future is going to provide them with numerous opportunities to experience the truth of his cleansing.

Peter still wanted to hold the line of honor and respect. He wasn't about to allow Jesus to wash his feet. But Jesus countered: "Unless I wash you, you have no part with me." Instantly Peter found himself backpedaling furiously: "If that's the case, then wash me all over!" Jesus responded with what is obvious in the physical realm but often lost in our spiritual dealings with God: The washing and cleansing of forgiveness that Jesus provides is complete, but we still get our feet dirty because we remain in the world. Repentance and forgiveness for the believer is spiritual foot washing, not repeated complete baths.

Getting Personal

Considering that both Judas and Peter would soon betray Jesus, what was so important about Jesus washing the feet of both men?

In what ways is washing the feet of others a symbol of forgiveness?

John points out that Jesus included an exception in his explanation to Peter. "And you are clean, though not every one of you." Judas was still at the table, among those whose feet Jesus washed. Judas's feet were washed, but he remained unclean.

THE WAY OF BLESSING

Setting the Scene

Apart from the brief exchange with Peter, little was said during the time Jesus went from disciple to disciple around the table, washing feet. But after those moments of action came the teaching. Jesus asked them a question he didn't expect them to answer. His question was another way to say, "You must understand what I have done for you."

First Jesus affirmed Peter's impulse: "You call Me Teacher and Lord, and you say well, for so I am" (John 13:13, NKJV). Then he used that fact as a basis for his instruction—if he could wash their feet, they ought to wash one another's feet. "I have set you an example," Jesus said, "that you should do as I have done for you." Jesus explains the obvious: "No servant is greater than his master, nor is a messenger greater than the one who sent him." He seems to be pointing out that there are distinctive roles within the Kingdom (servants, masters, messengers), yet no one is exempt from the duty of service. No menial task (foot washing being the example) is too low or insignificant to be out of the question for those with the most elevated responsibilities. If the Lord of lords didn't hesitate to put on the towel and do the work, neither should his followers.

Verse 17 gives a lasting challenge: "Now that you know these things, you will be blessed if you do them." Conversely, if we claim to understand what God says but don't put it into practice, we will not be blessed. Knowledge without application has limited benefits. We may be deeply moved along with the disciples in visualizing the servant example of Jesus, but if we do not respond to the needs around us, we have wasted a teachable moment.

Getting Personal

When have you received unexpected service?

What settings might give you opportunity for service?

We cross a significant threshold in spiritual maturity when we set aside our own needs and desires and watch for God's direction in meeting the needs of others.

READING THE WORD

✶ *John 13:12-20, NIV*

When he had finished washing their feet, he put on his clothes and returned to his place. "Do you understand what I have done for you?" he asked them. [13]"You call me 'Teacher' and 'Lord,' and rightly so, for that is what I am. [14]Now that I, your Lord and Teacher, have washed your feet, you also should wash one another's feet. [15]I have set you an example that you should do as I have done for you. [16]Very truly I tell you, no servant is greater than his master, nor is a messenger greater than the one who sent him. [17]Now that you know these things, you will be blessed if you do them. [18]I am not referring to all of you; I know those I have chosen. But this is to fulfill this passage of Scripture: 'He who shared my bread has turned against me.' [19]I am telling you now before it happens, so that when it does happen you will believe that I am who I am. [20]Very truly I tell you, whoever accepts anyone I send accepts me; and whoever accepts me accepts the one who sent me."

TALKING TO GOD

Acknowledge your human tendency to focus on your own needs. Ask God to give you a central focus of worshiping him and enjoying his presence, and a secondary focus on the needs of those around you.

LOVE ONE ANOTHER

READING THE WORD

❧ *John 13:33-35, NIV*
My children, I will be with you only a little longer. You will look for me, and just as I told the Jews, so I tell you now: Where I am going, you cannot come. 34A new command I give you: Love one another. As I have loved you, so you must love one another. 35By this everyone will know that you are my disciples, if you love one another.

TALKING TO GOD

Admit the extensive gap between Jesus' standard for loving and your own ability to love others. Ask the Lord to fill you with his love and compassion for those around you, beginning with your immediate family members. Ask him to help you love as he has loved.

Setting the Scene

Judas had gone into the night to further his betrayal. Jesus' tone became tender, almost paternal. He called the remaining disciples "my children" (*tekna*), a form of parental endearment that John later used in his letters. He told them again that their remaining time together was short. Once he departed, neither the disciples nor the rest of the Jews would be able to find him because he would be going where they could not go—yet.

The shift from "you cannot come" to "a new command" includes a sense of "meanwhile," as if Jesus were saying, "Realize that you can't come with me, but you will still have each other, so here's what I expect: Love one another." Jesus repeated the phrase "love one another" two more times in quick succession. But the question naturally arises, what is *new* about loving one another? Is it not the universal sentiment expressed in families and circles of friends? Any individual in such a matrix of relationships would express his or her love in part by encouraging love among the others. This command can certainly be found in the Old Testament (see Exodus 20:12-17; Leviticus 19:18, 33-34; Deuteronomy 5:16-21; 22:1-4).

What *is* new is the standard: "as I have loved you." Loving one another for the disciples and for us would no longer be left to intuition or guessing—we would have a supreme example to emulate, Jesus himself. As the indicator of discipleship, Jesus said, "By this everyone will know that you are my disciples, if you love one another." That standard still stands.

Getting Personal

What do you find particularly challenging or difficult about loving other believers as Jesus has loved you?

How does Jesus' example enable you to love in this way?

The temptation is always to define love by what we think we can easily do or what comes naturally. Genuine love means doing things we may not want to do. And Jesus' standard comes with his promise to help us live up to his example.

RASH PROMISES

Setting the Scene

All four Gospels record Jesus predicting that Peter would deny him before the night was over. Matthew and Mark write that Jesus knew that all the disciples would shortly abandon him (see Matthew 26:31; Mark 14:27). John's account offers an almost humorous sequence in which Jesus announced his impending departure (13:33), then he gave the new commandment to love one another (13:34-35), and Peter ignored the monumental challenge Jesus had just spoken by interrupting: "Lord, where are you going?" It's as if Peter hadn't even heard the new commandment; he was stuck trying to figure out what Jesus had said just before that. How often do we do the same, missing parts—important parts—of what Jesus is telling us?

Jesus' words of tough love for Peter pointed to the future when Jesus' presence would be in the person of the Holy Spirit. The term we can think about today is "follow." It's helpful to read, in conjunction with these passages predicting Peter's denial, the description of Peter's restoration in John 21:15-22, where "follow" is prominently featured. Peter was going to have to learn the hard way what it meant to follow Jesus when Jesus wasn't around.

The disciples were about to experience a rupture in their unique relationship with their Master. Jesus promised always to be with them—and with us—but the question is whether we will be with *him*.

Getting Personal

What does it mean to you today to have Jesus with you, as well as that you are with him?

What do you think was Jesus' purpose in being honest with Peter about his upcoming denial? Was it intended to help Peter somehow avoid the denial or to prepare Peter for his restoration?

We may wonder why Peter was not more conscious of the dangers once Jesus had warned him. In fact, Jesus' warning did not prevent his disciples from bolting when the arresting crowd showed up. The fact that God knows our shortcomings ahead of time should not only keep us humble before his sovereignty but should also fill us with wonder at his grace and forgiveness.

READING THE WORD

❈ *Matthew 26:31-35, NIV*
Then Jesus told them, "This very night you will all fall away on account of me, for it is written: 'I will strike the shepherd, and the sheep of the flock will be scattered.' 32But after I have risen, I will go ahead of you into Galilee." 33Peter replied, "Even if all fall away on account of you, I never will." 34"Truly I tell you," Jesus answered, "this very night, before the rooster crows, you will disown me three times." 35But Peter declared, "Even if I have to die with you, I will never disown you." And all the other disciples said the same.

❈ *John 13:36-38, NIV*
Simon Peter asked him, "Lord, where are you going?" Jesus replied, "Where I am going, you cannot follow now, but you will follow later." 37Peter asked, "Lord, why can't I follow you now? I will lay down my life for you." 38Then Jesus answered, "Will you really lay down your life for me? Very truly I tell you, before the rooster crows, you will disown me three times!"

TALKING TO GOD

Realize that God's Word holds numerous warnings that we tend to neglect from day to day. Ask the Lord to help you not to ignore these warnings, and for him to empower you to live up to his commands for how you should live. Thank him for his unlimited grace and forgiveness.

SIFTED LIKE WHEAT

READING THE WORD

✤ *Luke 22:31-34, NIV*

[Jesus said,] "Simon, Simon, Satan has asked to sift all of you as wheat. 32But I have prayed for you, Simon, that your faith may not fail. And when you have turned back, strengthen your brothers." 33But he replied, "Lord, I am ready to go with you to prison and to death." 34Jesus answered, "I tell you, Peter, before the rooster crows today, you will deny three times that you know me."

TALKING TO GOD

Express your willingness to be "sifted" if it's necessary for you to become a more faithful disciple of the Lord Jesus. Depend on his prayers for you, and ask him to help you, despite your weaknesses, to be part of strengthening your fellow believers.

Setting the Scene

How difficult it must have been for Jesus to say to Peter: "Satan has asked to sift all of you as wheat." To understand why Jesus said this to Peter, we must understand sifting. Sifting doesn't change wheat; it simply removes chaff and chunks of debris to prepare the wheat for effective use. Satan's purpose, of course, is to gather the chaff and highlight our impurities. He is the ultimate accuser (Revelation 12:10). God's purpose, however, is to prepare us for works of service that he has designed for us. As wheat, we may not enjoy being sifted, but we must endure the testing process in order to become useful for the Kingdom.

Jesus gave Peter several encouragements along with the news of his upcoming trial. First, he assured Peter that he had already prayed for Peter that his faith would not fail. What a stunning revelation: Denying Christ doesn't necessarily mean our faith has failed! It simply means that chaff has been revealed and it's time to immediately return to Jesus.

Second, Jesus assured Peter that he would indeed return by saying, "when you have turned back" (not "if"), a process that Jesus himself participated in (see John 21:15-22).

Third, Jesus assured Peter that the testing and sifting process—though he would fail it—would provide a lesson for others. Jesus told Peter to put his shocking example of weakness to good use by undertaking to "strengthen your brothers."

Getting Personal

What times in your life as a believer have you felt that Satan was sifting you as wheat?

What encouragement can you take from Peter's experience?

What helps you grow closer to God in times of testing?

Failures of one kind or another are our universal lot as members of the fallen human race. Failures are not good in and of themselves; but they can wake us from lethargy, force us to approach things differently, and allow us to be of encouragement to others, not only warning them of danger but also being there to help them "turn back" when failures come.

JESUS PROMISES THE HOLY SPIRIT
Week 41, Day 1

❉ *John 14:1-31*

After predicting betrayal by one of the Twelve and Peter's denial, Jesus reassured the disciples by affirming his true identity, confirming their future destination, and promising his presence and power for living. This week as we learn from Jesus' reassuring words, we'll find hope for facing each day's challenges.

TRUSTING

Setting the Scene

After hearing what Jesus had said about Judas's betrayal, Peter's denial, and his own imminent departure, the disciples must have been confused and "troubled" (see John 13:28). So Jesus told them to anchor their trust in him. Jesus indicated that he and the Father would prepare a place for the disciples while he was gone, and that he would return for them.

Jesus knew he would be taken forcefully from them, falsely accused, tortured, and crucified. He knew the disciples would scatter and hide, their faith severely tested. So he encouraged them to hold on to their trust in God and to trust in him.

Later, Jesus told the disciples why he had given them glimpses of the near future: "I have told you these things before they happen so that when they do happen, you will believe" (John 14:29, NLT). Even Judas's betrayal and the terrible events to follow should reassure them that Jesus was who he said he was. After all, he had predicted those very events. Thus the disciples could be confident that everything Jesus had predicted and promised would come true.

Jesus had said that he would "prepare a place" in his Father's house for the disciples, and he reaffirmed that promise, adding that eventually they would be reunited forever in heaven.

READING THE WORD

❉ *John 14:1-3, NLT*
Don't let your hearts be troubled. Trust in God, and trust also in me. 2There is more than enough room in my Father's home. If this were not so, would I have told you that I am going to prepare a place for you? 3When everything is ready, I will come and get you, so that you will always be with me where I am.

TALKING TO GOD

The Lord understands your questions and doubts about the future, so don't hesitate to bring them all to him. Ask him to help you focus on his love, his faithfulness, and his many promises regarding your future. Thank him for being such a perfect promise keeper.

Getting Personal

When do you feel your trust in God being undermined, with doubts creeping in?

What evidence do you have that you can trust Jesus to bring you through and to bring you home?

What difference should your trust make in how you live from day to day?

Jesus' words to the disciples should encourage us as well. Throughout his time with these followers, Jesus had warned them about opposition. He had always told them the truth, even the predictions of pain, separation, rejection, and persecution. And everything happened, just as he said. So we can believe his words about the future, too. What a glorious future that will be, together with Jesus forever! In the meantime, during our struggles and sorrows, we trust him. When we feel lonely and abandoned, we trust him. When we don't know what to do or which way to turn, we trust him. He is preparing a place, our place.

KNOWING

Setting the Scene

Thomas verbalized what all the disciples must have been thinking. They couldn't understand Jesus' words about going to "prepare a place" for them (John 14:2, NLT). Jesus answered by identifying himself not only as the disciples' eternal companion but also as the very means for them to see the Father. He claimed to be the unique and ultimate resource when he said: "I am the way, the truth, and the life. No one can come to the Father except through me." Jesus' response also showed that the destination is not a physical place but a person (the Father) and that the way to that destination is another person (the Son).

Jesus provides all we can know and need to know about God. He is the "way"—our path, bridge, transport, not just an example or road sign pointing the way. He is the "truth"—our source of intimate knowledge of the Father and the reality of all God promised. He is the "life," now and forever—our only source of eternal life.

Jesus' exclusive claim is unmistakable, forcing an unconditional response. His self-description invalidates alternative plans of salvation—he is the *only* way ("No one can come to the Father except through me"). Some say that a single way is too restrictive, too narrow. But the human condition is desperate. We are totally lost without him. That we have *a* way at all is evidence of God's grace and love. Those objecting to having a single way are like people drowning at sea who are graciously thrown a lifesaving rope but who respond by insisting that they deserve a choice of several ropes along with the option of swimming to safety.

Getting Personal

How does knowing Jesus is "the truth" help you love the Lord "with all your mind" (Luke 10:27)?

How does Jesus being "the life" affect both your eternal future after death and your life here on earth?

This passage dispels all doubt about Jesus claiming to be divine and the only way to heaven. Knowing that Jesus is the only way should encourage us to live boldly for him.

READING THE WORD

✤ *John 14:4-6, NLT*
[Jesus said,] "And you know the way to where I am going." 5"No, we don't know, Lord," Thomas said. "We have no idea where you are going, so how can we know the way?" 6Jesus told him, "I am the way, the truth, and the life. No one can come to the Father except through me."

TALKING TO GOD

Meditate on what it means for you that Jesus is "the way, the truth, and the life." Thank him for being your way to the Father, the truth to inform every aspect of your life, and the abundant life that will last forever.

SEEING

READING THE WORD

❈ *John 14:7-11, NLT*

[Jesus said,] "If you had really known me, you would know who my Father is. From now on, you do know him and have seen him!" 8Philip said, "Lord, show us the Father, and we will be satisfied." 9Jesus replied, "Have I been with you all this time, Philip, and yet you still don't know who I am? Anyone who has seen me has seen the Father! So why are you asking me to show him to you? 10Don't you believe that I am in the Father and the Father is in me? The words I speak are not my own, but my Father who lives in me does his work through me. 11Just believe that I am in the Father and the Father is in me. Or at least believe because of the work you have seen me do."

TALKING TO GOD

When you pray, you affirm the triune nature of God. You pray to God the Father, by the power of the Holy Spirit, in the name of Jesus, the Son. Thank God for being one, and for epitomizing love in that triune relationship. Thank him for drawing you into his family.

Setting the Scene

The disciples' response to Jesus' statement about himself reveals that they didn't understand his divine nature. In today's and tomorrow's readings, Jesus describes four aspects of his unique identity: (1) He and the Father share characteristics in such a way that anyone who has seen one has also seen the other; (2) he and the Father are united in such a way that Jesus could speak of either of them being "in" the other; (3) he gives special abilities to those who trust him to accomplish even greater signs than the disciples had already seen; and (4) requests to God made in his name will be answered.

To know Jesus is to know the Father (see John 1:18; Colossians 1:15; Hebrews 1:3). Jesus insisted that because the disciples knew him, they knew the Father. To the Jews, God was the sovereign Creator, holy and wholly separate from them. God loved them and chose them, but he was distant and mysterious. In the Incarnation, however, God put on flesh and became a human being. In effect Jesus was saying, "If you want to know what God is like, look at me!"

Jesus' statement beginning with "from now on" meant that from that time forward, people could know the Father personally through the Son. Jesus holds the way open for us today.

Getting Personal

How does studying the life of Jesus help you when you struggle with doubts about God?

How do the Word (Jesus) and God's Word (the Bible) work together to help you understand who God is and what pleases him?

This declaration conveys the complete unity between Jesus and the Father and affirms that Jesus fully reveals God to us. God has revealed himself generally in nature and specifically in the Bible, but he has revealed himself perfectly in his Son. If we want to know what God is like, we need only look at Jesus.

When you struggle with doubts about God and his love for you, look at Jesus. When you want to know how to live, look at Jesus. When you need to get your values and priorities straight, look at Jesus. When you desire hope for the future, look at Jesus.

LIVING

Setting the Scene

Jesus gave this promise about doing "the same works" and "even greater works" to the disciples, probably referring to the task of spreading the gospel (see John 15:7-8). The "greater works" would have two parts: a greater number of converts and a greater scope for the conversions.

Asking in Jesus' name means praying in agreement with Jesus' person and purpose, according to God's character and will. God will not grant requests contrary to his nature or desires, and we cannot use his name as a magic formula to fulfill our selfish desires. As John reminds us, whenever "we ask for anything that pleases him . . . he will give us what we ask for" (1 John 5:14-15, NLT).

In addition to evangelism and prayer, Jesus reminded the disciples to obey his commandments. When the disciples had Jesus with them, they could watch him and listen to him carefully. If they had questions, they could ask Jesus. During those three years, their understanding of Jesus was expanding and deepening. Eventually, they would carry the responsibility of taking his message to "all the nations" (Matthew 28:19, NLT). Jesus was preparing the disciples for life without his physical presence. They would have to pray ("ask"), live ("obey"), and tell ("greater works").

Getting Personal

How has a deeper acquaintance with Jesus' life and teaching changed the way you pray?

When do you find obeying Christ most difficult?

What can you do to be a more effective witness for Christ?

Three words summarize the Christian life: pray, live, and tell. Pray implies relationship, communication, and worship. We live in vital union with Christ and honestly share our dreams and desires. Live means doing what God wants us to do. This involves studying his Word to discover his commands and principles for living; then we obey. Tell means sharing with others the Good News about Jesus—what he did at the Cross and how he has changed our lives. Like the disciples, with the power of the Holy Spirit working through us, we can change the world.

READING THE WORD

✸ *John 14:12-15, NLT*
I tell you the truth, anyone who believes in me will do the same works I have done, and even greater works, because I am going to be with the Father. 13You can ask for anything in my name, and I will do it, so that the Son can bring glory to the Father. 14Yes, ask me for anything in my name, and I will do it! 15If you love me, obey my commandments.

TALKING TO GOD

Thank the Lord for the freedom you have to approach him in prayer. Praise him for revealing himself so thoroughly through his Son and through his Word. Pray for the power of his Spirit to live for him and share the truth.

SENSING

READING THE WORD

❊ *John 14:16-21, 25-26, NLT*
And I will ask the Father, and he will give you another Advocate, who will never leave you. 17He is the Holy Spirit, who leads into all truth. The world cannot receive him, because it isn't looking for him and doesn't recognize him. But you know him, because he lives with you now and later will be in you. 18No, I will not abandon you as orphans—I will come to you. 19Soon the world will no longer see me, but you will see me. Since I live, you also will live. 20When I am raised to life again, you will know that I am in my Father, and you are in me, and I am in you. 21Those who accept my commandments and obey them are the ones who love me. And because they love me, my Father will love them. And I will love them and reveal myself to each of them.... 25I am telling you these things now while I am still with you. 26But when the Father sends the Advocate as my representative—that is, the Holy Spirit—he will teach you everything and will remind you of everything I have told you.

TALKING TO GOD

It's part of being human to feel isolated or lonely at times. Thank God for the incredible gift of his constant nearness to you. Ask him to help you "practice" his presence by remembering him all through the day. Thank God for the gift of his Spirit to teach you, to convict you of sin, to lead you into all truth.

Setting the Scene

Jesus promised his followers they would experience his presence more fully and intimately because the Father would send them the Holy Spirit. The expression "another Advocate" implies that Jesus was the first and the Spirit would be the same kind of "Comforter." When Jesus would no longer be with the disciples physically, the Holy Spirit would be with them and in them, and he would lead them "into all truth."

The power of the Spirit came on the disciples just before his ascension (John 20:22), and the Spirit was poured out on all the believers at Pentecost (Acts 2), shortly after Jesus ascended to heaven. The Holy Spirit is the presence of God, helping all believers live as he wants and building Christ's church on earth. Jesus taught these truths about the Spirit:

- He will be with us forever (John 14:16).
- The world at large cannot accept him (John 14:17).
- He lives with us and in us (John 14:17).
- He teaches us (John 14:26).
- He reminds us of Jesus' words (John 14:26; 15:26).
- He convicts us of sin, shows us God's righteousness, and announces God's judgment on evil (John 16:8).
- He guides into truth and gives insight into future events (John 16:13).
- He brings glory to Christ (John 16:14).

This coming would be "soon," after Jesus' crucifixion, burial, and resurrection. After the Resurrection, the disciples would realize by their own experience that Jesus lived in his Father, they themselves lived in Jesus, and Jesus lived in them. They would begin to know what it meant to live in God and have God live in them. The Spirit would continue the ministry of teaching and would remind the disciples of what Jesus had taught.

Getting Personal

When do you sense the Holy Spirit working in and through you?

How has the Holy Spirit helped you understand and apply the Bible?

Jesus did not leave the disciples, and us, alone. He is with us through his Spirit, encouraging, assuring, convicting, guiding, enlightening, and empowering. We need to depend on him, listen to him, and follow his lead.

FINDING

Setting the Scene

Jesus' gift to the disciples was peace. Jesus wasn't promising the absence of trouble; in fact, in the coming hours he personally would endure great physical, emotional, and spiritual struggles. Instead, Jesus was promising to give these men peace *during* those conflicts and problems. They could know that he was with them, that what they stood for and lived for was true, that God was in control, and that their eternal destiny was secure.

As long as Jesus was present with the disciples physically, they could rely on the peace and security he brought them. But what would they do when they had to face problems *without* him? Along with his continued presence through the Holy Spirit, he promised his peace. This would be a vital resource for the disciples in the days and years to come. Later he told them, "I have told you all this so that you may have peace in me. Here on earth you will have many trials and sorrows. But take heart, because I have overcome the world" (John 16:33, NLT).

Jesus told the disciples about his imminent departure and return so they would not be surprised and fearful when these events occurred. Instead, they would recognize that Jesus knew what would happen, and they would have confidence in him. Jesus wanted them to have peace and not be "troubled and afraid."

Getting Personal

What conflicts and problems are you facing? How can remembering what Jesus experienced give you peace?

What threats, real or imagined, keep you up at night? How can knowing who Jesus is and what he has promised calm your fears and give you hope?

How do you rely on the Holy Spirit to keep you calm and confident during difficult times?

Jesus knew what would happen to the disciples—that their lives and dreams would be shattered. Jesus was preparing them for those difficult hours and days . . . and years. Every day, we face struggles, conflicts, tragedies, and broken dreams. At every turn, Jesus assures us of his presence and promise.

READING THE WORD

❋ *John 14:27-31, NLT*

I am leaving you with a gift—peace of mind and heart. And the peace I give is a gift the world cannot give. So don't be troubled or afraid. 28Remember what I told you: I am going away, but I will come back to you again. If you really loved me, you would be happy that I am going to the Father, who is greater than I am. 29I have told you these things before they happen so that when they do happen, you will believe. 30I don't have much more time to talk to you, because the ruler of this world approaches. He has no power over me, 31but I will do what the Father requires of me, so that the world will know that I love the Father. Come, let's be going.

TALKING TO GOD

God sees the big picture and retains control, even when circumstances or relationships are stressful. Thank God for his sovereignty over all things and ask him to help you rely on his strength in every situation.

JESUS TEACHES ABOUT THE TRUE VINE

Week 42, Day 1

❈ *John 15:1–16:33*

Chapters 15 and 16 of the Gospel of John continue the extended teaching Jesus gave his disciples during the Last Supper. These intimate comments are recorded nowhere else in the New Testament, though they harmonize with and deepen many of the themes Jesus touched on in other places. Key relationships are explored: with Christ, with other believers, and with the world. Jesus also declared and described the Holy Spirit who would continue to work in the world and indwell believers. And then he reminded his disciples—and us—that though tribulations and troubles would come, he has taken care of everything!

READING THE WORD

❈ *John 15:1-8, NKJV*

I am the true vine, and My Father is the vinedresser. 2Every branch in Me that does not bear fruit He takes away; and every branch that bears fruit He prunes, that it may bear more fruit. 3You are already clean because of the word which I have spoken to you. 4Abide in Me, and I in you. As the branch cannot bear fruit of itself, unless it abides in the vine, neither can you, unless you abide in Me. 5I am the vine, you are the branches. He who abides in Me, and I in him, bears much fruit; for without Me you can do nothing. 6If anyone does not abide in Me, he is cast out as a branch and is withered; and they gather them and throw them into the fire, and they are burned. 7If you abide in Me, and My words abide in you, you will ask what you desire, and it shall be done for you. 8By this My Father is glorified, that you bear much fruit; so you will be My disciples.

THE LIFE OF BRANCHES

Setting the Scene

By the time the Last Supper was over, Jesus had given the disciples some powerful and unforgettable verbal pictures to help them understand the radical change that was about to affect their ongoing relationship with him. The picture of a life-giving connection between a vine and its branches would sustain them in the time to come. Very soon, their world would turn upside down with Jesus' arrest, trial, and death. Then while they were still in shock from those developments, their world would be turned right side up again with Jesus' resurrection. Eventually they would treasure each of Jesus' lessons, indelibly confirmed by everything that happened.

Jesus began his teaching on the vine and the branches by identifying the vine. He had just introduced the disciples to the Counselor (John 14:15-18, 25-27), saying, "You know him, for he lives with you and will be in you" (John 14:17, NIV). When Jesus spoke of himself as the vine and his Father as the gardener, although the Counselor/Holy Spirit isn't specifically mentioned, his presence permeates the scene. The incarnate Son was speaking of his sustaining role in the disciples' lives that would continue in the Holy Spirit as surely as it had been while he was with them in the flesh. Jesus was speaking to his disciples as well as to all those "who will believe in me through their message" (John 17:20, NIV).

Three types of branches are addressed by Jesus: abiding branches, potential branches, and dead branches. Those who are potential branches (our initial state) find out they will soon be dead branches if no "abiding" connection is made to the vine. The claim of connection is proven true by fruitfulness. Ironically, both fruitful branches and dead ones might appear to get the same treatment from the Gardener. Getting pruned *back* may look and feel at times like getting pruned *off*. Generations of believers give us evidence that times of fruitfulness often follow the times of hardship and difficulty that might be described as pruning. The picture of remaining or abiding in the vine sets up the process of seasons of pruning, which Jesus alludes to in 15:3, "You are already clean," where the term "clean" translates the same word used in the previous verse for "pruning." This is not a onetime event, but an ongoing process tended to by the Gardener.

While fruitfulness is usually described as a picture of effective spiritual reproduction, it's worth noting the branches bear *fruit*, not other branches. Each fruit contains the seeds that might lead to more branches, but fruits are more than seeds. Items such as endurance, answered prayer, love, joy, peace, and more are described as fruit of our Spirit-empowered relationship with Jesus, the vine (see John 15:7, 11-12; Galatians 5:22-24; 2 Peter 1:5-8).

Getting Personal

What are current evidences of fruitfulness in your life?

When did your last round of pruning occur? What result have you seen from that work by the Gardener in your relationship with him?

Remaining or abiding in Christ is not a matter of remembering some time in the past when you were seeking to obey the Lord. The evidence of abiding lies in fruitfulness now, in the present. If you've been thinking some old commitment to Christ suffices, give yourself to abiding in Christ today.

TALKING TO GOD

Submit yourself to God, the Gardener, for whatever pruning he sees fit. But ask him to help you be aware of the work he is doing in your life, so that you may benefit fully from the "trimming," for your good and for his glory.

ABIDING IN LOVE

READING THE WORD

❊ *John 15:9-17, NKJV*

As the Father loved Me, I also have loved you; abide in My love. 10If you keep My commandments, you will abide in My love, just as I have kept My Father's commandments and abide in His love. 11These things I have spoken to you, that My joy may remain in you, and that your joy may be full. 12This is My commandment, that you love one another as I have loved you. 13Greater love has no one than this, than to lay down one's life for his friends. 14You are My friends if you do whatever I command you. 15No longer do I call you servants, for a servant does not know what his master is doing; but I have called you friends, for all things that I heard from My Father I have made known to you. 16You did not choose Me, but I chose you and appointed you that you should go and bear fruit, and that your fruit should remain, that whatever you ask the Father in My name He may give you. 17These things I command you, that you love one another.

TALKING TO GOD

Thank God for the gifts described in this passage: the dwelling place of his love, his guidance and direction, his joy, the ability to love others sacrificially with himself as an example, status as Christ's friend as well as servant, and a chosen place and purpose in his Kingdom.

Setting the Scene

Each verse in this passage can be unwrapped as a delightful gift that keeps on giving. The first gift is a dwelling place where we can live and remain—Christ's love. The way we appropriate this gift is by keeping his commandments. We abide in his love when we obey, and we abide in his Word when we trust that he loves us. Both these are aspects of abiding in him. The second gift contains Christ's commands, the gift of direction and application. We find this gift is true every day as we remain in Christ. The third gift overflows with joy. This joy is not generated from within us but is an overflow of Christ's joy. Since he is in us, his joy flows through us. This joy is immediate, ongoing, and intimately connected with the "things I have spoken to you." The absence of joy can often be traced to a disconnection from his Word.

The command to love others is the central command that flows out of our shared love from God and for God. When Jesus was asked to summarize all of God's law, he pointed out love for God and love for neighbor (see Matthew 22:34-40; Mark 12:28-34). These two are inseparable parts of the same package. When we read verse 13, we discover that the love Jesus is commanding us to exercise is sacrificial, exactly the kind of love Jesus is about to demonstrate at the Cross. The next package is the gift of close relationship with Jesus. Though we remain servants, we are now also friends. Another gift is the double assurance "I chose you and appointed you"; we were given a place and purpose.

Getting Personal

How do the promises of Christ bring you joy?

What can you do to show your friendship to Christ?

The dynamic relationship pictured by the attachment between branch and vine implies flow, action, and obedience. Every moment the branch remains, it receives life. Jesus pictured it as a constant, vibrant interaction.

OPPOSITION

Setting the Scene

Jesus previously warned those who wanted to be his disciples to count the cost of following him (see Matthew 8:18-22; Luke 9:57-62; 14:28-33). He indicated that we should expect the hatred of the world. If the world hated him and we are representing him, it shouldn't come as a surprise when hatred for the vine spills over to the branches. The point is not to seek rejection as a confirmation of our faith but to live for Christ and let the rejection chips fall where they may. Bearing fruit carries with it both the joy of acceptance and the risk of rejection of our message. If we never run the risk of rejection, we are probably not making much of an effort at living obediently for Christ.

Jesus made it clear that rejecting him means rejecting the Father. People have Jesus' words, his miracles, the convicting ministry of the Holy Spirit, and the example of his work in others' lives, so they are, in God's eyes, without excuse.

In a stunning note, Jesus warns of the coming time when "anyone who kills you will think they are offering a service to God" (John 16:2, NIV). This was literally true in the early church and is true in places today. An Islamic extremist who kills believes he is serving God. This is also true of those who would silence or intimidate Christians as "service" to their god, even if their "god" is merely their own will or a human system.

Getting Personal

What people in your life have no idea that you are a follower of Jesus Christ? What could you do to inform them?

When have you experienced animosity toward Christ?

How can your witness for Christ be both winsome and bold?

When we do experience rejection, we probably should ask ourselves if we were simply being obnoxious or insensitive. Speaking the truth into a situation does not automatically release us from responsibility for timing, tone, and compassion. But if we are using concerns about sensitivity as the primary reason for consistent silence, then we are probably covering fear with excuses. We need to speak up.

READING THE WORD

✵ *John 15:18-22, NIV*

If the world hates you, keep in mind that it hated me first. 19If you belonged to the world, it would love you as its own. As it is, you do not belong to the world, but I have chosen you out of the world. That is why the world hates you. 20Remember what I told you: "A servant is not greater than his master." If they persecuted me, they will persecute you also. If they obeyed my teaching, they will obey yours also. 21They will treat you this way because of my name, for they do not know the one who sent me. 22If I had not come and spoken to them, they would not be guilty of sin; but now they have no excuse for their sin.

✵ *John 16:2-3, NIV*

They will put you out of the synagogue; in fact, the time is coming when anyone who kills you will think they are offering a service to God. 3They will do such things because they have not known the Father or me.

TALKING TO GOD

Affirm your commitment to be identified with Jesus and with God's Kingdom. Ask the Lord to help you be loving and creative in the ways you express your faith to nonbelievers.

THE HELPER'S WORK

READING THE WORD

❋ *John 16:7-15, NKJV*

Nevertheless I tell you the truth. It is to your advantage that I go away; for if I do not go away, the Helper will not come to you; but if I depart, I will send Him to you. 8And when He has come, He will convict the world of sin, and of righteousness, and of judgment: 9of sin, because they do not believe in Me; 10of righteousness, because I go to My Father and you see Me no more; 11of judgment, because the ruler of this world is judged. 12I still have many things to say to you, but you cannot bear them now. 13However, when He, the Spirit of truth, has come, He will guide you into all truth; for He will not speak on His own authority, but whatever He hears He will speak; and He will tell you things to come. 14He will glorify Me, for He will take of what is Mine and declare it to you. 15All things that the Father has are Mine. Therefore I said that He will take of Mine and declare it to you.

TALKING TO GOD

Accept the Spirit's correction and conviction, as it comes in partnership with joy in your relationship with the Lord. Thank God for his compassionate work in your life and for giving you what you need even when you don't know you need it.

Setting the Scene

Up until this point in the table conversation, Jesus' description of the Helper, or Counselor, focused on the role of the Holy Spirit in the lives of believers. Jesus already indicated that his departure from physical ministry on earth would pave the way for the Counselor's arrival (John 14:15-16). But, Jesus added, he would continue to be involved in the lives of believers: "I will not leave you orphans; I will come to you" (John 14:18, NKJV).

Now Jesus reveals the broader purpose for the arrival of the Holy Spirit. This is not so much a description of new roles the Holy Spirit will fulfill, but a revelation of roles the Spirit has always played in the affairs of people, only now with open sanction in God's plan. First, the Holy Spirit will convict the world of sin, particularly in regard to their rejection of Jesus. Second, conviction will relate to righteousness, particularly in the absence of Jesus' physical example. Third, the Spirit's conviction will extend God's judgment over the "ruler of this world" to all those who side with him. Fourth, the Holy Spirit will guide believers into all truth, relating to God's Word ("whatever He hears") and including truth about "things to come." Fifth, the Spirit will reveal more of the glory of Jesus by allowing his followers to understand even more about him.

Getting Personal

When have you experienced the Holy Spirit's work in your life?

When have you avoided his presence in helping, guiding, or convicting? What can you do to welcome the Spirit's work?

Jesus promised unprecedented access to his Spirit while we live for him in this world. The spiritual sensitivity from the world that we long to see ultimately rests with the Holy Spirit, not us. The role of convicting "the world of sin, and of righteousness, and of judgment" is not ours. As believers, we can fully expect the Spirit to persistently bring us more and more into full awareness of who Jesus is.

SHORT GRIEF

Setting the Scene

During this Last Supper, the disciples were trying to cope with Jesus' loving actions and words at the same time they were trying to grasp his statements about his imminent departure. They weren't sure if he was going or coming, or both. They wouldn't understand most of what he said until they lived through it with him.

In John 16, Jesus held out the hope that the Resurrection would answer many of their questions. Jesus made the connection for the disciples between the reality of grief and the reality of prayer. He didn't take himself out of the prayer process (see Romans 8:34; Hebrews 7:25), but he emphasized that access to his Father would soon be direct. It was easy for the disciples (and we still make this error) to isolate Jesus as the intercessor to whom they directed their requests, grief, concerns, and needs. He then would take them before the Father. Is God the Father unaware or inattentive until Jesus approaches him? Of course not. What Jesus knows, the Father knows. Jesus was telling his disciples (and us) to continue addressing him in prayer and to use his name freely in expressing prayer, but to realize at all times that we are speaking to God: Father, Son, and Holy Spirit. We have Jesus' permission to place anything before God in prayer.

Getting Personal

When you use Jesus' name in prayer, what is your intention? What are your reasons for using or not using Jesus' name in prayer?

How would you distinguish between Jesus' dual roles as intercessor and facilitator in prayer? How does each role encourage prayer?

The power of Jesus' name is not the power of a secret code word or incantation; it is relational power. Jesus told his disciples that all who would believe in him could be assured that any approach to God in his name would be guaranteed a welcome.

READING THE WORD

❋ *John 16:21-28, NIV*
A woman giving birth to a child has pain because her time has come; but when her baby is born she forgets the anguish because of her joy that a child is born into the world. 22So with you: Now is your time of grief, but I will see you again and you will rejoice, and no one will take away your joy. 23In that day you will no longer ask me anything. Very truly I tell you, my Father will give you whatever you ask in my name. 24Until now you have not asked for anything in my name. Ask and you will receive, and your joy will be complete. 25Though I have been speaking figuratively, a time is coming when I will no longer use this kind of language but will tell you plainly about my Father. 26In that day you will ask in my name. I am not saying that I will ask the Father on your behalf. 27No, the Father himself loves you because you have loved me and have believed that I came from God. 28I came from the Father and entered the world; now I am leaving the world and going back to the Father.

TALKING TO GOD

Recognize the Father, Son, and Holy Spirit as you pray today. Thank the Father for making a way of direct access to him and for lovingly welcoming your prayers. Thank Jesus for being the way that provided bold access and for interceding for you as you pray. Thank the Spirit for translating your prayers when you don't know how to pray (Romans 8:26).

REASON FOR CHEER

Setting the Scene

In our experience, belief is always tenuous, with sparkling moments of certainty. Today's assurance deflates into tomorrow's apparently empty hope. We "arrive" one day, only to feel lost the next.

When Jesus paused after his comments about prayer, the disciples thought they had reached an important moment of understanding. Jesus was finally "speaking plainly." Their testimony in that moment is revealing: "Now we are sure that You know all things." They were willing to affirm, "You came forth from God." This is the last recorded statement by the disciples during the Last Supper.

Jesus gently challenged their statement of faith: "Do you now believe?" (NKJV), which perhaps is another way of saying, "Finally, you believe!" Jesus knew that what they believed at that moment would not be enough to prevent them from scattering under pressure. Then Jesus added some statements that have provided relief to countless believers over the centuries: "I have told you these things, so that in me you may have peace. In this world you will have trouble. But take heart! I have overcome the world" (John 16:33, NIV).

Getting Personal

How have you experienced Jesus' guarantee, "In the world you will have tribulation"?

What is your source of "good cheer," and what causes you to "take heart" when the world threatens to overcome you?

How did Jesus overcome the world?

Jesus gave those words of hope to his disciples because their faith was—as ours is—tenuous. Sometimes we hold on by a thread. Ultimately, our frail faith and our peace must be anchored to the one who did overcome the world. He gave that message to his disciples before he finished overcoming the world so that they could pass on the Good News to us who would come later. In him we can have peace; in him we can overcome the world. Any other means we try will prove inadequate.

READING THE WORD

❧ *John 16:29-33, NKJV*

His disciples said to Him, "See, now You are speaking plainly, and using no figure of speech! 30Now we are sure that You know all things, and have no need that anyone should question You. By this we believe that You came forth from God." 31Jesus answered them, "Do you now believe? 32Indeed the hour is coming, yes, has now come, that you will be scattered, each to his own, and will leave Me alone. And yet I am not alone, because the Father is with Me. 33These things I have spoken to you, that in Me you may have peace. In the world you will have tribulation; but be of good cheer, I have overcome the world."

TALKING TO GOD

Don't let the ups and downs of your feelings of faith keep you from coming to the Lord, no matter how you feel. Ask him to help you understand the confidence you can have that Jesus has overcome the world, and that it would give you "good cheer."

✦ *John 17:1-26*

Jesus knew that very soon in Gethsemane he would confront Judas and the soldiers and be taken, tried, convicted, and crucified. So he prayed—not just for himself but for his followers, the disciples and all future believers. This week we'll focus on that prayer, to hear Jesus' requests for us, to hear his heart.

KNOWING THE SON

Setting the Scene

The time for Jesus' glorification had arrived. If the Father would glorify the Son in the Crucifixion and Resurrection, the Son could, in turn, give eternal life to believers. In doing so, he would glorify the Father. Jesus clearly stated that people could have eternal life by "know[ing] you, the only true God, and Jesus Christ, the one you sent to earth." In this statement, Jesus affirmed that he had glorified the Father on earth by "completing the work" that the Father had given him to do. This work would be accomplished through his death on the cross. Then, looking beyond the Cross to his resurrection and ascension, Jesus asked the Father to restore the glory he had enjoyed with the Father "before the world began." Jesus' resurrection and ascension—and Stephen's dying exclamation (Acts 7:56)—attest that Jesus' prayer was answered. He returned to his exalted position at the right hand of God.

Paul explains . . .

> Though [Jesus] was God,
> > he did not think of equality with God
> > as something to cling to.
> Instead, he gave up his divine privileges;
> > he took the humble position of a slave
> > and was born as a human being.
> When he appeared in human form,
> > he humbled himself in obedience to God
> > and died a criminal's death on a cross.

READING THE WORD

✦ *John 17:1-5, NLT*

After saying all these things, Jesus looked up to heaven and said, "Father, the hour has come. Glorify your Son so he can give glory back to you. ²For you have given him authority over everyone. He gives eternal life to each one you have given him. ³And this is the way to have eternal life—to know you, the only true God, and Jesus Christ, the one you sent to earth. ⁴I brought glory to you here on earth by completing the work you gave me to do. ⁵Now, Father, bring me into the glory we shared before the world began."

TALKING TO GOD

Thank God for the crucifixion and resurrection of Jesus, which reconciles you to him and makes it possible for you to approach him in prayer. Bow at the wonderful name of Jesus, which means "Savior," and confess that he is Lord, to the glory of God.

Therefore, God elevated him to the place of highest honor
   and gave him the name above all other names,
that at the name of Jesus every knee should bow,
   in heaven and on earth and under the earth,
and every tongue confess that Jesus Christ is Lord,
   to the glory of God the Father.
         (Philippians 2:6-11, NLT)

Getting Personal

How did God glorify Jesus in his crucifixion and resurrection?

Who or what was most influential in helping you come to know Jesus?

What steps or resources help you continue to know Jesus?

Jesus knew who he was—the Son of God who had come to earth to redeem fallen humankind. Today, people have wide-ranging ideas of Jesus' identity. Some see him as an idealistic religious leader; others highlight his moral teachings and example. Some call him a radical, and others focus on his concern for the poor.

While some Jesus-views have a bit of truth, these are the most important facts about Jesus: He is fully divine and fully human; he died on the cross for our sins and rose from the dead; eternal life can be found only through faith in him. We can know a lot about various religious practices and the Bible. We can even live an exemplary life of morality and good works. But that means nothing unless we know Jesus.

ACCEPTING RESPONSIBILITY

Setting the Scene

Jesus began to pray for the men God had selected to be his disciples. Jesus had "revealed" the Father to these men, telling them, "Anyone who has seen me has seen the Father" (John 14:9, NLT). The disciples had received Jesus' words as coming from God; thus, they had come to believe that Jesus had been sent from the Father (see John 16:28-30). Jesus also said that he had "passed on" the gospel message, both in content and in calling. That is, he had told them about the Kingdom of God and how to obtain it, and he had entrusted to them the responsibility of spreading the Word. The disciples had accepted this responsibility, and through them the whole world would hear about Jesus—his life, death, and resurrection. Jesus was also declaring that the disciples were ready for the next lesson, as difficult as it might be.

Getting Personal

Who passed on God's message about eternal life to you?

How have you "kept his word"?

What makes passing on the gospel a struggle for you?

"Disciple" means "follower." The disciples believed in Jesus and gave up everything to follow him. They called him "Lord" and "Messiah," so they were willing to obey him, to do whatever he asked. Very soon they would learn that this would entail taking Christ's message to "all the nations" (Matthew 28:19, NLT)— and they did. Because of their faithfulness, we know about Jesus today.

Every generation needs to receive Jesus' words and pass them on. As modern disciples, we must accept our responsibility to tell others about God's gift of eternal life through his Son.

READING THE WORD

❋ *John 17:6-8, NLT*
I have revealed you to the ones you gave me from this world. They were always yours. You gave them to me, and they have kept your word. 7Now they know that everything I have is a gift from you, 8for I have passed on to them the message you gave me. They accepted it and know that I came from you, and they believe you sent me.

TALKING TO GOD

As your understanding of the Good News grows as you study Jesus' life and teaching, ask the Lord to give you opportunities to pass along the important truth of the gospel. Thank him specifically for those who have been faithful in bringing you the message of salvation.

REFLECTING GLORY

READING THE WORD

✤ *John 17:9-12, NLT*

My prayer is not for the world, but for those you have given me, because they belong to you. ¹⁰All who are mine belong to you, and you have given them to me, so they bring me glory. ¹¹Now I am departing from the world; they are staying in this world, but I am coming to you. Holy Father, you have given me your name; now protect them by the power of your name so that they will be united just as we are. ¹²During my time here, I protected them by the power of the name you gave me. I guarded them so that not one was lost, except the one headed for destruction, as the Scriptures foretold.

TALKING TO GOD

Pray that the Lord would allow others to see Christ in you through your attitudes, lifestyle, actions, and words. Confess the times when you have brought shame, rather than glory, to the name of Jesus. Ask for the Spirit's enabling to help all your choices be Christ-glorifying.

Setting the Scene

God loves the whole world, but here Jesus was focusing on his disciples. They belonged to both Jesus and the Father, and Jesus would be glorified in them after he had returned to the Father because their lives and words would reveal Jesus' essential character to the world. He would be present through them. The disciples would have the responsibility of spreading the news about Jesus and his Kingdom. They would encounter terrible opposition, so Jesus asked the Father to unite and protect them. During the time that Jesus was physically present with the disciples, they had been unified around him, and Jesus had carefully protected these disciples as a precious gift given to him from the Father. Soon Jesus would leave these men, and he knew their faith would be severely tested; yet they would glorify him through their lives and their testimony.

Getting Personal

What assurances do you have that you "belong" to Christ?

How do you feel "guarded" and "protected" by Christ?

What can you do to bring glory to Christ?

The disciples "belonged" to God—they had been chosen and bought with a price (see 1 Corinthians 6:20). And Jesus was leaving these men in the world, entrusting them with the great responsibility of taking his message to all the nations. The life purpose for these early disciples and for all who follow Christ should be to bring him glory. We do this through how we live and what we say. Jesus had said, "Anyone who has seen me has seen the Father!" (John 14:9, NLT); that is, "If you want to know what God is like, look at me." Here we find the next part of the equation: "If you want to know what Jesus is like, look at his followers."

Setting the Scene

The world hates Christ-followers. Because Christians don't cooperate with the world by joining in their sin, they are living accusations against the world's immorality. Thus believers have to endure hatred and opposition.

Like Jesus, the disciples didn't "belong to the world" but to God. Jesus asked the Father "to keep them safe from the evil one," not to isolate them from the world. They wouldn't be removed from evil people and temptations but were to *resist* evil. This would happen by making them "holy by [God's] truth." The word *holy* means "set apart." Thus Jesus was saying that his followers needed to live *in* the world but differently *from* the world in the way they thought and acted—set apart and focused on doing God's will. This happens when believers understand and apply God's truth.

Jesus came "into the world" on a mission for the Father; so he sent these disciples "into the world" on a mission. Jesus did not pray that the disciples would be removed from the hatred and persecution to come, rather that they would be protected through the difficult circumstances from falling prey to the devil. The only way believers can be witnesses *to* the world is to be witnessing for Christ *in* the world.

Getting Personal

When have you been tempted to withdraw from nonbelievers or to avoid them? Why?

How does God's Word set us apart? How does God fill us with his joy?

What makes living in the world so difficult for Christ-followers?

At times, Christians have tried to withdraw from the world, living in isolated communities or restricting their relationships and associations to other believers. Given the differences from the world, we can understand that reaction, but it's not God's way. His mission for us is to be a positive, dynamic influence for him. And he wants us to live with joy. He doesn't remove us from evil but delivers us (Matthew 6:13) by giving us the power to resist, through his Word and Holy Spirit.

READING THE WORD

❋ *John 17:13-19, NLT*
Now I am coming to you. I told them many things while I was with them in this world so they would be filled with my joy. 14I have given them your word. And the world hates them because they do not belong to the world, just as I do not belong to the world. 15I'm not asking you to take them out of the world, but to keep them safe from the evil one. 16They do not belong to this world any more than I do. 17Make them holy by your truth; teach them your word, which is truth. 18Just as you sent me into the world, I am sending them into the world. 19And I give myself as a holy sacrifice for them so they can be made holy by your truth.

TALKING TO GOD

The mission of all believers depends on our living in a holy way. Ask the Lord to set you apart in your attitudes and actions, so that in glorifying him in everyday ways you will make a difference for his Kingdom in this world.

READING THE WORD

❊ *John 17:20-21, NLT*
I am praying not only for these disciples but also for all who will ever believe in me through their message. ²¹I pray that they will all be one, just as you and I are one—as you are in me, Father, and I am in you. And may they be in us so that the world will believe you sent me.

TALKING TO GOD

Enjoy the intimacy of being fully known by God. Jesus prayed for you centuries before you were born, knowing you would belong to him. Thank God for this legacy of faith, and ask him to help you carry it on to your children and grandchildren and to young people in your neighborhood, community, and church. Pray that this next generation of young believers will stay strong and unified as they live for God.

PRAYING FORWARD

Setting the Scene
After praying for his disciples, Jesus prayed for all those who would believe in him "through their message." In reality, everyone who has become a Christian has done so through the apostles' message; after all, they wrote much of the New Testament and were the founders of the Christian church and served as the first evangelists. Thus, Jesus was praying for us and for those who would come to know him through our witness. We can easily replace "all" in the prayer with our own names and realize Jesus was thinking of us as he prepared for the Cross.

This prayer contains several lessons. First, everything Jesus prayed for the disciples in this chapter of the book of John also applies to us. Second, Jesus had us in mind two thousand years ago—he knew the gospel would spread through the disciples. Third, we should continue to tell others about Christ and pray for those, even yet to be born, who will follow us in following him.

Getting Personal
In what ways does knowing that Jesus included you in this prayer encourage and motivate you?

What aspects of Jesus' prayer do you most need today?

How can you join with others to spread the good news about Jesus to the next generation?

Knowing that Jesus prayed for us should give us confidence as we work for his Kingdom. Jesus expected his original disciples to come together after being scattered at his arrest and crucifixion. After Christ's resurrection, great commission, and ascension and the coming of the Holy Spirit, the disciples would spread the Good News courageously throughout the world. The message has continued to be spread, and we live in that legacy of faith. Now the mission to see succeeding generations of Christ-followers belongs to us.

BEING ONE

Setting the Scene

Perhaps the strongest, most repeated request in Jesus' prayer is for unity in the body of believers. Jesus asked that the disciples be "one"—he wanted to see a deep connection among those who were connected to him. Jesus said this would be possible because he had "given them the glory" the Father had given him. In other words, all believers share an intimate knowledge of who Jesus is and have the Holy Spirit residing in them.

Earlier, Jesus had challenged the disciples to "love each other" so that their "love for one another" would prove to the world that they were his disciples (John 13:34-35, NLT). Both "unity" and "love" have the same purpose—"that the world will know that you sent me and that you love them as much as you love me." Here Jesus was still referring to all his followers, not just the immediate disciples. When Christians demonstrate this oneness, they convince the world that the Father sent the Son and that the Father loves believers deeply and eternally, just as he loves the Son.

Getting Personal

In your experience, what kinds of issues cause division in churches or between churches?

How can we discover the way Christ is working in other believers?

As you meet Christians from other churches, what can you do to express your unity with them?

Too often Christians are known for what divides instead of what unites them. The multitude of denominations, minute theological distinctions, and worship expressions confuse outsiders. And consider the damage inflicted by church splits and lawsuits among believers. Instead, we should join ranks with all those who honor Jesus as Lord and affirm his Word. We should be united in our common belief in Jesus as the God-man, the only way to heaven, through faith, because of his death on the cross and resurrection. Instead of competing for members, churches should work together to spread the gospel community-wide.

READING THE WORD

✸ *John 17:22-26, NLT*
I have given them the glory you gave me, so they may be one as we are one. 23I am in them and you are in me. May they experience such perfect unity that the world will know that you sent me and that you love them as much as you love me. 24Father, I want these whom you have given me to be with me where I am. Then they can see all the glory you gave me because you loved me even before the world began! 25O righteous Father, the world doesn't know you, but I do; and these disciples know you sent me. 26I have revealed you to them, and I will continue to do so. Then your love for me will be in them, and I will be in them.

TALKING TO GOD

Pray for other churches in your community that preach the Word and believe in Jesus as the Savior—and pray for your own church's witness in your community. Ask the Father to give believers in your area a unity that allows for differences in giftedness and personality—and even in minor doctrinal beliefs. Pray that others will be drawn to the Savior because of the love and unity you demonstrate.

JESUS PRAYS FOR HIMSELF
Week 44, Day 1

❀ *Matthew 26:36-46; Mark 14:32-42; Luke 22:39-46*

The Gospel of John takes us from the Last Supper to the location of Judas's betrayal. Matthew, Mark, and Luke indicate that a certain amount of time transpired between the arrival of the group at the garden of Gethsemane and the approach by Judas and those who had come to make the arrest. During those moments, Jesus spent time in agonized prayer, the final time of preparation for the difficult hours that would follow. Jesus' prayer teaches us about the cost and the ultimate reward of seeking God with our whole being.

READING THE WORD

❀ *Matthew 26:36-38, NIV*
Then Jesus went with his disciples to a place called Gethsemane, and he said to them, "Sit here while I go over there and pray." 37He took Peter and the two sons of Zebedee along with him, and he began to be sorrowful and troubled. 38Then he said to them, "My soul is overwhelmed with sorrow to the point of death. Stay here and keep watch with me."

WATCH AND PRAY

Setting the Scene

The Gospels of John and Luke tell us that Jesus and his disciples regularly visited Gethsemane. That's why Judas knew where to lead the group that came to arrest Jesus. If Jesus spent his days in Jerusalem during the last week, then a stop in the olive grove on the other side of the valley between the city and the village of Bethany may well have been a nightly routine. It is certainly where Jesus took the disciples after his last supper with them.

Once they were in the grove, Jesus had eight of the disciples stay close to the entrance while he moved deeper among the trees to pray. He took James, John, and Peter with him, the same three who had accompanied him on the mountain when he was transfigured (Matthew 17:1-13). Those with him could clearly see that Jesus was "sorrowful and troubled." While there had been other times in their experience when Jesus had been troubled, this must have been disconcerting to the disciples. Then Jesus told the three who were with him, "My soul is overwhelmed with sorrow to the point of death. Stay here and keep watch with me." Jesus literally said, "I am very sad" or "grieved." This haunting revelation by Jesus takes us back to Isaiah's words about the Servant of the Lord whom God would eventually send to his people: "He was despised and rejected by mankind, a man of suffering, and familiar with pain. Like one from whom people hide their faces he was despised, and we held him in low esteem" (Isaiah 53:3, NIV). Whatever part of suffering and pain Jesus did not yet know, he was about to experience.

Jesus asked the three, "Stay here and keep watch with me." The term he used means "keep awake." Jesus wasn't asking them to do one thing while he did another; he was asking them to pray alertly as he was praying. It is not likely that Jesus closed his eyes during prayer, nor that he instructed his disciples to do so. We're told that before he raised Lazarus from the grave, "Jesus lifted up His eyes and said, 'Father, I thank You that You have heard Me'" (John 11:41, NKJV). John 17:1 describes how Jesus began his high priestly prayer: "Jesus spoke these words, lifted up His eyes to heaven, and said: 'Father, the hour has come. Glorify Your Son, that Your Son also may glorify You'" (NKJV). The keeping awake and watching that Jesus had in mind was prayer.

In those crisis moments, Jesus turned to prayer and he enlisted others to join him. He expressed his dependence on God and his dependence on others. He went to the Cross alone, but he invited others to walk there with him as far as possible. As we will see, that wasn't very far.

Getting Personal

From what you know of Jesus, what was causing him to grieve so deeply?

Do pressures and trouble make you more or less likely to turn to God for help? Why?

On whom can you depend for support in prayer?

People we depend on often let us down (and we let others down), but that's not necessarily a compelling reason to stop depending on them. Even though Jesus knew the shortcomings of these disciples, he trusted them in his hour of need. It was the only way they would eventually learn to be trustworthy. The most important lessons are rarely learned on the first try!

TALKING TO GOD

Praise the Lord that he gives his followers multiple opportunities to learn and obey, and that he understands your human frailty. With humility, ask him to improve your ability to follow him well, day by day.

JESUS THE HUMAN

TALKING TO GOD

Strip away any pretense and bring your truest feelings before the Lord, even when they are raw or hurt emotions, like those that Jesus expressed. Ask the Lord to make you willing to do whatever he asks of you and to give you courage and strength to obey.

Setting the Scene

Prayer was one of the most familiar practices the disciples observed in Jesus. He demonstrated each day the principle the apostle Paul later described as "pray without ceasing" (1 Thessalonians 5:17, NKJV). In today's language we might say that prayer was Jesus' default setting, and the program was running in the background of his thoughts at all times. So it is not at all surprising that Jesus would have met the most difficult time in his extended task on earth by relying on prayer.

In his prayer, Jesus made a request ("if it is possible, let this cup pass from Me") and declared his ongoing intentions ("not as I will, but as You will"). These are some of Jesus' finest human moments. He was anticipating suffering and death in ways that would be familiar to all of us. But the combination of Jesus' two statements tells us this wasn't a case of second thoughts, but genuine emotional "due diligence." Jesus wondered, but he didn't waver.

The term "cup" had an established use as a reference to suffering (Isaiah 51:17). What the cup contained would be bitter and difficult. The cup itself represented the voluntary nature of the experience. Jesus was already committed to drink the cup if and when it was presented to him.

Getting Personal

How would you characterize the times you spend alone with God? At what points in a crisis are you most likely to turn to God? Why?

When have you struggled to accept what clearly seemed to be God's will for you?

When he taught us to pray, Jesus gave us permission to ask God, "Lead us not into temptation" (Matthew 6:13, KJV) in the same sense that he prayed here. This is not "temptation" to sin, but "trials" that cause us to grow (the same Greek word is behind both of those terms). We can express our lack of enthusiasm for or our fear of training as long as down deep we understand that God's will comes first.

SPIRIT AND BODY

Setting the Scene

Although they knew Jesus was agitated before he left them and as he prayed close by in the darkness, it wasn't long before the evening breezes and the long day caught up with the disciples. Luke wrote that they were "exhausted from sorrow" (Luke 22:45, NIV). Jesus had asked them to "keep watch with me," but they drifted into sleep.

When Jesus approached them and found all three sound asleep, he spoke to Peter, but his disappointment included all of them: "Couldn't you men keep watch with me for one hour?" Jesus' rhetorical question rebuked the disciples in the light of their recent assurances. Peter in particular had testified that they could be counted on to stand with Jesus. This chance to put their commitment to the test resulted in dismal failure.

Before he returned to prayer, Jesus expanded his request, giving his disciples a compelling reason not only to watch, but also to pray. Jesus knew the immediate temptation to fall asleep was nothing compared to the trials and temptations that were already approaching.

Jesus intertwined several sentiments in his statements. He reproved them without rejecting them. His words urged them to do better even as he acknowledged their limitations. The "watch and pray" command urged them to enlist God's help in the process of identifying and resisting temptation as well as enduring trials. The willing spirit that overcomes the handicap of the flesh develops as a result of prayer. Neither our willing spirit nor our weak flesh in themselves are enough to sustain us in life's challenges. That inner strength comes from the indwelling Spirit as we depend on God.

Getting Personal

What have you discovered that assists you in the process of watching and praying?

What are the primary differences between a life of watchful prayer and a life of careless prayer?

If we don't take seriously the warnings about what will happen if we are not diligent in depending on God, then we must accept responsibility for the chaos that follows when we "fall into temptation."

READING THE WORD

✢ *Matthew 26:40-41, NIV*
Then he returned to his disciples and found them sleeping. "Couldn't you men keep watch with me for one hour?" he asked Peter. 41"Watch and pray so that you will not fall into temptation. The spirit is willing, but the flesh is weak."

TALKING TO GOD

Bring both your willing spirit and your weak flesh before God today, as you rely on him to help you remain alert to temptation and responsive to the Spirit's conviction.

RESPECTFUL REPETITION

READING THE WORD

✤ *Matthew 26:42, NKJV*
Again, a second time, He went away and prayed, saying, "O My Father, if this cup cannot pass away from Me unless I drink it, Your will be done."

✤ *Mark 14:39, NIV*
Once more he went away and prayed the same thing.

TALKING TO GOD

If necessary, wrestle your way in persistent prayer to the point of deep acceptance that God's ways are best. Praise God for drawing you into closer conformity with his will for you.

Setting the Scene

When is repeating yourself in prayer a good thing, and when is it redundant or evidence of unbelief? Jesus repeated a prayer he had uttered just a little while before. But Jesus also taught, "When you pray, do not use vain repetitions as the heathen do. For they think that they will be heard for their many words" (Matthew 6:7, NKJV). How do we harmonize Jesus' words about repetitive prayers with his words about prayer in the parable of the persistent widow (Luke 18:1-8)?

Vain repetitions come across as mindless incantations rather than conversation. Persistent prayer, however, is attentive praying, expecting an answer and using the multiple expressions of concern as an exercise in conforming to God's will. When we conclude a prayer as Jesus did, "Yet not as I will, but as you will" (Matthew 26:39, NIV), we are admitting that our wills are not yet the same as God's will, but we recognize the priority of his will.

In Matthew's record of Jesus' second prayer, Jesus was conforming his will to his Father's will. The first prayer was "If it is possible, may this cup be taken from me" (Matthew 26:39, NIV); the second one said, "If it is not possible for this cup to be taken away unless I drink it, may your will be done" (Matthew 26:42, NIV). The previous request has become an assertion. It may take time to move from knowing God's will to accepting God's will.

Getting Personal

How do you gauge the difference in your own practice between unnecessary repetition in prayer and persistent prayer?

What are some needs or concerns that have been matters for persistent prayer?

A vital component of spiritual growth involves becoming more and more conformed to God's will in every part of life. Yet the actual process may take several steps. Our initial acknowledgment of God's perfect will may take some time. Jesus told us we would have trouble in this life. Accepting this as God's will in a general way is very different when it becomes his specific will for us.

STRIKE TWO

Setting the Scene

None of the three accounts of this second visit from Jesus to the sleeping threesome records that Jesus said anything. Nothing needed to be said. Guilty silence may have filled the air. Jesus apparently recognized that further comments were not going to help or change the situation.

We might imagine ourselves doing better than those three men, but we would probably also have been hard pressed to maintain vigilance beyond what our "heavy eyes" would allow. Many of us who claim to be following Jesus are often "asleep at the wheel."

It is amazing that the disciples themselves recorded or reported these humiliating events. Only John's Gospel omits this episode in the sequence. In his account, Jesus' arrival in Gethsemane is followed immediately by the arrival of Judas and the mob. Apparently John felt that it would serve little good to rehash these moments given the subsequent history of the three disciples involved. By the time of John's writing, both James and Peter were dead. Their testimony was sealed, and God had done a lot with their willing spirits and weak flesh.

Getting Personal

As Jesus monitors your life today, in what state is he finding you—slumbering, watchful, or somewhere in between?

What aspects of your Christian life require the most diligence? What can you do to be more awake and watchful and less spiritually lethargic?

Settling into repetitive failure is easy. We are tempted to give in to those temptations that have tripped us up in the past. We become inattentive to patterns of disobedience or unbelief. In light of this, we ought to be thankful for the shock, embarrassment, and even shame that comes when we realize God has again shown us an area in which we can make progress. Giving up is no way to arrive where God wants us to be.

READING THE WORD

✿ *Mark 14:40, NIV*
When he came back, he again found them sleeping, because their eyes were heavy. They did not know what to say to him.

TALKING TO GOD

The Lord is already aware of areas of spiritual lethargy in your life. Ask him to show you these areas and to wake you into more diligent attention or watchfulness by his Spirit. Thank him for his nearness and his persistent investment of loving attention in your spiritual development.

IT'S TIME

Setting the Scene

Luke's account summarizes the event by picturing the disciples basically sleeping through those moments, but he adds a couple of significant notes. An angel was with Jesus at least part of the time and "strengthened" him. The detail that Jesus sweat drops of blood in his anguish is mentioned only by Luke.

Mark's version includes a definite conclusion to the sequence of prayer and sleep; he shifts into the arrival of Judas with those who would arrest Jesus. The sleeping and resting by the disciples was shattered by real temptation. The time for praying (or sleeping) was over; the hour appointed by God's will had come.

Jesus had just spent a third span of time in prayer, repeating what he had previously said to his Father. The tone of the prayers had fully shifted by this point from being about the inevitability of the cup to the necessity of being conformed to God's will. Jesus was ready to face the "hour" in which he would drink all that was in the cup. He willingly and deliberately stepped into the way of suffering.

Getting Personal

In what ways do you think the victory of the Cross was won in the shadows of the garden of Gethsemane?

Based on Jesus' experience in the garden, how would you say a Christian can best develop confidence to face whatever happens in life?

One of the key principles of handling temptations and trials in life is found in 1 Corinthians 10:13: "No temptation has overtaken you except what is common to mankind. And God is faithful; he will not let you be tempted beyond what you can bear. But when you are tempted, he will also provide a way out so that you can endure it" (NIV). When we apply this principle to Jesus' suffering, we may wonder where the "way out" was. But God was faithful and provided a way through, which was his will. God got his Son through the trial; and he will do the same for us.

READING THE WORD

✤ *Mark 14:41-42, NIV*
Returning the third time, he said to them, "Are you still sleeping and resting? Enough! The hour has come. Look, the Son of Man is delivered into the hands of sinners. 42Rise! Let us go! Here comes my betrayer!"

✤ *Luke 22:39-46, NIV*
Jesus went out as usual to the Mount of Olives, and his disciples followed him. 40On reaching the place, he said to them, "Pray that you will not fall into temptation." 41He withdrew about a stone's throw beyond them, knelt down and prayed, 42"Father, if you are willing, take this cup from me; yet not my will, but yours be done." 43An angel from heaven appeared to him and strengthened him. 44And being in anguish, he prayed more earnestly, and his sweat was like drops of blood falling to the ground. 45When he rose from prayer and went back to the disciples, he found them asleep, exhausted from sorrow. 46"Why are you sleeping?" he asked them. "Get up and pray so that you will not fall into temptation."

TALKING TO GOD

It's natural to feel reluctance at drinking a "cup" of suffering or trial that God may have for you. Bring all your anxiety and fear to the Lord, and ask him to provide a way out or great grace and strength for the way through. Thank him for being faithful in keeping his promises to sustain you.

JESUS IS ARRESTED
Week 45, Day 1

❀ *Matthew 26:47-56; Mark 14:43-52; Luke 22:47-53; John 18:1-11*

After celebrating the Passover with his beloved disciples, Jesus spent time teaching them and praying with and for them. He knew where he was going and what would happen, but he walked to Gethsemane anyway. This week, we'll see Jesus betrayed by Judas and taken by soldiers and a mob of religious leaders, their torches piercing the night. As we consider how Jesus and the disciples responded, we'll determine to follow our Savior more closely.

THE CLAIM

Setting the Scene

Judas had left the group in the upper room, not knowing for sure where Jesus and the disciples were going. But he surmised they would go to Gethsemane. So he guided a detachment of Roman soldiers and Temple guards to the garden. The Temple guards came because Jews had been given authority to make arrests for minor infractions. The soldiers probably did not participate in the arrest but came to make sure the situation didn't get out of control. Matthew states that these men had been "sent by the leading priests and elders of the people" (Matthew 26:47, NLT). Mark adds the "teachers of religious law" (Mark 14:43, NLT). These were the three groups that made up the Sanhedrin, the Jewish supreme court. Jesus had mentioned these three groups in his predictions of his death (Matthew 16:21; 20:18). The entire religious leadership together issued the warrant for Jesus' arrest.

"Jesus fully realized all that was going to happen to him," that his betrayal, arrest, and crucifixion would transpire according to divine plan. So he "stepped forward" to meet those who had come to arrest him and asked who they were looking for. When they answered, "Jesus the Nazarene," Jesus responded, "I Am he." Immediately the group of soldiers, guards, and religious leaders backed off and fell to the ground. This seems like a strange reaction by a large armed contingent confronting a single individual with a small band of followers. But Jesus was doing much more than identifying himself as the one they were seeking; he was identifying himself as God Almighty, the

READING THE WORD

❀ *John 18:1-9, NLT*

After saying these things, Jesus crossed the Kidron Valley with his disciples and entered a grove of olive trees. ²Judas, the betrayer, knew this place, because Jesus had often gone there with his disciples. ³The leading priests and Pharisees had given Judas a contingent of Roman soldiers and Temple guards to accompany him. Now with blazing torches, lanterns, and weapons, they arrived at the olive grove. ⁴Jesus fully realized all that was going to happen to him, so he stepped forward to meet them. "Who are you looking for?" he asked. ⁵"Jesus the Nazarene," they said. (Judas, who betrayed him, was standing with them.) ⁶As Jesus said "I Am he," they all drew back and fell to the ground! ⁷Once more he asked them, "Who are you looking for?" And again they replied, "Jesus the Nazarene." ⁸"I told you that I Am he," Jesus said. "And since I am the one you want, let these others go." ⁹He did this to fulfill his own statement: "I did not lose a single one of those you have given me."

TALKING TO GOD

This side of heaven, you may never fully grasp the meaning of what Jesus did for us. But stand in awe, or kneel in worship before him. Thank him for his great love and great courage. Ask him to help you make sacrifices for him in your daily choices, ones that honor his ultimate sacrifice.

God of Abraham, Isaac, and Jacob—the Creator and Sustainer of the universe. Jesus' response is literally, "I Am," the name for God. When Moses had wondered what he could possibly say to gain credibility with his people, God had replied, "I Am Who I Am. Say this to the people of Israel: I Am has sent me to you" (Exodus 3:14, NLT). This name signifies God's nature with the verb "to be"—he is, always was, and forever will be.

Jesus' reaction startled this mass of armed men. The Temple guards probably understood the significance of his claim. Perhaps the group was overcome by Jesus' obvious power and authority. Among them may have been some of the guards who earlier had concluded, "We have never heard anyone speak like this!" (John 7:46, NLT). The guards' response shows that Jesus could have exercised his power to thwart his arrest but chose not to.

Throughout the Gospels we find passages that describe Jesus proclaiming his divinity. Jesus knew he was all-powerful and could easily have stopped his arrest. Just seconds later he told his disciples, "Don't you realize that I could ask my Father for thousands of angels to protect us, and he would send them instantly? But if I did, how would the Scriptures be fulfilled that describe what must happen now?" (Matthew 26:53-54, NLT).

Jesus, God in the flesh, *chose* to go to the Cross, willingly submitting himself to these human authorities and their false accusations, phony trial, and verdict.

Getting Personal

As you reflect on the past weeks' studies, what other evidence for Christ's divinity do you remember?

In what ways should knowing who Jesus is and what he did for you affect your worship?

What differences might Jesus' choices for you make in your choices for him?

In the garden, we begin to see the full impact of the Incarnation—Jesus becoming man and becoming sin for us. Jesus didn't use his power to make a dramatic escape; instead, he humbled himself further, accepting a traitor's kiss and the soldiers' arrest.

THE CONFRONTATION

Setting the Scene

Judas, who left the Last Supper early (John 13:27-30), went to the religious leaders to whom he had spoken earlier (Matthew 26:14-16). With Judas acting as the official accuser, the leaders issued a warrant for Jesus' arrest. Judas led the group to one of Jesus' retreats, where no onlookers would interfere with them.

Judas, "the traitor," had told the crowd to arrest the man whom he would "kiss." A kiss on the cheek or hand was a common form of greeting in the Middle East, so this was not unusual. Greeting Jesus with feigned affection, Judas called him "Rabbi" and kissed him. A rabbi did not have an official ecclesiastical position like a pastor today, but the title was an unofficial sign of respect. Judas showed himself the ultimate traitor. He had eaten with Jesus only hours before, and here he used a sign of friendship and affection in his betrayal.

When Jesus addressed Judas as "my friend," he was demonstrating his love for this man who was pretending love and respect while betraying him. Both Jesus and Judas knew what was going on, yet Jesus was still in charge and gave Judas permission to proceed: "Go ahead and do what you have come for."

Getting Personal

When have you felt distant from God? What caused the problem in your relationship with him?

How does understanding Jesus' love for you affect how you respond to him?

What amazing love! Jesus accepted Judas's kiss and addressed him as "friend," knowing full well this was a one-way friendship. Judas was a traitor, pretending affection while betraying his "friend" and leader. The Bible is very clear that God loves the world (John 3:16) and would like everyone to repent and have eternal life (2 Peter 3:9). His love is constant and consistent, extended even to the Judases among us.

When you feel distant from God, remember Jesus in the garden extending his love to a traitor. He waits for you to return to him, with genuine repentance and faith, to greet you with the words "my friend."

READING THE WORD

❊ *Matthew 26:47-50, NLT*
And even as Jesus said this, Judas, one of the twelve disciples, arrived with a crowd of men armed with swords and clubs. They had been sent by the leading priests and elders of the people. 48The traitor, Judas, had given them a prearranged signal: "You will know which one to arrest when I greet him with a kiss." 49So Judas came straight to Jesus. "Greetings, Rabbi!" he exclaimed and gave him the kiss. 50Jesus said, "My friend, go ahead and do what you have come for." Then the others grabbed Jesus and arrested him.

TALKING TO GOD

Consider your attitudes and actions, and confess to the Lord any that may have damaged or interrupted your relationship. Acknowledge that he has never left you, and thank him for his persistent, forgiving love.

READING THE WORD

✤ *Matthew 26:49-51, NLT*
So Judas came straight to
Jesus. "Greetings, Rabbi!" he
exclaimed and gave him the
kiss. 50Jesus said, "My friend,
go ahead and do what you have
come for." Then the others
grabbed Jesus and arrested him.
51But one of the men with Jesus
pulled out his sword and struck
the high priest's slave, slashing
off his ear.

TALKING TO GOD

*It was Jesus' love that kept him
from retaliating or fighting back.
Ask the Father to give you his
love so that you can respond
creatively, and perhaps unexpectedly, when confronted with
trouble or an attack. Ask him to
help you make love your natural
response, through the enabling
of his Spirit.*

THE CONFLICT

Setting the Scene
The religious leaders had not arrested Jesus in the
Temple, because they were afraid that the people would
riot. Instead, they had come secretly at night, under the
influence of the prince of darkness, Satan himself. Jesus
offered no resistance. Everything was proceeding according to God's plan. The time had come for Jesus to suffer
and die.

But Peter tried to stop the authorities, pulling his
sword and swinging it toward the men, in the process
cutting off the right ear of "the high priest's slave," a man
named Malchus (John 18:10, NLT). Peter was loyally defending Jesus and trying to prevent what he saw as defeat. Luke 22:51 records that Jesus immediately healed
the man's ear and prevented any further bloodshed.
Although Peter could have been arrested, he wasn't—
because Jesus handled the matter by healing the man and
restraining Peter.

Impetuous Peter had declared that he was ready to
die for Jesus (John 13:37), and that's what it seems he
was trying to do at this point. But whether drawing his
sword and defending Jesus was a momentary act of loyalty and courage or foolishness, Peter soon fled into the
night with the rest of the disciples.

Getting Personal
*When you hear or read statements that attack Jesus,
how do you feel? How do you respond?*

*Why do we like to take matters into our own hands,
even if we're not sure it's how God would want us
to act?*

*What can you do to be more Christlike in responding
to "enemies"?*

*We can easily identify with Peter's reaction. He loved
Jesus, and this torch-lit mini-mob led by Judas the
traitor had arrived in the dark to take him away. Peter
thought he had to stop it or at least go down fighting,
but that was not Jesus' approach. His way is often
countercultural and the opposite of what we would
do naturally. Jesus said the last would be first, the
humbled would be exalted, and the greatest must be
a servant. He told his disciples to become like children,
love enemies, and turn the other cheek. His ways are
not our ways, but they lead to truth and life.*

THE COMEBACK

Setting the Scene

Jesus told Peter to put away his sword and allow God's plan to unfold. Although Jesus had told him and the others several times that he *had to* die in order to gain victory, Peter didn't get it. He may have listened carefully and even nodded as if he understood, but it made no sense to him. At one point, Peter had reprimanded Jesus for talking that way and Jesus had responded strongly (Matthew 16:22-23).

Jesus' words here, recorded only by Matthew, emphasize the difference between people's tendency to take matters into their own hands (and suffer the consequences) and God's more far-reaching actions. The reason for putting away the sword was that "those who use the sword will die by the sword." Jesus was probably quoting a local proverb. He meant that the law of vengeance is below the level of God's plans. Jesus clarified this by stating that if he so desired, he could summon "thousands of angels" to deliver him. Jesus was stating that he was in control. He did not need the help of a few sleepy disciples. He could easily get out of this situation, but he had already settled this matter with the Father during his previous hours of prayer.

Getting Personal

When have you felt as if the enemy were closing in and all was lost (for example, in relationships, finances, education, career, or health issues)?

What makes trusting God so difficult during those times?

What do you know about God—Father, Son, and Holy Spirit—that helps you trust him in every situation?

As finite human beings, our perspective is severely limited. We may think we know the sure outcome of a choice or action only to experience the opposite result. We can barely anticipate what will happen today, let alone in the years and decades to follow. That's why we must trust in our sovereign Father who knows us perfectly, and he knows the past, present, and future. Trusting isn't easy when we're faced with torches and swords in the night. But we aren't alone—Jesus is with us.

READING THE WORD

�֍ *Matthew 26:52-54, NLT*
"Put away your sword," Jesus told him. "Those who use the sword will die by the sword. 53Don't you realize that I could ask my Father for thousands of angels to protect us, and he would send them instantly? 54But if I did, how would the Scriptures be fulfilled that describe what must happen now?"

TALKING TO GOD

Identify issues that are hard for you to leave in God's hands. In your personal worship, focus on God's omniscience and omnipotence, and put your trust in his wisdom and control.

THE CONFIDENCE

READING THE WORD

❋ *Matthew 26:52-54, NLT*
"Put away your sword," Jesus told him. "Those who use the sword will die by the sword. 53Don't you realize that I could ask my Father for thousands of angels to protect us, and he would send them instantly? 54But if I did, how would the Scriptures be fulfilled that describe what must happen now?"

❋ *Luke 22:51-53, NLT*
But Jesus said, "No more of this." And he touched the man's ear and healed him. 52Then Jesus spoke to the leading priests, the captains of the Temple guard, and the elders who had come for him. "Am I some dangerous revolutionary," he asked, "that you come with swords and clubs to arrest me? 53Why didn't you arrest me in the Temple? I was there every day. But this is your moment, the time when the power of darkness reigns."

TALKING TO GOD

Spend some time in prayer remembering how God has blessed and protected you in past months and years, then move on to reaffirm your confident trust in his control of your future.

Setting the Scene

Jesus "touched the man's ear and healed him." Even as Jesus was being led away to face a trial, torture, and death, he stopped to care for this one who was coming to arrest him. Jesus pointed out the ridiculous tactics of these people who had come to arrest him. Twelve peaceful men in a garden, most of them asleep, would hardly prove much of a threat. They didn't have to come against him with "swords and clubs" because he was voluntarily surrendering. Jesus was not a revolutionary; he was a religious teacher who had been teaching in the Temple every day of the past week. On one of those days, he had cleared the place of merchants and money changers, but they hadn't tried to arrest him then. Instead, they came at night.

Jesus knew the events were unfolding as they were in order to fulfill the Scriptures. Judas's betrayal of Jesus, the coming mockery of a trial, and the trial's ultimate outcome had all been prophesied (see Psalms 22:7-8, 14, 16-17; 41:9; Isaiah 50:6; 53:7-8). Although Satan seemed to be gaining the upper hand, everything was proceeding according to God's plan. The time had come for Jesus to die. His time of prayer had made him serene in God's will.

Jesus moved confidently toward the future, knowing the incredible pain that lay in his path. He knew who he was, and he knew the Father. He knew that through these events the world would be saved.

Getting Personal

What issues keep you up at night?

What are your fears for the future?

How can God help you live with confidence?

Jesus could face his future without fear. We may worry about physical safety in a storm, stress out over a relationship confrontation, feel tension in a high-level meeting, be afraid of losing a prized possession, and express concern about financial investments. Other more serious fears include issues of health, safety, loved ones, and financial security. Jesus has gone before us and is with us. We can face the future without fear, as Jesus leads the way.

THE CHARACTERS

Setting the Scene

Shortly before this confrontation, the disciples had vowed never to desert Jesus (Mark 14:31). The *all* who had promised total allegiance were now the *all* who fled into the night. Judas's kiss marked a turning point for them. With Jesus' arrest, each one's life would be radically different. For the first time, Judas openly betrayed Jesus before the other disciples, and for the first time, Jesus' loyal disciples "deserted him and ran away." Their world was collapsing. Their teacher who had taught in the Temple was under arrest, and their treasurer had become a traitor. What confusion! The disciples' loyalty to Jesus should have kept them from running, but fear took its toll. One young man (probably Mark), who had been following the disciples, was so afraid that he left his clothes behind and ran away naked.

The band of fearful and dispirited disciples would be tested even more severely before being transformed from hesitant followers into dynamic leaders.

Getting Personal

Why do some people feel they're not qualified to do anything great for God?

Matthew was a despised tax collector. Thomas had his doubts. John and Andrew had bad tempers. Peter was impetuous and outspoken. They all ran away. How does knowing that God used flawed men and women to advance his Kingdom encourage you as you serve him?

When have you seen God use you, despite your imperfections?

This certainly was a low point for the disciples. And the fact that the writers of the Gospels included this incident confirms that they were recording the truth. These men did not present themselves as heroic in any sense of the word.

Despite their cowardly flight, this account of the disciples' behavior should encourage us and give us hope. Obviously God uses ordinary, weak people to accomplish his mission in the world. Sometimes we create a mental image of biblical characters as larger than life, strong, courageous, and dynamic. In reality, they were just like us: fallible, weak, and often cowardly. Yet God chose them, working in and through them, and they changed the world.

READING THE WORD

✣ *Mark 14:48-52, NLT*
Jesus asked them, "Am I some dangerous revolutionary, that you come with swords and clubs to arrest me? 49Why didn't you arrest me in the Temple? I was there among you teaching every day. But these things are happening to fulfill what the Scriptures say about me." 50Then all his disciples deserted him and ran away. 51One young man following behind was clothed only in a long linen shirt. When the mob tried to grab him, 52he slipped out of his shirt and ran away naked.

TALKING TO GOD

Don't hesitate to lay your weaknesses and fears before your heavenly Father; he knows them all already! Bring him your willingness to obey and to follow him. Give him your heart, and pray that he will grow in you a desire to serve his Kingdom.

✤ *Matthew 26:57-58, 69-75; Mark 14:66-72; Luke 22:54-62; John 18:12-27*

When Jesus was arrested in the garden of Gethsemane, all of his disciples ran away, deserting him in his hour of need. A few followed at a safe distance. This week we'll empathize with Peter as he watches Jesus in trouble but crumbles under pressure and denies even knowing him. Peter's actions serve as a warning to us who also follow Jesus.

READING THE WORD

✤ *John 18:12-18, NLT*
So the soldiers, their commanding officer, and the Temple guards arrested Jesus and tied him up. 13First they took him to Annas, the father-in-law of Caiaphas, the high priest at that time. 14Caiaphas was the one who had told the other Jewish leaders, "It's better that one man should die for the people." 15Simon Peter followed Jesus, as did another of the disciples. That other disciple was acquainted with the high priest, so he was allowed to enter the high priest's courtyard with Jesus. 16Peter had to stay outside the gate. Then the disciple who knew the high priest spoke to the woman watching at the gate, and she let Peter in. 17The woman asked Peter, "You're not one of that man's disciples, are you?" "No," he said, "I am not." 18Because it was cold, the household servants and the guards had made a charcoal fire. They stood around it, warming themselves, and Peter stood with them, warming himself.

DENIAL

Setting the Scene

Peter had run from the garden along with all the other disciples. But then he and another disciple had returned and joined those who were watching the events. The procession from the garden led to Annas's house where Annas questioned Jesus first.

Annas was the former high priest (from AD 6 to 15) and father-in-law of Caiaphas, the ruling high priest. After Annas had been deposed by Roman rulers, Caiaphas had been appointed high priest. According to Jewish law, the office of high priest was held for life, but the Roman government had taken over the process of appointing all political and religious leaders. Caiaphas served for eighteen years (AD 18 to 36/37), longer than most high priests, suggesting that he was gifted at cooperating with the Romans. Caiaphas was the first to recommend Jesus' death in order to save the nation (John 11:49-50). Many Jews, however, still considered Annas to be the high priest. Annas may have asked to question Jesus after his arrest and then been given permission to do so. John 18:12-24 describes this hearing. Annas and Caiaphas undoubtedly lived near each other, perhaps even sharing this same large residence in Jerusalem; thus, Jesus could easily have been questioned by both of them in a short amount of time.

This house was more like a compound surrounded by walls with a guarded gate. Evidently the unnamed disciple was an acquaintance of the high priest and thus was allowed to enter the courtyard. At this disciple's suggestion, the woman at the gate opened it for Peter.

As he entered the courtyard, Peter was immediately put on the defensive as this woman at the gate asked him if he was one of Jesus' followers. The construction of the question expects a negative answer: "You're not one of that man's disciples, are you?" We don't know how loud Peter spoke or his inflection, but he seems to have responded quickly, eager to remain anonymous and blend in. And Peter lied, "No, I am not," and joined those warming themselves at a fire. Jerusalem sits 2,500 feet above sea level and would have been chilly on this spring night. So those occupied in this terrible business under the cover of darkness were chilled. The fire kept the cold at bay.

Just a few hours earlier, Peter had declared that he would never abandon Jesus. We can imagine the bold confidence in Peter's voice: "I'll stand by you, Lord, even if I'm the only one!"

But then Jesus had predicted Peter's denials: "I tell you the truth, Peter—before the rooster crows tomorrow morning, you will deny three times that you even know me" (John 13:38, NLT).

And Peter had responded, "No! Even if I have to die with you, I will never deny you!" (Matthew 26:35, NLT).

Getting Personal

Why do you think Peter made such a bold declaration in the upper room?

When have you made a similar statement of loyalty to Christ? What happened?

When have you seen supposedly strong, confident believers turn their backs on Christ?

What can you do to be more honest and realistic in your professions of faith and more Christ-honoring in your actions?

Bold assertions of faith and loyalty are easy to make apart from life's pressures and temptations and when surrounded by like-minded believers. The true test comes in the real world, when following Christ isn't popular, when his people are threatened and bullied. Peter had said he would never leave Jesus, that he would even die for him. But he ran from the soldiers, kept his distance, and then distanced himself further from his Lord.

TALKING TO GOD

Acknowledge that it's at the times when you feel strong and able to resist temptation that you're most likely to fail or fall. Ask the Lord to help you depend on his strength in every circumstance.

READING THE WORD

✻ *Matthew 26:69-74, NLT*
Meanwhile, Peter was sitting outside in the courtyard. A servant girl came over and said to him, "You were one of those with Jesus the Galilean." 70But Peter denied it in front of everyone. "I don't know what you're talking about," he said. 71Later, out by the gate, another servant girl noticed him and said to those standing around, "This man was with Jesus of Nazareth." 72Again Peter denied it, this time with an oath. "I don't even know the man," he said. 73A little later some of the other bystanders came over to Peter and said, "You must be one of them; we can tell by your Galilean accent." 74Peter swore, "A curse on me if I'm lying—I don't know the man!" And immediately the rooster crowed.

TALKING TO GOD

Ask God to help you become sensitive to ways your actions, as well as your words, may be "denying" that you are a follower of Christ. Pray that the Lord will continue to transform you into his likeness.

Setting the Scene

Standing among the soldiers, Peter was in a difficult situation—in enemy territory—and he didn't want to be identified with the man on trial for his life. So Peter made a natural and impulsive response—he lied. Peter had been ready to fight with a sword but not to face the accusations of a servant girl.

Peter's second test came when another servant girl saw him. She told those nearby that Peter "was with Jesus of Nazareth." With more people drawn into the conversation, Peter lied again, but this time "with an oath."

After an hour or so, another bystander recognized Peter (Luke 22:59). This person was "a relative of the man whose ear Peter had cut off" (John 18:26, NLT). Not only did Peter look familiar, but he also had a "Galilean accent." Peter may have hoped to blend into the group by joining the conversation; instead, his speech gave him away.

Peter made the strongest denial he could think of by asserting that he did not "know the man" and invoking a curse on himself if his words were untrue. He was saying, in effect, "May God strike me dead if I am lying!"

The statements about Peter's identity and Peter's denials progressed in intensity. At first he pretended not to understand the question; then he denied being one of the disciples; finally he sealed his denial with an oath so there could be no doubt about it. Peter had slid to the point of completely denying his Lord and Savior.

Getting Personal

When have you found yourself on this slippery slope of temptation and rationalization? What happened?

When have you stood up for Christ after being identified as his follower? What happened?

What can you do to not give in to temptations, even the "small" ones?

Lies and temptations usually begin this way, with the first step so easy and seemingly small. But that becomes a slippery slope. Once we've started down that path, the next lie or sin comes easier. We rationalize: "It's just one look"; "It's just a few dollars"; "It's such a small lie"; "No one will ever know."

TRUE IDENTITY

Setting the Scene

That the trial should occur at the residence of the high priest was unprecedented. Normally the Sanhedrin would meet in a large hall in the Temple area, which would have been available because during the Passover, the Temple opened at midnight rather than at dawn. They may have chosen the more private setting to avoid causing a riot.

This "courtyard" was probably in a central area of the buildings that made up the high priest's residence. There "the guards lit a fire" around which the servants and soldiers were warming themselves against the early morning chill. After entering the compound, Peter joined the group at the fire.

"A servant girl," the woman who had opened the courtyard gate, saw Peter's face a little more clearly in the flickering light and thought she recognized him as someone close to Jesus.

Later, others at the fire wondered if Peter was a Jesus-follower because he seemed to be from Galilee (Matthew 26:73). His accent would have been closer to Syrian speech than to that of the Judean servants in the Jerusalem courtyard. The group concluded that Peter must have been with the Galilean on trial inside the palace.

Although in the pressure of the moment Peter tried to deny it, people could tell that he had been with Jesus. The evidence was superficial and circumstantial, but the servant girl and the others were correct in identifying Peter as a disciple.

Getting Personal

How do your relatives, close friends, and coworkers know you are a Christian? What "evidence" do they have?

What can you do to follow Christ more closely?

Christians can be identified in many ways. Church attendance reveals something about a person. And believers often have an "accent"; that is, they use certain words and expressions. But those are superficial signs that can be faked, rationalized, or denied. The most telling evidence that someone follows close to Jesus is how that person lives. The closer we are to Jesus— the more time we spend with him—the more we will be like him.

READING THE WORD

❉ *Luke 22:54-59, NLT*

So they arrested him and led him to the high priest's home. And Peter followed at a distance. 55The guards lit a fire in the middle of the courtyard and sat around it, and Peter joined them there. 56A servant girl noticed him in the firelight and began staring at him. Finally she said, "This man was one of Jesus' followers!" 57But Peter denied it. "Woman," he said, "I don't even know him!" 58After a while someone else looked at him and said, "You must be one of them!" "No, man, I'm not!" Peter retorted. 59About an hour later someone else insisted, "This must be one of them, because he is a Galilean, too."

TALKING TO GOD

Tell the Lord of your desire to be closely identified with him, to be known as one who belongs to him and is committed to his cause. Ask him to draw you close and to give you the courage to live for him.

READING THE WORD

✤ *Luke 22:60-62, NLT*
But Peter said, "Man, I don't know what you are talking about." And immediately, while he was still speaking, the rooster crowed. 61At that moment the Lord turned and looked at Peter. Suddenly, the Lord's words flashed through Peter's mind: "Before the rooster crows tomorrow morning, you will deny three times that you even know me." 62And Peter left the courtyard, weeping bitterly.

TALKING TO GOD

Express your gratitude to God that he doesn't look away from your sin or your denials. Thank him for the blessing of being fully known—and fully loved and forgiven.

Setting the Scene

As Peter spoke these words of his third denial, "the rooster crowed," signaling the early morning hour. The time between midnight and 3:00 a.m. was known as "cockcrowing." A rooster would crow first at about 12:30 a.m. and then, again, at about 1:30 a.m.

Immediately after this third denial, Jesus turned and looked at Peter; their eyes met. Either Jesus was on the upper story of the building or he was being led through the courtyard between visits with Annas and Caiaphas. In either case, Jesus knew where Peter was and what he had done.

This was not a chance meeting or a coincidence. Jesus seems to have been intentionally looking at Peter. Imagine the look in his eyes.

Peter had spent three years with Jesus—traveling, eating, conversing face-to-face, watching, and learning. He was arguably closer than anyone else to the Lord. So when he saw Jesus turn and look at him, he must have seen sadness in the eyes of his friend and leader, the pain of desertion and betrayal. But he also saw love. Peter's mind may have flashed back to when he walked on the water until he looked *away* from Jesus (Matthew 14:22-33) or when Jesus reprimanded him (Matthew 16:23) or when Jesus' face "shone like the sun" (Matthew 17:2, NLT) or when Jesus washed his feet in the upper room (John 13:6-9). Peter knew that face and that look of love.

Getting Personal

When by your actions or words have you denied knowing Jesus? What motivated you to act that way?

What else causes distance between you and Jesus?

Imagine Jesus looking at you across that courtyard. What do you see in his eyes? How do you respond?

Jesus never leaves us, as he told his disciples (see John 14:16 and Matthew 28:20); but often we pull away from him. Through our actions, attitudes, and even outright denials we distance ourselves from Jesus, but he hasn't left. He's still there, looking with his eyes of compassion, waiting for us to return.

REALITY CHECK

Setting the Scene

When Peter heard the rooster crow the second time and saw Jesus look at him, the realization of what he had done hit him full force. Peter had promised never to deny Jesus (Mark 14:31), but Jesus had predicted that Peter would, in fact, deny him three times that very night.

Peter "broke down and wept," not only because he hadn't kept his pledge, but also because he had turned his back on his Lord and his dear friend. Unable to stand by Jesus for even twelve hours, he felt like an utter failure.

Luke notes that Peter wept "bitterly" and left the courtyard (Luke 22:62). We can imagine him stumbling out and away, overcome by remorse for his failure mixed with grief for what was happening to Jesus. Proud and confident Peter had hit bottom; he had come to the end of himself. Peter's tears were of deep sorrow and repentance but not despair (which would consume Judas). Later, Peter would reaffirm his love for Jesus, and Jesus would forgive him (see Mark 16:7; John 21:15-19). Peter would be restored to fellowship and ministry and eventually become a fearless evangelist and powerful leader of the church.

Getting Personal

When confronted with a mistake or wrongdoing, how do you typically respond?

When recently have you experienced "godly sorrow"?

In what ways has God's acceptance and forgiveness affected how you live?

Many people feel bad when confronted with their sinful attitudes and actions. They may even express regret and apologize to an offended party. Often, however, they are simply sorry that they got caught. Others may be so distraught that their sorrow leads them to depression, despair, and even suicide—like Judas.

Peter experienced the redemptive sorrow that Paul later described: "The kind of sorrow God wants us to experience leads us away from sin and results in salvation. . . . But worldly sorrow, which lacks repentance, results in spiritual death" (2 Corinthians 7:10, NLT). Christ always stands ready to forgive, but he wants us to admit, confess, and repent (1 John 1:8-9).

READING THE WORD

✤ *Mark 14:66-72, NLT*

Meanwhile, Peter was in the courtyard below. One of the servant girls who worked for the high priest came by [67]and noticed Peter warming himself at the fire. She looked at him closely and said, "You were one of those with Jesus of Nazareth." [68]But Peter denied it. "I don't know what you're talking about," he said, and he went out into the entryway. Just then, a rooster crowed. [69]When the servant girl saw him standing there, she began telling the others, "This man is definitely one of them!" [70]But Peter denied it again. A little later some of the other bystanders confronted Peter and said, "You must be one of them, because you are a Galilean." [71]Peter swore, "A curse on me if I'm lying—I don't know this man you're talking about!" [72]And immediately the rooster crowed the second time. Suddenly, Jesus' words flashed through Peter's mind: "Before the rooster crows twice, you will deny three times that you even know me." And he broke down and wept.

TALKING TO GOD

Truthfully analyze your own remorse and repentance before the Lord. Ask him to help you turn away from sin and turn toward a life of deeper submission to his commands and calling.

Setting the Scene

Fortunately, the story of Peter doesn't end with his denials and tears. Soon he would rush to the empty tomb, see his risen Lord behind closed doors, and then converse with him on the beach, where Jesus would restore Peter to fellowship and ministry (John 21:15-19). And the book of Acts describes Peter, rather than running from trouble, courageously preaching, teaching, healing, and confronting the authorities.

Peter had to come to the end of himself before he could be an effective disciple. In fact, this event—Peter's failure—became part of the process of Peter's sanctification. From this humiliating experience of denying Christ, Peter grew in his faith and relationship with God and learned much that would help him when he became leader of the young church. The fact that this episode is reported in all four Gospels shows its importance to the early church, both as a warning of the dangers of yielding to persecution and as an example of Jesus' power to forgive.

Getting Personal

When do you tend to rely on yourself instead of God? How might that change for you?

When have you experienced God transforming something bad into good?

At this point in his life, Peter had hit bottom. But we know the rest of the story, what he became from that point on. In what ways does Peter's story give you hope?

Peter had tried to follow Christ on his own, in his own strength, and he discovered the truth about himself— that he was weak and a sinner. He needed to trust Christ completely and rely on him alone.

Peter's experience also demonstrates that our failures are not final. God forgives and forgets, and God can transform us. Romans 8:28 reminds us that "God causes everything to work together for the good of those who love God and are called according to his purpose for them" (NLT). When we confess our sins, he forgives and restores . . . and he uses even those negative experiences for our good and his glory.

READING THE WORD

❋ *John 18:25-27, NLT*
Meanwhile, as Simon Peter was standing by the fire warming himself, they asked him again, "You're not one of his disciples, are you?" He denied it, saying, "No, I am not." 26But one of the household slaves of the high priest, a relative of the man whose ear Peter had cut off, asked, "Didn't I see you out there in the olive grove with Jesus?" 27Again Peter denied it. And immediately a rooster crowed.

TALKING TO GOD

God's purposes cannot be thwarted. Thank him that even your failures and mistakes are being redeemed for his purposes and his glory. Thank him for working everything together for your good.

JESUS IS TRIED BY PILATE
Week 47, Day 1

❋ *Matthew 27:11-26; Mark 15:1-15; Luke 23:1-25; John 18:28-40*

After the arrest in the garden of Gethsemane, Jesus was taken to the home of Caiaphas, the high priest, where he faced a phony trial before the teachers of religious law and elders. After finally "convicting" him of blasphemy, they brought him to the Roman governor. This week, as Jesus stands in judgment, we'll note how Pilate struggled with his choices, wondering how to respond to the religious leaders and the crowd, wondering what to do with this King of the Jews. We'll also consider Jesus and marvel at *his* choice and his sacrifice for us.

JUDGING JESUS

Setting the Scene

The Romans had taken away the Jews' right to inflict capital punishment; Jesus had to be sentenced by a Roman official. So the Jewish leaders brought him to Pontius Pilate, the Roman governor for the regions of Samaria and Judea (from AD 26 to 36). Because of the large crowds in the city for the Passover festival, Pilate and his soldiers had come to Jerusalem to keep the peace. He was staying at his headquarters, called the Praetorium. Pilate was a harsh governor who intensely disliked the Jews. Although the Jewish religious leaders felt antagonistic toward Pilate, they had no other way to get rid of Jesus than to go to him. So early Friday morning they brought before him a man whom they accused of treason against the hated Romans!

Because the charge was treason, Pilate asked Jesus directly if he claimed to be "the king of the Jews." Jesus did claim to be a king, but he wasn't claiming kingship that would threaten Pilate, Caesar, or the Roman Empire. The religious leaders were trying to build a case on this political twist, but what Jesus said and how he said it alerted Pilate to the discrepancy between indictment and reality. He must have sensed the Jewish leaders' jealousy of Jesus. Pilate certainly had seen or heard about Jesus' glorious entry into Jerusalem a few days earlier, so he understood the motives of these religious leaders. Pilate could sense that the Sanhedrin's case was weak and could see that the man standing before him was unlikely to lead a revolt against Rome. Pilate's reluctance to

READING THE WORD

❋ *Matthew 27:11-14, NLT*
Now Jesus was standing before Pilate, the Roman governor. "Are you the king of the Jews?" the governor asked him. Jesus replied, "You have said it." 12But when the leading priests and the elders made their accusations against him, Jesus remained silent. 13"Don't you hear all these charges they are bringing against you?" Pilate demanded. 14But Jesus made no response to any of the charges, much to the governor's surprise.

❋ *John 18:29-31, NLT*
So Pilate, the governor, went out to them and asked, "What is your charge against this man?" 30"We wouldn't have handed him over to you if he weren't a criminal!" they retorted. 31"Then take him away and judge him by your own law," Pilate told them. "Only the Romans are permitted to execute someone," the Jewish leaders replied.

READING THE WORD

❈ *Luke 23:13-16, NLT*
Then Pilate called together the leading priests and other religious leaders, along with the people, ¹⁴and he announced his verdict. "You brought this man to me, accusing him of leading a revolt. I have examined him thoroughly on this point in your presence and find him innocent.... ¹⁵Nothing this man has done calls for the death penalty. ¹⁶So I will have him flogged, and then I will release him."

TALKING TO GOD

Ask God to make you sensitive about speaking for God or holding too strong an opinion that you claim is his. Being wise and discerning is important, but we are not judges. Ask him to help you leave all judging to him, the ultimate Judge.

prosecute Jesus, however, was undoubtedly due more to his contempt for the Jews than for any particular consideration of Jesus.

Pilate's low regard for the Jewish leadership sank even lower as their frenzied testimony continued. Pilate knew the charges were preposterous, and he expected Jesus to defend himself against the false accusations. Roman law required listing the charges against a person, and hearing the person's defense and eyewitness testimony. Then the judge would retire with his advisers, consider the evidence, and render the verdict, which would be carried out immediately.

Yet Jesus "made no response." Pilate was surprised that Jesus, facing the death penalty, would not defend himself because if Jesus did not answer, Pilate would have to judge him guilty. Pilate wanted to release Jesus, but he was under pressure from Rome to keep peace in his territory. The last thing Pilate needed was a rebellion over this quiet, seemingly insignificant man.

Pilate said he would punish Jesus and release him. He probably hoped that flogging Jesus would appease the crowd—that they would pity Jesus and let him go.

Getting Personal

When Jesus stood before Pilate, what do you think Pilate saws in Jesus' eyes? Imagine standing there—what do you see in Jesus' eyes?

What are some of the judgments people today render about Jesus? Why do they think they have the right to do so?

When recently have you taken Jesus for granted or made an assumption about him? How should seeing Jesus as he really is—Savior and Judge—affect how you live?

Pilate thought he held full power over Jesus as judge, jury, and executioner, and that Jesus was a hopeless, helpless victim of petty Jewish religious conflicts.

But we know Jesus is God and could have triumphed in an instant. And we know that much more was playing out in Pilate's court, a drama with eternal significance. Yet people, even believers, still judge Jesus, expressing condescending opinions about his identity and what he can and cannot do. In reality, Jesus is the judge—and he will judge.

EXPECTING A SHOW

Setting the Scene

Jesus grew up in Nazareth and later had made Capernaum his base, so he was, indeed, "under Herod's jurisdiction." This was the Herod Antipas who had killed John the Baptist (see Matthew 14:1-12). He, too, was in Jerusalem that weekend for the Passover.

Herod was ecstatic. He apparently saw Jesus as no more than a traveling sideshow. However, Jesus would not answer Herod's questions, much less perform any miracles. Herod is the only person to whom Jesus said nothing at all. Herod had not listened to John the Baptist, and Jesus had nothing to add to what John had said. Jesus remained silent, so Herod simply "sent him back to Pilate."

Herod had two advantages over Pilate: He had come from a part-Jewish monarchy and had held his position much longer. But Pilate had two advantages over Herod: He was a Roman citizen and an envoy of the emperor, and his position had been created to replace Herod's ineffective half brother. So the two men were uneasy around each other. Jesus' trial, however, brought them together. Because Pilate had recognized Herod's authority over Galilee, Herod had stopped feeling threatened by the Roman politician. And because neither man knew what to do in this predicament, their common problem united them.

Getting Personal

What examples can you remember of people wanting Jesus to perform for them?

When have you used prayer as sort of a magic formula, expecting God to meet your need because you asked him in the right way?

Instead of trying to use Jesus, how should you approach him?

Another popular way to "judge" Jesus is to see him as just a miracle worker. Many hope that Jesus will put on a show for them, saying they will believe in Jesus if he'll do a miracle. Others act like Herod by expecting Jesus to respond to their command, to answer a prayer for physical healing, instant riches, romance, or some other desire or dream. But Jesus will not perform at our whim. In reality, he "is able, through his mighty power at work within us, to accomplish infinitely more than we might ask or think" (Ephesians 3:20, NLT).

READING THE WORD

❋ *Luke 23:4-12, NLT*
Pilate turned to the leading priests and to the crowd and said, "I find nothing wrong with this man!" 5Then they became insistent. "But he is causing riots by his teaching wherever he goes—all over Judea, from Galilee to Jerusalem!" 6"Oh, is he a Galilean?" Pilate asked. 7When they said that he was, Pilate sent him to Herod Antipas, because Galilee was under Herod's jurisdiction, and Herod happened to be in Jerusalem at the time. 8Herod was delighted at the opportunity to see Jesus, because he had heard about him and had been hoping for a long time to see him perform a miracle. 9He asked Jesus question after question, but Jesus refused to answer. 10Meanwhile, the leading priests and the teachers of religious law stood there shouting their accusations. 11Then Herod and his soldiers began mocking and ridiculing Jesus. Finally, they put a royal robe on him and sent him back to Pilate. 12(Herod and Pilate, who had been enemies before, became friends that day.)

TALKING TO GOD

Confess that sometimes your prayers slip into a long list of requests or demands, or that you have seen God as a way to help you get what you want. Ask God to fill you with his love and his purposes, so that what you want lines up with his plans. Tell him you depend on his mighty power to accomplish more than you might ask or think.

SEEING THE KING

READING THE WORD

❋ *Luke 23:3, NLT*

So Pilate asked him, "Are you the king of the Jews?" Jesus replied, "You have said it."

❋ *John 18:33-37, NLT*

Then Pilate went back into his headquarters and called for Jesus to be brought to him. "Are you the king of the Jews?" he asked him. 34Jesus replied, "Is this your own question, or did others tell you about me?" 35"Am I a Jew?" Pilate retorted. "Your own people and their leading priests brought you to me for trial. Why? What have you done?" 36Jesus answered, "My Kingdom is not an earthly kingdom. If it were, my followers would fight to keep me from being handed over to the Jewish leaders. But my Kingdom is not of this world." 37Pilate said, "So you are a king?" Jesus responded, "You say I am a king."

❋ *Mark 15:9-12, NLT*

"Would you like me to release to you this 'King of the Jews'?" Pilate asked. 10(For he realized by now that the leading priests had arrested Jesus out of envy.) 11But at this point the leading priests stirred up the crowd to demand the release of Barabbas instead of Jesus. 12Pilate asked them, "Then what should I do with this man you call the king of the Jews?"

TALKING TO GOD

If you have never called God your Lord and King, humble yourself before your Sovereign today, acknowledging his reign over all creation and his authority over you.

Setting the Scene

The Jewish religious leaders hoped to have Pilate condemn Jesus by telling Pilate that Jesus had claimed to be "a king" (Luke 23:2, NLT). So Pilate asked Jesus directly, "Are you the king of the Jews?" This question is identical in all four Gospels, and the word *you* is emphatic. Jesus answered clearly, "You have said it" (Matthew 27:11, NLT).

Pilate used the title "king of the Jews" several times in his interaction with Jesus. These words mocked the Jews—the meek and silent man standing on the platform beside him was about as powerful as any Jew could be against the might and power of Rome.

During his ministry, Jesus had often spoken of his Kingdom, describing its nature and importance. Many, including the disciples, had interpreted this to mean an earthly kingdom—to throw off the Romans and restore the glory of Israel. But as Jesus had taught previously, he stated clearly to Pilate, "My Kingdom is not an earthly kingdom . . . not of this world."

Getting Personal

Today people seem to have no problem honoring Jesus as a baby, but they cannot accept him as King. Why do you think that is?

What makes submitting to Christ so hard?

What areas of your life do you find difficult turning over to his control?

When Jesus spoke of his Kingdom, he was referring to all that is under his authority, especially people. When believers are born again, they become subjects of this spiritual Kingdom. It doesn't make sense to most people, then or now. How could Jesus be a King on a cross? But he is, and he has changed our lives and rules in our hearts.

To acknowledge someone as a "ruler," "sovereign," or "king" implies authority and submission. That person has the power and authority, and our response should be to submit and obey. Yet many who claim Jesus as their "Lord," "Master," and "King" resist his authority over their lives.

GOING WITH THE CROWD

Setting the Scene

Pilate was losing ground; the huge crowd seemed ready to riot. No doubt he did not want to risk losing his position, which may have been shaky, by allowing a riot to occur in his province. As a career politician, he knew the importance of compromise, and Pilate saw Jesus more as a political threat than as a human being. So he tried again, this time offering to release Jesus in an act of Passover mercy. But the leaders wouldn't relent, and they whipped up the crowd, calling for the release of Barabbas. Then, when Pilate simply asked, "What should I do with Jesus who is called the Messiah?" they screamed, "Crucify him!"

The people made their choice, stated their preference, and confirmed their sin. This was just what the Jewish religious leaders wanted. If Jesus were crucified, he would die the death of a rebel and slave, not of the king he claimed to be. Crucifixion would also put the responsibility for killing Jesus on the Romans, so the crowds would not blame the religious leaders. Pilate gave in, and "to pacify the crowd, [he] released Barabbas to them. He ordered Jesus flogged with a lead-tipped whip, then turned him over to the Roman soldiers to be crucified."

The object of flogging was to cause as much pain and suffering as possible. The soldiers would bare the upper half of the victim's body and tie his hands to a pillar. Then they would lash him with a three-pronged whip made of leather thongs that connected pieces of bone and metal like a chain. Flogging before crucifixion was a way to weaken the prisoner so he would die more quickly on the cross.

Getting Personal

What recent examples have you seen or heard reported of mob action?

When have you experienced group pressure? What was the group pressuring you to do? How did you respond?

What might be the cost to you for taking a stand for truth against a lie or for morality versus sin—for Christ?

Pilate had little conviction and even less courage. He gave in to the pressure of the angry crowd, releasing a murderer while ordering the execution of an innocent man.

READING THE WORD

❊ *Matthew 27:22-23, NLT*
Pilate responded, "Then what should I do with Jesus who is called the Messiah?" They shouted back, "Crucify him!" 23"Why?" Pilate demanded. "What crime has he committed?" But the mob roared even louder, "Crucify him!"

❊ *Mark 15:12-15, NLT*
Pilate asked them, "Then what should I do with this man you call the king of the Jews?" 13They shouted back, "Crucify him!" 14"Why?" Pilate demanded. "What crime has he committed?" But the mob roared even louder, "Crucify him!" 15So to pacify the crowd, Pilate released Barabbas to them. He ordered Jesus flogged with a lead-tipped whip, then turned him over to the Roman soldiers to be crucified.

❊ *Luke 23:18-22, NLT*
Then a mighty roar rose from the crowd, and with one voice they shouted, "Kill him, and release Barabbas to us!" 19(Barabbas was in prison for taking part in an insurrection in Jerusalem against the government, and for murder.) 20Pilate argued with them, because he wanted to release Jesus. 21But they kept shouting, "Crucify him! Crucify him!" 22For the third time he demanded, "Why? What crime has he committed? I have found no reason to sentence him to death. So I will have him flogged, and then I will release him."

TALKING TO GOD

Ask the Lord to strengthen your mind and spirit as you open yourself to his influence and close yourself against the insistent messages of cultural norms or society's pressure. Ask him to bring you alongside believers who live wholeheartedly for him and will help you stand for truth.

AVOIDING RESPONSIBILITY

READING THE WORD

❋ *John 18:37-38, NLT*
Jesus responded, "You say I am a king. Actually, I was born and came into the world to testify to the truth. All who love the truth recognize that what I say is true." 38"What is truth?" Pilate asked.

❋ *Matthew 27:24-26, NLT*
Pilate saw that he wasn't getting anywhere and that a riot was developing. So he sent for a bowl of water and washed his hands before the crowd, saying, "I am innocent of this man's blood. The responsibility is yours!" 25And all the people yelled back, "We will take responsibility for his death— we and our children!" 26So Pilate released Barabbas to them. He ordered Jesus flogged with a lead-tipped whip, then turned him over to the Roman soldiers to be crucified.

TALKING TO GOD

Make no excuses as you come to the Lord in full confession today. In his great love and mercy, you are already forgiven, thanks to Christ's act of redemption.

Setting the Scene

When Jesus said he had come to "testify to the truth," Pilate cynically responded, "What is truth?" He was beginning to rationalize away his responsibility for whatever happened to Jesus. If truth is unknowable, then he couldn't be held responsible for what he would decide about this man standing before him. When we have no basis for truth, then we have no basis for moral right and wrong. Justice becomes whatever works or whatever helps those in power. Certainly that must have been the underlying motivation for most of Pilate's decisions as a Roman politician.

Pilate performed the act of washing his hands as a gesture of innocence. It was a Jewish custom, not a Roman one, to illustrate that a person had nothing to do with a murder (see Deuteronomy 21:6-9). Pilate may have done this to show his utter contempt for the Jews and their demand for Jesus' crucifixion. In excusing himself and placing the responsibility for an innocent man's death on them, he followed the path already taken by the religious leaders as they had dealt with Judas when they said, "That's your problem" (Matthew 27:4, NLT). Pilate washed his hands, but the guilt remained.

Getting Personal

What excuses have you heard given by individuals caught in illegal or illicit behavior?

Why do we try rationalizing instead of taking responsibility or admitting guilt?

For what mistakes and sins do you often make excuses?

Pilate was looking out for himself and not worrying about justice. He rationalized and took no responsibility for his actions.

We're all like Pilate. We may know we should or shouldn't do something—our conscience and the Holy Spirit tell us—but we make the wrong, more convenient and self-serving choice, rationalizing along the way. Instead, we should make the right decision, even if it costs us, and we should stop making excuses for our sin. We need to realize that every sin is serious; our sins put Jesus on the Cross. He doesn't condemn us for them; he forgives. But he wants us to be honest with him and confess.

TAKING HIS PLACE

Setting the Scene

Either as an effort to improve relations with the people or to help cover his many wrongful acts, Pilate had established the custom of releasing any prisoner the people requested. Whatever his motivation, this was a small act of mercy from the Roman overseer.

Barabbas had taken part in a rebellion against the Roman government. He had been convicted of murder and was awaiting execution. Ironically, Barabbas was guilty of the crime of which Jesus was accused. Some early manuscripts say his name was "*Jesus* Barabbas," which is quite possible because Jesus was a common name. The name "Barabbas" means "son of the father," which, of course, is Jesus' position with his Father.

Pilate really wanted to release Jesus. Even Pilate's wife had urged him to let Jesus go. Pilate must have felt the pressure of the situation because he put himself in the position of bargaining with the crowd. He had the authority to let Jesus go and then get on with his day; instead, he appealed to them again but to no avail. They wanted Jesus crucified. So Pilate gave in to the crowd and released Barabbas.

Getting Personal

What do you imagine Barabbas felt and thought about Jesus, the one who died in his place?

What does it mean to you that Christ died in your place?

Faced with a clear choice, the people chose Barabbas, a revolutionary and murderer, over the Son of God. Faced with the same choice today, people are still choosing "Barabbas." They would rather have the tangible force of human power than the salvation offered by the Son of God.

Although his name means "son of the father," Barabbas could have been anybody's son; thus he represents all sinners. Barabbas, son of an unnamed father, committed a crime. Because Jesus died in his place, this man was set free. All people are sinners who have broken God's holy law. Like Barabbas, we deserve to die. But Jesus died in our place, for our sins, and by faith we have been set free.

READING THE WORD

❊ *Matthew 27:15-21, NLT*

Now it was the governor's custom each year during the Passover celebration to release one prisoner to the crowd—anyone they wanted. 16This year there was a notorious prisoner, a man named Barabbas. 17As the crowds gathered before Pilate's house that morning, he asked them, "Which one do you want me to release to you—Barabbas, or Jesus who is called the Messiah?" 18(He knew very well that the religious leaders had arrested Jesus out of envy.) 19Just then, as Pilate was sitting on the judgment seat, his wife sent him this message: "Leave that innocent man alone. I suffered through a terrible nightmare about him last night." 20Meanwhile, the leading priests and the elders persuaded the crowd to ask for Barabbas to be released and for Jesus to be put to death. 21So the governor asked again, "Which of these two do you want me to release to you?" The crowd shouted back, "Barabbas!"

TALKING TO GOD

Let gratitude overwhelm you as you worship the Savior, who took your place, receiving the punishment and death that you will never suffer because Christ Jesus is the resurrection and the life.

JESUS IS CRUCIFIED
Week 48, Day 1

✹ *Matthew 27:31-44; Mark 15:21-32; Luke 23:26-43; John 19:16-27*

This will be a difficult week. Many people find it hard to consider in detail what Jesus endured on our behalf at the Cross. The whole idea of public execution via crucifixion is both foreign and abhorrent to us. Each of the Gospel writers included a glimpse of the grisly scene, and each one revealed something unique in his account. The descriptions of Jesus' suffering on the cross leave us stunned and silent. Most of the talking on Golgotha was done by onlookers, not by the three men on crosses. Their statements were brief. Both their silence and their few words take us into the heart of the meaning of the Cross.

READING THE WORD

✹ *Luke 23:26-33, NIV*
As the soldiers led him away, they seized Simon from Cyrene, who was on his way in from the country, and put the cross on him and made him carry it behind Jesus. 27A large number of people followed him, including women who mourned and wailed for him. 28Jesus turned and said to them, "Daughters of Jerusalem, do not weep for me; weep for yourselves and for your children. 29For the time will come when you will say, 'Blessed are the childless women, the wombs that never bore and the breasts that never nursed!' 30Then 'they will say to the mountains, "Fall on us!" and to the hills, "Cover us!"' 31For if people do these things when the tree is green, what will happen when it is dry?" 32Two other men, both criminals, were also led out with him to be executed. 33When they came to the place called the Skull, they crucified him there, along with the criminals—one on his right, the other on his left.

STATIONS OF SUFFERING

Setting the Scene

Once the mockery of justice was over in Jesus' manipulated trial, the sentence was immediately set in motion. Jesus began to walk the Via Dolorosa (the way of suffering). Over the centuries, believers meditating on Jesus' experience have developed a sequence, partly based on the biblical account and partly based on tradition, called "the stations of the Cross." These snapshots of the journey to the Cross are often depicted in stained-glass windows, paintings, carvings, and occasionally an extended walking experience with statuary that allows pilgrims to sense the movement in Jesus' greatest act. The stations can be as many as fourteen, but ten mark events leading to the moment when Jesus was nailed to the cross: (1) Jesus is formally condemned to death (John 19:16); (2) Jesus sets out bearing his cross (Matthew 27:31; John 19:17); (3) Jesus falls; (4) Jesus meets his mother along the way; (5) Simon is recruited to help Jesus (Matthew 27:32; Mark 15:21; Luke 23:26); (6) Veronica wipes the face of Jesus; (7) Jesus falls again; (8) Jesus consoles the women of Jerusalem (Luke 23:27-31); (9) Jesus falls a third time; (10) Jesus is stripped of his garments for which the guards will gamble (Matthew 27:35; Mark 15:24; Luke 23:34; John 19:23-24).

Condemned men were required to carry their own crosses to the execution site, but beatings had weakened Jesus so that apparently he needed assistance. The Roman soldiers recruited Simon of Cyrene to assist Jesus. Mark's note that Simon was "the father of Alexander and

Rufus" (Mark 15:21) seems to indicate that the man and his family were known among the believers in Jerusalem. We don't know if Simon was a displaced Jew in town for the Passover or whether he was a Jewish proselyte from Africa, since Cyrene is in Libya. Simon's action points toward the significance of Jesus' teaching about faithful discipleship being similar to bearing a cross. What Simon was required to do every believer should be willing to do, take up the cross assigned to us by God and serve Christ (see Luke 14:27).

Luke records that there was a group of believers who followed Jesus to Calvary, weeping. Jesus spoke to the women briefly, urging them to join him in grieving for Jerusalem. Their grief for him would be short-lived, but the city would soon face destruction by Rome.

Once Jesus was nailed to the cross, he was three hours from the finish line. During those hours of excruciating suffering, Jesus made several brief statements, though breathing was very difficult. Jesus' crucified companions soon became silent. But he had some important things to say. Seven times he spoke. Three times, his words were prayers: He prayed for those who had just nailed him to the cross (Luke 23:34); he prayed as he realized God's abandonment (Matthew 27:46; Mark 15:34); and his final words were a prayer (Luke 23:46). Twice he had brief conversations with others: the two thieves beside him (Luke 23:39-43) and then his mother and John (John 19:26-27). And twice he spoke to the people gathered at the foot of the cross: "I am thirsty" (John 19:28, NIV), and "It is finished" (John 19:30, NIV). His last, brief words still speak into our lives today.

Getting Personal

Knowing how the story turns out, what benefit do you find in revisiting the events of Jesus' crucifixion? How do you respond to the fact of his suffering?

With whom do you identify most in the events of Jesus' last hours?

What words of Jesus from the cross speak most directly to you?

When we think about the cross of Jesus, our memories of suffering can help, but we haven't seen the Cross until we can truthfully say, "I belong there, but because of Jesus, I won't be going there!"

TALKING TO GOD

Meditate on the suffering of your Savior, cherishing what he did at the Cross on your behalf. Ask him to help you show your gratitude to him through your personal worship and obedience today.

READING THE WORD

❂ *Mark 15:24-26, NKJV*
And when they crucified Him, they divided His garments, casting lots for them to determine what every man should take. 25Now it was the third hour, and they crucified Him. 26And the inscription of His accusation was written above: THE KING OF THE JEWS.

❂ *John 19:23-24, NIV*
When the soldiers crucified Jesus, they took his clothes, dividing them into four shares, one for each of them, with the undergarment remaining. This garment was seamless, woven in one piece from top to bottom. 24"Let's not tear it," they said to one another. "Let's decide by lot who will get it." This happened that the scripture might be fulfilled that said, "They divided my clothes among them and cast lots for my garment." So this is what the soldiers did.

TALKING TO GOD

Don't be afraid to consider the Cross, in all its terror and glory, because it was God's design for reconciling you to himself. Worship your Savior today, thanking God for the extremes he went to in order to make you his own.

CRUCIFIED

Setting the Scene

Crucifixion was a lonely, painful, gruesome way to die. It killed—slowly and with agony. In fact, it often prolonged life longer than pain could be felt. Victims would simply go into shock and remain barely alive, breathing by unconscious will. At this point, the executioners broke the legs of the condemned and caused them to finish dying swiftly.

Though we find it hard and even repulsive to imagine, Jesus was only one of many people who had been executed this way by the Romans. His experience on the cross included several added sobering features, making it a unique death for a unique man.

First, the crucifixion was shameful. He was stripped of his clothing and pinned naked between heaven and earth. He was mocked by the crowds and taunted by one of the criminals crucified beside him. A sign posted over his head made fun of his claim to be king.

Second, Jesus was absolutely innocent. He was there, every moment of his agony, by choice. The nails didn't keep him on the cross. His decision to remain there was stronger than his desire to avoid the pain. He had said: "Greater love has no one than this, than to lay down one's life for his friends" (John 15:13, NKJV).

Third, Jesus bore the sins of the world—including yours and mine—on the cross.

Fourth, Jesus sensed God's abandonment when his Father turned away from him, covered as he was in our sins. When Jesus said, "My God, my God, why have You forsaken Me?" (Matthew 27:46, NKJV), he was experiencing firsthand the full separation that sin creates between God and man. He prayed that prayer so we never have to pray it.

Getting Personal

What does the phrase "Jesus is my Savior" mean to you?

In what sense would you say that, for you, the Cross was a necessity?

We can picture ourselves in various positions relative to the Cross. When we get close enough to see ourselves on the cross, we can begin to understand why it was crucial for Jesus to take our place.

FORGIVE THEM

Setting the Scene

In the shocking first moments after being elevated between earth and sky—as the criminals cursed, the crowd mocked, and the soldiers prepared to gamble for his clothes—Jesus made his first statement. Perhaps there was a moment of silence as the crowd watched him take a painful breath. Jesus said the last thing that was on anyone's mind: "Father, forgive them, for they do not know what they are doing."

There are many people Jesus could have had in mind when he prayed for "them" and asked his Father for forgiveness on their behalf, beginning with the soldiers below his feet, more intent on the value of his clothes than feeling any regret over the task they had just performed. Their callous ignorance was included in Jesus' forgiveness. Then there were the jeering crowds, the conspirators who thought they had succeeded in eliminating the threat Jesus represented. They did not know what they did. As Paul put it later, "None of the rulers of this age understood it, for if they had, they would not have crucified the Lord of glory" (1 Corinthians 2:8, NIV).

Applied to its broadest possible audience, Jesus' prayer includes us, whose sin required that he pay with his perfect life. The prayer is not precise in terms of time, so the forgiveness requested has no bounds. Forgiveness was provided long before we knew enough to accept it!

Getting Personal

How can someone fully experience Jesus' forgiveness of his or her sins? What does that mean for you?

If forgiveness of others is such a crucial part of the life in Christ, why is it so difficult to do?

Who's on your "I can't forgive" list, and how might that change based on Jesus' words and example?

The road to justifying our own lack of forgiveness is swift and easy. The realization that Jesus was willing to extend forgiveness demands that we reconsider why we may be so unwilling to forgive. How can we claim to have received forgiveness for ourselves if we won't extend it to others?

READING THE WORD

✤ *Luke 23:34-38, NIV*
Jesus said, "Father, forgive them, for they do not know what they are doing." And they divided up his clothes by casting lots. 35The people stood watching, and the rulers even sneered at him. They said, "He saved others; let him save himself if he is God's Messiah, the Chosen One." 36The soldiers also came up and mocked him. They offered him wine vinegar 37and said, "If you are the king of the Jews, save yourself." 38There was a written notice above him, which read: THIS IS THE KING OF THE JEWS.

TALKING TO GOD

Thank the Lord that he forgave even those who had no interest in being forgiven. Ask him to give you a deep awareness of how much you have received because of his grace, so that it will help you extend God's grace to others.

ROLLING THE DICE

Setting the Scene

Two groups had a vested interest in the events surrounding the Cross but had no interest at all in understanding their actual significance.

The soldiers efficiently carried out their duties, expressing little concern over the agony of the men they put to death. Perhaps they had done this so often they had become hardened to the specter of human cruelty. They drafted Simon to help Jesus carry the cross, not because they wanted to make things easier for Jesus, but because they wanted to keep the process moving. They probably offered the narcotic mixture of myrrh and wine not to ease pain but to make the men easier to handle. The only apparent perk for these soldiers was access to the condemned men's personal belongings. John tells us that from Jesus the soldiers had several dividable items and a seamless garment, which became the prize they gambled for at the foot of his cross. John also notes that their behavior actually fulfilled a prophecy recorded in Psalm 22:18: "They divide my clothes among them and cast lots for my garment" (NIV).

The second group, Pilate and the Jewish leadership, squabbled over the wording of the charges on the sign in three languages over Jesus' head. Pilate expressed his irritation over the way he had been manipulated into condemning Jesus by refusing to edit what he had inscribed: "King of the Jews." Ironically, the words were true in ways no one present could imagine!

READING THE WORD

❀ *John 19:19-24, NIV*

Pilate had a notice prepared and fastened to the cross. It read: JESUS OF NAZARETH, THE KING OF THE JEWS. 20Many of the Jews read this sign, for the place where Jesus was crucified was near the city, and the sign was written in Aramaic, Latin and Greek. 21The chief priests of the Jews protested to Pilate, "Do not write 'The King of the Jews,' but that this man claimed to be king of the Jews." 22Pilate answered, "What I have written, I have written." 23When the soldiers crucified Jesus, they took his clothes, dividing them into four shares, one for each of them, with the undergarment remaining. This garment was seamless, woven in one piece from top to bottom. 24"Let's not tear it," they said to one another. "Let's decide by lot who will get it." This happened that the scripture might be fulfilled that said, "They divided my clothes among them and cast lots for my garment." So this is what the soldiers did.

TALKING TO GOD

Give glory to God because nothing and no one can sidetrack his plans and nothing can interfere in his purposes for you. Your times are in good hands, the very best!

Getting Personal

How is God's sovereignty evident even in the actions of those who did not have God's interests in mind in the execution of Jesus?

In what ways can you identify with Jesus' humiliation on the cross? Why is this a significant spiritual exercise?

How have you experienced any humiliating aspects of being a follower of Jesus?

When looking closely at the Cross, we can discern two overlapping scenes occurring simultaneously. The world was busy carrying on its plans and intentions; meanwhile, in the eternal realms, Jesus was dying to save sinful humans. What we believe about Jesus puts us in one of those two scenes.

CONVERSION

Setting the Scene

Conversations with eternal consequences occur all the time. Such a conversation occurred that day among the three men hanging together on crosses, while they waited to die.

The two criminals heard Jesus say, "Father, forgive them, for they do not know what they are doing" (Luke 23:34, NIV). This statement probably provoked and in some way steered the conversation that followed.

The conversation began with one of the dying criminals lashing out verbally: "Aren't you the Messiah? Save yourself and us!" The statement was a dare of sorts, similar to one Jesus had faced in the wilderness with Satan, "If you are the Son of God . . ." (Luke 4:3, 9).

Before Jesus could answer, the other criminal weighed in: "'Don't you fear God,' he said, 'since you are under the same sentence? We are punished justly, for we are getting what our deeds deserve. But this man has done nothing wrong.'" While the first man had gruffly identified Jesus as the Messiah, the second one managed to summarize his own condition and Jesus' uniqueness in his brief words. He recognized the fundamental need to fear God. He acknowledged his own sinfulness while pointing out Jesus' innocence.

Then he requested (but didn't demand) from Jesus something only the Messiah could give: "Jesus, remember me when you come into your kingdom." Jesus' response was immediate and unqualified: "Truly I tell you, today you will be with me in paradise." That brief interchange brought a new citizen into the Kingdom of Heaven.

Getting Personal

What caused you to put your faith in Jesus Christ? How would you describe your turning point?

Is anything missing from the faith exercised by the criminal who asked Jesus for admittance to the Kingdom? If so, what?

Why was the form of the criminal's "sinner's prayer" effective?

The knowledge required for conversion must be a profound understanding of sinfulness and helplessness, coupled with a desperate, no-holds-barred surrender to Christ. If you have done that, you have been promised a place with Jesus one day in paradise. Perhaps even today.

READING THE WORD

❧ *Luke 23:32-33, 39-43, NIV*
Two other men, both criminals, were also led out with him to be executed. 33When they came to the place called the Skull, they crucified him there, along with the criminals—one on his right, the other on his left. . . . 39One of the criminals who hung there hurled insults at him: "Aren't you the Messiah? Save yourself and us!" 40But the other criminal rebuked him. "Don't you fear God," he said, "since you are under the same sentence? 41We are punished justly, for we are getting what our deeds deserve. But this man has done nothing wrong." 42Then he said, "Jesus, remember me when you come into your kingdom." 43Jesus answered him, "Truly I tell you, today you will be with me in paradise."

TALKING TO GOD

God is so quick to forgive those who put their hope in him! Thank him for his readiness to respond to the thief on the cross, and thank him for specific ways he drew you to himself.

THE OTHERS

Setting the Scene

Jesus was crucified on a public thoroughfare. Crucifixions were much like the reality entertainment of that day. The mixed crowd seemed to dismiss the two dying thieves as not worth bothering about, but they found a certain satisfaction in heaping abuse on Jesus as he hung from the cross. The theme of the crowd's taunts misquoted Jesus' statement about the Temple and a three-day reconstruction project. They blatantly misapplied it by asking him to come down from the cross—overlooking the three-day time period Jesus had mentioned.

Meanwhile, the religious leaders, who believed they had engineered the circumstances, stood mocking Christ "among themselves." Their statement is strangely ironic: "'He saved others,' they said, 'but he can't save himself!'" They were so close to the truth, and yet so far. He did save others, and in order to save many, he chose not to save himself.

As far as we know, of the Twelve, only John was present at the Cross. Most of the disciples were still hiding in fear; Peter was hiding in shame; Judas had taken his own life.

Several women were close to the cross. Jesus made eye contact with his mother, Mary, and John. In his last act as her human son, Jesus insured her safekeeping by entrusting her to John. Jesus didn't leave any loose ends.

READING THE WORD

✾ *Mark 15:29-32, NIV*
Those who passed by hurled insults at him, shaking their heads and saying, "So! You who are going to destroy the temple and build it in three days, 30come down from the cross and save yourself!" 31In the same way the chief priests and the teachers of the law mocked him among themselves. "He saved others," they said, "but he can't save himself! 32Let this Messiah, this king of Israel, come down now from the cross, that we may see and believe."

✾ *John 19:25-27, NIV*
Near the cross of Jesus stood his mother, his mother's sister, Mary the wife of Clopas, and Mary Magdalene. 26When Jesus saw his mother there, and the disciple whom he loved standing nearby, he said to her, "Woman, here is your son," 27and to the disciple, "Here is your mother." From that time on, this disciple took her into his home.

TALKING TO GOD

Take a minute to marvel at the way Jesus, the God-man, managed all his duties—earthly and spiritual—even while he was dying. Come to the Lord today without any excuses, but simply with a willingness to follow his lead in accepting responsibility in your various roles—as a child, a spouse, a parent, a friend, an employer or employee, etc. Ask him to help you be wise in discerning which duties are yours to manage—and which are his.

Getting Personal

How does Jesus' tying up loose ends in his human relationships influence your thinking about responsibilities you may have to your earthly family?

How would you compare John's and Peter's behavior as disciples during this time? What do you learn from each of them?

When Jesus took on human nature, he took on all the baggage that came with it. He dealt with all those complicated family relationships that can be such a challenge in our lives. His example guides our efforts in maintaining integrity in our relationships, honoring him in every way.

JESUS DIES AND IS BURIED

Week 49, Day 1

❁ *Matthew 27:45-66; Mark 15:33-47; Luke 23:44-56; John 19:28-42*

After being sentenced to death, Jesus was flogged and then forced to carry his cross to the execution site. There he was crucified between two common criminals. During his time on that cross and in excruciating pain, Jesus forgave his executioners, promised eternal life to a dying criminal, and made sure his mother was cared for. This week, as we consider Jesus' final moments on the cross and see how witnesses responded to his death and burial, we'll learn more about our Savior and how we can respond to him.

THE CRY

Setting the Scene

Jesus was crucified at 9:00 a.m. Death by crucifixion was slow and excruciating, and sometimes could take days. For three hours, Jesus put up with abuse from bystanders. Then, "at noon, darkness fell" over the land for three hours, and an earthquake shook the ground (Matthew 27:51). The darkness on that Friday afternoon was both physical and spiritual as all nature seemed to mourn over the death of God's Son.

Then Jesus cried out, "My God, my God, why have you abandoned me?" Jesus was quoting the first line of Psalm 22, not asking in surprise or despair. The psalm is a prayer of expectation for deliverance, not a cry of abandonment, and the whole psalm is a prophecy expressing the deep agony over the Messiah's death for the world's sin.

In becoming sin for us, Jesus was temporarily separated from his Father because God cannot look on sin (see Habakkuk 1:13). This was the "cup" that Jesus had agonized over in the garden of Gethsemane (Matthew 26:39).

Some of those standing nearby thought Jesus was "calling for the prophet Elijah." Because Elijah had ascended into heaven without dying (2 Kings 2:11), a popular belief held that he would return to rescue the righteous from great trouble (Malachi 4:5). Elijah was associated with the final appearance of God's Kingdom, and in the annual Passover feast, Jewish families still set an extra place at the table for Elijah in expectation of his return.

READING THE WORD

❁ *Matthew 27:45-49, NLT*

At noon, darkness fell across the whole land until three o'clock. 46At about three o'clock, Jesus called out with a loud voice, *"Eli, Eli, lema sabachthani?"* which means "My God, my God, why have you abandoned me?" 47Some of the bystanders misunderstood and thought he was calling for the prophet Elijah. 48One of them ran and filled a sponge with sour wine, holding it up to him on a reed stick so he could drink. 49But the rest said, "Wait! Let's see whether Elijah comes to save him."

TALKING TO GOD

Bring to Jesus the whole mixture of emotions stirred up by considering his crucifixion—sympathy and sorrow, remorse and repentance, and gratitude for the depth of his grace. "Thank you" seems far less than adequate, but thank God anyway, and ask him to help you thank him with your whole being—heart, soul, mind, and strength.

One of the bystanders put a wine-soaked sponge on a long stick and held it up to Jesus' lips, probably to help ease his pain. The others told him not to give Jesus any relief for his thirst but to wait and see if Elijah would come to rescue him.

Getting Personal

What does this passage teach about what Jesus endured for you?

How does remembering Christ's suffering highlight the reality of our sin?

In what ways can you express your gratitude to Jesus for taking your place at the Cross?

The physical and emotional agony suffered by Jesus during the whole process of crucifixion was horrible, almost unimaginable—being flogged, having nails driven through hands and feet, hanging from those nails, enduring insults and ridicule, being abandoned by his disciples, and more. But being ripped from his Father—the spiritual alienation from God—was the ultimate torture. Separation from God is "hell," and Jesus experienced this, a double death actually, so that we wouldn't have to.

We can easily read over words such as "the Crucifixion" and "hell" because we have heard them so often. But as we focus on Jesus' agony on the cross and consider his cry of incredible pain, we begin to understand the depth of his suffering. And he did this for us.

THE TEAR

Setting the Scene

The Temple curtain being "torn in two, from top to bottom" symbolized what Christ had finished on the Cross (Matthew 27:50-52, NLT). The Most Holy Place in the Temple housed the Ark of the Covenant and could only be entered once a year on the Day of Atonement, and even then, only by the high priest (Leviticus 16:1-34). Symbolically, the curtain separated holy God from sinful people. By tearing the curtain in two, God showed that Christ had opened the way for sinners to come to God directly.

In committing his spirit to the Father, Jesus died. He did not faint or become unconscious—he "breathed his last." John presents more evidence for his death. Because the Jewish leaders did not want to desecrate their Sabbath (Deuteronomy 21:22-23) by allowing the bodies of three crucified Jews to remain hanging on crosses overnight, they asked Pilate to make sure the victims were dead so "their bodies could be taken down." Breaking the legs would assure death because this would stop the crucified person from using his legs to lift his body in order to take more oxygen into his collapsing lungs. When the soldiers came to Jesus, however, they found that he had already died.

Getting Personal

With his death on the cross, what barrier did Christ remove between you and God?

How should the fact that you have direct access to God affect how you live?

What keeps you from using more often the privilege of going directly to the Father?

In an effort to deny the Resurrection, some say Jesus didn't actually die. They say he only appeared to do so and was revived later. But Jesus' death was confirmed by the Roman soldiers, Pilate, Joseph of Arimathea, Nicodemus, the religious leaders, the apostle John, and the women who witnessed his death and burial. Jesus suffered actual physical death on the cross. And he gave his life; no one took it from him.

God was in complete control of our salvation to the last detail. Jesus' sacrifice was complete and effective. And because of Jesus' death on the cross, the curtain has been torn; we have direct access to God.

READING THE WORD

✣ *Luke 23:44-46, NLT*

By this time it was about noon, and darkness fell across the whole land until three o'clock. 45The light from the sun was gone. And suddenly, the curtain in the sanctuary of the Temple was torn down the middle. 46Then Jesus shouted, "Father, I entrust my spirit into your hands!" And with those words he breathed his last.

✣ *John 19:31-35, NLT*

It was the day of preparation, and the Jewish leaders didn't want the bodies hanging there the next day, which was the Sabbath (and a very special Sabbath, because it was the Passover). So they asked Pilate to hasten their deaths by ordering that their legs be broken. Then their bodies could be taken down. 32So the soldiers came and broke the legs of the two men crucified with Jesus. 33But when they came to Jesus, they saw that he was already dead, so they didn't break his legs. 34One of the soldiers, however, pierced his side with a spear, and immediately blood and water flowed out. 35(This report is from an eyewitness giving an accurate account. He speaks the truth so that you also can believe.)

TALKING TO GOD

Confess to the Lord that sometimes you act as if his door were closed to you, even though Christ's death has given you direct access to God. Ask him to give you a hunger for time with him and that he would deepen the bond of relationship between you.

READING THE WORD

❃ *Mark 15:39-41, NLT*
When the Roman officer who stood facing him saw how he had died, he exclaimed, "This man truly was the Son of God!" 40Some women were there, watching from a distance, including Mary Magdalene, Mary (the mother of James the younger and of Joseph), and Salome. 41They had been followers of Jesus and had cared for him while he was in Galilee. Many other women who had come with him to Jerusalem were also there.

❃ *Luke 23:47-49, NLT*
When the Roman officer overseeing the execution saw what had happened, he worshiped God and said, "Surely this man was innocent." 48And when all the crowd that came to see the crucifixion saw what had happened, they went home in deep sorrow. 49But Jesus' friends, including the women who had followed him from Galilee, stood at a distance watching.

TALKING TO GOD

What is a stumbling block to others is the message of life for believers. Thank God for his perfect sacrifice and for opening your mind and heart to understand and accept the gift of salvation through Christ.

THE RESPONSE

Setting the Scene

A Roman officer had accompanied the soldiers to the execution site. He probably had done this many times, yet this crucifixion was completely different—the unexplained darkness, the earthquake, even the one who had uttered, "Father, forgive them, for they don't know what they are doing" (Luke 23:34, NLT). The officer may have mocked Jesus earlier (Luke 23:36-37), but now he realized that Jesus had been no ordinary person.

This Roman officer and the other soldiers at the cross (Matthew 27:54), all of them Gentiles, realized what most of the Jewish nation had missed, that Jesus was innocent and "truly was the Son of God!" The centurion may not have understood the implications of that statement, but he "worshiped God." While the Jewish religious leaders were celebrating Jesus' death, a small group of Gentiles were the first to proclaim Jesus as the Son of God after his death.

The male disciples had made great promises of loyalty to Jesus, but the women among Jesus' followers waited at the cross and went to the tomb.

Getting Personal

Put yourself in the story. Where would you have been at Jesus' crucifixion? With which person or group do you most identify: centurion, soldiers, religious leaders, Jewish crowd, women followers, or male disciples?

Why do you think the Roman centurion responded the way he did?

As you have matured in your faith, how has your appreciation for Christ's death deepened?

The Roman centurion had probably not had previous contact with Jesus—to him this man was just another religious zealot. But God broke through, and the hardened soldier recognized that Jesus was different.

The Cross still draws some close while pushing others away. Those who recognize Jesus as innocent but dying for them, turn to him and worship the Son of God. But many, often religious people, are put off by this gruesome display. Some who claim to be Christ's followers are embarrassed and don't bring up the Crucifixion.

But the essence of Christianity is the Cross. That's why Paul exclaimed, "We preach Christ crucified: a stumbling block to Jews and foolishness to Gentiles" (1 Corinthians 1:23, NIV).

THE FULFILLMENT

Setting the Scene

Jesus had carried out his mission (John 17:4), so he surrendered his life to his Father. Jesus fulfilled Scripture when he expressed his thirst and was given the soaked sponge (see Psalm 42:2 and Psalm 69:21). This "sour wine" was not the same as the drugged wine offered to Jesus earlier, which he had refused (Mark 15:23).

The Greek word *tetelestai* translated as "it is finished" actually means "it is accomplished," "it is fulfilled," or "it is paid in full." Jesus' death accomplished redemption and fulfilled all the Old Testament prophecies. Until Jesus sacrificed himself at the Cross, sin could be atoned only through a complicated system of sacrifices. With his death, that sacrificial system ended, because Jesus took all sin upon himself.

When the soldiers pierced Jesus with a spear instead of breaking his legs (John 19:33-34), they fulfilled two biblical prophecies. Exodus 12:46 and Numbers 9:12 speak of the bones of the Passover lamb that should not be broken. Because Jesus was the final sacrifice, those verses apply to him. Also, Zechariah 12:10 (NLT) states, "They will look on me whom they have pierced" (see also Revelation 1:7).

Christ finished his work at the Cross, fully accomplishing our salvation, paying in full our debt.

Getting Personal

Why do people have difficulty understanding and accepting that they are saved by grace and not by works?

When did you come to realize how the work of Christ at the Cross paid your debt in full and made you complete?

Why do you, at times, act as if your relationship with God depends on what you do for him?

We are saved by grace (undeserved favor or love) alone through faith alone. We can't earn our forgiveness; we can't work our way to heaven. And we can't add anything to what Christ has done. It is finished. Yet many believers act as if their salvation depends on them. We don't gain God's favor by keeping commandments. Instead, obedience should flow out of our love for Christ as we understand what he has done for us and that we belong to him. Jesus did the "work" of salvation— completely fulfilled, totally finished!

READING THE WORD

✤ *John 19:28-30, 36-37, NLT*
Jesus knew that his mission was now finished, and to fulfill Scripture he said, "I am thirsty." 29A jar of sour wine was sitting there, so they soaked a sponge in it, put it on a hyssop branch, and held it up to his lips. 30When Jesus had tasted it, he said, "It is finished!" Then he bowed his head and released his spirit.... 36These things happened in fulfillment of the Scriptures that say, "Not one of his bones will be broken," 37and "They will look on the one they pierced."

TALKING TO GOD

What little we have to offer in comparison to what he has given! Thank God that your position in his family doesn't depend on your own righteous behavior but on the perfect behavior of Jesus, the sacrificed Lamb. Thank him for the grace that has saved you.

THE REQUEST

READING THE WORD

✱ *Mark 15:42-47, NLT*
This all happened on Friday, the day of preparation, the day before the Sabbath. As evening approached, 43Joseph of Arimathea took a risk and went to Pilate and asked for Jesus' body. (Joseph was an honored member of the high council, and he was waiting for the Kingdom of God to come.) 44Pilate couldn't believe that Jesus was already dead, so he called for the Roman officer and asked if he had died yet. 45The officer confirmed that Jesus was dead, so Pilate told Joseph he could have the body. 46Joseph bought a long sheet of linen cloth. Then he took Jesus' body down from the cross, wrapped it in the cloth, and laid it in a tomb that had been carved out of the rock. Then he rolled a stone in front of the entrance. 47Mary Magdalene and Mary the mother of Joseph saw where Jesus' body was laid.

TALKING TO GOD

Ask God to remove your fears about what others will think of you or say about you. Ask for the courage and strength to stand up for your faith and for Christ Jesus.

Setting the Scene

Some of the women at the Cross had come from Galilee with Jesus for the Passover. These women had been faithful to Jesus' ministry, following him and providing for his material needs (see Luke 8:1-3). Mary Magdalene was from Magdala, a town near Capernaum in Galilee. Jesus had released her from demon possession (Luke 8:2). Matthew distinguishes another Mary by identifying her sons, who may have been well known in the early church (Matthew 27:56). Salome, the mother of the disciples James and John, was there, too. John wrote that Jesus' mother, Mary, was present and that, from the cross, Jesus told John to take care of her (John 19:25-27).

Because Jewish law forbade allowing a dead body to remain exposed overnight (Deuteronomy 21:23), Joseph of Arimathea "asked for Jesus' body" so he could give it a proper burial. Although he was an honored member of the Sanhedrin (Mark 15:43), Joseph was a "secret disciple" of Jesus (John 19:38, NLT). As evening and the Sabbath approached, Joseph had to hurry. Fortunately he had help. Nicodemus, another member of the Sanhedrin, brought spices with which to wrap Jesus' body in the linen cloth provided by Joseph (John 3:1; 19:38-42).

Joseph and Nicodemus wrapped Jesus' body, placed it in the tomb, and rolled a heavy stone across the entrance. The religious leaders also watched where Jesus was buried, along with Mary Magdalene and Mary the mother of Joseph.

Getting Personal

When have you been tempted to keep your faith a secret?

What do you risk in letting others know how you feel about Jesus?

Jesus' eleven closest disciples ran away when he was taken. But his secret followers Joseph and Nicodemus stepped forward. In asking for Jesus' body, they were exposed, their secret revealed. Joseph risked his safety and reputation to give Jesus a proper burial; he went against propriety and expectations.

It would be easiest and safest to keep quiet about our beliefs and convictions. But Christ calls us to follow him boldly, standing for the truth and doing what is right. When you think your Christian witness will endanger your reputation or security, remember Joseph and Nicodemus.

THE SEAL

Setting the Scene

The day before the Sabbath was used to prepare for the Sabbath because no work was allowed from sunset on Friday to sunset on Saturday. The Pharisees went to Pilate on the Sabbath, clearly violating their own laws.

Apparently these religious leaders knew where Jesus was buried. They also remembered he had said "after three days I will rise from the dead." Jesus had only spoken these words to his disciples (Matthew 16:21; 17:9; 20:19), so Judas may have provided this information. The leading priests and Pharisees asked Pilate to "seal the tomb."

The grieving disciples might have forgotten about Jesus' promise of resurrection, but these religious leaders hadn't. They did not believe Jesus' claims, but they were afraid of fraud. They wanted to make sure no one would steal Jesus' body and claim he had risen from the dead.

Hewn out of rock in the side of a hill, the tomb had only one entrance. It was made "secure" by stringing a cord across the stone that was rolled over the entrance and sealing the cord at each end with clay. Pilate gave the leaders permission to post a guard at the tomb as a further precaution. These may have been some Roman soldiers or the Temple police who were at the Jewish leaders' disposal (see John 18:3). With such precautions, the only way the tomb could be empty would be for Jesus to rise from the dead. The Pharisees failed to understand that no power could prevent the Son of God from rising again.

Getting Personal

When have you seen others try to stop the spread of the gospel? What happened?

When have you felt opposition because of your faith in Christ?

What aspects of today's lesson give you hope and courage?

The religious leaders thought they had the situation under control, but no tomb, rock, seal, or army could withstand God's will and power.

Centuries later, we still encounter people, some religious, who believe they can prohibit God's work in the world. They may be able to silence us, but they can never stop God.

READING THE WORD

❀ *Matthew 27:62-66, NLT*
The next day, on the Sabbath, the leading priests and Pharisees went to see Pilate. 63They told him, "Sir, we remember what that deceiver once said while he was still alive: 'After three days I will rise from the dead.' 64So we request that you seal the tomb until the third day. This will prevent his disciples from coming and stealing his body and then telling everyone he was raised from the dead! If that happens, we'll be worse off than we were at first." 65Pilate replied, "Take guards and secure it the best you can." 66So they sealed the tomb and posted guards to protect it.

TALKING TO GOD

Bring to the Lord any circumstances or relationships that seem troubled beyond resolution, remembering God's power over every aspect of life and this world. Praise him for his power and goodness!

JESUS IS RESURRECTED

Week 50, Day 1

❋ *Matthew 28:1-15; Mark 16:1-6; Luke 24:1-12; John 20:1-18*

Jesus was taken, tried, condemned, tortured, and executed—crucified between two criminals. The Jewish leaders, the Roman officials, the Jerusalem crowd, and his followers thought Jesus' ministry was over. Most of Jesus' friends had fled and now huddled in fear and despair, wondering about their future. But the Cross is the symbol of victory, not defeat; of the beginning, not the end. This week we'll see Jesus conquering death and changing the world—and our lives—forever.

READING THE WORD

❋ *Matthew 28:1-7, NLT*
Early on Sunday morning, as the new day was dawning, Mary Magdalene and the other Mary went out to visit the tomb. 2Suddenly there was a great earthquake! For an angel of the Lord came down from heaven, rolled aside the stone, and sat on it. 3His face shone like lightning, and his clothing was as white as snow. 4The guards shook with fear when they saw him, and they fell into a dead faint. 5Then the angel spoke to the women. "Don't be afraid!" he said. "I know you are looking for Jesus, who was crucified. 6He isn't here! He is risen from the dead, just as he said would happen. Come, see where his body was lying. 7And now, go quickly and tell his disciples that he has risen from the dead, and he is going ahead of you to Galilee. You will see him there. Remember what I have told you."

THE EVENT

Setting the Scene

Jesus had died on that cross—the Romans had made sure of it. His lifeless body had been lovingly cared for by a formerly "secret" follower, Joseph of Arimathea (Matthew 27:57-61; John 19:38). Then, observed by "Mary Magdalene and the other Mary," Joseph had placed Jesus in a nearby tomb. Everyone involved in the crucifixion—rulers, leaders, guards, followers, and onlookers— knew Jesus was dead. And many, in particular these three (Joseph, Mary, and Mary), knew where he was buried.

The Jewish leaders, remembering that Jesus had said something about coming back to life, had convinced the Romans to secure the tomb to make sure no one would even think about removing the body.

Yet the tomb is empty. Jesus did, in fact, rise from the dead. This event happened in space and time. That is, in AD 33, a real corpse, wrapped and laid in a real tomb outside ancient Jerusalem and guarded by real men, came back to life. This was not some "idea" or "spiritual" event: Jesus actually arose bodily.

Those who don't want to believe in the Resurrection have proposed a number of theories for the empty tomb (for example, the women went to the wrong tomb; Jesus didn't really die—he was just in very bad shape; followers somehow stole the body; everyone who saw Jesus alive was hallucinating; the Gospel writers made up the story; etc.), all of which can be disproved and dismissed.

Jesus' resurrection is unique. Other religions have strong ethical systems, concepts about the afterlife, and writings that they consider holy. Only Christianity has a God who became human, literally died for his people, and was raised again in power and glory to rule his church forever.

The Resurrection stands as the central fact of Christian history, and on it the church is built. Christians can look very different from one another, and they can hold widely varying beliefs about politics, lifestyle, and even theology. But one central belief unites and inspires all true Christians: Jesus Christ rose from the dead!

Getting Personal

What makes Jesus coming back to life difficult for some people to believe?

What evidence bolsters your belief in the Resurrection?

In what ways does the Resurrection give you confidence and assurance in your faith?

Believing that someone who has died can come back to life is nearly impossible. Consider the disciples. They had seen Jesus bring dead people back to life on at least three occasions (Jairus's daughter—Matthew 9:18, 23-26; a widow's son—Luke 7:11-16; and Lazarus—John 11:1-45), yet they couldn't believe Jesus himself had been raised, even after hearing reports from eyewitnesses. So we shouldn't be surprised when people today struggle with this event; bodies just don't get up and walk out of graves after three days.

But Jesus did—all the evidence points to this amazing event, this turning point in history. And what a difference the Resurrection makes. Because Jesus arose, just as he said he would, we know that he is who he said he was—God in the flesh and our Savior—and that all he taught is true.

Jesus arose, and he lives today!

TALKING TO GOD

Bring your doubts to the Lord, and any feelings that your faith is vague and intangible. Ask God to help you remember that your faith is anchored on the truth about Jesus Christ, who entered real human history as a real, human person. Praise him that you don't base your faith solely on ancient accounts, but in a living, active Savior.

THE POWER

✤ *Matthew 28:1-4, NLT*
Early on Sunday morning, as the new day was dawning, Mary Magdalene and the other Mary went out to visit the tomb. 2Suddenly there was a great earthquake! For an angel of the Lord came down from heaven, rolled aside the stone, and sat on it. 3His face shone like lightning, and his clothing was as white as snow. 4The guards shook with fear when they saw him, and they fell into a dead faint.

✤ *Mark 16:5-7, NLT*
When they entered the tomb, they saw a young man clothed in a white robe sitting on the right side. The women were shocked, 6but the angel said, "Don't be alarmed. You are looking for Jesus of Nazareth, who was crucified. He isn't here! He is risen from the dead! Look, this is where they laid his body. 7Now go and tell his disciples, including Peter, that Jesus is going ahead of you to Galilee. You will see him there, just as he told you before he died."

TALKING TO GOD

Bring to the Lord any situations that are currently leaving you feeling weak or powerless. Thank him for the power of his Holy Spirit, and reaffirm your confidence in his sovereignty and goodness.

Setting the Scene

After the Crucifixion, the women had returned to their homes to keep the Sabbath as the law required (from sundown Friday to sundown Saturday). Anointing a body was a sign of devotion and respect, and bringing spices to the tomb would be like bringing flowers to a grave today. Since Jesus had been buried so rapidly after his death, the women had been unable to perform the anointing before his burial. They were determined to get to the burial site with their spices and perfumes.

Before the women arrived, however, another supernatural event took place—a "great earthquake." Either the earthquake occurred as the angel of the Lord descended or was the means by which the stone was rolled away from the tomb's entrance. The stone was not rolled back so Jesus could get out but so others could get in and see that Jesus had risen.

The Resurrection was a display of God's mighty power. Because we believe in God, we shouldn't be too surprised at this. After all, he created all that is (John 1:1-4); he controls the universe and beyond. How could any person or group think they could keep Jesus in the grave? The religious leaders failed to do it; the power of the Roman army and justice system could not hold him; even lack of faith on the part of the disciples couldn't keep Jesus dead. God's power to raise Jesus is greater than any power in the universe.

We can trust God's promises. He is greater than all our problems or infirmities. The Resurrection assures us that Christ is alive and real.

Getting Personal

Jesus demonstrated his power over sin and over death. What does that mean for you personally?

How can you rely on God's power from day to day?

Often we feel weak and powerless—and we are! But our God is all-powerful. That's why Paul could proclaim, "He is far above any ruler or authority or power or leader or anything else—not only in this world but also in the world to come" (Ephesians 1:21, NLT).

THE WITNESSES

Setting the Scene

Mary Magdalene and Mary the mother of James and Joseph (or Joses) had been at the Crucifixion and had followed Joseph of Arimathea, the man who had taken Jesus' body to the tomb (Mark 15:47). So they knew where Jesus had been buried. Salome, probably the mother of the disciples James and John, had also been at the cross. Along with other women, Mary Magdalene had been a longtime follower of Jesus, traveling with the disciples and helping provide for the financial needs of the group (Luke 8:1-3).

At first, Mary was shocked and confused at the absence of Jesus' body, so she ran to Peter and John, who then ran to see for themselves. John arrived first and saw the linen wrappings. Peter also saw the graveclothes and noted that the headpiece was folded up separately from the other wrappings. A grave robber couldn't possibly have made off with the body and left the linens as if they were still shaped around it.

Peter and John did not fabricate this story about the Resurrection; in fact, they were surprised that the body was missing. The fact of the Resurrection opened the disciples' minds to see that God had foretold his plan through the prophets. Although John and Peter "believed" something miraculous had occurred, they weren't sure what they should do next. So they went home. Later, they joined the other disciples behind locked doors (John 20:19).

Getting Personal

When confronted with the evidence for the Resurrection, why do some people refuse to believe?

When have you seen evidence of God's work in your life but didn't recognize it until much later? What kept you from "seeing and believing"?

Evidence of God permeates our world and personal experience. We can see his fingerprints in creation, in relationships, and in our own thoughts and desires. We recognize him as he gives comfort and peace and guides us daily—through his Word, godly teachers, and circumstances. The evidence surrounds us. May we come close, see the empty clothes, and believe.

READING THE WORD

❋ *Mark 16:1, NLT*
Saturday evening, when the Sabbath ended, Mary Magdalene, Mary the mother of James, and Salome went out and purchased burial spices so they could anoint Jesus' body.

❋ *John 20:1-10, NLT*
Early on Sunday morning, while it was still dark, Mary Magdalene came to the tomb and found that the stone had been rolled away from the entrance. 2She ran and found Simon Peter and the other disciple, the one whom Jesus loved. She said, "They have taken the Lord's body out of the tomb, and we don't know where they have put him!" 3Peter and the other disciple started out for the tomb. 4They were both running, but the other disciple outran Peter and reached the tomb first. 5He stooped and looked in and saw the linen wrappings lying there, but he didn't go in. 6Then Simon Peter arrived and went inside. He also noticed the linen wrappings lying there, 7while the cloth that had covered Jesus' head was folded up and lying apart from the other wrappings. 8Then the disciple who had reached the tomb first also went in, and he saw and believed— 9for until then they still hadn't understood the Scriptures that said Jesus must rise from the dead. 10Then they went home.

TALKING TO GOD

Ask God to open your eyes to evidence of his presence and activity today. As you think of him, praise him throughout the day for being a personal God, who reveals himself to those who seek him.

THE COVER-UP

READING THE WORD

❊ *Matthew 28:11-15, NLT*
As the women were on their way, some of the guards went into the city and told the leading priests what had happened. 12A meeting with the elders was called, and they decided to give the soldiers a large bribe. 13They told the soldiers, "You must say, 'Jesus' disciples came during the night while we were sleeping, and they stole his body.' 14If the governor hears about it, we'll stand up for you so you won't get in trouble." 15So the guards accepted the bribe and said what they were told to say. Their story spread widely among the Jews, and they still tell it today.

TALKING TO GOD

Approach the living Savior and ask him to give you insight and wisdom for interacting with those who deny the Resurrection. Praise him for being the source of all that is true.

Setting the Scene

The women hurried to tell the disciples the amazing news about the empty tomb. At the same time, the guards were on their way to the "leading priests," not to Pilate. If these were Roman guards, under Roman law, they would pay with their lives for falling asleep on the job. But they had been assigned to the Jewish authorities, so they went to the religious leaders badly in need of a cover-up.

The religious leaders' worst fears had been realized (Matthew 27:63-64)—Jesus' body had disappeared from the tomb! Instead of even considering that Jesus was the risen Messiah, they chose to "give the soldiers a large bribe" to lie.

The "stolen body" story may have seemed like a logical explanation, but they didn't think through the details. Why would Jesus' disciples, who had deserted him at his arrest, risk a return to a guarded and sealed tomb to remove a body—an offense that could incur the death penalty? And even if they had done so, would they have taken the time to unwrap the body and leave the graveclothes? Also, if this had occurred while the guards were asleep, how could the guards possibly have known the disciples were the thieves? The story was full of holes, and the guards would have to admit to negligence. So getting them to spread this rumor required the large bribe.

Apparently the plan worked, because the soldiers took the bribe. The story circulated, and many people believed the lie, apparently not thinking through the information carefully. The story was still being circulated when Matthew wrote his Gospel.

Getting Personal

What theories or arguments have you heard that try to undermine or refute the Resurrection?

How might you lovingly point to the truth—that Jesus did rise from the dead, that he lives, and that he has changed your life?

Because the Resurrection is difficult to believe, people still try to explain the empty tomb. No twisting of facts or rationalizing can cover up the truth: Jesus was dead but is alive! Hallelujah!

THE MEANING

Setting the Scene

Understandably, the women were frightened by the angels at the tomb. An angel spoke reassuringly and reminded them of Jesus' prediction about the Resurrection. The words "He has risen" or "He is risen" are literally, "He is raised." God raised Jesus from the dead as a vindication of Jesus' divinity. The angel invited the women to see that the tomb was empty and then sent them to the disciples with the amazing news.

Jesus' resurrection is the key to the Christian faith. Because Jesus rose from the dead, we know that Jesus is the Truth, God incarnate, not a false prophet or impostor. He is ruler of God's eternal Kingdom.

Because Jesus was raised from the dead, we know that the Kingdom of Heaven has broken into earth's history. Our world is now headed for redemption, not disaster. God's mighty power is at work destroying sin, creating new lives, and preparing us for Christ's second coming.

Because Jesus arose just as he said he would, we can be confident that he will accomplish all that he has promised, including bringing us to heaven.

Because of Jesus' resurrection we can be certain of our own resurrection. Death has been conquered and is not the end. We will be raised from the dead to live forever with Christ.

Getting Personal

In what ways has the truth of the Resurrection bolstered your confidence?

How has it given you hope?

Why should the Resurrection be a reason for joy?

The apostle Paul knew the importance of the Resurrection. He wrote: "And if Christ has not been raised, then your faith is useless and you are still guilty of your sins. In that case, all who have died believing in Christ are lost! And if our hope in Christ is only for this life, we are more to be pitied than anyone in the world" (1 Corinthians 15:17-19, NLT).

Christ has been raised from the dead. Christianity is not a "religion," it is a relationship with a living Savior. The Resurrection enables us to live with confidence, hope, and joy!

READING THE WORD

✱ *Matthew 28:5-10, NLT*
Then the angel spoke to the women. "Don't be afraid!" he said. "I know you are looking for Jesus, who was crucified. 6He isn't here! He is risen from the dead, just as he said would happen. Come, see where his body was lying. 7And now, go quickly and tell his disciples that he has risen from the dead, and he is going ahead of you to Galilee. You will see him there. Remember what I have told you." 8The women ran quickly from the tomb. They were very frightened but also filled with great joy, and they rushed to give the disciples the angel's message. 9And as they went, Jesus met them and greeted them. And they ran to him, grasped his feet, and worshiped him. 10Then Jesus said to them, "Don't be afraid! Go tell my brothers to leave for Galilee, and they will see me there."

TALKING TO GOD

Thank God for the confidence you feel because of his faithfulness in keeping his word. Thank him for the hope you have for your future in him. Thank him for the joy you experience in relationship with him.

READING THE WORD

❈ *John 20:11-18, NLT*

Mary was standing outside the tomb crying, and as she wept, she stooped and looked in. 12She saw two white-robed angels, one sitting at the head and the other at the foot of the place where the body of Jesus had been lying. 13"Dear woman, why are you crying?" the angels asked her. "Because they have taken away my Lord," she replied, "and I don't know where they have put him." 14She turned to leave and saw someone standing there. It was Jesus, but she didn't recognize him. 15"Dear woman, why are you crying?" Jesus asked her. "Who are you looking for?" She thought he was the gardener. "Sir," she said, "if you have taken him away, tell me where you have put him, and I will go and get him." 16"Mary!" Jesus said. She turned to him and cried out, "Rabboni!" (which is Hebrew for "Teacher"). 17"Don't cling to me," Jesus said, "for I haven't yet ascended to the Father. But go find my brothers and tell them, 'I am ascending to my Father and your Father, to my God and your God.'" 18Mary Magdalene found the disciples and told them, "I have seen the Lord!" Then she gave them his message.

TALKING TO GOD

Take some time to remember what God has done for you personally in your life. Ask him to help you feel glad about sharing the truth about the Savior everywhere you can.

THE MISSION

Setting the Scene

The women mentioned in yesterday's Scripture portion had heard Jesus' predictions of his death, and suddenly their memories and the facts came together. Everything had occurred just as Jesus had predicted. The women rushed to the sorrowing disciples saying exactly what the angel had told them to say. The fact that the message was carried by women gives credibility and persuasive force to this account. No ancient person making up such a story would list women as the official witnesses. And by Jewish law, women could not give evidence.

John and Peter had run back to the tomb and Mary apparently returned with them. When the two disciples left, she was there alone, still crying. John reports that as she stooped to look into the tomb, she saw two angels. They asked Mary why she was crying. Mary answered, "Because they have taken away my Lord, and I don't know where they have put him."

As Mary turned to leave, she found Jesus standing there but didn't recognize him. Perhaps her eyes were so filled with tears that she could not see clearly.

Thinking this man must be the gardener, Mary asked if he knew the location of Jesus' body. Then Jesus simply spoke her name, "Mary," and she identified his voice immediately. Mary's instinctive response was to cling to Jesus—joyous in the reunion and fearful of losing him again. But Jesus stopped her and gave her a message to give to his "brothers," the disciples.

Getting Personal

What tends to keep you from spreading the news about this greatest event in history?

What can you do to stay focused on mission?

The women and then the disciples were assigned the mission of telling people that Jesus is alive. It's our mission as well. People who hear about the Resurrection for the first time may need time before they can comprehend this amazing story (after all, the disciples had trouble believing). But we need to share this truth with joy, accepting individuals' need to think through, to wonder, and to investigate the facts for themselves.

JESUS APPEARS TO THE DISCIPLES
Week 51, Day 1

✤ *Mark 16:12-13; Luke 24:13-43; John 20:19-29*

Jesus had been taken, tried, judged guilty, and crucified, and the disciples had scattered, confused, despairing, and fearing for their lives. But Jesus conquered death and arose. He lives! This week we'll focus on how Jesus reconnected with his beloved friends and followers, walking and breaking bread with them, reassuring them, and explaining what they should do next. We'll begin to grasp the implications of serving a living Savior.

QUESTIONING THE FACTS

Setting the Scene

This interaction of Jesus with two of his followers on the road occurred on the same day as the Resurrection. We know very little about these disciples except that one man's name was Cleopas and the other man also was not one of the eleven. As these men were walking the seven miles to Emmaus, "they were talking about everything that had happened." Cleopas and his friend may have taken part in the Triumphal Entry and may later have heard the crowds call for Jesus' death. Perhaps they had witnessed Jesus' final walk through Jerusalem and even his execution. They were discussing these events as they left the city and were returning home.

Jesus began walking with the two men, "but God kept them from recognizing him." Joining their intense conversation, Jesus asked what they had been discussing. At his question, they stopped, "sadness written across their faces," and responded. Apparently the two hadn't been able to understand what had just occurred in Jerusalem and were still upset about what they had seen and heard.

The men rehearsed the facts and expressed their feelings about the recent events, describing Jesus as a powerful "prophet" and "mighty teacher" (Luke 24:19) who had been condemned to death and crucified. They had hoped that Jesus was the Messiah, their Redeemer. As far as they knew, however, he had died like all the other prophets before him. So when Jesus died, they lost all hope. These men didn't understand that Jesus' death offered the greatest hope and redemption possible.

READING THE WORD

✤ *Luke 24:13-17, 19-24, NLT*
That same day two of Jesus' followers were walking to the village of Emmaus, seven miles from Jerusalem. 14As they walked along they were talking about everything that had happened. 15As they talked and discussed these things, Jesus himself suddenly came and began walking with them. 16But God kept them from recognizing him. 17He asked them, "What are you discussing so intently as you walk along?" They stopped short, sadness written across their faces. . . . 19"The things that happened to Jesus, the man from Nazareth," they said. . . . 20"Our leading priests and other religious leaders handed him over to be condemned to death, and they crucified him. 21We had hoped he was the Messiah who had come to rescue Israel. This all happened three days ago. 22Then some women from our group of his followers were at his tomb early this morning, and they came back with an amazing report. 23They said his body was missing, and they had seen angels who told them Jesus is alive! 24Some of our men ran out to see, and sure enough, his body was gone, just as the women had said."

TALKING TO GOD

As you pray today, shift your focus from the problems and conflicts that seem so pressing to considering who God is and what he has done for you and what he is doing for you.

Although they had heard an amazing report from some women about the tomb being empty and meeting angels there, which was confirmed by Peter and John, the two travelers left the city still believing their hopes in Jesus and his Kingdom had died with him.

Getting Personal

What makes reports of modern-day miracles so difficult to believe?

When have you heard someone tell of God's amazing work in his or her life? How did you feel about what that person said?

What would Jesus say to you today that would give you hope and life in your sadness?

These followers of Jesus, walking sadly toward their homes in Emmaus, had read the Prophets and had heard Jesus say that "on the third day he would be raised from the dead" (Matthew 16:21). Then, on that third day after the Crucifixion, they had heard the women tell of a missing body and the angels' message that Jesus was alive. Yet they walked in sadness, not believing the reports or bothering to find out if they were true.

Many believers respond like the two men on the way to Emmaus. We know the verses about God's power and have our theology straight about God's sovereignty. We may even have heard or read testimonies of God's amazing work in people's lives. Yet still we wonder if those reports are true, and we pray timidly. Then we are surprised when God answers. And when confronted with difficult circumstances, we quickly lose hope. Instead, we should remember that the God who raised Jesus wants to work in us and through us—and he walks with us.

BELIEVING THE WORD

Setting the Scene

Jesus called these two disciples "foolish" because they hadn't been able to believe what had been predicted in the Scriptures: that "the Messiah would have to suffer . . . before entering his glory." Evidently these men, like most of Jesus' followers, had been caught off guard by the Crucifixion and then probably had expected God to rescue Jesus from the cross. They hadn't expected the Messiah to suffer the way Jesus had.

So Jesus reintroduced these disciples to the teachings of Scripture about him, no doubt beginning with the promised offspring in Genesis (3:15) and going through the suffering Servant in Isaiah (chapter 53), the pierced one in Zechariah (12:10), the messenger of the covenant in Malachi (3:1), and other passages in between.

The Jewish religious leaders had spent their lives studying Scripture but had ignored or disregarded the idea of a suffering Servant. Jesus showed the men how the recent events in Jerusalem had fulfilled every prophecy regarding the Messiah. Jesus may have taken the two followers through Old Testament history, pointing out the problem of sin and how it would have to be solved through the sacrificial death of God's own Son.

Getting Personal

What biblical principle gleaned from a sermon, small group, class, or personal Bible study have you been recently trying to apply in your life?

What Bible promises or teachings do you have difficulty believing?

Jesus told the two men they were "foolish" for not believing what the Bible clearly teaches. Today we have an amazing array of Bible translations, study tools, commentaries, and devotionals. We certainly have no excuse for not reading, studying, and understanding Scripture. Our greater struggle is truly believing and applying what we read.

The two men leaving Jerusalem behind were so focused on their plight and what they perceived as catastrophic events that they failed to believe what they had read in Scripture—no wonder they couldn't believe the women's report of an empty tomb. What Scripture had predicted they had seen fulfilled, and they should have been eagerly expecting God's next move.

READING THE WORD

✸ *Luke 24:25-27, NLT*

Then Jesus said to them, "You foolish people! You find it so hard to believe all that the prophets wrote in the Scriptures. 26Wasn't it clearly predicted that the Messiah would have to suffer all these things before entering his glory?" 27Then Jesus took them through the writings of Moses and all the prophets, explaining from all the Scriptures the things concerning himself.

TALKING TO GOD

Actions speak louder than words, so ask your heavenly Father to help you live according to the truths you are learning from the example and teachings of Jesus. Ask him to help your belief in the value of his Word lead to a transformed life.

READING THE WORD

✤ *Luke 24:28-34, NLT*
By this time they were nearing Emmaus and the end of their journey. Jesus acted as if he were going on, 29but they begged him, "Stay the night with us, since it is getting late." So he went home with them. 30As they sat down to eat, he took the bread and blessed it. Then he broke it and gave it to them. 31Suddenly, their eyes were opened, and they recognized him. And at that moment he disappeared! 32They said to each other, "Didn't our hearts burn within us as he talked with us on the road and explained the Scriptures to us?" 33And within the hour they were on their way back to Jerusalem. There they found the eleven disciples and the others who had gathered with them, 34who said, "The Lord has really risen! He appeared to Peter."

TALKING TO GOD

Acknowledge that God is with you, as near as if he were walking beside you as he did with the men on the road to Emmaus. Ask the Lord to increase your awareness of his presence, so that you practice living with him and for him.

SEEING JESUS

Setting the Scene

The travelers were impressed with everything Jesus had been telling them. They wanted to talk with Jesus further, so they invited him to stay. They were also being hospitable because traveling after dark would have been dangerous. Jesus accepted their invitation and went home with them.

During the meal, Jesus blessed and broke the bread, a task usually done by the host. Immediately the men recognized Jesus. These two disciples had not been at the Last Supper, so that's not what sparked recognition. God opened their eyes at the exact time he wanted them to recognize Jesus. Then Jesus disappeared, leaving the two disciples to wonder at what they had just experienced. Jesus had walked *with* them and had walked them through the Scriptures. They understood and felt the truth. Their doubts had been dispelled and their hope rekindled.

Although evening had come, the men couldn't wait until morning to spread the news, so they hurried back to Jerusalem.

Getting Personal

What keeps us from seeing Jesus in our lives and in others?

If you knew Jesus was walking with you, how would your thoughts, words, and actions change?

How would that affect your relationships and your use of time and other resources?

After the two men realized the identity of the stranger who had walked with them, they reflected on the experience: "Didn't our hearts burn within us?" That's what happens when we encounter the Savior. Jesus promised never to abandon us (Hebrews 13:5), to be with us "always, even to the end of the age" (Matthew 28:20, NLT). We can see him in hurting people (see Matthew 25:34-40) and in Communion as the bread is broken and the bread and wine are blessed. We can see him in church, in other believers—"Christ's body" (Romans 12:5, NLT). And he lives in us through his Spirit.

EXPERIENCING PEACE

Setting the Scene

The disciples, still confused and afraid, were gathered "behind locked doors." They probably were discussing the reports of the women, Peter, and John, and Mary's claim that she had seen Jesus. More news arrived with the two men from Emmaus, who breathlessly told the rest of the group they had met Jesus on the road and had spent the day with him.

Luke wrote that this was when Jesus made his first appearance to his gathered disciples (although Thomas was missing from the group). Suddenly Jesus stood among them. His first words to his group of followers and disciples, all of whom had deserted him in his time of greatest need, were, "Peace be with you." This was a standard Hebrew greeting, but Jesus repeated it for emphasis and with profound meaning: Jesus' presence brought deep and lasting peace to their troubled hearts.

Getting Personal

At what times in life have you felt that your life was in chaos?

What recent events and concerns threaten to steal your peace of mind and heart?

Isaiah wrote, "You will keep in perfect peace all who trust in you, all whose thoughts are fixed on you!" (Isaiah 26:3, NLT). How can you access that peace today?

Imagine the chaos of Jerusalem during those recent days—Passover pilgrims, angry mob, soldiers, crucifixions, darkness at noon, earthquake, and disillusioned and terrified followers of Jesus, huddled in fear. But Jesus came and brought peace. Jesus had told his disciples, "I am leaving you with a gift—peace of mind and heart. And the peace I give is a gift the world cannot give. So don't be troubled or afraid" (John 14:27, NLT).

Through Jesus' death and resurrection, he brought peace with God. And through his presence by the Holy Spirit, he brings the peace of God—the confident assurance that all is well because he is in control and because he loves us and is with us (see Romans 8).

READING THE WORD

✵ *Luke 24:33-37, NLT*
And within the hour they were on their way back to Jerusalem. There they found the eleven disciples and the others who had gathered with them, 34who said, "The Lord has really risen! He appeared to Peter." 35Then the two from Emmaus told their story of how Jesus had appeared to them as they were walking along the road, and how they had recognized him as he was breaking the bread. 36And just as they were telling about it, Jesus himself was suddenly standing there among them. "Peace be with you," he said. 37But the whole group was startled and frightened, thinking they were seeing a ghost!

✵ *John 20:19-21, NLT*
That Sunday evening the disciples were meeting behind locked doors because they were afraid of the Jewish leaders. Suddenly, Jesus was standing there among them! "Peace be with you," he said. 20As he spoke, he showed them the wounds in his hands and his side. They were filled with joy when they saw the Lord! 21Again he said, "Peace be with you. As the Father has sent me, so I am sending you."

TALKING TO GOD

God has promised peace to those who fix their thoughts on him. Prayer focuses on the Lord and who he is. As you focus on him today, reaffirm your trust in him and ask for the blessing of his peace, which comes from being in his presence.

KNOWING THE TRUTH

READING THE WORD

✸ *Luke 24:38-43, NLT*
"Why are you frightened?" he asked. "Why are your hearts filled with doubt? 39Look at my hands. Look at my feet. You can see that it's really me. Touch me and make sure that I am not a ghost, because ghosts don't have bodies, as you see that I do." 40As he spoke, he showed them his hands and his feet. 41Still they stood there in disbelief, filled with joy and wonder. Then he asked them, "Do you have anything here to eat?" 42They gave him a piece of broiled fish, 43and he ate it as they watched.

TALKING TO GOD

Take some time to review the story of your own changed life, not just so that you are prepared to answer those who may ask you about it. Pray through the details of your transformed life, thanking God for his work in your life at every step and remembering the sacrifice of Jesus that made it all possible.

Setting the Scene

Jesus had risen physically from the dead. Suddenly he appeared in bodily form to the gathered disciples. At first they wondered what they were seeing: Was this a vision? An apparition? Jesus dispelled those notions and questions by inviting them to touch him. Jesus had a real, tangible body with flesh and bones, and his hands, feet, and side still bore the scars of the crucifixion. Then Jesus ate a piece of fish to show he was real and not a ghost or a figment of their imagination. We don't know the actual makeup of Jesus' body, though we do know he wasn't limited by locked doors or walls. But his actions established for the disciples—and for us—that he had a physical body.

The Resurrection was not a fable or wishful thinking; it was the truth, a historical fact—and now the disciples knew it. They had seen Jesus, alive.

Getting Personal

What makes the Resurrection so difficult for most people to believe?

The fact that Jesus rose from the dead became the central point of the disciples' preaching. Why is the Resurrection so important to Christianity?

How can the experience of these first-century Christ-followers and their strong witness give you confidence and hope?

The close followers of Jesus ran for their lives from the garden and then kept their distance from the trial and Crucifixion. Peter denied even knowing Jesus. Two of them walked sadly away from Jerusalem, hopeless of seeing Jesus again. Then this same group hid from the authorities in a locked room. But soon they would be boldly proclaiming the Good News about Jesus. What changed these confused and disillusioned men and women? The Resurrection! They saw Christ alive—they knew the truth—and their lives were forever changed. This is perhaps the greatest proof that Christ did, in fact, rise from the dead: the disciples' changed lives.

DISPELLING ALL DOUBTS

Setting the Scene

Thomas had missed the gathering, so he still had his doubts when the others told him about Jesus' appearance, stating unequivocally, "I won't believe it unless I see the nail wounds in his hands, put my fingers into them, and place my hand into the wound in his side." Thomas wanted proof.

We tend to remember this doubting episode in Thomas's life. But Thomas is the one who earlier had exclaimed, "Let's go, too—and die with Jesus" (John 11:16, NLT). Thomas was committed to Jesus, even if he tended to be pessimistic. And remember, some of the other disciples were also skeptical (Matthew 28:17). Part of Thomas's character was a tendency to put into words what everyone was feeling. The other disciples also only fully believed after they had seen the risen Christ in person.

Eight days later, Thomas was present when Jesus appeared. Turning directly to Thomas, Jesus told him to look, touch, and believe. Then, when *doubting* Thomas saw Jesus, he became *believing* Thomas, as he confessed his faith in Jesus.

Jesus didn't criticize Thomas for doubting but affirmed him for his confession of faith. Then Jesus left a message for all believers who would follow, including us: "Blessed are those who believe without seeing me."

Getting Personal

What doubts do you have about God, Jesus, and the Christian faith?

Where can you go to find answers to your questions?

What can you do to help others who express serious questions about Jesus and the Resurrection?

God wants us to be honest with him, to express our feelings, to confess our sins, and to ask our questions. When Thomas said he had doubts about Jesus being alive and would need proof, he was expressing what others in the group had thought. After all, they had heard the reports from the women and the travelers on the road to Emmaus but hadn't believed until they saw Jesus. Having doubts isn't a problem, but what we do with those doubts can be. When we have questions, we should be looking for answers. Then we should be as bold and open as Thomas in our confession of Jesus as Lord and God.

READING THE WORD

❋ *John 20:24-29, NLT*
One of the disciples, Thomas (nicknamed the Twin), was not with the others when Jesus came. 25They told him, "We have seen the Lord!" But he replied, "I won't believe it unless I see the nail wounds in his hands, put my fingers into them, and place my hand into the wound in his side." 26Eight days later the disciples were together again, and this time Thomas was with them. The doors were locked; but suddenly, as before, Jesus was standing among them. "Peace be with you," he said. 27Then he said to Thomas, "Put your finger here, and look at my hands. Put your hand into the wound in my side. Don't be faithless any longer. Believe!" 28"My Lord and my God!" Thomas exclaimed. 29Then Jesus told him, "You believe because you have seen me. Blessed are those who believe without seeing me."

TALKING TO GOD

Confess that at times you question God's presence or doubt aspects of the gospel message. Affirm your desire to trust in God fully, and ask him to lead you to the answers you need.

JESUS GIVES FINAL INSTRUCTIONS
Week 52, Day 1

❋ Matthew 28:16-20; Mark 16:15-18; Luke 24:44-49; John 21:1-25

The days following Jesus' resurrection must have been indescribable. We are not told much about how the disciples felt or what they thought. The four Gospels focus on what Jesus told his followers before he departed. Some of the same confusion his friends felt before his death now came back to haunt those who couldn't stop talking about his resurrection. If he had conquered death, why did he have to leave? Jesus let them know that the Resurrection had been a great gift of assurance for believers, but Jesus still needed to depart from this place so the Holy Spirit could do his job among believers and around the world.

READING THE WORD

❋ John 21:3-10, NKJV

Simon Peter said to them, "I am going fishing." They said to him, "We are going with you also." They went out and immediately got into the boat, and that night they caught nothing. 4But when the morning had now come, Jesus stood on the shore; yet the disciples did not know that it was Jesus. 5Then Jesus said to them, "Children, have you any food?" They answered Him, "No." 6And He said to them, "Cast the net on the right side of the boat, and you will find some." So they cast, and now they were not able to draw it in because of the multitude of fish. 7Therefore that disciple whom Jesus loved said to Peter, "It is the Lord!" Now when Simon Peter heard that it was the Lord, he put on his outer garment (for he had removed it), and plunged into the sea. 8But the other disciples came in the little boat (for they were not far from land, but about two hundred cubits), dragging the net with fish. 9Then, as soon as they had come to land, they saw a fire of coals there, and fish laid on it, and bread. 10Jesus said to them, "Bring some of the fish which you have just caught."

SHORE LUNCH

Setting the Scene

At the beginning of the book of Acts, Luke tells us that Jesus "presented himself to them and gave many convincing proofs that he was alive. He appeared to them over a period of forty days and spoke about the kingdom of God" (Acts 1:3, NIV). The disciples were in a daze of joy and confusion, still shaken by Jesus' death and the way his final hours had revealed how weak they were. They were also overwhelmed by the reality of his resurrection.

With Jesus intent on leaving, the disciples were somewhat at a loss about what to do. So some of them went back to what was familiar. Peter decided to go fishing. Six other disciples joined him. The results of the trip weren't much of an indication that Peter should resume his old career. After a night on the water the fishermen came up with nothing.

The setting may have reminded Peter of one of his first encounters with Jesus (Luke 5:1-11). The boats were hauled up on shore after a fruitless night of fishing, and Simon Peter and the others had been listening to Jesus teach as they cleaned their nets. Jesus had asked Simon if he could use his boat as a teaching platform and they pushed out a little from shore. After the teaching, Jesus suggested some fishing. Simon said, "Master, we've worked hard all night and haven't caught anything. But because you say so, I will let down the nets" (Luke 5:5, NIV). After a wasted night, what would another cast of the nets hurt? Their catch burdened their equipment and they had to call for help.

Now Peter was back on the same water, experiencing the same lack of success. He was about to call it quits when a voice called from shore to suggest tossing the nets over the right side of the boat. Peter must have found himself thinking again, "One more cast. What could it hurt?" Again, the net came alive with fish. All hands struggled to control the catch. At that point, John turned to Peter and said, "It's the Lord!" (John 21:7, NLT). Peter jumped overboard and rushed to the beach. Jesus was busy at the fire, arranging the bread and fish he already had there. The other six got the boat and the bulging net to shore.

Jesus broke the ice with a simple invitation, "Come and have breakfast" (John 21:12, NIV). Suddenly it was back to the routine of the last three years, Jesus passing out the bread and fish, and the men enjoying easy company around a simple meal.

John notes this was their third encounter with Jesus following the Resurrection. The disciples were tongue-tied, unsure what to say or ask. They were simply enjoying Jesus' presence. They were rediscovering what believers eventually must discover about the Lord—that Jesus longs for us to apply ourselves to him, giving ourselves attentively to him, seeking to know him more and more.

Getting Personal

Why do you think Peter's decision to go fishing was a good idea?

When in your life has Jesus provided an interruption that changed everything and brought results you never expected?

What have been your best moments of simple fellowship with Christ?

We don't know if Peter's original reason for going fishing was his intention to resume his work as a fisherman or whether he found it hard to wait in inactivity. By fishing, he stayed in motion and he wasn't being disobedient. Those are attitudes God loves to work with. Fishing is not a bad way to wait on the Lord.

TALKING TO GOD

Take a cue from this breakfast picnic and spend some simple time with the Savior. Try to come to him without a big agenda today, but with an openness to enjoying being in his presence and hoping to know him better.

RESTORATION

READING THE WORD

❉ *John 21:15-19, NIV*
When they had finished eating, Jesus said to Simon Peter, "Simon son of John, do you love me more than these?" "Yes, Lord," he said, "you know that I love you." Jesus said, "Feed my lambs." 16Again Jesus said, "Simon son of John, do you love me?" He answered, "Yes, Lord, you know that I love you." Jesus said, "Take care of my sheep." 17The third time he said to him, "Simon son of John, do you love me?" Peter was hurt because Jesus asked him the third time, "Do you love me?" He said, "Lord, you know all things; you know that I love you." Jesus said, "Feed my sheep. 18Very truly I tell you, when you were younger you dressed yourself and went where you wanted; but when you are old you will stretch out your hands, and someone else will dress you and lead you where you do not want to go." 19Jesus said this to indicate the kind of death by which Peter would glorify God. Then he said to him, "Follow me!"

TALKING TO GOD

Don't hold back from coming to the Lord, even if you feel burdened by regrets or remorse. Bring all your weaknesses and failures to Jesus, the Great Restorer. Ask him to redeem your wrong choices and help you to walk with him.

Setting the Scene

It's helpful to pause and imagine John as an old man recording these memories after a lifetime of experiences. By the time he wrote about these events, Peter and the other disciples were probably all dead. John knew he had to include this crucial moment in the life of the brash disciple who had been so confident during the Last Supper that nothing could keep him from being faithful to Christ. Then he had discovered that a little servant girl's question was enough to cause him to deny Christ.

So on this morning, Jesus pulled Peter aside for a probing question posed three times: "Simon son of John, do you love me?" Simon had denied Jesus three times; the Lord gave him three opportunities to declare his love. Peter's answers were not the boisterous affirmations he might have voiced earlier. There was a painful humility in the fisherman's responses: "Yes, Lord, you know that I love you." By the third time, Peter was wondering what was up. John suggests he was hurt by the repetitions. His third answer was a slightly revised version of the previous ones: "Lord, you know all things; you know that I love you." Peter was helplessly saying, "Look, I'm only trying to tell you what you already know, Lord."

Each time, Jesus told Peter, "Feed my sheep." He was restoring the disciple's role as someone who could serve him. He was assuring Peter he had work to do with others.

Getting Personal

How would you answer Jesus' question, "Do you love me?" Why?

If Jesus said to you, "Feed my sheep," what relationships and responsibilities might he be directing?

If you have been avoiding restoration in relationship with Jesus because of pain or shame, what keeps you from coming to him right now?

Despite Peter's shocking failure, Jesus wasn't done with him. Peter becomes our prime example of how grace overcomes failure and sin. It's not the gravity of the sin that matters but the willingness of a sinner to be restored by the only one who can restore him, Jesus.

KEEPING ON

Setting the Scene

No sooner was Peter on his feet faith-wise than he was back to his impulsive ways. John was following the two and must have been a little surprised when Peter pointed toward him and asked Jesus, "What about him?" Peter may simply have wanted to include John in the conversation, but it's likely he was practicing the time-honored tactic of shifting weight. *Lord, I'm feeling a lot of responsibility right now with the "Feed my sheep" command. So what's John going to have to do?*

Jesus basically told Peter that his plans for John were none of Peter's business. The underlying point is that we get distracted from our purpose when we compare others' assignments with ours. Our task is not to figure out what God wants others to do, but to be sure we are doing what he wants us to do.

Next, Jesus echoed one of the very first statements he ever said to Peter: "Follow me." This is an unchanging word from Jesus to each of us: Follow me. It takes belief and gives it the action of trust. Jesus isn't looking for a nod of agreement from us; he's looking for a life of obedience and learning. If we're not following, we may not be trusting either.

John must have chuckled as he noted that a rumor had spread because of Jesus' words that he would be alive at Christ's return, which John gently deflected. John would have been quick to make the same point Peter had needed to hear: "Follow Jesus!"

Getting Personal

What is the evidence from your life that you are following Jesus?

Why should you keep your relationship with Jesus current rather than think of it as a decision made sometime in the past?

If Jesus were to come back today, what things about your life would he find pleasing?

We are not to waste our time comparing what God has called us to do with what God has called others to do. Our task is simple: Follow.

READING THE WORD

✱ *John 21:20-25, NIV*

Peter turned and saw that the disciple whom Jesus loved was following them. (This was the one who had leaned back against Jesus at the supper and had said, "Lord, who is going to betray you?") 21When Peter saw him, he asked, "Lord, what about him?" 22Jesus answered, "If I want him to remain alive until I return, what is that to you? You must follow me." 23Because of this, the rumor spread among the believers that this disciple would not die. But Jesus did not say that he would not die; he only said, "If I want him to remain alive until I return, what is that to you?" 24This is the disciple who testifies to these things and who wrote them down. We know that his testimony is true. 25Jesus did many other things as well. If every one of them were written down, I suppose that even the whole world would not have room for the books that would be written.

TALKING TO GOD

Explore Christ's command, "Follow me," today. Ask the Lord to make you aware of next steps that you should be taking. Affirm your willingness to submit to God's leadership.

TO THE ENDS OF THE EARTH

❧ *Matthew 28:16-20, NIV*
Then the eleven disciples went to Galilee, to the mountain where Jesus had told them to go. 17When they saw him, they worshiped him; but some doubted. 18Then Jesus came to them and said, "All authority in heaven and on earth has been given to me. 19Therefore go and make disciples of all nations, baptizing them in the name of the Father and of the Son and of the Holy Spirit, 20and teaching them to obey everything I have commanded you. And surely I am with you always, to the very end of the age."

❧ *Mark 16:15-18, NIV*
He said to them, "Go into all the world and preach the gospel to all creation. 16Whoever believes and is baptized will be saved, but whoever does not believe will be condemned. 17And these signs will accompany those who believe: In my name they will drive out demons; they will speak in new tongues; 18they will pick up snakes with their hands; and when they drink deadly poison, it will not hurt them at all; they will place their hands on sick people, and they will get well."

TALKING TO GOD

Consider how the truth about Christ's resurrection and the good news of salvation have traveled through so many generations to reach your own. Thank God for the priceless gift of these precious truths, and ask him to make you a generous steward of the Good News.

Setting the Scene

Forty days after the Resurrection, Jesus called a meeting in Galilee. The time had come to leave, as he had told his disciples repeatedly. He would still be with them, but not in the same way he had been for the last three years.

Matthew wrote, "Some doubted." All of us struggle with doubt sometimes. The struggles of the early disciples reach across the centuries and provoke us to pay attention. Our assumption that given the same undeniable proofs of Jesus' resurrection and identity we would be unflinchingly faithful is wishful thinking. God doesn't ever have to do more to prove himself to us.

Jesus stated his supreme authority and then exercised that authority by telling his disciples to spread the gospel to the ends of the earth. They were to reproduce themselves—disciples making disciples, who in turn make more disciples. The target audience, "all nations," confirms God's eternal purpose is reaching the world with a message for all people (Genesis 12:3; Luke 2:10). In both Matthew's and Mark's accounts, baptism is the symbolic aspect of discipleship while belief and obedience are the required signs of authentic discipleship.

Because of his previous promise of the Holy Spirit, Jesus could say, "I am with you always, to the very end of the age." That presence of Jesus is what still marks the lives of authentic believers today.

Getting Personal

In what ways are you taking Jesus' commission seriously?

Who made you a disciple, and how have you passed on the gift to others?

Why is Jesus' promise of his continual presence important to you?

Jesus' final command was not for a chosen few designated to be missionaries, but for all those who claim to follow Jesus. The point of Jesus' promise to be with us is not primarily for personal well-being and companionship but to accomplish the ongoing purpose to evangelize and disciple the world.

EMPOWERED

Setting the Scene

What Jesus did for two disciples on the road to Emmaus, he did again for the disciples gathered in Jerusalem. He assured them they could count on his teaching to come true. He showed them how all that God had already revealed in his Word had been fulfilled or would be fulfilled in him. Then he "opened their understanding, that they might comprehend the Scriptures." He made it possible for them to see for themselves what had always been there in God's Word but was hidden by distortion or unbelief. What Jesus did for his disciples he continues to do today. Our need to comprehend the Scriptures is the same as theirs. Much of the authority of the New Testament writings can be traced to understanding the Old Covenant Jesus gave his disciples in preparation for recording the New Covenant. The new understanding will not only help us recognize Jesus throughout Scripture, but also remind us of God's offer of salvation to the world: "Repentance and remission of sins should be preached in His name to all nations."

Jesus confirmed his promise of indwelling power that would soon arrive and become the energizing life of his church—the Holy Spirit. The task of spreading the gospel to all the nations would begin in Jerusalem, so he commanded them to stay there until they were "endued with power from on high." They waited attentively and were empowered. Today, all who ask the Holy Spirit to empower them find that same outpouring.

Getting Personal

To what degree would you say your life is steeped in God's Word?

As you have experienced these applied devotions on the life of Jesus, how has your view of God's Word been affected?

How are you experiencing the Holy Spirit's power in your life?

What Jesus described and promised for the disciples was not any easier for them to accept or understand than it is for us today. The challenge of genuine discipleship continues to be as real, dangerous, and thrilling as it has ever been.

READING THE WORD

✤ *Luke 24:44-49, NKJV*
Then He said to them, "These are the words which I spoke to you while I was still with you, that all things must be fulfilled which were written in the Law of Moses and the Prophets and the Psalms concerning Me." 45And He opened their understanding, that they might comprehend the Scriptures. 46Then He said to them, "Thus it is written, and thus it was necessary for the Christ to suffer and to rise from the dead the third day, 47and that repentance and remission of sins should be preached in His name to all nations, beginning at Jerusalem. 48And you are witnesses of these things. 49Behold, I send the Promise of My Father upon you; but tarry in the city of Jerusalem until you are endued with power from on high."

TALKING TO GOD

Come to the Lord with a spirit of expectation, looking attentively for the Spirit to provide direction and empowering. Be ready to set aside your preconceived ideas about what your obedience might look like, in order to receive whatever guidance the Lord has for you today.

UNTIL LATER

READING THE WORD

❁ *Mark 16:19-20, NIV*
After the Lord Jesus had spoken to them, he was taken up into heaven and he sat at the right hand of God. 20Then the disciples went out and preached everywhere, and the Lord worked with them and confirmed his word by the signs that accompanied it.

❁ *Luke 24:50-53, NIV*
When he had led them out to the vicinity of Bethany, he lifted up his hands and blessed them. 51While he was blessing them, he left them and was taken up into heaven. 52Then they worshiped him and returned to Jerusalem with great joy. 53And they stayed continually at the temple, praising God.

TALKING TO GOD

Adapt one of the apostle Paul's prayers, that "Christ will make his home in your heart as you trust in him; that your roots would grow down into God's love and keep you strong; and that you may have the power to understand, as all God's people should, how wide, how long, how high, and how deep his love is; that you may experience the love of Christ, though it is too great to understand fully; and that you will be made complete with all the fullness of life and power that comes from God" (see Ephesians 3:17-19, NLT).

Setting the Scene

The final glimpse of Jesus was yet another surprise in a long line of startling developments for his disciples. During the previous forty days Jesus had been appearing and disappearing unexpectedly, so this departure was markedly different. Both Mark and Luke report that he was "taken up." He didn't disappear; he went away, leaving the distinct impression that what he said about returning might happen at any time. In the book of Acts, when Luke continued his account of what happened next, he added: "They were looking intently up into the sky as he was going, when suddenly two men dressed in white stood beside them. 'Men of Galilee,' they said, 'why do you stand here looking into the sky? This same Jesus, who has been taken from you into heaven, will come back in the same way you have seen him go into heaven'" (Acts 1:10-11, NIV).

Clearly, the spreading of the gospel to the nations was not going to happen by disciples stuck on the Mount of Olives looking up to the sky. Luke's closing note is that they returned to Jerusalem with great joy. The power was coming, but the message was already planted. They would soon set the world on fire with the unstoppable Good News that any life can be eternally altered by the forgiving power of God, to the glory of God.

Getting Personal

In what ways do other people recognize your joy? How does the joy of the Lord affect your daily life?

How often would you say you delight in anticipating Christ's return? What does that privilege mean to you?

Just as his first disciples, fresh from the scene of Jesus' ascension, anticipated Christ's return, we live today in similar anticipation. The believer knows that none of us has to live longer than a lifetime to see Jesus. We will leave through death to meet him, or he will come for us. Either way, our task is to live with joy, letting others know why it is that we can't stop praising God.

TOPICAL INDEX

ABIDING IN CHRIST
Week 42, Day 1
Week 42, Day 2
Week 42, Day 3
Week 42, Day 4
Week 42, Day 5

ACCOUNTABILITY
Week 15, Day 2

ADULTERY
Week 10, Weekend

ANGER
Week 35, Day 1

ANOINTING
Week 33, Day 1
Week 33, Day 3

ATONEMENT
Week 47, Weekend

ATTENTION
Week 20, Day 2

BAPTISM
Week 24, Day 4

BEATITUDES
Week 10, Day 1
Week 10, Day 2

BELIEF
Week 3, Day 2
Week 6, Day 2
Week 50, Day 3
Week 50, Weekend
Week 51, Day 1
Week 51, Day 2

BELONGING
Week 1, Day 4

BETRAYAL
Week 38, Day 3
Week 38, Day 4
Week 38, Weekend
Week 39, Day 3
Week 39, Day 4
Week 45, Day 2

BLASPHEMY
Week 12, Day 5

BLESSING
Week 15, Day 2

BLINDNESS
Week 31, Day 1

BORN AGAIN
Week 6, Day 3

BURIAL
Week 49, Day 5
Week 49, Weekend

CARING FOR OTHERS
Week 8, Day 5

CELEBRATION
Week 27, Weekend

CHANGE
Week 35, Day 2

CHANGED LIVES
Week 51, Day 5

CHILDREN
Week 21, Day 2

CHRISTLIKENESS
Week 20, Day 3

CHRIST'S AMBASSADORS
Week 43, Day 3

CHRIST'S AUTHORITY
Week 36, Day 1

THE CHURCH
Week 12, Day 1
Week 12, Day 2
Week 18, Weekend
Week 33, Day 2
Week 35, Day 3
Week 35, Day 5

CLEANSING
Week 4, Day 4

COMMITMENT
Week 4, Weekend
Week 22, Day 1

COMMUNION
Week 39, Weekend

COMMUNITY
Week 10, Day 3
Week 15, Day 2

COMPARISON
Week 30, Day 5

COMPASSION
Week 9, Day 4
Week 16, Day 1
Week 23, Day 3
Week 23, Day 4
Week 23, Weekend
Week 26, Day 2
Week 27, Day 4
Week 29, Day 3
Week 34, Day 4

CONFESSION
Week 47, Day 5

CONVERSION
Week 32, Day 4
Week 48, Day 5

CONVICTION
Week 42, Day 4

CORNERSTONE
Week 36, Day 4

CORRECTION
Week 21, Day 5

COST
Week 10, Day 2
Week 15, Weekend
Week 19, Day 1
Week 19, Day 4
Week 22, Day 1
Week 22, Day 2
Week 23, Day 5

COVENANT
Week 39, Day 5

COVER-UP
Week 50, Day 4

CREATION
Week 1, Day 1

CRITICISM
Week 17, Day 1

THE CROSS
Week 19, Day 5
Week 48, Day 1
Week 48, Day 2
Week 48, Day 3
Week 48, Day 4
Week 48, Day 5
Week 48, Weekend
Week 49, Day 3

CRUCIFIXION
Week 49, Day 1

CURIOSITY
Week 32, Day 2

DANGER
Week 14, Day 2

DEATH
Week 15, Weekend
Week 19, Day 2

DEATH OF JESUS
Week 49, Day 2

DECISION
Week 36, Day 4

DEITY OF CHRIST
Week 1, Day 1
Week 18, Day 2
Week 25, Day 5
Week 25, Weekend
Week 41, Day 3
Week 45, Day 1

DEMONS
Week 8, Day 1
Week 8, Day 2
Week 12, Day 3
Week 12, Day 4

DENIAL
Week 39, Day 3
Week 40, Day 5
Week 40, Weekend
Week 46, Day 1
Week 46, Day 2
Week 46, Day 4

DESIRE
Week 5, Day 3

DISCIPLESHIP
Week 15, Day 1
Week 17, Day 5
Week 19, Day 1

Week 19, Day 4
Week 19, Day 5
Week 19, Weekend
Week 20, Day 3
Week 20, Day 4
Week 22, Day 1
Week 22, Day 2
Week 22, Day 3
Week 22, Day 4
Week 22, Day 5
Week 22, Weekend
Week 25, Day 3
Week 40, Day 4
Week 42, Day 2
Week 43, Day 2
Week 44, Day 1
Week 46, Day 3
Week 52, Day 3

DIVERSITY
Week 12, Day 1
Week 12, Day 2
Week 13, Weekend

DIVISION
Week 24, Day 4
Week 24, Day 5

DIVORCE
Week 10, Weekend

DOUBT
Week 23, Day 1
Week 42, Weekend
Week 51, Weekend

ECUMENISM
Week 43, Weekend

EMOTIONS
Week 28, Day 4

ENCOURAGEMENT
Week 41, Day 1

END TIMES
Week 37, Day 2
Week 37, Weekend
Week 24, Day 1
Week 24, Day 2
Week 24, Day 3
Week 37, Day 3
Week 37, Day 4
Week 37, Day 5

ETERNAL LIFE
Week 1, Weekend
Week 6, Day 5
Week 23, Day 1
Week 29, Day 1
Week 29, Day 4
Week 29, Weekend

EVIDENCE
Week 25, Weekend

EVIL
Week 3, Day 5

EXPECTATIONS
Week 28, Day 1

FAILURE
Week 14, Weekend
Week 46, Weekend

FAITH
Week 3, Day 2
Week 3, Weekend
Week 6, Weekend
Week 8, Day 1
Week 12, Day 4
Week 14, Day 4
Week 14, Day 5
Week 15, Day 1
Week 16, Day 2
Week 20, Day 4
Week 28, Day 2
Week 28, Day 3
Week 31, Day 3
Week 31, Day 4
Week 31, Day 5
Week 42, Weekend
Week 51, Weekend

FAITHFULNESS
Week 37, Weekend

FALSE TEACHERS
Week 25, Day 2
Week 25, Day 4
Week 37, Day 3

FAMILY
Week 12, Day 2

FASTING
Week 5, Day 2

FEAR
Week 14, Day 2
Week 14, Day 3
Week 14, Day 4
Week 14, Day 5
Week 14, Weekend
Week 15, Day 4
Week 45, Weekend

FEEDING OF THE FIVE THOUSAND
Week 16, Day 5

FELLOWSHIP
Week 1, Day 3
Week 33, Day 2

FOCUS
Week 4, Day 2

FOLLOWING JESUS
Week 15, Weekend
Week 52, Day 3

FOOT WASHING
Week 40, Day 2

FORGIVENESS
Week 8, Weekend
Week 11, Day 5
Week 12, Day 5
Week 21, Day 5
Week 21, Weekend
Week 40, Weekend
Week 46, Day 5
Week 47, Day 5
Week 48, Day 3
Week 52, Day 2

FRIENDSHIP
Week 45, Day 2

FRUIT
Week 13, Day 1
Week 13, Day 4

FRUIT OF THE SPIRIT
Week 12, Weekend
Week 42, Day 1

FUTURE
Week 2, Day 1
Week 2, Day 3
Week 3, Day 1
Week 19, Day 1
Week 24, Day 1
Week 38, Day 1
Week 45, Day 5

GENEROSITY
Week 23, Day 3
Week 23, Day 5
Week 26, Day 4
Week 30, Weekend

GENTILES
Week 49, Day 3

GIVING
Week 16, Day 3

GOD WITH US
Week 2, Day 3

GOD'S CARE
Week 15, Day 5

GOD'S FAMILY
Week 1, Day 4

GOD'S GLORY
Week 28, Day 1

Week 28, Day 2
Week 28, Day 5
Week 43, Day 1

GOD'S JUDGMENT
Week 24, Weekend

GOD'S LOVE
Week 6, Day 5
Week 27, Day 2
Week 27, Day 4

GOD'S PLANS
Week 39, Day 4

GOD'S PRESENCE
Week 14, Day 1
Week 18, Day 1
Week 19, Day 3
Week 51, Day 3

GOD'S SOVEREIGNTY
Week 48, Day 4

GOD'S WILL
Week 1, Day 2
Week 2, Day 4
Week 3, Day 1
Week 4, Day 1
Week 12, Day 2
Week 38, Day 2
Week 44, Day 2
Week 44, Day 4
Week 46, Weekend

GOD'S WORD
Week 34, Weekend
Week 52, Day 5

GOOD NEWS
Week 52, Day 4

GOOD SAMARITAN
Week 23, Day 4
Week 23, Day 5

GOOD SHEPHERD
Week 25, Day 4
Week 25, Day 5

GRACE
Week 9, Day 1
Week 9, Day 2
Week 9, Day 3
Week 9, Day 4
Week 9, Day 5
Week 9, Weekend
Week 18, Day 5
Week 29, Day 1
Week 29, Day 5
Week 30, Day 1
Week 30, Day 4

Week 49, Day 4
Week 52, Day 2

GREAT COMMISSION
Week 52, Day 4
Week 52, Day 5

GREATNESS
Week 21, Day 1

GREED
Week 33, Day 4

GRIEF
Week 28, Day 4

GROWTH
Week 13, Day 3
Week 13, Day 5

GUIDANCE
Week 2, Day 2
Week 16, Day 4
Week 20, Day 2

HABITS
Week 8, Day 4

HARVEST
Week 13, Day 3
Week 13, Day 4
Week 30, Day 3

HEALING
Week 8, Day 1
Week 8, Day 3
Week 8, Day 5
Week 8, Weekend
Week 9, Day 5
Week 12, Day 3
Week 12, Day 4
Week 16, Day 1
Week 31, Day 1
Week 31, Day 2
Week 31, Day 3
Week 31, Day 4
Week 31, Day 5
Week 31, Weekend

HEART
Week 17, Day 5
Week 17, Weekend

HEAVEN
Week 26, Day 5
Week 26, Weekend
Week 30, Day 5
Week 41, Day 1

HERITAGE
Week 20, Day 4
Week 43, Day 5

HOLINESS
Week 11, Day 3
Week 43, Day 4

HOLY SPIRIT
Week 12, Day 5
Week 12, Weekend
Week 18, Day 5
Week 34, Weekend
Week 41, Day 5
Week 41, Weekend
Week 42, Day 4

HOLY WEEK
Week 47, Day 1

HONESTY WITH GOD
Week 7, Day 3
Week 7, Day 4

HONORING CHRIST
Week 1, Day 4

HOSPITALITY
Week 8, Day 3
Week 26, Day 1
Week 26, Day 4

HUMILITY
Week 2, Day 5
Week 10, Day 5
Week 11, Day 1
Week 21, Day 2
Week 26, Day 3
Week 26, Day 5
Week 31, Day 2
Week 45, Day 3

HYPOCRISY
Week 11, Day 1
Week 17, Day 2
Week 17, Day 4
Week 36, Day 5

IDENTITY OF CHRIST
Week 16, Weekend
Week 18, Day 3
Week 18, Day 4

IDOLS
Week 29, Day 2

INCARNATION
Week 1, Day 2

INTEGRITY
Week 10, Weekend

INVITATION
Week 26, Weekend
Week 32, Day 3

ISOLATION
Week 10, Day 3

JOURNEY
Week 19, Weekend

JOY
Week 4, Day 5
Week 52, Weekend

JUDGING
Week 17, Day 1
Week 27, Day 5

JUDGMENT
Week 47, Day 1

JUSTICE
Week 30, Weekend
Week 36, Day 3

KING
Week 47, Day 3

KINGDOM OF GOD
Week 13, Day 1
Week 13, Day 3
Week 13, Day 4
Week 13, Day 5
Week 13, Weekend
Week 21, Day 1
Week 21, Day 2
Week 24, Weekend
Week 29, Weekend

KNOWLEDGE
Week 32, Day 2

LAMB OF GOD
Week 38, Day 1

LAST SUPPER
Week 39, Weekend

LAW
Week 10, Day 4
Week 17, Day 3

LEADERSHIP
Week 17, Day 4
Week 18, Weekend
Week 20, Day 1

LEARNING
Week 6, Day 4
Week 14, Weekend

LEGALISM
Week 9, Day 1
Week 9, Day 2
Week 9, Day 3
Week 9, Day 4
Week 9, Day 5
Week 9, Weekend

LORD'S DAY
Week 35, Day 4

LORDSHIP
Week 22, Day 4

LOST AND FOUND
Week 32, Day 5

LOVE
Week 4, Day 5
Week 40, Day 4

LOVE FOR ENEMIES
Week 10, Weekend

LOVE ONE ANOTHER
Week 40, Day 1

LOYALTY
Week 38, Weekend
Week 46, Day 1
Week 46, Day 2
Week 46, Day 4

MERCY
Week 9, Day 1
Week 9, Day 2
Week 9, Day 3
Week 9, Day 4
Week 9, Day 5
Week 9, Weekend
Week 17, Day 3
Week 27, Day 4
Week 31, Day 1

MESSIAH
Week 18, Day 3
Week 18, Day 4
Week 18, Day 5
Week 28, Day 3

MIRACLES
Week 14, Day 1
Week 14, Day 2
Week 14, Day 3
Week 14, Day 4
Week 14, Day 5
Week 14, Weekend
Week 16, Day 5
Week 31, Weekend
Week 47, Day 2
Week 51, Day 1

MISSION
Week 15, Day 1
Week 15, Day 2
Week 15, Day 3
Week 43, Day 4
Week 50, Weekend

MUSTARD SEED
Week 13, Day 5

NATIVITY
Week 2, Day 1
Week 2, Day 4

NEEDS
Week 11, Day 2
Week 16, Weekend
Week 23, Day 4

NEIGHBOR
Week 23, Day 2
Week 23, Day 5
Week 23, Weekend

NEW LIFE
Week 6, Day 3
Week 6, Day 4
Week 28, Day 5

OBEDIENCE
Week 1, Day 1
Week 1, Day 5
Week 2, Day 2
Week 3, Day 4
Week 4, Day 1
Week 4, Day 3
Week 10, Day 4
Week 16, Day 4
Week 17, Day 3
Week 20, Day 2
Week 20, Weekend
Week 22, Weekend
Week 23, Day 2
Week 33, Day 1
Week 36, Day 2
Week 36, Weekend
Week 39, Day 1
Week 41, Day 4
Week 44, Day 2
Week 51, Day 2

OPPOSITION
Week 9, Weekend
Week 24, Day 4

PASSION
Week 10, Day 5

PASSOVER
Week 34, Day 2
Week 38, Day 1

PATH
Week 25, Day 3

PEACE
Week 24, Day 5
Week 51, Day 4

PEACEMAKING
Week 10, Day 1
Week 21, Weekend

PERSECUTION
Week 10, Day 1
Week 15, Day 3
Week 15, Day 4
Week 19, Day 5
Week 29, Weekend
Week 33, Weekend
Week 37, Day 2
Week 37, Day 4
Week 45, Day 3
Week 47, Day 4

PERSEVERANCE
Week 4, Weekend

PERSONAL TESTIMONY
Week 7, Day 5

PERSPECTIVE
Week 7, Weekend

PLAN OF SALVATION
Week 28, Weekend

PLANS
Week 2, Day 1
Week 2, Day 4

POSSESSIONS
Week 16, Day 3
Week 16, Day 5
Week 29, Day 2
Week 29, Day 3
Week 29, Day 4
Week 32, Day 1
Week 34, Day 1

POWER
Week 50, Day 2

PRAISE
Week 3, Day 2
Week 31, Weekend
Week 34, Day 2
Week 34, Day 3

PRAYER
Week 8, Day 4
Week 11, Day 1
Week 11, Day 2
Week 11, Day 3
Week 11, Day 4
Week 11, Day 5
Week 11, Weekend
Week 12, Day 5
Week 41, Day 4
Week 42, Day 5
Week 43, Day 1
Week 44, Day 1
Week 44, Day 2
Week 44, Day 3

Week 44, Day 4
Week 44, Day 5
Week 44, Weekend
Week 47, Day 2
Week 49, Day 2

PREJUDICE
Week 7, Day 1
Week 35, Day 5

PRESSURE
Week 47, Day 4

PRETENSE
Week 33, Day 4

PRIDE
Week 5, Day 4

PRIORITIES
Week 8, Day 4
Week 22, Day 3
Week 22, Day 5
Week 29, Day 2
Week 36, Weekend

PROBLEMS
Week 14, Day 5

PRODIGAL SON
Week 27, Day 3
Week 27, Day 4
Week 27, Day 5
Week 27, Weekend

PROMISE
Week 39, Day 5

PROPHECY
Week 28, Weekend
Week 34, Day 3
Week 35, Weekend
Week 37, Day 1
Week 49, Day 4

PROTECTION
Week 43, Day 3

PROVISION
Week 11, Day 4

PUBLIC CONFESSION
Week 32, Weekend

PURPOSE
Week 19, Day 3

QUESTIONS
Week 6, Day 1

QUIET TIME
Week 39, Day 2

RATIONALIZATION
Week 23, Day 2

REACTIONS/RESPONSES
Week 2, Day 2
Week 9, Weekend

REBUKE
Week 21, Day 5

RELATIONSHIP WITH GOD
Week 39, Day 2

RELIGION
Week 50, Day 5

REMORSE
Week 38, Day 5

REPENTANCE
Week 4, Day 3
Week 4, Day 4
Week 35, Day 2
Week 38, Day 5
Week 46, Day 5

RESOURCES
Week 16, Day 3
Week 16, Day 5

RESPONSE
Week 18, Day 4

RESPONSIBILITIES
Week 22, Day 3

RESTORATION
Week 21, Day 5
Week 32, Day 5
Week 52, Day 2

RESURRECTION
Week 19, Day 2
Week 28, Day 3
Week 28, Day 5
Week 49, Weekend
Week 50, Day 1
Week 50, Day 2
Week 50, Day 3
Week 50, Day 4
Week 50, Day 5
Week 51, Day 3
Week 51, Day 5

REVENGE
Week 45, Day 4

REVERENCE
Week 11, Day 3

REWARD
Week 10, Day 2
Week 29, Weekend

RIGHTEOUSNESS
Week 10, Day 4

RULES
Week 26, Day 2

SABBATH
Week 9, Day 1
Week 9, Day 2
Week 9, Day 3
Week 9, Day 4
Week 9, Day 5
Week 9, Weekend
Week 26, Day 2

SACRIFICE
Week 17, Day 3
Week 29, Weekend
Week 32, Day 4
Week 33, Day 3

SALT
Week 10, Day 3

SALVATION
Week 1, Day 1
Week 1, Day 3
Week 2, Day 5
Week 2, Weekend
Week 3, Weekend
Week 6, Day 5
Week 27, Day 1
Week 27, Day 3
Week 28, Weekend
Week 29, Day 5
Week 29, Weekend
Week 30, Day 3
Week 30, Day 4
Week 30, Day 5
Week 30, Weekend
Week 33, Day 5
Week 36, Day 2
Week 41, Day 2
Week 49, Weekend

SATAN
Week 5, Day 1
Week 5, Day 2
Week 5, Day 3
Week 5, Day 4
Week 5, Day 5
Week 5, Weekend
Week 8, Day 2

SAVIOR
Week 48, Day 2

SCRIPTURE
Week 5, Day 5
Week 13, Day 1
Week 35, Weekend

SEA OF GALILEE
Week 14, Day 1

SECOND COMING
Week 24, Day 1
Week 24, Day 2
Week 24, Day 3
Week 37, Day 1
Week 37, Day 5
Week 52, Weekend

SECURITY
Week 32, Day 1

SEEKING
Week 3, Day 3

SELF-CENTEREDNESS
Week 4, Day 2

SELF-DENIAL
Week 19, Weekend

SELF-RIGHTEOUSNESS
Week 27, Day 5

SEPARATION FROM GOD
Week 49, Day 1

SERVANT LEADERSHIP
Week 21, Day 1
Week 40, Day 2

SERVICE
Week 21, Day 3
Week 23, Day 3
Week 23, Weekend
Week 24, Day 3
Week 40, Day 1
Week 40, Day 3

SHARING THE GOSPEL
Week 24, Weekend

SHEPHERD
Week 25, Day 1
Week 25, Day 3

SIN
Week 3, Day 5
Week 10, Day 5
Week 17, Weekend
Week 21, Day 4
Week 27, Day 1
Week 38, Day 4

SINCERITY
Week 11, Day 2
Week 36, Day 5

SINNERS
Week 32, Day 3

SON OF MAN
Week 18, Day 1
Week 18, Day 2
Week 22, Day 2

SPIRITUAL DARKNESS
Week 12, Day 3

SPIRITUAL GROWTH
Week 8, Day 4

SPIRITUAL LETHARGY
Week 44, Day 5

SPIRITUAL THIRST
Week 7, Day 2

SPIRITUAL WARFARE
Week 8, Day 2
Week 38, Day 3

STATIONS OF THE CROSS
Week 48, Day 1

STEREOTYPES
Week 6, Day 1

STEWARDSHIP
Week 34, Day 1
Week 36, Day 3

SUBMISSION
Week 1, Day 2
Week 3, Day 3
Week 4, Day 3
Week 7, Day 4
Week 11, Day 4
Week 39, Day 1

SUBSTITUTION
Week 47, Weekend

SUFFERING
Week 19, Day 2
Week 19, Day 3
Week 28, Day 1
Week 44, Weekend

TALENTS
Week 16, Day 5

TEMPLE
Week 34, Day 5
Week 35, Day 1
Week 35, Day 3

TEMPTATION
Week 5, Day 1
Week 5, Day 2
Week 5, Day 3
Week 5, Day 4
Week 5, Day 5
Week 5, Weekend
Week 11, Weekend
Week 21, Day 4
Week 44, Day 3

TESTIMONY
Week 15, Day 3
Week 32, Weekend
Week 33, Day 5
Week 33, Weekend

TESTING
Week 16, Day 2

TRADITION
Week 17, Day 1
Week 17, Day 2
Week 17, Day 3

TRANSFIGURATION
Week 20, Day 1
Week 20, Day 3
Week 20, Day 5
Week 20, Weekend

TRANSFORMATION
Week 20, Day 3
Week 31, Day 5
Week 32, Day 4
Week 32, Day 5

TREASURE
Week 13, Weekend

TRIALS
Week 41, Weekend

THE TRINITY
Week 1, Weekend
Week 25, Day 5
Week 25, Weekend
Week 41, Day 3

TRIUMPHAL ENTRY
Week 34, Day 3
Week 34, Day 5

TRUST
Week 3, Day 4
Week 14, Day 2
Week 14, Day 3
Week 14, Weekend
Week 45, Day 4

TRUTH
Week 17, Day 2
Week 31, Day 2
Week 41, Day 2

UNBELIEF
Week 12, Day 4

UNBELIEVERS
Week 26, Day 1

UNDERSTANDING
Week 13, Day 2
Week 17, Day 5

UNITY
Week 21, Day 3
Week 43, Day 5
Week 43, Weekend

WAITING
Week 3, Day 2
Week 52, Day 1

WEAKNESS
Week 45, Weekend

WEALTH
Week 29, Day 2
Week 29, Day 3
Week 29, Day 4
Week 32, Day 1

WITNESS
Week 15, Day 4
Week 33, Day 5
Week 42, Day 3
Week 49, Day 5
Week 50, Weekend

WITNESSING
Week 1, Weekend
Week 2, Weekend
Week 4, Day 2
Week 6, Day 2
Week 6, Weekend
Week 7, Day 2
Week 7, Day 5
Week 7, Weekend

WORK
Week 30, Day 4

WORRY
Week 3, Day 1
Week 11, Day 4
Week 15, Day 5
Week 45, Day 5

WORSHIP
Week 26, Day 3
Week 33, Day 2
Week 33, Day 3
Week 34, Day 2
Week 35, Day 4
Week 35, Day 5

SCRIPTURE INDEX

EXODUS 3:14
Week 45, Day 1

EXODUS 20:8-11
Week 9, Day 1

DEUTERONOMY 6:16
Week 5, Days 4–5

PSALM 19:1
Week 34, Day 3

PSALM 22:18
Week 48, Day 4

PSALM 56:3
Week 14, Day 4

PSALM 103:13
Week 27, Day 4

PSALM 118:26-27
Week 34, Day 2

PSALM 121:1-2
Week 20, Day 2

PROVERBS 16:9
Week 38, Day 2

ISAIAH 26:3
Week 51, Day 4

ISAIAH 53:3
Week 44, Day 1

ISAIAH 53:6
Week 25, Day 3

ISAIAH 64:6
Week 10, Day 4

EZEKIEL 36:26
Week 17, Weekend

MATTHEW 1:18
Week 2, Day 1

MATTHEW 1:19-21
Week 2, Day 2

MATTHEW 1:22-23
Week 2, Day 3

MATTHEW 1:24-25
Week 2, Day 2

MATTHEW 2:1-6
Week 3, Day 3

MATTHEW 2:9-11
Week 3, Day 3

MATTHEW 2:13-15
Week 3, Day 4

MATTHEW 2:16-18
Week 3, Day 5

MATTHEW 2:19-23
Week 3, Day 4

MATTHEW 3:3
Week 4, Day 2

MATTHEW 3:4
Week 4, Day 2

MATTHEW 3:13
Week 4, Day 1

MATTHEW 3:13-15
Week 4, Day 3

MATTHEW 3:15
Week 4, Weekend

MATTHEW 3:16-17
Week 4, Weekend

MATTHEW 4:1-4
Week 5, Day 2

MATTHEW 4:6-7
Week 5, Day 5

MATTHEW 4:10-11
Week 5, Weekend

MATTHEW 5:1-10
Week 10, Day 1

MATTHEW 5:11-12
Week 10, Day 2

MATTHEW 5:13
Week 21, Weekend

MATTHEW 5:13-16
Week 10, Day 3

MATTHEW 5:16
Week 13, Day 2

MATTHEW 5:17-20
Week 10, Day 4

MATTHEW 5:21-28
Week 10, Day 5

MATTHEW 5:31-34
Week 10, Weekend

MATTHEW 5:37-39
Week 10, Weekend

MATTHEW 5:43-45
Week 10, Weekend

MATTHEW 6:5-6
Week 11, Day 1

MATTHEW 6:7
Week 44, Day 4

MATTHEW 6:7-8
Week 11, Day 2

MATTHEW 6:9
Week 11, Day 3

MATTHEW 6:10-11
Week 11, Day 4

MATTHEW 6:12, 14-15
Week 11, Day 5

MATTHEW 6:13
Week 11, Weekend

MATTHEW 8:19-20
Week 22, Day 2

MATTHEW 8:21-22
Week 22, Day 3

MATTHEW 8:26
Week 14, Day 4

MATTHEW 10:1-8
Week 15, Day 1

MATTHEW 10:9-15
Week 15, Day 2

MATTHEW 10:16-20
Week 15, Day 3

MATTHEW 10:21-28
Week 15, Day 4

MATTHEW 10:29-31
Week 15, Day 5

MATTHEW 10:32-40
Week 15, Weekend

MATTHEW 10:37
Week 12, Day 2

MATTHEW 11:11
Week 36, Day 2

MATTHEW 12:1-2
Week 9, Day 1

MATTHEW 12:9-13
Week 9, Day 5

MATTHEW 12:14
Week 9, Weekend

MATTHEW 12:22-23
Week 12, Day 3

MATTHEW 12:23
Week 12, Day 4

MATTHEW 12:24-29
Week 12, Day 4

MATTHEW 12:30-32
Week 12, Day 5

MATTHEW 12:33-37
Week 12, Weekend

MATTHEW 13:3-12
Week 13, Day 1

MATTHEW 13:24-30
Week 13, Day 4

MATTHEW 13:36-39
Week 13, Day 4

MATTHEW 13:43
Week 13, Day 4

MATTHEW 13:44-53
Week 13, Weekend

MATTHEW 14:19-21
Week 16, Day 5

MATTHEW 15:3-9
Week 17, Day 2

MATTHEW 15:12-14
Week 17, Day 4

MATTHEW 15:15-20
Week 17, Day 5

MATTHEW 15:32
Week, 18, Day 1

MATTHEW 16:13
Week 18, Days 1–2

MATTHEW 16:13-14
Week 18, Day 3

MATTHEW 16:13-15
Week 18, Day 4

MATTHEW 16:15-17
Week 18, Day 5

MATTHEW 16:16
Week 19, Day 1

MATTHEW 16:18-20
Week 18, Weekend

MATTHEW 16:21
Week 19, Day 1
Week 38, Day 1

MATTHEW 16:22-23
Week 19, Day 3

MATTHEW 16:24-26
Week 19, Day 4

MATTHEW 17:1-3
Week 20, Day 2

MATTHEW 17:2-4
Week 20, Day 3

MATTHEW 17:3-7
Week 20, Day 4

MATTHEW 17:4-7
Week 20, Day 5

MATTHEW 17:8-13
Week 20, Weekend

MATTHEW 17:22-23
Week 38, Day 1

MATTHEW 18:3-4
Week 21, Day 2

MATTHEW 19:14
Week 21, Day 2

MATTHEW 19:30
Week 30, Day 1

MATTHEW 20:1
Week 30, Day 1

MATTHEW 20:1-2
Week 30, Day 2

MATTHEW 20:3-7
Week 30, Day 3

MATTHEW 20:8
Week 30, Day 4

MATTHEW 20:9-15
Week 30, Day 5

MATTHEW 20:15
Week 30, Weekend

MATTHEW 20:16
Week 30, Day 1
Week 30, Weekend

MATTHEW 20:18-19
Week 33, Day 1
Week 38, Day 1

MATTHEW 20:34
Week 31, Day 5

MATTHEW 21:1-3
Week 34, Day 1

MATTHEW 21:4-9
Week 34, Day 2

MATTHEW 21:10-11
Week 34, Day 5

MATTHEW 21:12-13
Week 35, Day 3

MATTHEW 21:13, 16
Week 35, Weekend

MATTHEW 21:14-16
Week 35, Day 5

MATTHEW 21:23-27
Week 36, Day 1

MATTHEW 21:28-32
Week 36, Day 2

MATTHEW 21:33-41
Week 36, Day 3

MATTHEW 21:42
Week 36, Day 4

MATTHEW 21:43-44
Week 36, Day 5

MATTHEW 21:45-46
Week 36, Weekend

MATTHEW 24:4-5
Week 37, Day 3

MATTHEW 24:4-14
Week 37, Day 2

MATTHEW 24:15-22
Week 37, Day 4

MATTHEW 24:23-26
Week 37, Day 3

MATTHEW 24:30-36
Week 37, Day 5

MATTHEW 24:43-44
Week 37, Day 5

MATTHEW 24:45-51
Week 37, Weekend

MATTHEW 26:1-2
Week 38, Day 1

MATTHEW 26:3-5
Week 38, Day 2

MATTHEW 26:6
Week 33, Day 2

MATTHEW 26:8-9
Week 33, Day 4

MATTHEW 26:14-15
Week 38, Day 4

MATTHEW 26:16
Week 38, Day 5

MATTHEW 26:20-22
Week 39, Day 3

MATTHEW 26:26-30
Week 39, Day 5

MATTHEW 26:31-35
Week 40, Day 5

MATTHEW 26:36-38
Week 44, Day 1

MATTHEW 26:39
Week 44, Day 2

MATTHEW 26:40-41
Week 44, Day 3

MATTHEW 26:42
Week 44, Day 4

MATTHEW 26:47-50
Week 45, Day 2

MATTHEW 26:49-51
Week 45, Day 3

MATTHEW 26:52-54
Week 45, Days 4–5

MATTHEW 26:53-54
Week 45, Day 1

MATTHEW 26:57-58
Week 46, Day 2

MATTHEW 26:69-74
Week 46, Day 2

MATTHEW 27:11-14
Week 47, Day 1

MATTHEW 27:15-21
Week 47, Weekend

MATTHEW 27:22-23
Week 47, Day 4

MATTHEW 27:24-26
Week 47, Day 5

MATTHEW 27:45-49
Week 49, Day 1

MATTHEW 27:62-66
Week 49, Weekend

MATTHEW 28:1-4
Week 50, Day 2

MATTHEW 28:1-7
Week 50, Day 1

MATTHEW 28:5-10
Week 50, Day 5

MATTHEW 28:11-15
Week 50, Day 4

MATTHEW 28:16-20
Week 52, Day 4

MATTHEW 28:20
Week 14, Day 1
Week 20, Day 5
Week 37, Day 1

MARK 1:7
Week 5, Day 1

MARK 1:10-11
Week 4, Day 4

MARK 1:11
Week 5, Day 1

MARK 1:12-13
Week 5, Day 1

MARK 1:32-34
Week 8, Day 1

MARK 1:37-38
Week 8, Day 4

MARK 2:2-12
Week 8, Weekend

MARK 3:1-4
Week 9, Day 4

MARK 3:6
Week 9, Weekend

MARK 3:20-21
Week 12, Day 2

MARK 3:31-35
Week 12, Day 2

MARK 4:21-25
Week 13, Day 2

MARK 4:26-29
Week 13, Day 3

MARK 4:35-36
Week 14, Day 1

MARK 4:35-38
Week 14, Day 3

MARK 4:37-41
Week 14, Weekend

MARK 4:39-40
Week 14, Day 4

MARK 4:41
Week 14, Day 5

MARK 6:30-34
Week 16, Day 1

MARK 6:37
Week 16, Day 3

MARK 7:1-5
Week 17, Day 1

MARK 7:14-15
Week 17, Day 3

MARK 7:17-19
Week 17, Day 5

MARK 7:20-23
Week 17, Weekend

MARK 8:34-38
Week 19, Day 5

MARK 8:36
Week 36, Day 1

MARK 9:24
Week 22, Day 1

MARK 9:33-35
Week 21, Day 1

MARK 9:36-37, 42
Week 21, Day 2

MARK 9:38-41
Week 21, Day 3

MARK 9:43-48
Week 21, Day 4

MARK 9:49-50
Week 21, Weekend

MARK 10:17-18
Week 29, Day 1

MARK 10:19-22
Week 29, Day 2

MARK 10:21
Week 29, Day 3

MARK 10:22
Week 29, Day 4

MARK 10:23-26
Week 29, Day 4

MARK 10:26
Week 29, Day 5

MARK 10:27
Week 29, Day 5

MARK 10:28-31
Week 29, Weekend

MARK 10:49-51
Week 31, Day 3

MARK 11:11
Week 34, Day 5

MARK 11:15-16
Week 35, Day 1

MARK 11:17
Week 35, Day 4

MARK 13:1-4
Week 37, Day 1

MARK 14:1-2
Week 38, Day 2

MARK 14:3, 6-9
Week 33, Day 3

MARK 14:10-11
Week 38, Weekend

MARK 14:12-16
Week 39, Day 1

MARK 14:22-25
Week 39, Day 5

MARK 14:35-36
Week 44, Day 2

MARK 14:39
Week 44, Day 4

MARK 14:40
Week 44, Day 5

MARK 14:41-42
Week 44, Weekend

MARK 14:48-52
Week 45, Weekend

MARK 14:66-72
Week 46, Day 5

MARK 15:9-12
Week 47, Day 3

MARK 15:12-15
Week 47, Day 4

MARK 15:24-26
Week 48, Day 2

MARK 15:29-32
Week 48, Weekend

MATTHEW 15:32
Week 18, Day 1

MARK 15:39-41
Week 49, Day 3

MARK 15:42-47
Week 49, Day 5

MARK 16:1
Week 50, Day 3

MARK 16:5-7
Week 50, Day 2

MARK 16:15-18
Week 52, Day 4

MARK 16:19-20
Week 52, Weekend

LUKE 1:30-38
Week 1, Day 2

LUKE 2:1-4
Week 2, Day 4

LUKE 2:5-7
Week 2, Day 5

LUKE 2:8-17
Week 2, Weekend

LUKE 2:14
Week 24, Day 5

LUKE 2:21-24
Week 3, Day 1

LUKE 2:25-38
Week 3, Day 2

LUKE 2:39-40
Week 3, Day 1

LUKE 2:41-49
Week 3, Weekend

LUKE 2:48-49
Week 12, Day 2

LUKE 2:49
Week 4, Weekend

LUKE 2:52
Week 4, Day 1

LUKE 3:21-22
Week 4, Day 5

LUKE 4:5-8
Week 5, Day 3

LUKE 4:9-12
Week 5, Day 4

LUKE 4:13
Week 5, Weekend

LUKE 4:31-37
Week 8, Day 2

LUKE 4:38-39
Week 8, Day 3

LUKE 4:42-44
Week 8, Day 4

LUKE 5:5
Week 52, Day 1

LUKE 5:12-16
Week 8, Day 5

LUKE 5:27-28
Week 27, Day 1

LUKE 5:30
Week 27, Day 1

LUKE 5:31-32
Week 27, Day 1

LUKE 6:1-5
Week 9, Day 2

LUKE 6:6-9
Week 9, Day 3

LUKE 6:11
Week 9, Weekend

LUKE 8:1-3
Week 12, Day 1

LUKE 8:23
Week 14, Day 2

LUKE 8:25
Week 14, Day 5

LUKE 9:12-14
Week 16, Day 3

LUKE 9:14-15
Week 16, Day 4

LUKE 9:22
Week 19, Day 2

LUKE 9:23-25
Week 19, Weekend

LUKE 9:27-28
Week 20, Day 1

LUKE 9:57
Week 22, Day 1

LUKE 9:58
Week 22, Day 5

LUKE 9:59-60
Week 22, Day 3, Weekend

LUKE 9:60
Week 22, Day 5

LUKE 9:61-62
Week 22, Day 4

LUKE 9:62
Week 22, Day 5

LUKE 10:25-28
Week 23, Day 1

LUKE 10:27
Week 23, Day 5

LUKE 10:28
Week 23, Day 2

LUKE 10:29
Week 23, Day 2

LUKE 10:30-32
Week 23, Day 3

LUKE 10:33-34
Week 23, Day 4

LUKE 10:35
Week 23, Day 5

LUKE 10:36-37
Week 23, Weekend

LUKE 11:42
Week 6, Day 1

LUKE 12:35-36
Week 24, Day 1

LUKE 12:35-40
Week 24, Day 2

LUKE 12:41-43
Week 24, Day 3

LUKE 12:48
Week 24, Day 3

LUKE 12:49-53
Week 24, Day 4

LUKE 12:51
Week 24, Day 5

LUKE 12:54-59
Week 24, Weekend

LUKE 13:18-21
Week 13, Day 5

LUKE 14:1
Week 26, Day 1

LUKE 14:1-5
Week 26, Day 2

LUKE 14:7-11
Week 26, Day 3

LUKE 14:11
Week 26, Day 5

LUKE 14:12-14
Week 26, Day 4

LUKE 14:15-17
Week 26, Day 5

LUKE 14:18-24
Week 26, Weekend

LUKE 14:24
Week 26, Day 5

LUKE 15:1-2
Week 27, Day 1

LUKE 15:3-10
Week 27, Day 2

LUKE 15:7, 10
Week 27, Weekend

LUKE 15:11-19
Week 27, Day 3

LUKE 15:20-24
Week 27, Day 4

LUKE 15:25-30
Week 27, Day 5

LUKE 15:31-32
Week 27, Weekend

LUKE 17:3-4
Week 21, Day 5

LUKE 18:19
Week 25, Day 4

LUKE 18:35-43
Week 31, Day 1

LUKE 18:39
Week 31, Day 2

LUKE 18:41-42
Week 31, Day 4

LUKE 18:43
Week 31, Weekend

LUKE 19:1-2
Week 32, Day 1

LUKE 19:2-4
Week 32, Day 2

LUKE 19:5-6
Week 32, Day 3

LUKE 19:7-8
Week 32, Day 4

LUKE 19:8-10
Week 32, Weekend

LUKE 19:9-10
Week 32, Day 5

LUKE 19:10
Week 27, Day 2

LUKE 19:29-34
Week 34, Day 1

LUKE 19:39-40
Week 34, Day 3

LUKE 19:41-44
Week 34, Day 4

LUKE 19:45
Week 35, Day 2

LUKE 20:16-18
Week 36, Day 4

LUKE 20:19
Week 36, Weekend

LUKE 22:3
Week 38, Day 3

LUKE 22:4-5
Week 38, Day 4

LUKE 22:6
Week 38, Day 5

LUKE 22:14-16
Week 39, Day 2

LUKE 22:17-20
Week 39, Weekend

LUKE 22:31-34
Week 40, Weekend

LUKE 22:33
Week 22, Day 1

LUKE 22:39-46
Week 44, Weekend

LUKE 22:42
Week 4, Day 3

LUKE 22:51-53
Week 45, Day 5

LUKE 22:54-59
Week 46, Day 3

LUKE 22:60-62
Week 46, Day 4

LUKE 23:3
Week 47, Day 3

LUKE 23:4-12
Week 47, Day 2

LUKE 23:13-16
Week 47, Day 1

LUKE 23:18-22
Week 47, Day 4

LUKE 23:26-33
Week 48, Day 1

LUKE 23:32-33
Week 48, Day 5

LUKE 23:34
Week 49, Day 3

LUKE 23:34-38
Week 48, Day 3

LUKE 23:39-43
Week 48, Day 5

LUKE 23:44-46
Week 49, Day 2

LUKE 23:47-49
Week 49, Day 3

LUKE 24:13-17
Week 51, Day 1

LUKE 24:19-24
Week 51, Day 1

LUKE 24:25-27
Week 51, Day 2

LUKE 24:28-34
Week 51, Day 3

LUKE 24:33-37
Week 51, Day 4

LUKE 24:38-43
Week 51, Day 5

LUKE 24:44-49
Week 52, Day 5

LUKE 24:50-53
Week 52, Weekend

JOHN 1:1-4, 14
Week 1, Day 1

JOHN 1:10-13
Week 1, Day 3

JOHN 1:11
Week 36, Day 1

JOHN 1:12-13
Week 1, Day 4

JOHN 1:14-17
Week 1, Day 5

JOHN 1:18
Week 1, Weekend

JOHN 1:19-23
Week 4, Day 2

JOHN 1:27
Week 4, Day 2

JOHN 1:29
Week 5, Day 1
Week 38, Day 1

JOHN 2:13-16
Week 35, Day 2

JOHN 3:1
Week 6, Day 1

JOHN 3:2
Week 6, Day 2

JOHN 3:2-8
Week 6, Day 3

JOHN 3:9-15
Week 6, Day 4

JOHN 3:16
Week 6, Day 5

JOHN 3:17-21
Week 6, Weekend

JOHN 4:1-9
Week 7, Day 1

JOHN 4:10-15
Week 7, Day 2

JOHN 4:16-18
Week 7, Day 3

JOHN 4:19-26
Week 7, Day 4

JOHN 4:27-30
Week 7, Day 5

JOHN 4:35-42
Week 7, Weekend

JOHN 5:25
Week 28, Day 5

JOHN 6:1-6
Week 16, Day 2

JOHN 6:8-9
Week 16, Day 3

JOHN 6:14-15
Week 16, Weekend

JOHN 6:66-68
Week 22, Day 5

JOHN 6:68
Week 8, Day 1
Week 14, Weekend

JOHN 10:1-9
Week 25, Day 1

JOHN 10:3-5
Week 25, Day 3

JOHN 10:8-10
Week 25, Day 2

JOHN 10:11-18
Week 25, Day 4

JOHN 10:14-16
Week 25, Day 3

JOHN 10:19-33
Week 25, Day 5

JOHN 10:34-42
Week 25, Weekend

JOHN 11:1-6
Week 28, Day 1

JOHN 11:7-16
Week 28, Day 2

JOHN 11:17-27
Week 28, Day 3

JOHN 11:18-19
Week 33, Day 5

JOHN 11:25-26
Week 28, Day 1

JOHN 11:28-37
Week 28, Day 4

JOHN 11:38-44
Week 28, Day 5

JOHN 11:41
Week 44, Day 1

JOHN 11:45
Week 33, Day 5

JOHN 11:45-53
Week 28, Weekend

JOHN 12:1, 3
Week 33, Day 1

JOHN 12:2
Week 33, Day 2

JOHN 12:3
Week 33, Day 3

JOHN 12:4-6
Week 33, Day 4

JOHN 12:6
Week 38, Day 3

JOHN 12:7-8
Week 33, Day 1

JOHN 12:9-11
Week 33, Day 5

JOHN 12:10-11
Week 33, Weekend

JOHN 12:16-19
Week 34, Weekend

JOHN 13:1-5
Week 40, Day 1

JOHN 13:2
Week 38, Day 3

JOHN 13:3
Week 40, Day 1

JOHN 13:6-11
Week 40, Day 2

JOHN 13:12-20
Week 40, Day 3

JOHN 13:21-30
Week 39, Day 4

JOHN 13:33-35
Week 40, Day 4

JOHN 13:36-38
Week 40, Day 5

JOHN 13:38
Week 46, Day 1

JOHN 14:1-3
Week 41, Day 1

JOHN 14:4-6
Week 41, Day 2

JOHN 14:6
Week 1, Day 2
Week 25, Day 1

JOHN 14:7-11
Week 41, Day 3

JOHN 14:8
Week 1, Weekend

JOHN 14:9
Week 1, Weekend

JOHN 14:12-15
Week 41, Day 4

JOHN 14:16-26
Week 41, Day 5

JOHN 14:18
Week 42, Day 4

JOHN 14:26
Week 34, Weekend

JOHN 14:27
Week 24, Day 5
Week 51, Day 4

JOHN 14:27-31
Week 41, Weekend

JOHN 14:29
Week 41, Day 1

JOHN 15:1-8
Week 42, Day 1

JOHN 15:9-17
Week 42, Day 2

JOHN 15:13
Week 48, Day 2

JOHN 15:18-22
Week 42, Day 3

JOHN 16:2-3
Week 42, Day 3

JOHN 16:7-15
Week 42, Day 4

JOHN 16:8-9
Week 12, Day 5

JOHN 16:21-28
Week 42, Day 5

JOHN 16:29-33
Week 42, Weekend

JOHN 16:33
Week 24, Day 5
Week 41, Weekend

JOHN 17:1
Week 44, Day 1

JOHN 17:1-5
Week 43, Day 1

JOHN 17:6-8
Week 43, Day 2

JOHN 17:9-12
Week 43, Day 3

JOHN 17:13-19
Week 43, Day 4

JOHN 17:20-21
Week 43, Day 5

JOHN 17:22-26
Week 43, Weekend

JOHN 18:1-9
Week 45, Day 1

JOHN 18:12-18
Week 46, Day 1

JOHN 18:25-27
Week 46, Weekend

JOHN 18:29-31
Week 47, Day 1

JOHN 18:33-37
Week 47, Day 3

JOHN 18:37-38
Week 47, Day 5

JOHN 19:19-24
Week 48, Day 4

JOHN 19:23-24
Week 48, Day 2

JOHN 19:25-27
Week 48, Weekend

JOHN 19:28-30
Week 49, Day 4

JOHN 19:31-35
Week 49, Day 2

JOHN 19:36-37
Week 49, Day 4

JOHN 20:1-10
Week 50, Day 3

JOHN 20:11-18
Week 50, Weekend

JOHN 20:19-21
Week 51, Day 4

JOHN 20:24-29
Week 51, Weekend

JOHN 21:3-10
Week 52, Day 1

JOHN 21:15-19
Week 52, Day 2

JOHN 21:20-25
Week 52, Day 3

JOHN 21:22
Week 20, Day 1

ACTS 1:3
Week 52, Day 1

ACTS 1:10-11
Week 52, Weekend

ACTS 2:34
Week 35, Day 4

ROMANS 5:8
Week 6, Day 5

ROMANS 8:28
Week 46, Weekend

ROMANS 10:9
Week 38, Day 1

ROMANS 10:9-10
Week 32, Weekend

ROMANS 12:2
Week 20, Day 3

I CORINTHIANS 1:23
Week 49, Day 3

I CORINTHIANS 2:8
Week 48, Day 3

I CORINTHIANS 3:6
Week 13, Day 3

I CORINTHIANS 10:13
Week 11, Weekend
Week 44, Weekend

I CORINTHIANS 11:23-25
Week 39, Weekend

I CORINTHIANS 15:17-19
Week 50, Day 5

2 CORINTHIANS 7:10
Week 46, Day 5

GALATIANS 2:20
Week 19, Day 5

GALATIANS 5:22-23
Week 12, Weekend

EPHESIANS 1:21
Week 50, Day 2

EPHESIANS 2:8
Week 18, Day 5

EPHESIANS 2:8-9
Week 29, Day 5

EPHESIANS 3:17-19
Week 52, Weekend

EPHESIANS 4:26
Week 35, Day 1

EPHESIANS 6:11-12
Week 38, Day 3

PHILIPPIANS 1:21
Week 19, Day 5

PHILIPPIANS 2:6-8
Week 4, Day 5

PHILIPPIANS 2:6-11
Week 43, Day 1

COLOSSIANS 4:6
Week 10, Day 3

HEBREWS 4:15
Week 4, Day 1
Week 28, Day 4
Week 34, Day 4

HEBREWS 12:2
Week 1, Day 5

JAMES 1:13-14
Week 11, Weekend

JAMES 4:10
Week 26, Day 3

I PETER 3:15
Week 15, Day 3

I PETER 5:7
Week 15, Day 5

I PETER 5:8-9
Week 5, Weekend

2 PETER 3:8-11, 14
Week 37, Weekend

I JOHN 1:1
Week 1, Day 1

I JOHN 1:1-3
Week 1, Day 3

I JOHN 2:22
Week 25, Day 2

REVELATION 3:20
Week 39, Day 2

REVELATION 22:20
Week 24, Day 2

Take Your Bible Study
to the Next Level

The **Life Application Study Bible** helps you apply truths in God's Word to everyday life. It's packed with nearly 10,000 notes and features that make it today's #1–selling study Bible.

Life Application Notes: Thousands of Life Application notes help explain God's Word and challenge you to apply the truth of Scripture to your life.

Personality Profiles: You can benefit from the life experiences of over a hundred Bible figures.

Book Introductions: These provide vital statistics, an overview, and a timeline to help you quickly understand the message of each book.

Maps: Over 200 maps next to the Bible text highlight important Bible places and events.

Christian Worker's Resource: Enhance your ministry effectiveness with this practical supplement.

Charts: Over 260 charts help explain difficult concepts and relationships.

Harmony of the Gospels: Using a unique numbering system, the events from all four Gospels are harmonized into one chronological account.

Daily Reading Plan: This reading plan is your guide to reading through the entire Bible in one unforgettable year.

Topical Index: A master index provides instant access to Bible passages and features that address the topics on your mind.

Dictionary/Concordance: With entries for many of the important words in the Bible, this is an excellent starting place for studying the Bible text.

Available in the New Living Translation, New International Version, King James Version, and New King James Version. Take an interactive tour of the *Life Application Study Bible* at
www.NewLivingTranslation.com/LASB